# Criminal Justice

*Contemporary Literature in Theory and Practice*

Series Editors

Marilyn McShane
Frank P. Williams III
*California State University – San Bernardino*

GARLAND PUBLISHING, INC.
*New York & London*
*1997*

# Contents of the Series

# Victims of Crime and the Victimization Process

Edited with introductions by

Marilyn McShane
Frank P. Williams III
*California State University – San Bernardino*

GARLAND PUBLISHING, INC.
*New York & London*
*1997*

**Library of Congress Cataloging-in-Publication Data**

Victims of crime and the victimization process / edited with
introductions by Marilyn McShane and Frank P. Williams III.
p.   cm. — (Criminal justice ; v. 6)
Includes bibliographical references.
ISBN 0-8153-2513-4 (alk. paper)
1. Victims of crimes—United States. I. McShane, Marilyn D.,
1956–   . II. Williams, Franklin P. III. Series: Criminal justice
(New York, N.Y.) ; v. 6.
HV6250.3.U5V35  1997
362.88—dc21                                          96-39140
                                                        CIP

Printed on acid-free, 250-year-life paper
Manufactured in the United States of America

# Contents

# Series Introduction

At the turn of the century the criminal justice system will be confronting many of the same demons, although the drugs of choice, the technology of crime fighting, and the tools and techniques of management have evolved. Despite the enhancements of twenty-first century technologies, funding, crowding, and public concerns about effectiveness continue to be discussed in "crisis" terminology, and criminal justice scholars remain somewhat cynical about the ability to reform the criminal justice system. This pessimistic attitude may be fueled, at least in part, by the drama of real-life crime that plays itself out in courtrooms, newspapers, and talk shows across America every day. The combination of emotional political maneuvering and campaigning on punitive rhetoric assures us of a steady stream of legislation designed to reflect a zero tolerance for crime.

Testing the constitutional limits of our times, we have devised even more ways of imposing severe punishments, seizing assets, reinstituting corporal punishment, and penalizing the parents of delinquents. We have also created new offenses, such as recruiting someone into a gang, transmitting "indecent" images on the Internet, and knowingly passing along a disease. Despite these politically popular solutions to crime, problems of enforcement, equity, and affordability remain. The public's preoccupation with "what works?" and quick fixes to crime problems have never been reconciled with the more realistic ideas of "what can we live with?" and long-range preventive solutions.

Ironically, despite public perceptions that crime has been getting worse, statistics seem to indicate that the rates for virtually all offenses are either no worse than they were in 1980 or are now lower. Drug-related arrests and the rates for most forms of adult crime (in particular, most violent crimes) have actually decreased. Against this general backdrop, the rate of violent juvenile crime appears to be the sole increasing trend, leading to a situation in which risks of victimization by violent crime have also increased for juveniles. The contrary public perception of a massive and growing crime problem has created a situation in which the number of cases of juveniles transferred to adult court has increased, as has the proportion of inmates facing life sentences, life in prison without parole, and death sentences. On the other hand the risk of incarceration also appears to have increased for minorities, directing attention to questions of racial and economic disparity in the quality of protection and justice available in this country today.

While all this has been happening over the past two decades, academia has rather quietly developed an entire discipline dedicated to the study of crime and the criminal justice system. Though crime policy is still dominated largely by political interests swayed by public opinion, crime scholars have begun to have an impact on how crime is viewed and what can be done about it. While this impact is not yet a major one, it continues to gain weight and shows promise of some day achieving the influence that economists have come to wield in the realm of public policy-making.

Simultaneously with this growing scholarship comes an irony: academic journals, the major repository of scholarly wisdom, are being discontinued by libraries. Access, although ostensibly available in an electronic form, is decreasing. In many academic libraries, only a few select, "major" journals are being retained. Clearly, there is so much being done that the few "top" journals cannot adequately represent current developments (even if these journals were not focused in particular directions). Thus, the knowledge of the field is being centralized and, at the same time, more difficult to obtain. The multitude of criminal justice and criminology degree programs now face an interesting dilemma: how do students and faculty access current information? Or put differently, how does the field distribute its hard-gained knowledge to both assure quality of education and pursue efforts to offset the often ill-informed myths of public opinion?

Electronic access would appear to be one possible answer to the problem, especially with libraries facing yet another squeeze, that of space. On-line and media-based (CD-ROM) services promise quick availability of periodical literature, but remain futuristic. The costs associated with downloading articles can approximate the cost of the journal subscriptions themselves and many libraries cannot afford to participate in on-line periodical services. In addition, there is the inconvenience of translating the electronic images into the user's still-preferred paper-based format. Moreover, the paper-based serendipitous value of "browsing" decreases as only specific articles appear on-line, without surrounding materials.

An alternative solution is to review the range of journals and collect the "best" of their articles for reprinting. This is the approach this criminal justice periodical series has taken. By combining both depth and scope in a series of reprints, the series can offer an attractive, cost-effective answer to the problem of creating access to scholarship. Moreover, such a compact format yields the added advantage that individuals searching for a specific topic are more likely to experience the serendipity of running across related articles. Each of the six volumes presents a comprehensive picture of the state of the art in criminal justice today and each contains articles focused on one of the major areas of criminal justice and criminology: Police, Drugs, Criminological Theory, Corrections, Courts, and Victimology. Each volume contains approximately twenty articles.

## The Article Selection Process

The articles appearing in the series represent the choices of the editors and a board of experts in each area. These choices were based on four criteria: (1) that the articles were from the time period of 1991–1995, (2) that they represent excellent scholarship, (3) that collectively they constitute a fair representation of the knowledge of the period, and (4) that where there were multiple choices for representing a knowledge area, the articles appeared in journals that are less likely to be in today's academic library holdings. We believe the selection criteria and the board of experts were successful in compiling truly representative content in each topical area. In addition, the authors of the selected articles constitute a list of recognizable experts whose work is commonly cited.

Finally, there is one other advantage offered by the volumes in this series: the articles are reprinted as they originally appeared. Scholars using anthologized materials are commonly faced with having to cite secondary source pages because they do not have access to the original pagination and format. This is a difficulty because mistakes in reprinting have been known to alter the original context, thus making the use of secondary sources risky (and synonymous with sloppy scholarship). In order to overcome this problem, the series editors and the publisher made the joint decision to photoreproduce each article's original image, complete with pagination and format. Thus, each article retains its own unique typesetting and character. Citations may be made to pages in confidence that the reproduced version is identical in all respects with the original. In short, the journal article is being made available exactly as if the issue had been on a library shelf.

We believe this series will be of great utility to students, scholars, and others with interests in the literature of criminal justice and criminology. Moreover, the series saves the user time that would have otherwise been spent in locating quality articles during a typical literature search. Whether in an academic or personal library, the only alternative to this collection is having the journals themselves.

# Volume Introduction

Many will agree that the field of victimology has only recently developed a wide range of publication outlets. Courses in this area are still quite new in some criminal justice programs and, in addition, libraries are just now beginning to reflect a respectable collection of works on victims and the study of the process of victimization. This compilation of articles attempts to fill gaps in existing resources with some of the best current statements on the topic. Subjects include the characteristics of victims, the effects of crime on victims, and some contemporary theories of victimization. Also included are evaluations of a variety of victim-oriented policies and programs, such as victim assistance, peacemaking, and victim-impact statements. Historically, studies of victims have reflected a narrow street-crime bias. However, as these articles show, the incorporation of domestic violence, white-collar crime, and hate crime have broadened our image of both offenders and victims.

## Victim Legislation

James Jacobs and Barry Eisler review the Hate Crimes Statistics Act of 1990 and conclude that it has been all but ignored by criminal attorneys and criminologists. Its greatest effect will be on police policy and the way we think about crime, thus redefining concepts of prejudice as criminal behavior.

Ezzat Fattah writes on the need to move to a new penal and sentencing policy. After reviewing 1980's legislative changes to improve victim rights, he shows that virtually all were enacted with little supportive information and with little opposition. Unfortunately, the evidence of success is also limited. Fattah believes that a new philosophy is needed that emphasizes reparation, mediation, and conciliation. Moreover, offenses should be treated as violations of victim rights rather than as outmoded transgressions against the state.

## Research on Victimization

One of the little researched areas in victimology is advice to victims on whether to report a crime. In one of these infrequent studies, Barry Ruback examines the factors that are associated with people who assume the role of victim advisor. Using two statewide surveys, he asked who had a family member who was a victim of a sexual assault, domestic assault, or robbery and whether those respondents provided advice. He also asked about the appropriateness of reporting crimes to the police. Important variables predicting reporting advice were gender of the victim/advisor, victim/offender relationship, and seriousness of the offense. Females, however, were much more likely to advise reporting for domestic assault.

Finn Esbensen and David Huizinga focus on juvenile victimization, conducting interviews with 11- to 15-year-olds who lived in high-risk urban neighborhoods. Males experienced higher rates of victimization, particularly for crimes against the person. Higher rates were also associated with older age, areas of social disorganization, and nontraditional family arrangements. No differences were found by ethnicity.

Victims who defend themselves during a crime are also a little-researched group. Chris Marshall and Vincent Webb use National Crime Survey data from 1987 to examine victims who used a gun, other weapon, or fists and feet in their defense. Kicking, hitting, biting, and pushing emerged as the most common mode of resistance and young white males were the most common age/racial group. As expected, they found that offender characteristics affected the likelihood and type of victim resistance, as well as the presence of a weapon and prior relationships with the offender.

Similarly, Ronet Bachman and Diane Carmody ask about the effect of victim resistance, particularly where strangers or intimate associates are concerned. Using National Crime Survey data, they analyze those victims who resisted crime. They find a higher rate of injury with intimate perpetrators when either physical or verbal resistance is used. Where strangers are concerned, resistance made no difference to extent of injury. However, higher rates of injury occurred when the stranger had a weapon, regardless of resistance. Bachman and Carmody conclude that fighting back in domestic violence situations serves to escalate the risk of injury.

In one of the relatively rare analyses of white-collar crime and victimization, Neal Shover, Greer Fox, and Michael Mills explore long-term consequences of fraud in a financial institution. Using data from a collapsed bank's accounts and interviews with those who lost funds, they find little long-term effect, while the impact of victimization ranged from minimal to severe. Some short-term loss of confidence in economic and political leaders resulted, although much of that was produced by those who sought to alleviate the impact of the bank's collapse.

In a study that examines victimization-produced psychological distress, Fran Norris and Krzysztof Kaniasty interviewed violent crime victims, property crime victims, and nonvictims at points over a fifteen-month period. Seven different "distress" measures were reviewed and results indicated that while victims decreased their distress levels from three to nine months, no change took place after nine months. There was some effect, however, attributed to victimizations subsequent to the original one. The highest level of distress belonged to violent crime victims, followed by property crime victims and, finally, by nonvictims.

Another study of psychological distress was conducted by John Freedy, Heidi Resnick, Dean Kilpatrick, Bonnie Dansky, and Richie Tidwell. They examine crime victims and family members for signs of post-traumatic stress disorder (PTSD). Among their findings are a higher propensity for females, violent crime victims, and those physically injured to be diagnosed as suffering from PTSD. In addition, they found that victim services rarely address PTSD, an obvious shortcoming of victim health-care programs.

## Victim Programs

Consistent with growing enthusiasm for the victim's movement, criminal justice agencies and political figures have been creating and funding various "victim's programs." Many of these have been little more than ways to get more funds into prosecutors' offices or provide fodder for political campaigns. Robert McCormack examines the history of the victim's movement, linking the baby boom, rising crime rates in the 1960s, more conservative court decisions, and the rise of feminist organizations to the emergence of victim's programs. He believes the first of these programs, violent crime compensation boards, was critical in setting the stage for other forms of national, state, and local victim assistance. With two decades of success behind them, McCormack believes the programs now need to move beyond a retributive stance to one that embraces general welfare, thus widening the movement's political power.

Victim impact statements, used at sentencing, have been touted as a way to make sure the victim's voice is heard and that punishment is commensurate with the harm done to the victim. The programs are now so widely spread that other areas of the criminal justice system, such as parole boards, are borrowing their concepts. Robert Davis and Barbara Smith report on the effect of victim impact statements for common felony crimes in an experiment conducted in Bronx County, New York. They judge that including the statements in the sentencing process has done little to increase consideration of harm done to victims and has had little effect on sentencing.

One promising approach has been victim-offender mediation programs. Mark Umbreit and Robert Coates evaluate four of these programs, collecting data by observation and interview, and comparing the results with two nonparticipating sites. They find that victims overwhelmingly felt the experience was fair and satisfactory. Moreover, offenders were significantly more likely to complete restitution.

Police response to domestic violence and programs created for abused spouses are among the earliest of victim-sensitive strategies. Eve Buzawa and Thomas Austin examine police response to domestic violence to see whether victim preferences affect decisions to arrest. Using data from Detroit, they conclude that victim satisfaction increases when police respond favorably to their desires and preferences. Buzawa and Austin believe that police sensitivity to victim preference is superior to such measures as mandatory arrest policies, thereby improving police domestic violence and spouse abuse programs.

## Theoretical Positions

Most of the theoretical approaches to victimization derive from routine activities or opportunity theories. James Lynch and David Cantor look at the latter using the Victim Risk Supplement of the National Crime Survey. Using both behavioral and ecological measures to predict burglary and household larceny, they find that environmental design measures are ineffective and that other ecological and behavior measures differ by the type of victimization. A major part of their analysis is the use of different levels of aggregation in measuring the ecological concepts and controlling for levels of dangerousness in housing blocks. Their results suggest opportunity theories should be revised.

Marilyn McShane and Frank Williams critique contemporary victimology by suggesting that victims have largely been used by the political system to further a conservative crime-control agenda. In the process, certain victim "images" are presented that in reality do not accurately reflect the bulk of real victims. They present ways that analyses derived from radical criminology may be used to understand the role of victims in the American criminal justice system and the media industry. Radical approaches would serve victimology in general by adding dimensions of understanding that do not now exist.

Further extending the argument that theoretical work in victimology is needed, Robert Meier and Terance Miethe suggest that crime theory and victim theory be integrated. They note that the two have similar problems: poor conceptualization, poor theory-data linkage, inattention to different types of crime, and poorly defined relationships. Better theorizing would incorporate victims, offenders, and situations into one integrated theory of crime.

In the volume's final essay, Daniel Van Ness explores one of the newest philosophies: restorative justice. Based on the concept that true justice should bring about healing, restorative justice involves a reworking of the entire criminal justice system, and victims become an integral part. Van Ness examines several of the challenges to implementing such a system and concludes that restorative justice is a worthwhile goal.

* * * * * *

We would like to thank the board members of this volume who assisted us in the selection of articles. Because only a limited number of pieces could be selected for this volume, an expanded bibliography is included to provide additional materials. Articles marked with an asterisk (*) are included in this anthology.

Alba, Richard, John Logan, and Paul Bellair (1994). Living with crime: The implications of racial/ethnic differences in suburban location. *Social Forces* 73(2): 395–434.

Arthur, John (1992). Criminal victimization, fear of crime, and handgun ownership among blacks: Evidence from national survey data. *American Journal of Criminal Justice* 16(2): 121–41.

*Bachman, Ronet and Dianne Carmody (1994). Fighting fire with fire: The effects of victim resistance in intimate versus stranger perpetrated assaults against females. *Journal of Family Violence* 9(4): 317–31.

Bachman, Ronet and Bruce Taylor (1994). The measurement of family violence and rape by the redesigned national crime victimization survey. *Justice Quarterly* 11(3): 499–512.

Badovinac, Kimberly (1994). The effects of victim impact panels on attitudes and intentions regarding impaired driving. *Journal of Alcohol and Drug Education* 39(3): 113–18.

Braithwaite, John (1994). Comment: Republican criminology and victim advocacy. *Law and Society Review* 28(4): 765–76.

Brandl, Steven and Frank Horvath (1991). Crime-victim evaluation of police investigative performance. *Journal of Criminal Justice* 19(2): 109–21.

Brewer, Victoria and Dwayne Smigh (1995). Gender inequality and rates of female homicide victimization across U.S. cities. *Journal of Research in Crime and Delinquency* 32(2): 175–90.

*Buzawa, Eve and Thomas Austin (1993). Determining police response to domestic violence victims: The role of victim preference. *The American Behavioral Scientist* 36(May/June): 610–23.

Cao, Liqun and David Maume Jr. (1993). Urbanization, inequality, lifestyles and robbery: A comprehensive model. *Sociological Focus* 26(1): 11–26.

Conaway, Mark and Sharon Lohr (1994). A longitudinal analysis of factors associated with reporting violent crimes to the police. *Journal of Quantitative Criminology* 10(1): 23–39.

Cooley, Dennis (1993). Criminal victimization in male federal prisons. *Canadian Journal of Criminology* 35 (Oct): 479–95.

Daly, Kathleen (1994). Comment: Men's violence, victim advocacy, and feminist redress. *Law and Society Review* 28(4): 777–87.

*Davis, Robert and Barbara Smith (1994). The effects of victim impact statements on sentencing decisions: A test in an urban setting. *Justice Quarterly* 11(3): 453–512.

Elias, Robert (1993). Police as victims of law and order. *Social Justice* 19(3): 67–76.

Elias, Robert (1994). Has victimology outlived its usefulness? *Journal of Human Justice* 6(1): 4–25.

Erez, Edna and Pamela Tontodonato (1992). Victim participation in sentencing and satisfaction with justice. *Justice Quarterly* 9(3): 393–417.

*Esbensen, Finn-Aage and David Huizinga (1991). Juvenile victimization and delinquency. *Youth and Society* 23(2): 202–28.

*Fattah, Ezzat (1991). From crime policy to victim policy: The need for a fundamental policy change. *International Annals of Criminology* 29(1-2): 43–60.

Finn-DeLuca, Valerie (1994). Victim participation at sentencing. *Criminal Law Bulletin* 30(5): 403–28.

Fitzpatrick, Kevin, Mark LaGory, and Ferris Ritchey (1993). Criminal victimization among the homeless. *Justice Quarterly* 10(3): 353–68.

Ford, David (1991). Prosecution as a victim power resource: A note on empowering women in violent conjugal relationships. *Law and Society Review* 25(2): 313–34.

*Freedy, John, Heidi Resnick, Dean Kilpatrick, Bonnie Dansky, and Ritchie Tidwell (1994). The psychological adjustment of recent crime victims in the criminal justice system. *Journal of Interpersonal Violence* 9(4): 450–68.

Gelles, Richard (1992). Poverty and violence toward children. *American Behavioral Scientist* 35(3): 258–74.

Goodey, Jo (1994). Fear of crime: What can children tell us? *International Review of Victimology* 3(3): 195–210.

Hall, Donald (1991). Victims' voices in criminal court: The need for restraint. *American Criminal Law Review* 28(2): 233–66.

Harry, Bruce, Timothy Pierson, and Andrei Kuznetsov (1993). Correlates of sex offender and offense traits by victim age. *Journal of Forensic Sciences* 38(5): 1068–74.

Hennessy, James and Laurie Kepecs-Schlussel (1992). Psychometric scaling techniques applied to rates of crime and victimization— I: Major population centers. *Journal of Offender Rehabilitation* 18(1-2): 1–80.

*Jacobs, James and Barry Eisler (1993). The Hate Crime Statistics Act of 1990. *Criminal Law Bulletin* 29(2): 99–123.

Koss, Mary (1993). Detecting the scope of rape: A review of prevalence research methods. *Journal of Interpersonal Violence* 2: 198–222.

Kposowa, Augustine, Gopal Singh, and K.D. Breault (1994). The effects of marital status and social isolation on adult male homicides in the United States. *Journal of Quantitative Criminology* 10(3): 277–89.

Lindner, Charles and Richard Koehler (1992). Probation officer victimization: An emerging concern. *Journal of Criminal Justice* 20(1): 53–62.

Lohr, Sharon and Joanna Liu (1994). A comparison of weighted and unweighted analyses in the National Crime Victimization Survey. *Journal of Quantitative Criminology* 10(4): 343–60.

*Lynch, James and David Cantor (1992). Ecological and behavioral influences on property victimization at home: Implications for opportunity theory. *Journal of Research in Crime and Delinquency* 29(3): 335–62.

Lurigio, Arthur and Dennis Rosenbaum (1992). The travails of the Detroit police-victims experiment: Assumptions and important lessons. *American Journal of Police* 11(3): 1–34.

*Marshall, Chris and Vincent Webb (1994). A portrait of crime victims who fight back. *Journal of Interpersonal Violence* 9(1): 45–74.

Marshall, Chris and Vincent Webb (1994). The impact of gender and race upon armed victim resistance: Some findings from the National Crime Survey. *Criminal Justice Policy Review* 6(3): 241–60.

*McCormack, Robert (1991). Compensating victims of violent crime. *Justice Quarterly* 8(3): 329–46.

McCormack, Robert (1994). United States crime victim assistance: History, organization and evaluation. *International Journal of Comparative and Applied Criminal Justice* 18(2): 209–20.

McDermott, Joan (1994). Criminology as peacemaking, feminist ethics and the victimization of women. *Women and Criminal Justice* 5(2): 1–20.

*McShane, Marilyn and Frank Williams III (1992). Radical victimology: A critique of the concept of victim in traditional victimology. *Crime and Delinquency* 38(2): 258–71.

*Meier, Robert and Terance Miethe (1993). Understanding theories of criminal victimization. *Crime and Justice: A Review of Research* 17: 459–99.

Miethe, Terance (1991). Citizen-based crime control activity and victimization risks: An examination of displacement and free-rider effects. *Criminology* 29(3): 419–39.

Miethe, Terance and David McDowall (1993). Contextual effects in models of criminal victimization. *Social Forces* 71(3): 741–60.

*Norris, Fran and Krzysztof Kaniasty (1994). Psychological distress following criminal victimization in the general population: Cross sectional, longitudinal, and prospective analyses. *Journal of Consulting and Clinical Psychology* 62(1): 111–23.

North, Carol, Elizabeth Smith, and Edward Spitznagel (1994). Post traumatic stress disorder in survivors of a mass shooting. *American Journal of Psychiatry* 151(1): 82–88.

Padgett, Deborah and E.L. Struening (1992). Victimization and traumatic injuries among the homeless: Associations with alcohol, drug, and mental problems. *American Journal of Orthopsychiatry* 62(Oct): 525–34.

Palermo, George, Maurice Smith, John DiMotto, and Thomas Christopher (1992). Victimization revisited: A national statistical analysis. *International Journal of Offender Therapy and Comparative Criminology* 36(3): 187–201.

Parsonage, William, Frances Bernat, and Jacqueline Helfgott (1994). Victim impact testimony and Pennsylvania's parole decision making process: A pilot study. *Criminal Justice Policy Review* 6(3): 187–206.

Rountree, Pamela, Kenneth Land, and Terance Miethe (1994). Macro-micro integration in the study of victimization: A hierarchical logistic model analysis across Seattle neighborhoods. *Criminology* 32(3): 387–414.

*Ruback, Barry (1994). Advice to crime victims: Effects of crime, victim, and advisor factors. *Criminal Justice and Behavior* 21(4): 423–42.

Scheingold, Stuart, Toska Olson, and Jana Pershing (1994). Republican criminology and victim advocacy. *Law and Society Review* 28(4): 729–64.

*Shover, Neal, Greer Fox, and Michael Mills (1994). Long-term consequences of victimization by white-collar crime. *Justice Quarterly* 11(1): 75–98.

Smith, Brent and Ronald Huff (1992). From victim to political activist: An empirical examination of a statewide victims' rights movement. *Journal of Criminal Justice* 20(3): 201–15.

Smith, Dwayne and Ellen Kuchta (1993). Trends in violent crime against women, 1973–89. *Social Science Quarterly* 74(1): 28–45.

Sohn, Ellen (1994). Anti-stalking statutes: Do they actually protect victims. *Criminal Law Bulletin* 30(3): 203–41.

Thompson, Martie and Fran Norris (1992). Crime, social status and alienation. *American Journal of Community Psychology* 20(1): 97–119.

Titus, Richard, Fred Heinzelmann, and John Boyle (1995). Victimization of persons by fraud. *Crime and Delinquency* 41(1): 54–72.

Tobolowsky, Peggy (1993). Restitution in the federal criminal justice system. *Judicature* 77(2): 90–95.

Umbreit, Mark (1995). Holding juvenile offenders accountable: A restorative justice perspective. *Juvenile and Family Court Journal* 46(2): 31–42.

Umbreit, Mark and Robert Coates (1992). The impact of mediating victim offender conflict: An analysis of programs in three states. *Juvenile and Family Court Journal* 43(1): 21–28.

*Umbreit, Mark and Robert Coates (1993). Cross-site analysis of victim-offender mediation in four states. *Crime and Delinquency* 39(4): 565–85.

Unnithan, Prabha (1994). Children as victims of homicide: Making claims, formulating categories and constructing social problems. *Deviant Behavior* 15(1): 63–83.

*Van Ness, Daniel (1993). New wine and old wineskins: Four challenges of restorative justice. *Criminal Law Forum* 4(2): 251–306.

Walklate, Sandra (1994). Can there be a progressive victimology. *International Review of Victimology* 3(1-2): 1–16.

Wooldredge, John, Francis Cullen, and Edward Latessa (1992). Victimization in the workplace: A test of routine activities theory. *Justice Quarterly* 9(2): 325–35.

Young, Vernetta (1992). Fear of victimization and victimization rates among women: A paradox. *Justice Quarterly* 9(3): 419–41.

*Journal of Family Violence, Vol. 9, No. 4, 1994*

# Fighting Fire with Fire: The Effects of Victim Resistance in Intimate Versus Stranger Perpetrated Assaults Against Females[1]

Ronet Bachman[2] and Dianne Cyr Carmody[3]

*The consequences of violence against woman are myriad, ranging from extreme psychological trauma to severe physical injury and even death. Utilizing the National Crime Victimization Survey, this paper explored the extent to which victim resistance, either physical or verbal/passive, during an assault differentially produced injury between intimate and stranger perpetrated assaults. It was found that female victims of assaults perpetrated by intimates were nearly twice as likely to sustain injury if they used either physical or verbal self-protective behavior. The only significant predictor of injury sustained by female victims of stranger perpetrated assaults, however, was presence of a weapon.*

**KEY WORDS:** intimate assaults; stranger assaults; self-protection; resistance; injury.

## INTRODUCTION

Over the past 2 decades, it has clearly been established that women in this country are at the highest risk of being assaulted *not* by the hands of a stranger, but in the once presumed "safety of their own homes," by an intimate. Estimates from a national survey concluded that approximately 1 out of 8 husbands carried out 1 or more violent acts during a given year against their partners (Straus and Gelles, 1990). Even more disturbing,

[1]Points of view or opinions expressed in this manuscript do not necessarily reflect those of the Bureau of Justice Statistics of the United States Department of Justice. An earlier version of this paper was presented at the 1992 American Society of Criminology meeting in New Orleans, LA.
[2]Bureau of Justice Statistics, 633 Indiana Ave. NW, Washington, DC 20531 Phone (202)616-3625.
[3]Department of Sociology, Western Washington University, Bellingham, Washington 98226.

0885-7482/94/1200-0317$7.00/0 © 1994 Plenum Publishing Corporation

however, is the finding that nearly 1.8 million of these women experienced incidents that had the potential of causing severe injury such as kicking, punching, or choking. Although other studies utilizing nonprobability samples have estimated higher rates of wife assault, estimates drawn from random samples are generally consistent with those found by Straus and Gelles (for a review of this literature, see Bachman and Pillemer, 1992).

In addition to the emotional and psychological trauma that women endure as the result of these assaults, many sustain severe physical injuries ranging from bruises and cuts to concussions and broken bones (Bachman, 1994; Browne, 1987). In fact, the National Center for Disease Control reports that attacks by husbands on wives result in more injuries to women requiring medical treatment than rapes, muggings, and auto accidents combined (NCADV, 1985). In addition, other research has shown that battering relationships account for approximately 1 in 4 of all female suicide attempts seen at emergency rooms (Stark, Flitcraft, Zuckerman, Grey, Robinson, and Frazier, 1981).

What contextual circumstances of a domestic assault increase the probability of a women sustaining injury? Are there differences between those factors that increase this probability for assaults perpetrated by intimates and those perpetrated by a stranger? While there is a plethora of research documenting the serious consequences that domestic violence has for women in this country, there have been few attempts to explore those factors of characteristics of an assaultive incident which may put women at greater risk of sustaining serious physical injury.

The purpose of this paper is twofold. We will first explore those factors present during an intimate assault that may increase the probability that a woman will sustain an injury. Specifically, we will predict the extent to which circumstances and behavior on the part of both the victim and offender increase the probability that the victim will sustain a serious injury as the result of the assault. In the analyses, we include such factors as weapon use, alcohol or drug use, and prior history of violence on the part of the offender in addition to physical or verbal self-protective behavior that was utilized by the victim. We will next examine the extent to which these same factors affect the probability of sustaining injury from stranger perpetrated assaults.

## THE CONSEQUENCES OF FIGHTING BACK

While there have been no systematic attempts to document the effects of utilizing resistance in domestic assaults, there is a wide body of literature that has investigated the consequences of resistance in stranger perpetrated crimes of violence (Block and Skogan, 1986; Block and Skogan, 1985; Cook, 1986; Kleck and Sayles, 1990). With the exception of rape, this literature has generally found that although forceful resistance less often results in the crime being completed, those who forcefully resist do more often risk being physically attacked and injured, particularly in crimes of robbery. A recent study of stranger perpetrated rapes, however, has found that women who physically resist their attackers not only decrease the probability that the rape will be completed but also do *not* appear to increase their likelihood of being injured (Kleck and Sayles, 1990).

Although there are no previous works that specifically examine outcomes of victim resistance in assaults perpetrated by intimates, there are a few studies that are inextricably related. Some very poignant insights into this issue are offered by deterrence researchers, who have examined those factors that both decrease and increase a husband's propensity to abuse his wife. For example, after examining the deterrent effects of a variety of legal and extralegal sanctions for wife assault, Carmody and Williams (1987) found that the more likely husbands perceived the certainty that they would be arrested for assaulting their wives, the less likely they were to engage in such behavior. Of more interest here, however, is the fact that in addition to this finding, Carmody and Williams (1987) also discovered that the more likely husbands perceived it was that their wife would hit them back, the *more* likely they were to abuse her. Thus, it appears that fighting back by women in this sample only increased the probability that they would continue to be assaulted.

Other research supports this supposition as well. After investigating the techniques used by women to successfully end their husband's battering, Bowker (1983) found that of 146 women, only 10% replied that aggressively defending oneself during an assault worked to stop the battering. The majority of women in Bowker's study said that talking to significant others or a formal agency worked best (nearly 70%) in ending the violence. Further, when these same women were asked to give advice to battered women on how to end violence in a relationship based on their own experiences, only 3% recommended fighting back aggressively. Overwhelmingly, most women advised getting out and contacting a formal social service agency (72%).

More direct evidence of the effects of physical self-protection comes from The Family Violence Survey, a nationally representative sample of American couples. In this sample, Gelles and Straus (1988) found that over 25% of victims of wife assault reported that fighting back actually escalated the level of violence they experienced. These authors point out that the futility of this method of "fighting with fire" is supported by the fact that the willingness of men to use force does *not* protect *them* from assault. They offer other national statistics as further rationale for this argument.

For example, three times as many men are murdered as women (UCR, 1991) and three times as many men are victims of assault (Bureau of Justice Statistics, 1991). Therefore, it appears that the readiness to use force does not provide security for *either* men or women.

These questions beg closer examination. "How does utilization of self-protective behavior such as physically fighting back during an assaultive situation affect the level of injury sustained during an assault?" "Are there differences in effects of self-protective behavior between stranger and intimate perpetrated assaults?" Utilizing a sample of female victims of intimate (husband/exhusband/boyfriend) and stranger perpetrated assaults obtained by the National Crime Victimization Survey, this study explores the answers to these questions. Based on the above literature, it is hypothesized that a women's use of physical self-protective behavior during an assault by an intimate will only serve to undermine her efforts and actually increase the probability that she will sustain injury.

## METHODOLOGY

The results reported in this study are based on data taken from the National Crime Victimization Survey (NCVS) for the years 1987-1990. (Prior to August of 1991, this survey was known as the National Crime Survey. It was renamed the National Crime Victimization Survey to emphasize more clearly the measurement of both reported and unreported victimizations experienced by respondents.) The NCVS is the nation's largest continuing survey of American households on their experience with criminal victimization. The survey obtains information about crimes, including incidents not reported to the police, from a continuous, nationally representative sample of households in the United States. Except for those who are crew members of merchant vessels, Armed Forces personnel living in military barracks, institutionalized persons, and U.S. citizens residing abroad or foreign visitors to this country, all individuals age 12 or older living in units designated for the sample were eligible to be interviewed for the survey. (More information on the NCVS sampling and estimation procedures can be obtained from Appendix III of Criminal Victimization in the United States, Annual reports from the NCVS. Bureau of Justice Statistics, U.S. Department of Justice, Washington, DC.) The response rate for the NCVS during the 1987-1990 period has ranged from 96 to 98%. The most recent year of 1990 yielded a response rate of approximately 97%, which represented about 95,000 persons being interviewed.

The operational definition of "assault" utilized by the NCVS is as follows: "An unlawful physical attack or threat of attack." Assaults may be classified as aggravated or simple. Rape and attempted rape are excluded from this category, as well as robbery and attempted robbery. The severity of assaults range from a minor threat to incidents which are nearly fatal (Bureau of Justice Statistics, 1992).

Accuracy of the NCVS for estimating incidence rates of domestic assault has been criticized (see particularly Straus and Gelles, 1990) because the survey does not directly ask respondents about assaultive incidents that were perpetrated by family members. However, this paper does *not* purport to offer estimates of incidence levels of domestic violence. The purpose here is to identify the contextual circumstances of an intimate perpetrated assault which place a female victim at greater risk of sustaining a serious injury and to compare these factors to those that predict injury in stranger perpetrated assaults. The NCVS was, therefore, the only nationally representative sample with enough cases of both intimate and stranger perpetrated assaults in which to provide an exploratory examination of these important questions. It should be noted here, however, that the NCVS, as the result of a 10-year redesign project, now asks respondents more specific questions about violent acts perpetrated by family members and intimates (Bachman and Taylor, 1994).

To investigate the relationship between self-protection measures and injuries sustained from intimate and stranger perpetrated assaults, this study utilizes a sample of 656 women who reported single offender assaults that were perpetrated by intimates (husbands/exhusbands/boyfriends) and 265 women who reported single offender assaults which were perpetrated by strangers. (The total unweighted number of women who reported assaults perpetrated by intimates during the 1987-1900 time period was 979; 742 women reported stranger perpetrated assaults to NCVS interviewers during this same time period. Because of missing data on the other variables of interest here (e.g., injury, self-protective behavior utilized, etc.), the sample selected for use in this research was restricted to 656 women assaulted by intimates and 265 women assaulted by strangers.)

Because we are trying to estimate the effects of self-protection behavior on the probability of injury to the victim, it is important to control the temporal order of initiated violence. For example, as Kleck and Sayles (1990) state, "While victim resistance may stimulate or deter aggression from the [offender], his inflicting of injury may also stimulate or inhibit resistance from the victim" (p. 154).

For purposes of this study, we were only interested in the self-protection measures used by women in response to violence that was initiated by the offender. For this reason, the sample used for multivariate analysis was further restricted to those women who told interviewers that the offender was the first to use or threaten to use physical force. This resulted in a sample consisting of 647 (8 cases deleted) women who had experienced assaults perpetrated by intimates and 257 (9 cases deleted) who had experienced assaults by strangers.

## Independent Variables

### *Self-Protection Measures*

To assess the extent to which victims engaged in self-protection during the commission of the assault, they were asked: "Was there anything you did or tried to do about the incident while it was going on?" If respondents answered yes, they were asked what measures were taken. For purposes of this study, answers to this question were categorized into two dichotomous variables that indicated use of physical action or passive/verbal action.

Because this question in the NCVS is a multiple response question, it was hierarchically categorized based on levels of resistance. If victims *only* utilized physical behavior or they utilized *both* physical *and* verbal/passive behavior, the self-protective variable was categorized as "physical." If the victim *only* engaged in verbal or passive behavior and did not engage in any physical resistance, the self-protective variable was categorized "passive/verbal." More specifically, the "Physical Action" variable was coded 1 if the victim engaged in any of the following behaviors: physically attacked or threatened to injure the offender, physically resisted offender, chased offender, ran away or called police. Because use of a weapon or threat of weapon use by victims only represented about 1% of self-protection measures used by victims, these cases were also included in the "Physical Action" variable. Victims who, in addition to these physical actions, utilized other verbal or passive responses were also coded 1 in the "Physical Action" variable. If victims did not engage in any physical self-protection measures, the "Passive/Verbal" variable was coded 1 if the victim engaged in any of the following behaviors: stalled, argued or reasoned with the offendee, tried to get the attention of others, or screamed and yelled. [Operationally, self-protective behavior was characterized as "physical" if it involved any type of physical action on the part of the victim and "passive/verbal" if it involved *only* a verbal or passive response. Of course, running away from the offender or calling the police are somewhat ambiguous types of behavior to classify. In the abstract, arguments could be made to classify them as either physical or verbal/passive behaviors. Because they do involve some type of motor activity (e.g., running or calling), they were classified in the physical category. In reality, however, it made no statistical difference which way we classified them. Results of the regression analyses were equivalent regardless of which classification scheme we utilized for these two self-protective behaviors. That is, self-protective behavior variables did not become insignificant in intimate related assaults when these two behaviors were dropped from the physical category and added to the verbal, nor did they become significant when predicting injury in stranger perpetrated assaults.]

### Offender Characteristics

In addition to use of self-protection measures employed by victims, certain contextual characteristics of the situation or offender characteristics may also effect the probability of injury sustained by victims of assault. The following variables were also controlled in the analyses: (1) if the offender was under the influence of alcohol/drugs; (2) if the offender had a weapon; and (3) if the offender had a history of assaultive behavior (this variable was only included in analyses of intimate assaults as over 80% of stranger perpetrated assault victims did not know the violent history of their perpetrators).

Each of these variables was operationalized by the victim's *perceptions* of the situation. Specifically, to assess the offender's use of alcohol or drugs, victims were asked, "Was the offender drinking or on drugs, or don't you know?" If victims replied yes, drug/alcohol use was coded 1, and 0 otherwise. Similarly, the questions, "Did the offender have a weapon such as a gun or knife, or something to use as a weapon, such as a bottle or wrench?" and "Was this the only time this offender committed a crime or made threats against you or your household?" measured the weapon presence and violent history on the part of the offender, respectively. If offenders were armed with a weapon, this variable was coded 1, and 0 if no weapon were present. The violent history variable was coded 1 if there were other times in which the offender victimized the respondent, and 0 if this was the only offense known to the victim.

### Demographic Controls

In addition to the above variables, racial and socioeconomic characteristics have also been shown to be related to incidence rates of domestic violence (Straus and Gelles, 1990). To control for the potential effects of these demographic characteristics on injury levels, the racial and socioeconomic status of victims was included in all logistic regression analyses. A dichotomous race measure was included in the models which coded black victims as 1 and nonblacks as 0. A 14 category variable measuring the victim's family income was also included which ranged from less than $5000 to a high of $75,000 and over.

## Dependent Variables

### Injury

Our primary focus will be on the extent to which self-protective behavior affects the likelihood that female victims of intimate and stranger perpetrated assaults sustain injuries. To assess the extent of injury incurred, victims were asked "What were the injuries you suffered, if any?" If any injury code was marked yes, this variables was coded 1. If no injuries were sustained, the injury variable was coded 0. Injuries could have included knife or gunshot wounds, broken bones, internal injuries, and bruises or cuts. Because one psychological response to being battered, however, may be minimization or denial of both the battering and/or any consequences of battering such as injury, an additional indicator of injury (medical treatment) was also analyzed. Walker (1979, 1984) provides a detailed account of the "battered woman syndrome," which includes such psychological responses as denial and minimization of the battering.

### Medical Treatment

Because victims assaulted by an intimate may have been reluctant to report any injuries sustained as the result of the assault, we also predicted the extent to which a victim needed medical care as a result of the attack. This was operationalized by the question "Were you injured to the extent that you received any medical care, including self treatment?" If victims responded yes, this variable was coded 1, and 0 if no medical treatment was received. In addition to providing a second proxy for our dependent variable of interest, medical treatment will also serve as a "severity" measure of the injury sustained. It is logical to assume that those women requiring medical treatment for injuries sustained more serious ones than those who did not require such treatment.

### Procedure

For simple random samples, there is a straightforward relationship between the variance of a variable in the population and the variance of an estimate of the sample mean for that variable. However, when the sam-

8

ple design is not a simple random sample, but a more complex design, the relationship between the sample estimates and the population parameters is more complex. Such is the case when utilizing the NCVS. Because the NCVS employs a stratified, multistage cluster sample, the effects of this complex sampling design must be taken into consideration when performing significance tests [for a detailed account of variance estimation issues, see Wolter (1985)].

Specifically, because the sample is not a simple random sample but one based on clusters, variance estimates must be adjusted upward to account for any correlation which may exist between respondents in any given cluster area. Put another way, the effect of a large sample taken from a multistage cluster design may not be equivalent to the same size sample taken from a simple random design because of the correlation that may exist between respondents in given clusters. Therefore, to determine the statistical significance of the hypothesized independent variables on the dependent variables of injury and medical case, all variances and standard errors and resulting significance tests reported in this paper were adjusted to reflect the complex sample design and weighting procedures used by the NCVS. Specifically, the sample design effect for the NCVS has been estimated to be approximately 1.92 for personal crimes of violence. That is, the variances are approximately twice as large as they would be for a simple random sample. Based on this, $t$ statistics used for significance testing in the logistic regression analyses reported in this paper were divided by 1.92 before the significance of each predictor variable was determined. [For a detailed discussion of general issues regarding these adjusting procedures, see Rao and Scott (1984) and Nguyen and Alexander (1987). Also, see Alexander and Hubble (1990) for a discussion of these adjusting procedures as they relate to the NCVS.]

## RESULTS

Before we examine the variables that best predict injury sustained by female victims, we will first describe the extent to which victims used self-protection measures, the extent to which these measures either helped the situation or made the situation worse, and the extent to which victims sustained injury and received medical attention from these injuries. Table I presents the percentage distribution of intimate and stranger assault victims on these outcome variables.

From Table I we can see that a greater proportion of intimate assault victims utilized some form of self-protection (78%) compared to stranger perpetrated assault victims (69%). It also appears that stranger perpetrated

| | Intimate Assaults | Stranger Assauts |
|---|---|---|
| Took self-protective action | 78% | 69% |
|   With weapon | 1 | 1 |
|   Physical action | 60 | 70[a] |
|   Verbal action | 39 | 29[a] |
| Self-protection helped | 52 | 76[a] |
| Self-protection made situation worse | 19 | 10%[a] |
| Injured | 82 | 50%[a] |
|   Received medical care | 43 | 51[a] |

[a]Indicates difference between intimate and stranger proportions is significant at $p < .05$. Percentage of Respondents who believed the self-protection measures helped or made situation worse do not total 100% as some respondents did not know the effects of their self-protection measures. The types of self-protection used include: With Weapon could have been used or threatened offender with gun or other weapon; Physical Action could have been physically attakced or threatened to injure offender, physically resisted, chased, ran or tried to run away; Verbal Action could have been stalled, argued or reasoned with offender, tried to get attention or screamed and yelled.

assault victims were more likely to believe that their self-protection actions actually helped the situation compared to victims of intimate assault (76% compared to 52%). Consistent with this, those who were victims of intimate assaults were more likely to believe that self-protective measures employed made the situation worse (19% compared to 10%).

Table I also reveals that intimate assault victims were significantly more likely to be injured (82%) compared to victims of stranger perpetrated assaults (50%). However, of those victims who sustained injury, victims of stranger perpetrated assaults were more likely to receive medical care for their injuries compared to victims of intimate assaults (51% and 43% respectively).

### Multivariate Analysis

Our inquiry next focused on examining multivariate relationships to uncover the variables that best predicted whether or not female victims of assault sustained injuries or needed medical care as a result of attacks perpetrated by intimate and strangers. Logistic regression analysis were performed separately for intimate and stranger perpetrated assaults, using both injury and medical treatment as our dependent variables.

10

Table II. Logistic Regression Results Predicting Whether Victim Sustained Injury During Commission of Assault From an Intimate and Whether Victim Received Medical Treatment for Injuries Sustained, NCVS 1987-1990 ($n = 647$)

|  | B | S.E. | Sig. | Exp(B) |
|---|---|---|---|---|
| Prediciting injury to victim |  |  |  |  |
| Black victim | -.1182 | .3090 | .7021 | .8885 |
| Family income | .0107 | .0285 | .7071 | 1.010 |
| Violent history | .3638 | .2443 | .1365 | 1.438 |
| Offender using drugs/alcohol | .1470 | .2144 | .4929 | 1.158 |
| Offender had weapon | .3586 | .3152 | .2553 | 1.431 |
| Victim used physical self-protection | .5312 | .2565 | .0383 | 1.702 |
| Victim used verbal self-protection | .6824 | .2828 | .0158 | 1.978 |
| Predicting medical treatment |  |  |  |  |
| Black victim | .7591 | .2647 | .0041 | 2.136 |
| Family income | .0151 | .0239 | .5274 | 1.015 |
| Violent history | .2984 | .2293 | .1931 | 1.347 |
| Offender using drugs/alcohol | .2308 | .1819 | .2044 | 1.259 |
| Offender had weapon | .8094 | .2421 | .0008 | 2.246 |
| Victim used physical self-protection | .0099 | .2443 | .9677 | 1.009 |
| Victim used verbal self-protection | .4089 | .2547 | .1084 | 1.505 |

Table II displays results of the logistic analyses predicting these dependent variables for assaults which were perpetrated by intimates. From the first panel of Table II, we see that the victim's use of both measures of self-protection, physical and verbal/passive, increased the probability that she sustained injury in cases of intimate assault. To better interpret the regression coefficients, the factor by which the odds of either sustaining injury or receiving medical treatment when the independent variables increase by one unit are displayed in the Exp(B) column. From this we can see that the odds of sustaining injury from intimate assaults increased by a factor of 1.7 if the victim used any physical self-protection measure. Further, the odds of the victim sustaining injury almost doubled (a factor of 1.978) if she responded to her assaulter verbally (e.g., pleading or arguing). No other variables included in the model were significant in predicting injury resulting from intimate assaults.

The second panel of Table II displays results of the logistic regression predicting the necessity for medical treatment resulting from injury from intimate assaults using these same predictor variables. From this it appears that use of self-protective behavior did not increase the extent to which female victims of intimate perpetrated assaults needed medical care. However, the odds of needing medical treatment were increased if the offender had a weapon and if the victim was black. In fact, the odds of needing

**Table III.** Logistic Regression Results Predicting Whether Victim Sustained Injury During Commission of Assault From a Stranger and Whether Victim Received Medical Treatment for Injuries Sustained, NCVS 1987-1990 ($n$ = 257)

|  | B | S.E. | Sig. | Exp(B) |
|---|---|---|---|---|
| Predicitng injury to victim |  |  |  |  |
|   Black victim | −.4028 | .4441 | .3644 | .6685 |
|   Family income | −.0605 | .0329 | .0661 | .9413 |
|   Offender using drugs/alcohol | −.0534 | .2787 | .8481 | .9480 |
|   Offender had weapon | .9223 | .3373 | .0063 | 2.515 |
|   Victim used physical self-protection | −.4566 | .3076 | .1377 | .6334 |
|   Victim used verbal self-protection | −.1384 | .3650 | .7046 | .8708 |
| Predicting medical treatment |  |  |  |  |
|   Black victim | .5759 | .6244 | .3564 | 1.778 |
|   Family income | .0443 | .0457 | .3321 | 1.045 |
|   Offender using drugs/alcohol | .0771 | .3916 | .8440 | 1.080 |
|   Offender had weapon | .2065 | .3935 | .5997 | 1.229 |
|   Victim used physical self-protection | .0547 | .4143 | .8949 | 1.056 |
|   Victim used verbal self-protection | .0611 | .4694 | .8964 | 1.063 |

medical treatment were over 2 to 1 if the offender was armed compared to intimate assaults perpetrated by unarmed offenders.

The next issue we investigated was the extent to which these same relationships were present for female victims of assault when the offender was a stranger. Table III presents the logistic regression results of the same independent and dependent variables in cases of stranger perpetrated assaults. From the top panel of Table III, it can be seen that the victim's use of self-protection in cases of stranger assaults did *not* increase the probability of sustaining injury. The only significant predictor of injury in assaults perpetrated by strangers was presence of a weapon on the offender. If the offender had a weapon, victims were more than 2 times as likely to sustain injuries (a factor of 2.515) compared to stranger assaults where the offender was unarmed.

When these same variables were used to predict the necessity for medical treatment, no coefficient attained significance. As the bottom panel of Table III indicates, none of the independent variables predicts severity of injury sustained by victims who were assaulted by strangers.

## DISCUSSION

Given the frequency and severity of assaults against women by intimates, it is of central importance to explore those factors of an assault that increase the probability that a woman will sustain serious injury from an assault. This study has be.  . initial attempt to explore the extent to which utilization of resistance (both physical and verbal) by victims of intimate and stranger perpetrated assaults increased the likelihood that they would sustain injury or require medical care. The results suggest that the dynamics and consequences of employing self-protective behavior in stranger versus intimate assaults may be very different.

While victims of intimate assaults were more likely to use self-protective behavior, they were also more likely to report that this behavior made the assaultive situation worse. In fact, when multivariate models were analyzed, the odds of sustaining an injury in an intimate assault nearly doubled if the victim used any self-protective measure. Unlike intimate perpetrated assaults, female victims of stranger perpetrated assaults did not increase the likelihood that they would sustain injury by employing either physical or verbal resistance. The only contextual circumstance that significantly predicted an increased risk to injury in stranger perpetrated assaults was presence of a weapon by the offender.

Self-protective behavior did not, however, predict the extent to which victims of either intimate or stranger perpetrated assaults received medical treatment for their injuries. It should be remembered here that although females assaulted by intimates were more likely to sustain injuries, they were *not* more likely to seek medical treatment for these injuries compared to females assaulted by strangers. It may be that female victims of stranger perpetrated assault in this sample suffered a greater proportion of injuries that required medical care than those sustained at the hands of intimates. However, it may also be that female victims of domestic assault do not seek medical treatment for other reasons. For example, women may fear retaliation from their abuser for seeking public assistance with their injuries or they may suffer embarrassment and shame as the result of their victimization. Each of these factors could prevent victims of intimate assaults from seeking the medical care they need.

Although this has been an exploratory attempt to investigate the effects of victim resistance in domestic assaults, the findings are consistent with results from earlier research related to this issue. In particular, others have eluded to the fact that women who fight back during a domestic assault more often serve to escalate the level of violence already present (Carmody and Williams, 1987; Gelles and Straus, 1988). Further, fighting back in a battering relationship has not been found to be an effective technique for ending the violence (Bowker, 1983). Results of the present work coupled with this earlier research suggests that "fighting fire with fire" during an assault perpetrated by an intimate may not only increase the "blaze" of violence, but also increase the risk of sustaining injury.

Implications of these findings should not go unnoticed. However, it is important to keep in mind that this has been an initial and exploratory attempt to unravel relationships between victim resistance and injury sustained from assaults perpetrated by intimates and strangers. Specific policy recommendations are premature at this point, particularly given the fact that the consequences of such policy recommendations are so serious to the lives of women. Clearly, additional research must address these issues with samples more representative of all domestic assaults. We hope that this work will be a catalyst for others to investigate these important and potentially life-threatening issues.

## REFERENCES

Alexander, C. H., and Hubble, D. L. (1990). Sample weights for the NCVS and NCVS estimation. Paper presented at the Workshop on the Design and use of the National Crime Survey, University of Maryland, College Park, June, 1990. Sponsored by the Bureau of Justice Statistics and the Committee on Law and Justice Statistics, American Statistical Association.

Bachman, R. (1994). Violence Against Women (NCJ #145325). Bureau of Justice Statistics, U.S. Department of Justice, Washington, D.C.: U.S. Government Printing Office.

Bachman, R., and Pillemer, K. A. (1992). Epidemiology and family violence involving adults. In Ammeman, R. T., and Hersen, M. (eds.), Assessment of Family Violence, Wiley, New York, NY.

Bachman, R., and Taylor, B. (1994). The Measurement of Family Violence and Rape by The Redesigned National Crime Victimization Survey. Justice Quarterly, 11(3).

Block, R., and Skogan, W. G. (1986). Resistance and nonfatal outcomes in stranger-to-stranger predatory crime, Viol. Vict. 1(4): 241-23.

Block, R., and Skogan, W. G. (1985). Dynamics of violence between strangers: Victim resistance and outcomes in rape, robbery and assault, Research Report, National Institute of Justice, US Department of Justice (NIJ Publ. No. 81-IJ-CX-0069.

Bowker, L. H. (1983). Beating Wife Beating, Lexington Books, Lexington, MA.

Browne, A. (1987). When Battered Women Kill, Free Press/Macmillan, New York, NY.

Bureau of Justice Statistics. (1992). Criminal Victimization in the United States, 1991: A National Crime Victimization Survey Report, Washington, DC: U.S. Government Printing Office.

Carmody, D. C., and Williams, K. R. (1987). Wife assault and perceptions of sanctions, Viol. Vict. 2(1).

Cook, P. J. (1986). Relationship between victim resistance and injury in noncommercial robbery. J. Legal Studies 15: 405-416.

Gelles, R. J., and Straus, M. A. (1988). Intimate violence: The Causes and Consequences of Abuse in the American Family, Touchstone, New York, NY.

Kleck, G., and Sayles, S. (1990). Rape and Resistance. Social Prob. 37(2): 149-162.

National Coalition Against Domestic Violence (1985). Understanding the Dynamics of Domestic Violence.

Rao, J. N. K., and A. J. Scott (1984). On Chi-Squared tests for multiway contingency tables with cell proportions estimated from survey data. Annals Stat. 12: 46-60.

Stark, E., Flitcraft, A., Zuckerman, D., Grey, A., Robinson, J., and Frazier W. (19810. Wife Abuse in the Medical Setting: An Introduction to Health Personnel, National Clearinghouse on Domestic Violence, Monograph Series #7.

Straus, M. A., and Gelles, R. J. (1990). *Physical Violence in American Families: Risk Factors and Adaptions to Violence in 8,145 Families*, Transaction Publishers, New Brunswick, NJ.
Wolter, Kirk M. (1985). *Introduction to Variance Estimation*, Springer-Verlag, New York.

# Determining Police Response to Domestic Violence Victims

## The Role of Victim Preference

EVE S. BUZAWA
THOMAS AUSTIN

**This article examines** when and if victim preferences affect the decision to arrest. As extensively discussed earlier, arrest of domestic violence offenders is not the normal predicted outcome after police intervention. In those relatively few circumstances where police are called, arrest usually does not occur.

Many variables have been found to affect the frequency of officer arrest decisions. These are briefly stated in the Introduction to this special issue and more fully explicated in Buzawa and Buzawa (1990). This article reports the results of one research project that explored several factors that affected the decision to arrest, including the impact of victim preferences.

It has long been known that the behavioral interaction between the officer and the participants, *both* victim and offender, clearly affects the decision to arrest. Police are, for example, far less likely to make arrest in cases where the victim is married and living with the offender (Dobash & Dobash, 1979; Martin, 1976; Worden & Pollitz, 1984). Similarly, if the victim's life-style is perceived (often inaccurately or as a result of racial or class stereotypes) to include violence as a normal way of life, arrests are made far less frequently (Black, 1980; Ferraro, 1989; Stanko, 1989). Similarly, if a victim's conduct is not appropriate, police appear far less willing to aggressively intervene (Manning, 1978; Skolnick, 1975). This is especially true if the victim is perceived as being quarrelsome or demanding in front of the officer as opposed to being rational and deferential (Ford, 1983; Pepinsky, 1975).

**Authors' Note:** *Portions of this article are from Domestic Violence: The Changing Criminal Justice Response edited by Eve Buzawa and Carl Buzawa, 1992, Westport, CT: Greenwood. Copyright © 1992 by Greenwood Publishing Group, Inc. Reprinted by permission.*

AMERICAN BEHAVIORAL SCIENTIST, Vol. 36 No. 5, May 1993 610-623
© 1993 Sage Publications, Inc.

The foregoing implicitly concedes that the decision to arrest is not based on the seriousness of the crime nor on the strength of the evidence against the offender. In any event, many prior studies have reported that victim preferences by themselves do not significantly effect decisions due to the overwhelming police bias against arrest. In fact, Bayley (1988) reported that assailant arrest was not even correlated with victim wishes. The collective impact renders the victim powerless. Her role is as a passive victim rather than an active participant in the decision-making process.

There have, however, been several studies reporting that victim preference does affect officer actions. These suggested that when jurisdictions had a policy that actively discouraged arrest, only victim preferences to press charges could mediate such a policy, although on relatively few occasions. In short, victim preference was a necessary condition but not a sufficient reason to make an arrest (Bell, 1984; Berk & Loseke, 1980-1981; Worden & Pollitz, 1984).

It is not surprising that victim preferences would be considered a valid discriminator for agency action. Given the known police desire to obtain "good" arrests, defined as those that result in felony convictions, the importance of this factor is obvious. Officers "know" that without victim cooperation, any charge will either be dismissed by the prosecutor or result in an acquittal for failure of evidence. They may also believe that if the victim is unwilling to expend the effort to initiate a complaint, the seriousness of the attack or the victim's account may not warrant any police effort. Further, because domestic assault is usually charged as a misdemeanor assault, the arrest does not have the same meaning in the police subculture.

However, the continued relevance of these research studies is not clear because there has been a well-documented change in the emphasis of police departments toward arrest. Under these conditions, it is possible that victim preference may not be salient in the current decision to arrest. By conducting this research, we sought to explore what impact victim preference had among other factors in a modern department.

## RESEARCH DESIGN

This effort arose as a reaction to the results of an initial project conducted by the Massachusetts Anti-Crime Council. That project indirectly explored officer attitudes toward domestic violence incidents by an examination of official police reports. After examining police reports from eight representative departments, it was found that over 75% failed to state the victim's preference regarding arrest. Not surprisingly, those failing to note victim preferences rarely made arrests. In short, in Massachusetts, even when such information was requested on a report form, this was not considered worthy of inquiry nor necessary for administrative compliance. Although suggestive of a lack of concern for victim desires, the former research clearly was only of a very preliminary nature. No systematic effort was made in the Massachusetts research to ascertain the reason for failure to report the requested information.

In this research, the authors received the active cooperation of the Detroit Police Department. The City of Detroit was selected for a variety of reasons. First, the authors have done considerable past research with the police department and have extensive background knowledge of the city and the department's administrators and officers. Further, the department has shown a commitment to appropriately handling domestic violence incidents. The authors wish to extend their profound gratitude to Executive Deputy Chief James Bannon and Commander James Jackson who enabled us to obtain full access to their department.

We incorporated several features to increase the validity of the data obtained in this study. We told participants that the project was designed to improve future officer training on domestic assault. Four precincts representative of the city's demographic characteristics were selected: two from the Eastern Division and two from the Western Division. The deputy chief in charge of each division was given Supplemental Arrest Reports, and officers in the selected precincts were instructed to complete these forms for all domestic assaults to which they responded. Officers were assured that responses would be kept confidential and would not serve in any way as an evaluative criteria. The instrument collected background information on the victim and offender, characteristics of the incident, seriousness of injury to victim, offender, and officer, and the nature of the victim preference and actual police response.

Approximately 165 reports were completed in a 4-month period. Information was requested concerning victims' address and telephone numbers for both them and a friend or relative who would know how to reach them should they relocate. Subsequently, 110 victims were randomly selected for a follow-up visit. Extensive efforts were made to contact all selected victims, and repetitive contacts at varying times of day were conducted, resulting in a sample of 90 victims. Due to the sensitivity of the information sought and the initial realization that much of the information could not be predetermined and subjected to an interview format, the first author personally conducted all the interviews. The interviewer traveled in an unmarked patrol car accompanied by a plainclothes officer, usually a woman from the training section. To lessen respondent distrust, efforts were made to be as non-threatening as possible. Victims were accurately told that a study was being conducted to determine their satisfaction with the police response to the incident and that all information would be confidential. Although we were unable to reach 10 of the original victims selected, not one prospective interviewee actually contacted declined to participate. Some, in fact, were pleased that there was an interest in following up on their case.

To minimize possible bias, the accompanying officer remained at a comfortable distance, usually talking with children, neighbors, or the assailant. If the assailant was present, the officer would engage him or her in conversation out of the victim's hearing. Alternately, the victim was taken into an area where she could feel certain that the conversation would not be overheard.

Victims generally appeared relaxed, and a few even thanked the interviewer for the visit. Some stated they were either surprised or felt it admirable to have the police department interested in following up with a personal visit. No hostility or anger was encountered by victims, except for one incident involving an intoxicated assailant.

There were two chief goals of the interview. First, an attempt was made to determine the accuracy of police reports, especially as to the officer's statements concerning the victim's preferred police action. A second objective was to obtain the victim's perspective about the dynamics of the domestic violence incidence, the police-citizen encounter, and the recurrence of violence.

## DATA ANALYSIS

### THE SUPPLEMENTAL ARREST REPORT

The results of the police questionnaire demonstrated a somewhat complex pattern of factors that were correlated with decisions to arrest/not arrest offenders. The three primary determinants appeared to be the presence of others at the scene of the crime, whether the victim lived with the offender, and the victim's preference. In addition, the seriousness of the injury definitely affected the decision to arrest but in a nonlinear manner.

The presence of bystanders during the abuse dramatically increased the chances that an arrest would be made (see Table 1). In approximately 50% of the 49 cases where witnesses were present, an arrest was made. However, in the far more typical case of an assault without witnesses (e.g., at the victim and/or offender's abode) arrests occurred less than one quarter of the time.

TABLE 1:    Percentage Bystanders/Witnesses Present, by Offender Arrested

|  | Bystanders/Witnesses Present | |
| --- | --- | --- |
| Offender Arrested | Yes (n) | No (n) |
| Yes | 49 (24) | 22 (21) |
| No | 51 (25) | 79 (83) |

$\chi^2 = 11.2, p < .01, \phi = .29$

It is instructive that very similar results occurred when children were present during the assault (see Table 2). The only difference was that the presence of children apparently had somewhat less effect than other witnesses.

The reason for this finding is probably closely related to the concept of spousal abuse as a "hidden crime." It has long been a truism in the literature that a sizable body of criminal justice personnel view domestic violence as inappropriate for intervention by criminal law (Hartog, 1976; Pleck, 1979, 1989; Rothman, 1980). The presence of witnesses, especially bystanders, and those independent of the victim and offender might therefore convert the offense into a significant matter for many of these people. Alternately, the importance of witnesses may be due to the fact that they corroborate the victim. In this light, the presence of children who may not be reliable witnesses might be theorized as not being as significant as the presence of truly independent outside witnesses. The legitimacy of this position as a policy, is of course, questionable.

As might be anticipated, the presence of weapons affected how the officer handled the incident. Table 3 indicates that when guns or sharp objects, such as knives, were used, arrests occurred in 45% of the cases. This declined to slightly more than 25% when either blunt objects or bodily weapons, such as hands or feet, were used.

Table 4 demonstrates that in this sample the nature of the injury was significantly related to the probability of arrest. When an offender was seriously injured, over 50% of the offenders were arrested. This, in fact, constituted the only subsample in this study with an arrest rate in excess of 50%. The arrest rate, as expected, declined, with 37% arrested in the case of minor but apparent injuries and 10% with minor injuries that were claimed but not observable. The only anomaly in the data was the rise for those that did not have any injury where 29% of the offenders were arrested.

The third factor that appears to be associated with rates of offender arrest is whether the victim lived with the offender. The association between arrest

TABLE 2:    Percentage Children Present, by Offender Arrested

| Offender Arrested | Children Present | |
|---|---|---|
| | Yes (n) | No (n) |
| Yes | 42 (28) | 22 (19) |
| No | 58 (39) | 78 (66) |

$\chi^2 = 5.7, p < .02, \phi = .20$

TABLE 3:    Percentage Weapon Type Involved, by Offender Arrested

| Offender Arrested | Type of Weapon Involved | | |
|---|---|---|---|
| | Gun/Sharp Object | Blunt Object/Other | Bodily Weapon |
| Yes | 45 (17) | 26 (21) | 27 (7) |
| No | 55 (21) | 74 (61) | 73 (19) |

$\chi^2 = 4.7, p = .09$, Cramer's V = .19

NOTE: Number of respondents is shown in parentheses.

TABLE 4:    Percentage Seriousness of Injury to Victim, by Offender Arrested

| Offender Arrested | Seriousness of Injury to Victim | | | |
|---|---|---|---|---|
| | Serious | Minor-Apparent | Minor-Claimed | None |
| Yes | 57 (16) | 37 (17) | 10 (5) | 29 (9) |
| No | 43 (12) | 63 (29) | 90 (46) | 71 (22) |

$\chi^2 = 20.8, p < .01$, Cramer's V = .36

NOTE: Number of respondents is shown in parentheses.

and living with the offender, as demonstrated in Table 5, is both clear and expected. In this case, arrests were more than twice as likely where the offender and victim shared the same residence.

The sample did not show a statistically significant difference between treatment of assaults involving married couples compared to others. This was very surprising in light of previous research and the findings concerning the relationship of arrests for offenders/victims living together.

In fact, a markedly different picture emerged when we examined the relationship of the offender to the victim and arrest. We found that

TABLE 5:   Percentage Victim Living With Offender, by Offender Arrested

|  | Victim Living With Offender | |
| --- | --- | --- |
| Offender Arrested | Yes (n) | No (n) |
| Yes | 39 (36) | 17 (10) |
| No | 61 (56) | 83 (48) |

$\chi^2 = 7.0, p < .01, \phi = .23$

regardless of the marital/domestic status—whether the offender was the victim's "spouse/ex-spouse," "boyfriend," "relative" such as in-law or "other" (primarily acquaintance)—the likelihood of the offender being arrested remained just about the same: 31% for spouse/ex-spouse compared to 29% for assaults involving acquaintances. This result is quite surprising and failed to confirm previous literature that had suggested that victim's marital status was a major predictor of police response (see esp. Black, 1980).

We are uncertain of the reason why this behavior deviated so markedly from expectations. We hypothesized that when the overall domestic violence arrest rate climbs from the 5% to 10% level reported in most samples in the previous literature to over the 30% level shown in this research, it is a profile of a more activist police department. The effect in that type of department of marital differences in offenders/victims then becomes (properly) submerged while the impact of living together still remains a key factor that discriminates among probable police actions.

Further research in high arrest jurisdictions, such as Detroit, clearly is needed to measure the permanence and validity of this very tentative finding. If reinforced, it will demonstrate that victim's residence and not marital status may be the key to predicting police response.

The other key factor associated with the decision to arrest is the victim's preferences (see Table 6). Of the 101 cases, 34 (34%) of the victims desired prosecution. In these cases, arrests were made 44% ($n = 15$) of the time. However, when the victim's preference was to do nothing or merely to talk or be advised of her rights, arrests were made in only 21% (14 out of 67) of the cases. This demonstrates that victim preference remains significant in the decision to arrest.

Finally, the data were examined to determine if there were significant differences in the profiles of incidents involving male victims of violence versus the more typical occurrence of male violence against females. Of the 162 cases where the gender of victim was specified, 138 (85%) were female.

22

TABLE 6: Percentage Victim Preference for Police Response, by Offender Arrested

| | Victim Preference for Police Response | |
|---|---|---|
| Offender Arrested | Prosecute | Do Nothing or Talk |
| Yes | 44 (15) | 21 (14) |
| No | 56 (19) | 79 (53) |

$\chi^2 = 7.1$, $p = .03$, Cramer's V = .26

NOTE: Number of respondents is shown in parentheses.

TABLE 7: Percentage of Victim, by Seriousness of Injury to Victim

| | Sex of Victim | |
|---|---|---|
| Seriousness of Injury | Male | Female |
| Serious | 37 (9) | 14 (19) |
| Minor-apparent | 25 (6) | 30 (42) |
| Minor-claimed | 21 (5) | 34 (47) |
| None | 17 (4) | 22 (30) |

$\chi^2 = 8.2$, $p = .04$, Cramer's V = .23

NOTE: Number of respondents is shown in parentheses.

Table 7 demonstrates that the profile of injuries to men shows that they reported almost three times the rate of serious injury as did their female counterparts—38% compared to 14%.

It is unclear why the male victims reported such high rates of serious injury. It is possible that the reluctance of male victims to report domestic violence results in only severe assaults ever being brought to police attention. As more fully discussed later, male victims were the only identifiable subgroup dissatisfied with police intervention. This may, at least partially, explain the disproportionate underreporting by male victims.

Despite differences in the rates of severe injury in male versus female victims and the differences in satisfaction reported by such victims, arrest rates of male and female offenders were very similar—31% compared to 26%. Unfortunately, the relatively small number of female offenders ($n = 19$) precluded an analysis of such cases. However, the relatively similar rates of arrest may mask differential treatment of male and female defendants when the severity of the injury is controlled.

Several other potential relationships that might mediate arrest rates were also examined. No tables depicting these relationships are presented because neither the level of statistical significance nor the degree of association are as strong as those generated in Tables 1 through 7.

The results of this research project tended to cast doubt on the continued validity of a "well known" relationship—the reluctance of the police to make arrests in cases of "Black on Black" violence. We instead found that Black offenders were somewhat more likely to be arrested than their White counterparts—33% as compared to 24%. This pattern remained valid when the victim was also Black, the offender's arrest rate being 32% compared to 26%. Because the patrol force of Detroit is about 70% minority, it is unlikely that this pattern is due to a prejudicial White police force. We instead believe that Black officers are *less* tolerant of Black crimes and criminals than are Whites (Black, 1980).

Finally, we found that arrest of the offender was only slightly more likely when it involved a "repeated problem" at the address—26% compared to 19%. If confirmed in subsequent research, this substantiates that there is only a very weak relationship between repeated problems at an address and officer conduct. Officers may not be aware of previous calls or, alternately, do not care that such offenses have occurred in the past. The importance of this is that it contradicts existing research in nondomestic violence areas that had suggested that known recidivists are more likely to receive a severe response by the criminal justice system.

### THE VICTIM INTERVIEW

Analysis of victim interviews suggests a populace that is highly satisfied with the responses of the police department; 93 of 110 interviewees (85%) stated that they were generally satisfied with the police response.

Aspects of the police response that most satisfied these victims were that the police responded in accordance with their preferences (e.g., when the victim wanted an offender arrested, this was generally done even if no visible injury was present). It is noteworthy that in 37% of cases, an arrest was made without any visible injury. Whereas previous research indicated that this is probably due to offender demeanor and officer/offender interaction (Manning, 1978; Skolnick, 1975), our data revealed the role of a second factor: victim preference.

Conversely, when the victim wanted the officers to simply end the violence by either removing or talking to the offender, they were largely satisfied when the police followed this course of action. Interviews revealed that even when the victim had been seriously injured, many did not wish to have the offender arrested and confirmed the officer's report stating that the victim's preference was in fact nonarrest.

TABLE 8:    Percentage Satisfaction With Police Response, by Sex of Victim

| Satisfied With Police Response | Sex of Victim | |
| --- | --- | --- |
| | Male | Female |
| Yes | 0 (0) | 94 (93) |
| No | 100 (12) | 6 (5) |

$\chi^2 = 37.4, p < .01, \phi = .82$

NOTE: Number of respondents is shown in parentheses.

An analysis of the variance in the satisfaction of victims suggests several dichotomies. Of primary importance was the sex of the victim. Results from this analysis is depicted in Table 8.

Clearly, the victim population was divided along lines of gender. Whereas most women were satisfied, *not one* male victim was pleased with the police response. They instead stated that preferences were not adhered to by the officers nor was their victimization taken seriously. The lack of police responsiveness occurred regardless of the degree of their injury.

For example, one male reported requiring hospitalization for treatment of a stab wound that just missed puncturing his lungs. Despite his request to have the offending woman removed (not even arrested), the officers simply called an ambulance and refused formal sanctions against the woman, including her removal. Indeed, all the men who were interviewed consistently reported having the incident trivialized and being belittled by the officers.

It is, of course, unclear whether the male victims are responding through the prism of misperception. It is possible they feel somewhat more self-conscious about having the police intervene. As discussed earlier, the police data indicated that males as a group were three times more likely to be seriously injured, so it is possible that police are only called in dire necessity. Moreover, interview data suggested that in cases of male victims, the call was far less likely to be made by the victim. When males were less seriously injured, the police were more likely to have been called by neighbors or other parties and not by the victim. Therefore, there may be a defined subpopulation of victims: namely, males who are less likely to call police due to perceptions or the reality of police indifference.

Under such circumstances, police actions are likely to be more strongly criticized for any real or perceived slight, however minor. Male victims may also be embarrassed when a female officer, present in high numbers in this sample, responded. Despite this, we believe there is some differential treat-

25

ment by officers. Reported conversations between male victims and officers appeared to confirm that officers were substantively less sympathetic to the plight of a male victim.

Another obvious and interesting implication is that male victims may consequently be disproportionately underreported in victimization statistics. This was previously suggested by Steinmetz (1977-1978, 1980). The fact that male victims were three times as likely to sustain serious injury requiring calling police for assistance, were less likely to initiate the call themselves, and were dissatisfied with the police response tends to indicate a general reluctance for involvement with the criminal justice systems related to expectations of trivialization/denigration of their injury and a failure to honor their preferences.

A study of the 5 female victims who were dissatisfied also strongly supports the proposition that dissatisfaction is related to the failure to follow victim preferences. These women all stated that they wanted a more aggressive police response, including, on occasion, arrest. When these preferences were ignored, they became dissatisfied.

Parenthetically, we tried to determine why these victims had their preferences ignored. We are unsure, however, whether behavioral aspects of the police-citizen encounter appear to predominate. For example, in one instance the victim described continually calling the police, and when they arrived, "yelling at officers for not doing their job." The officer accompanying the interviewer wryly observed that many officers would instantly dislike her and probably discount anything she said due to her belligerence and hostility.

It is also important to realize that not all cases of failure to follow victim preferences are unreasonable. One woman was not satisfied with the adequacy of an arrest. She recounted how she emphatically asked the police to beat the offender because an arrest would have no effect. He apparently had been frequently arrested for other offenses. When the police refused and left with the arrested offender, she had her brother come back and beat him up after his return home. She believed that that action alone was responsible for having deterred future violence.

Although it is possible that the variance in satisfaction among victims might be based on sociodemographic characteristics, such as race, ethnicity, age of victim, and social class, the relatively homogeneous sample and the small number ($n = 17$) of dissatisfied respondents precluded such an analysis.

The actions of the police officers were, however, studied to determine if making an arrest versus other activity appeared to significantly influence levels of satisfaction. This sample did not show any such correlation. Instead, it appeared to be wholly dependent on whether the officers followed victim

26

preference. Similarly, we found no difference based on officer gender or race. In this sample, the actions of Black and White and male and female officers were consistently rated highly.

## CONCLUSION

We recognize that use of a generic term "satisfied" is somewhat simplistic. It is difficult to assert with any degree of accuracy the varying ways in which victims determine whether they are satisfied. The term is, of course, largely dependent on victim expectations of "proper" police conduct and the expected impact that police action should have on future offender conduct. For some victims, this will merely mean coming when called, especially in the setting of a poor inner city where many calls are never answered. On the opposite extreme, it is possible—though not likely in this sample—that others may deem themselves "satisfied" only when the police action can be directly tied to an immediate arrest followed by sustained cessation of violence.

For this reason, any study of victim satisfaction with police responses has only limited external validity. Subsequent studies therefore need to focus on variances in departmental response, victim expectations, including variations in departmental response, and victim expectations, including variations based on victim sociodemographic characteristics and urban/suburban/rural distinctions. In addition, although situational determinants, such as the type of police response, did not greatly affect the very high levels of victim satisfaction found in this sample, the finding that males were not as satisfied nor as likely to contact the police must be studied further to determine whether it relates to failed expectations of police conduct (e.g., the police refusing to take cues from the victim) or, instead, whether it is related to the attitude/performance of the responding officer in the situational context of dealing with males as victims. It is possible that male victims have been neglected in efforts to provide more responsive police actions.

There are major policy implications in this research. Specifically, despite new controversy over the deterrent effect of arrest as a result of the replication studies, there will undoubtedly remain a continued emphasis on the role of sanctions (i.e., making arrests). This is exemplified by the growing number of local jurisdictions and states mandating arrests. This denigrates the traditional role of officer discretion and, to an extent, the primacy of victim preferences. Whereas the legislative intent may be to remove police discretion and thereby to provide greater responsiveness to victim needs, a collateral consequence may be the concurrent removal of victim discretion.

27

For this reason, we support an alternative approach. We believe that police should increase their responsiveness to the desires of victims. Such a policy may not automatically lead to higher rates of arrest. It is, in many cases, unlikely to be related to the seriousness of victim injury.

In stating this policy preference, we recognize that some analysts reject the primacy of victim preference in determining the appropriate criminal justice response. They believe that a victim who has frequently suffered repeated injuries is often unable to escape the psychological constraints of tolerating violence without outside intervention. Also, such researchers believe that violence in itself should be punished as an offense against society, not only due to the impact on the victim but also because of the long-term effects on other family members and because failure to punish indicates societal tolerance of further male domination.

We cannot answer such a normative position except to state that in responding to other aspects of interpersonal violence (with the obvious exception of murder and violence against legal incompetents, such as children), victim preference has long been recognized and generally accepted as the primary factor in determining proper police action.

If we adopt the position that victim preference should be of primary importance, then the policy issue becomes how to ensure that this occurs. Perhaps this is best done by increasing police accountability. To some extent, this is already happening in the form of lawsuits against police for failure to honor victim preferences. However, because these lawsuits may properly lead to multi-million-dollar judgments against nearly bankrupt municipalities, they cannot be regarded as inherently the best method to ensure police accountability. Instead, this could be accomplished at a minimal cost by relatively modest modifications of police procedures. For example, police reports might mandate that the officer request and report victim preferences and, if necessary, explain in detail why the officer refuses to follow such preferences. This single act would dramatically cut the incidence of non-responsive police action. Similarly, regulations could also provide that victims actually sign the report and receive a copy. On the back of the victim's copy, a list of referral agencies and sources of victim assistance could be stated in English or any other appropriate language.

Finally, we must realize that effective police action depends on police attitudes toward domestic violence. As explained in many other research monographs, proper training and support by senior police administrators may greatly affect subsequent police actions. In any event, it appears critical to increase the police officer's level of consciousness to the serious nature of domestic violence crimes and provide clear consistent direction to the officers to act in appropriate cases. When this is done, as in Detroit, there is a relatively high correlation between the officer's perceptions of victim desires and the actual expressed victim concerns. If such knowledge is then acted on and the victim's legitimate requests are followed, there may be no need for more drastic remedies, such as the imposition of a mandatory arrest policy.

## REFERENCES

Bayley, D. H. (1986). The tactical choices of police patrol officers. *Journal of Criminal Justice, 14*, 320-348.

Bell, D. (1984). The police responses to domestic violence: A replication study. *Police Studies, 7*, 136-143.

Berk, S. F., & Loseke, D. R. (1980-1981). "Handling" family violence: Situational determinants of police arrests in domestic disturbances. *Law and Society Review, 18*(3), 479-498.

Black, D. (1980). *The manners and customs of the police.* New York: Academic Press.

Buzawa, E., & Buzawa, C. (1990). *Domestic violence: The criminal justice response.* Newbury Park, CA: Sage.

Dobash, R. E., & Dobash, R. (1979). *Violence against wives: A case against the patriarchy.* New York: Free Press.

Ferraro, K. (1989). Policing women battering. *Social Problems, 36*(1), 61-74.

Ford, D. A. (1983). Wife battery and criminal justice: A study of victim decision making. *Family Relations, 32*, 463-475.

Hartog, H. (1976). The public law of a county court: Judicial government in eighteenth century Massachusetts. *American Journal of Legal History, 20*, 282-329.

Manning, P. (1978). The police: Mandate, strategies and appearances. In P. Manning & J. Van Mannen (Eds.), *Policing a view from the street.* Santa Monica, CA: Goodyear.

Martin, D. (1976). *Battered wives.* San Francisco: Glide.

Pepinsky, H. E. (1976). Police patrolman's offense-reporting behavior. *Journal of Research in Crime and Delinquency, 13*(1), 33-47.

Pleck, E. (1979). Wife beating in nineteenth century America. *Victimology, 4*(1), 60-74.

Pleck, E. (1989). Criminal approaches to family violence, 1640-1980. In L. Ohlin & M. Tonry (Eds.), *Crime and justice: A review of research* (Vol. 2, pp. 19-58). Chicago: University of Chicago Press.

Rothman, D. J. (1980). *Conscience and convenience: The asylum and its alternatives in progressive America.* Boston: Little, Brown.

Skolnick, J. H. (1975). *Justice without trial.* New York: Wiley.

Stanko, E. A. (1989). Missing the mark? Police battering. In J. Hanmewr, J. Radford, & B. Stanko (Eds.), *Women, policing and male violence.* London: Routledge & Kegan Paul.

Steinmetz, S. (1977-1978). The battered husband syndrome. *Victimology, 2*, 499-509.

Steinmetz, S. (1980). Women and violence. *American Journal of Psychotherapy, 34*(3), 334.

Worden, R. E., & Pollitz, A. A. (1984). Police arrests in domestic disturbances: A further look. *Law and Society Review, 18*, 105-119.

# THE EFFECTS OF VICTIM IMPACT STATEMENTS ON SENTENCING DECISIONS: A TEST IN AN URBAN SETTING*

ROBERT C. DAVIS
BARBARA E. SMITH
Victim Services Agency
New York, NY

Many reforms have been initiated in an effort to assure victims participation in the justice process. Although these reforms appear to represent great progress, it remains unclear to what extent victims actually have benefited. The present study examines one widely heralded reform measure—victim impact statements—and seeks to determine whether they have resulted in sentences more congruent with the harm done to victims and/or in sentences generally harsher on convicted defendants. These questions were examined in a field test implemented in Bronx County, NY. The study concludes that impact statements neither increased officials' consideration of harm to victims nor resulted in generally harsher sentencing decisions.

The victim movement, begun two decades ago, has matured. More than 5,000 programs now provide services to victims in crisis and victims involved in the criminal justice system (Davis and Henley 1990). The great majority of these programs are no longer tenuously funded demonstration projects, but entities with established places in local, state, and federal government budgets. As part of this maturation process, victim supporters have advocated not only that victims in the criminal justice system be treated well and kept informed, but also that they receive rights to participate in the court process (e.g., DuBow and Becker 1976; Goldstein 1982).

Early attempts to allow greater participation to victims were implemented without supporting legislation. Reformers persuaded criminal court officials to listen to victims' statements or to inform them of key decisions. Often these efforts were implemented as limited-term experiments (see, for example, Clark et al. 1984; Kerstetter and Heinz 1979). As time passed, however, victim advocates

---

* This research was funded under Grant 7-0483-0-NY-IJ of the National Institute of Justice. The views herein reflect those of the authors, and are not necessarily those of NIJ.

JUSTICE QUARTERLY, Vol. 11 No. 3, September 1994
© 1994 Academy of Criminal Justice Sciences

become more and more strongly convinced of the need for legislation mandating that officials listen to victims and/or inform them of court actions (e.g., Davis, Kunreuther, and Connick 1984).

## Victims' Rights Legislation and Victim Impact Statements

During the 1980s, state and federal governments implemented a vast array of legislation guaranteeing rights to victims in the criminal justice process. In 1981 the federal government took the initiative by declaring a Victims' Rights Week, to focus national attention on victim issues. Soon after that time, provisions were made to inform victims of proceedings in their cases and, in some instances, to consult them about the course of prosecution.

In 1982 the federal government established a Presidential Task Force on Victims of Crime. The Task Force recommended that victim impact statements—assessments of the physical, financial, and psychological effects of crime on individual victims—be taken and distributed to judges before sentencing. That recommendation was implemented when the 1982 Omnibus Victim and Witness Protection Act became law; it mandated that victim impact statements be provided at sentencing in federal cases.

By the mid-1980s, victim impact statements had become a popular vehicle for increased participation by victims. Victims' involvement at sentencing had been endorsed by the American Bar Association and the National Judicial College (Kelly 1990). By 1982, 12 states had passed impact statement laws (Hudson 1984). By 1984 the number had climbed to 22 (Davis, Fischer, and Paykin 1985); as of August 1987, 48 states had provisions authorizing some form of victim participation in conjunction with imposition of sentence (McLeod 1988:3).

Victim impact statements offer victims the opportunity to relate the harm done to them by the crime and (in some states) to express their concerns, in the expectation that this information will be considered in sentencing decisions. Supporters of victim impact statements have argued that the introduction of such statements will improve the sentencing process by making decisions conform more closely to the community's interests (Henderson 1985), by reminding officials of the human costs of crime (Kelly 1987), and by making sentences more proportional to the actual harm done by the offender (Rubel 1986).

Victim impact statements have met with criticism on several fronts, however. Some writers have expressed fear that allowing victims to participate may reduce judges' ability to withstand unreasonable public pressure (Rubel 1986). Others have been concerned about the potential for adding costs to the justice system or contributing to delay (Carrington and Younger 1979).

The most significant concern about victim impact statements—and about victims' participation generally—is that gains for victims will result in costs for defendants. Some legal scholars have expressed fear that victim impact statements may reduce uniformity in sentencing and may introduce a greater degree of arbitrariness (Abramovsky 1986; Henderson 1985; Talbert 1988), or that they will result in harsher treatment of convicted offenders across the board (American Bar Association 1981). These issues have formed the basis of court challenges to the constitutionality of victim impact statements. In June 1987 the United States Supreme Court ruled in a 5-4 decision (*Booth v. Maryland* 1987) that victim impact statements are unconstitutional in capital cases. The court contended that "such information is irrelevant to a capital sentencing decision, and its admission creates a constitutionally unacceptable risk the jury may impose the death penalty in an arbitrary and capricious manner."

In June 1989, in a further development, the United States Supreme Court upheld a ruling by the South Carolina Supreme Court, overturning a death sentence for the murderer of a "self-styled" minister. Although *South Carolina v. Gathers* (1989) did not directly involve victim impact statements, the court's decision extended and reaffirmed the *Booth v. Maryland* decision by reiterating that "a sentence of death must be related to the moral culpability of the defendant." The Supreme Court upheld the lower court ruling, which maintained that the prosecution's description of the religious articles found near the minister's body constituted information about the victim's personal character, and as such was irrelevant to the sentencing decision.

Most recently, the Court revised itself and upheld state's rights to allow victim impact statements. In *Payne v. Tennessee* (1991) the court decided that the Eighth Amendment erects no bar to victim impact evidence per se. The decision, however, still left open the possibility of excluding victim impact evidence if the evidence "is so unduly prejudicial that it tenders the trial fundamentally unfair."

Clearly, the arguments against victim impact statements are not frivolous, and public debate on their appropriateness is useful. That debate, however, underscores the need for a fuller understanding of whether and how such statements affect sentences. The concerns raised by opponents of victim impact statements—

that they may result in more disparate or harsher sentences—can be subjected to empirical scrutiny by using social research methods.

To date we know of two attempts to bring empirical evidence to bear in examining how victim impact statements affect sentencing patterns. An earlier study by our research group (Davis 1985) attempted to look at the effect of these statements on sentences by using a quasi-experimental design. An impact statement procedure was introduced by the District Attorney's office in one of two felony court parts in Brooklyn that handled essentially identical cases. (Assignment of cases to one part or the other alternated, depending on the week when the cases were arraigned.) Comparison of the effects of victim impact statements on sentencing was thwarted, however, because of prosecutors' resistance to the program. Statements reached the judge in only one of the 10 cases designated to include impact statements. In the other nine cases, either prosecutors failed to obtain an impact statement or the statements never were forwarded to the presiding judge.

More significant is a correlational study by Erez and Tontodonato (1990). These authors looked at 500 Ohio felony cases; victim impact statements were taken in some of these but not in others, according to prosecutors' files. (The authors state that impact statements were solicited only when prosecutors expected a case to be tried.) Erez and Tontodonato compared sentencing in cases with and cases without impact statements after controlling for a number of potential confounding variables (e.g., seriousness of charge, defendant's record). They found that cases in which a victim impact statement was taken were more likely than those without a statement to result in a prison sentence than in probation. A second analysis showed no association between length of sentence, among those incarcerated, and whether a victim impact statement was taken.

The correlational approach used by Erez and Tontodonato makes the results of their study difficult to interpret. These researchers found large differences in offense seriousness and in many other measures between cases that had impact statements taken and cases without statements. Although the study controlled for many observed differences between the two groups of cases, the authors acknowledged that "[T]o completely control for such bias, it would be necessary to accurately model all previous selection decisions" (1990:462).

*The Current Study*

The only way to be confident that treatments are not confounded with outcomes is to assign cases randomly to treatments

34

(Boruch and Wothke 1985). That approach was used in the current research. In this study, implemented in the Bronx County, New York Supreme (Felony) Court, cases were assigned randomly[1] to one of three treatments: 1) impact statements were taken and distributed to officials; 2) impact statement interviews were conducted, but no statement was prepared; and 3) no interview was conducted.

The most obvious approach to examining how victim impact statements affect sentences is by comparing sentences in cases in which court officials had access to victim impact statements with cases in which they did not have access. By framing the question in this way (as did Erez and Tontodonato), one addresses the defense issue of whether impact statements may lead officials to make harsher sentencing decisions generally.

Upon reflection, however, we thought it unlikely that cases with victim impact statements would routinely receive more severe sentences than those without. In the cases with impact statements, court officials should know more about the effect of crime on the victims. Sometimes that effect will be major, and officials will become more aware of the luridness of crimes, as Henderson (1985) suggests. Experience has shown, however (e.g., Davis 1985), that for many victims the impact of crime is relatively slight and short-lived; this is reflected in impact statements. Thus impact statements can either intensify or detract from officials' perceptions of the seriousness of a crime. (Erez & Tontodonato 1990 similarly point out that impact statements may increase proportionality in sentencing.) Impact statements, *on average*, could induce officials to impose harsher sentences only if officials normally assumed—in the absence of impact statements—that the effect of crime on victims was minimal. In other words, sentences would be harsher only if impact statements awakened officials to the fact that the cases they had been sentencing actually were considerably more heinous than they had imagined.

We thought this only a remote possibility. We believe that if victim impact statements affect sentences, their influence is likely to be more subtle. We think these statements have the potential to produce sentences that are more congruent with the harm done to victims. That is, the effect of crime on victims ought to be a more accurate predictor of sentences when impact statements are available to officials than when they are not. In cases in which the effect

---

[1] In fact, we began the random assignment process after the first 32 cases had been taken into the sample. As described below, all of the first 32 cases were assigned to one of the treatment conditions.

of crime on victims is serious, impact statements may induce officials to impose stiffer sentences than they would have imposed otherwise. (In particular we expected that restitution awards might be affected by victim impact information; this point was suggested by our earlier work. See Davis et al. 1984.) Conversely, in cases in which the effect of crime on victims is slight, impact statements may induce officials to impose lesser sentences than they would otherwise have imposed. Thus the net effect of impact statements on the overall harshness of sentences may be nil; at the same time, impact statements may result in sentences that reflect more accurately the harm done to victims, whether large or small.

With these thoughts in mind, we decided to examine whether impact statements altered the distribution of sentences—how many offenders were sentenced to conditional discharges versus probation versus short or long terms of incarceration. We then investigated whether impact statements result in sentences that reflect more accurately the harm done to victims.

## METHOD

We conducted the experiment in the Bronx (New York) Supreme Court. Between July 1988 and April 1989, 293 victims of robbery, nonsexual assault, and burglary went through the intake procedure. We chose these crimes rather than homicides or rapes in order to obtain the sample size we needed for analysis.

Sixty-nine percent of the sample were victims of robbery, 21 percent were victims of physical assault or attempted homicide, and 10 percent were victims of burglary. Twenty percent of the victims knew the offender before the crime was committed. Only one in two of the victims had completed high school; 52 percent had household incomes of less than $15,000 per year. The median age of the sample was 25 years.

*Treatments*

Each victim was assigned to one of three treatments as follows: 1) the victim was interviewed, and a victim impact statement was written and distributed (104 victims); 2) the victim was interviewed, but no statement was written (100 victims); 3) only the victim's name and address were recorded (89 victims).

*Victims interviewed, statement written.* Victims who received victim impact statements were told by a caseworker (hired by the research project specifically to prepare impact statements) that they would be interviewed and that a statement, based on the answers they gave to the questions in the interview, would be written up and distributed to the judge, the defense attorney, and the prosecutor. It was explained to these victims that because an impact statement would be prepared for them, court officials might have more information about how they were affected by the crime. Victims also were told that judges would have this information during sentencing. In addition, they were informed that someone would try to contact them by phone or letter in about one month in order to update the information in their statement.

The victim impact interview typically took 5 to 10 minutes. Victims were asked about the impact the of crime in five areas of their lives: physical impact, property loss or damage that occurred as a direct result of the crime, any subsequent financial loss (such as hospital bills or pay lost from time missed from work), psychological impact, and behavioral impact (any changes in routines or habits as a result of the crime—for example, whether they now had trouble sleeping, or took a different route to work). The victims' responses to the interview questions were rated on a scale of 1 to 3 according to the magnitude of the impact of the crime (from no impact to much impact in each category of response).

Victims in the impact statement group (like all the victims, regardless of their treatment group) were given a pamphlet from the victim assistance unit located in the Bronx Criminal Court. They were told that they could go to the victim assistance office if they needed information, referrals, or counseling.

The impact interview, containing the ratings of harm to the victim, was copied immediately, and a copy was turned over to the prosecutor assigned to the case. The caseworker then wrote a victim impact statement based on the victim's responses to the interview questions, and distributed it to the prosecutor and the defense attorney through the head of the Supreme Court Bureau. Copies of the statement also were forwarded to the appropriate judge for each case. One copy was mailed out as soon as a judge was assigned to the case. Another copy was delivered to the chief clerk of the Supreme Court Bureau, who enclosed the statement with the file containing the presentence report and delivered it to the judge just before sentencing.

*Victims interviewed, no statement written.*  This treatment provided a comparison group for determining whether the impact statement procedure resulted in sentences that reflected more accurately the harm done to the victim. The victims in this treatment group were administered the same interview as the victims for whom statements were written. The caseworker explained to them that she was conducting research to learn more about the experiences of crime victims and that she would like some background information about the effects of the crime on their lives. The interview questions were asked, but none of the descriptive responses were written down; victims' responses were rated on the same scale as was used for victims who went through the impact statement procedure.

These victims, like those in the first group, were given a victim assistance pamphlet. The prosecutor received a copy of a form that reflected only the victim's and the defendant's name, the charge, the docket number, and the ratings of harm to the victim. The prosecutors required this form, which defined the victim's role in the study, to document the fact that the victim had not disclosed discoverable information to the research project caseworker.

*Victims in the control group.* Only the names and addresses of these victims were recorded. The prosecutor received a memo saying that each of these victims was a control in our study, and that only his or her name and address were recorded. Like the victims in the other two groups, these victims received a victim assistance pamphlet.

### Procedures

*Intake.* All victims were brought by the prosecutor assigned to their case to the research project office after their grand jury testimony. Victims were assigned to treatments according to a log sheet that was prenumbered with victims' ID numbers and a corresponding treatment group for each number. The treatments were preassigned on the basis of a table of random numbers.

The random assignment was not begun, however, until after the first 32 victims were interviewed. These initial victims, all of whom gave impact statements, were intended originally to be a pretest group. We were forced to include them in the experiment, however, when intake proved to be far slower than anticipated. Analyses revealed no significant differences between these 32 victims and later victims assigned to the impact statement group in terms of type of charge (chi-square = 2.43, df = 3, n.s.), severity of charge ($t$ [98] = 0.09, n.s.), victim's education ($t$ [72] = 0.75, n.s.), income ($t$ [30] = $-1.13$, n.s.), or age ($t$ [75] = $-1.26$, n.s.).

*Rating system.* As explained above, we developed a rating system to rank the severity of the various effects of the crime. This system included five categories for which the victim received a rating (physical injury, immediate property loss or damage, subsequent financial loss, psychological impact, and behavioral change). Victims in the impact statement and interview-only groups were rated in these five categories on a scale of 1 to 3: 1 represented no impact or not applicable, 2 represented some impact, and 3 represented major impact. For example, a victim who reported having suffered no physical injury received a rating of 1 for the injury category, a victim with minor injuries received a 2, and a victim who had been hospitalized received a 3.

After much debate about how to rank psychological distress, we decided to ask the victims to rate themselves. As part of the interview we asked victims whether they had been feeling upset since the crime. If they said no, they received 1 on the rating scale. If they said, yes, we asked them to say whether they would describe themselves as "somewhat" or "very" upset, and subsequently gave them a 2 or a 3 on the scale, depending on their answer.

From these five individual measures of harm to the victim—physical harm, short-term financial impact, long-term financial impact, psychological harm, and behavioral changes—we created a composite harm measure. This summary variable was produced by summing the scores for the five component items.

*Follow-up.* Approximately one month after case intake, we attempted to contact victims from whom victim impact statements had been taken, in order to update the information in their statements. When new information was discovered, the impact statements were revised and an updated version was given to the judge at the time of sentencing. We tracked cases; when they had been disposed, we gathered information on sentences from files of the district attorney's office.

### Subgroup Differences

We examined the three treatment groups to ensure that they were comparable before undergoing the experimental manipulation. We found no differences between the three conditions in terms of type of charge (dichotomized as personal crimes, attempted murder and assault, versus property crimes, robbery and burglary: chi-square = 8.10, df = 6, n.s.); severity of charge (coded from 1 to 5, corresponding to the felony class of the charge, A through E: $F$ = 0.78, df = 2,283, n.s.); victim/offender relationship (dichotomized as strangers versus acquaintances: chi-square = 0.26, df = 2, n.2.); offender's prior record (number of felony convictions: $F$ = 0.29, df = 2,286, n.s.); victim's age ($F$ = 0.13, df = 2,212, n.s.); victim's years of education ($F$ = 1.66, df = 2,209, n.s.); or victim's annual household income ($F$ = 0.67, df = 2,103, n.s.).

We further compared the impact statement group with the interview-only group on ratings of crime impact, based on information provided by victims during the interview. We found no differences between the two groups on the overall measure of crime impact ($F$ = 1.96, df = 1,200, n.2.); behavioral impact ($F$ = 0.48, df = 1,201, n.2.); immediate financial impact ($F$ = 0.09, df = 1,201, n.s.); subsequent financial impact ($F$ = 0.05, df = 1,201, n.s.); or psychological impact ($F$ = 1,26, df = 1,200, n.s.). The differences between the two groups on physical impact fell just short of statistical significance ($F$ = 3.59, df = 1,201, .05 < $p$ < .10).

*Interviews with Criminal Justice Officials*

We asked assistant district attorneys to complete a 10-item survey concerning their experiences with and opinions of victim impact statements. Surveys were completed and returned by 22 of the 24 assistants in the unit. We also conducted semistructured interviews face-to-face with all seven judges who had received victim impact statements in at least three of their cases. Interviews averaged 20 to 30 minutes in length.

## RESULTS

Case dispositions for the 293 cases in the sample were as follows: 3 percent ended in bench warrants, 14 percent were dismissed, 3 percent were acquitted, 10 percent were sentenced to probation, 14 percent were sentenced to less than one year in jail, 7 percent were sentenced to one to three years in state prison, 32 percent were sentenced to three to six years in prison, and 14 percent were sentenced to more than six years in prison. Each of the analyses described below on the effects of victim impact statements uses the 229 cases in the sample in which convictions were won and sentences imposed.

*Effects on Overall Sentencing Patterns of Victim Impact Statements*

Table 1 compares sentences for cases in the three treatment groups. The table shows only minor variations between the groups in the frequencies of conditional discharges, sentences of probation,

40

and various lengths of prison terms. The differences in the distribution of sentences between the groups did not approach statistical significance (chi-square=10.86, df=8, n.s.).[2],[3]

**Table 1.   Effects of Treatments on Sentencing Patterns[a]**

|  | Victim Impact Statement | Interview Only | Control |  |
|---|---|---|---|---|
| Conditional Discharge | 2% | 1% | 8% |  |
|  | (2) | (1) | (5) | n=8 |
| Probation | 15% | 11% | 12% |  |
|  | (13) | (8) | (8) | n=29 |
| 0-1 Years' Incarceration | 20% | 22% | 10% |  |
|  | (17) | (17) | (7) | n=41 |
| 1-3 Years' Incarceration | 12% | 7% | 6% |  |
|  | (10) | (5) | (4) | n=19 |
| 3-6 Years' Incarceration | 41% | 37% | 42% |  |
|  | (35) | (28) | (28) | n=91 |
| 6+ Years' Prison | 11% | 22% | 22% |  |
|  | (9) | (17) | (15) | n=41 |
|  | 100% | 100% | 100% |  |
|  | (n=86) | (n=76) | (n=67) | N=229 |

[a] Excludes open cases, bench warrants, dismissals, and acquittals.

As a further check on the effects of impact statements on sentence patterns, we conducted a multivariate logistic regression analysis. We dichotomized the sentence variable as "incarcerated" and "not incarcerated" and the treatment variable as "impact statement present in file" and "impact statement not present in file." (We combined cases in which no impact interview was held with cases in which an interview was held, but an impact statement was not produced.)

We introduced into the analysis extraneous variables that were likely to influence the decision to incarcerate, including seriousness of the charge, type of charge, offender's prior record (number of convictions), and overall harm to the victim (the sum of the five individual impact measures—physical, psychological, behavioral,

---

[2] In calculating the chi-square value, we combined conditional discharges and probation sentences (the first two rows of Table 1) in order to avoid expected cell frequencies less than 5.

[3] Our thanks to an anonymous reviewer who pointed out that at least one partitioning of the data would lead to an alternate conclusion. If sentences are dichotomized into six or fewer years in prison versus more than six years and if the two control groups are combined, sentences involving victim impact statements are *less* likely to be long-term than sentencing decisions reached without victim impact statements (chi-square = 5.1, df=1, *p.*=.05).

short-term financial, and long-term financial—each measured on a three-point scale).

The results of the logit analysis are displayed in Table 2. Type of charge, severity of charge, and prior convictions all exerted significant influences on the decision to incarcerate. Yet neither the presence of an impact statement in the court file (the treatment variable) nor the overall victim harm measure approached statistical significance in the analysis.

**Table 2.   Multivariate Analysis of the Effects of Treatments on the Decision to Incarceration[a]**

| Effect | Estimated Coefficient | SE | Significance |
|---|---|---|---|
| Charge Type | −1.39 | 0.61 | .02 |
| Charge Severity | −0.50 | 0.25 | .05 |
| Convictions | 0.43 | 0.21 | .04 |
| Victim Impact | 0.16 | 0.14 | .26 |
| Treatment | 0.68 | 0.56 | .22 |

[a] Model chi-square = 16.12, df=5, $p<.01$

Finally, we found no indications that victim impact statements increased the use of special conditions in sentencing. Restitution was not ordered in *any* case in our sample. We encountered only two judicial admonishments to offenders to keep away from victims, and one order for an offender to undergo drug rehabilitation.

*Effects of Victim Impact Statements (VIS) on the Congruence between Victim Harm and Sentence Severity*

To determine whether impact statements result in sentences that reflect harm to victims more clearly, we compared treatment groups in terms of the relationship between harm to the victim and sentence severity, after controlling for other factors related to sentencing. If impact statements affected sentencing, we would expect to see a stronger relationship between harm to the victim and sentence severity in the group in which impact statements were taken than in the other two treatments, in which statements were not taken or distributed to officials.

To determine whether victim impact exerted a significant effect on sentence severity, we conducted a hierarchical regression analysis. In this case we were interested in differences, according to treatment group, in the effects of harm to the victim on severity of sentence (a six-point ordinal variable, coded as displayed in Table 1). Again, we controlled statistically for the effects of extraneous

variables likely to influence sentence severity, including seriousness of the charge, type of charge, and number of convictions. On
the first step of the analysis, we entered nature of the charge, seriousness of the charge, and offender's prior record. On the next step,
we entered the overall measure of harm to the victim.

The results are displayed in Table 3. This table shows that seriousness of the charge and (for VIS cases only) nature of the charge
are associated with sentence severity: sentences were more severe
when charges were more serious and (for VIS cases only) when the
charge involved an assault or attempted murder rather than a robbery or burglary. Harm to the victim, however, played little role in
sentencing decisions after charge and criminal history were taken
into account. Adding victim impact to the regression model increased the model's explanatory power by less than 2 percent. This
was true for the victim impact statement group ($F$ [1,77] = 1.64,
n.s.) as well as for cases where no impact statement was taken or
forwarded to officials ($F$ [1,66] = 1.00, n.s.).

**Table 3.  Effects of Victim Impact on Sentence Severity, by
Treatment Group**

| Standardized Regression Coefficients | Regression Coefficients for VIS Cases | Regression Coefficients for Interview Only Cases |
|---|---|---|
| Step 1 | | |
| Prior convictions | 0.10 | 0.09 |
| Seriousness of charge | 0.32* | 0.56* |
| Nature of charge | 0.21* | 0.05 |
| Step 2 | | |
| Victim impact | 0.09 | 0.07 |
| Increase in Variance Explained by Adding Victim Impact to Model | <2% | <1% |
| | $F$ (1,77) = 1.64, ns | $F$ (1,66) = 1.00, ns |

\* $p < .01$

We conducted the same type of analyses using the separate indicators of victim impact (representing physical, psychological, behavioral, and short- and long-term financial impact), and achieved
essentially the same results: victim impact measures bore no consistent relationship to sentencing decisions, either for cases with or
cases without victim impact statements.

*Court Officials' Reactions to Victim Impact Statements*

Interviews with prosecutors revealed that 15 of the 22 thought it appropriate to consider the impact of crime on victims in negotiating dispositions, but they did not think that victim impact statements added substantially to their knowledge of impact on the victim: only three prosecutors believed that impact statements usually contained more accurate or more detailed information than they would have obtained from their files on personal interviews with victims. Moreover, 13 of the 22 prosecutors thought that procedures for taking victim impact statements were problematic (some were worried that the defense could use the statements to point up inconsistencies in victims' testimony) or inconvenient (some expressed concern about subjecting victims to "yet another interview").

Interviews with the seven judges suggested that they had received and read our victim impact statements. All of the seven believed it was helpful to learn through the statements how victims were affected by crime. Unlike prosecutors, the judges stated that they did not normally receive information on victim impact through other channels, either from prosecutors or from victims themselves.

Yet prosecutors expressed skepticism about judges' interest in the impact of crime on victims. Only three of the 22 prosecutors believed that judges usually considered victim impact in sentencing decisions.

We inspected files from the district attorney's office to determine whether the copies of impact statements given to prosecutors had been placed in the files, and whether the envelopes containing the statements had been opened. We found that impact statements were missing in 37 percent of the files where they ought to have been included. In the files that contained impact statements, 53 percent of the statements had never been opened.

## CONCLUSIONS

We began this study to address some of the controversial issues surrounding the use of victim impact statements. Do impact statements result in harsher sentences? In sentences that reflect more accurately the harm done to victims?

In one important respect, our results back up the advocates of victim impact statements: we found no support for those who argue against these statements on the grounds that their use places defendants in jeopardy and may result in harsher sentences. In this respect, our data stand in contrast to the findings reported by Erez and Tontodonato (1990), who found that victim impact statements were associated with an increased likelihood of incarceration. The discrepancy between the two studies may reflect differences between courts in receptivity to such statements. Again, it may exist because Erez and Tontodonato used a weaker, correlational research design: their study gives no guarantee that cases in which victim impact statements were taken were equivalent in other respects to cases without impact statements, even after the researchers controlled for some potential confounding variables.

Our data, however, also may give advocates of victim impact statements cause for concern. These statements did not produce sentencing decisions that reflected more clearly the effects of crime on victims. Nor did we find much evidence that—with or without impact statements—sentencing decisions were influenced by our measures of the effects of crime on victims, once the charge and the defendant's prior record were taken into account. (This finding replicates the results of a study by Hernon and Forst 1983, which concluded that harm to the victim had little effect on sentencing decisions.) Yet it is also true that the impact of crime on victims is incorporated into charging decisions: more serious charges tend to reflect greater harm to victims, and our analysis found severity of charge to be highly predictive of sentences.

Interviews conducted with officials helped to explain why impact statements had no discernible effect on sentencing. Although judges professed to be interested in the impact of crime on victims, prosecutors thought, at best, that judges considered such information only occasionally. Also, although most of the prosecutors interviewed said that victim impact ought to be considered regularly, judges reported that prosecutors rarely related such information to them. Moreover, prosecutors clearly believed that information contained in victim impact statements was not especially useful to them, as evidenced by their frequent failure to incorporate the statements into their case files and their failure to open the statements that had been placed in case files.[4]

Probably the truth is that officials have established ways of making decisions which do not call for explicit information about

---

[4] One could argue that the experiment is invalidated by the fact that many impact statements were not read by prosecutors. We disagree for several reasons. First, judges also received copies of the statements, and judges are the officials who directly pass sentence on convicted offenders. Second, even if statements had been present and opened in prosecutors' files in all cases in the experiment, one still could question whether prosecutors gave them serious attention. (Indeed, prosecutors' or judges' apathy toward impact statements is an important factor that would have gone undetected in earlier studies of the effects of victim impact statements on sentencing.) In our opinion, our finding that prosecutors often did not attend to statements when they were available is a legitimate and interesting outcome of the intervention we designed.

the impact of crime on victims. They make sentencing decisions according to established norms based on the nature of the charge and the defendant's character (Rosett and Cressey 1976): in this process, officials may believe that the charge itself often conveys enough information about harm to the victim to meet the purposes of sentencing. Inducing officials to consider specific measures of victim impact entails changing well-established habits, and a brief experiment is not likely to do that.

Our conclusions about the effects of impact statements on sentencing are limited by the fact that we conducted the research on a new rather than a well-established program. Possibly it takes a long time for officials to accept and incorporate impact statements into the sentencing process—not the few short months available to us in this experiment. Moreover, the results we obtained in the Bronx may not apply equally well to lower-volume suburban or rural courts. Thus replications of our experiment are needed at other sites. Moreover, we examined common felony crimes—robbery, assault, and burglary—so that we could generate a sample large enough to permit tests of statistical inference. It may be that impact statements have greater effects for the most serious crimes—homicides, rapes, and aggravated assaults.

Pending additional research, our experiment raises troubling questions about the viability of impact statements as a vehicle for victims' participation in the court process. These statements have become the preferred method for allowing victims greater participation. They are less controversial than other means of victim participation might be, and they are relatively inexpensive to administer. For these reasons, victim advocates have pushed hard for statutes to mandate their use. But if impact statements do not give victims a meaningful voice, what gains have victims really made over the past 20 years in having their concerns represented to the court? This question deserves to be considered carefully by those interested in making the justice process responsive to the concerns of victims and other citizens.

## REFERENCES

Abramovsky, A. (1986) "Crime Victims' Rights." *New York Law Journal*, February 3, pp. 1 and 3.

American Bar Association (1981) *Victim/Witness Legislation*. Report of the Victim Witness Assistance Project, Criminal Justice Section. Washington, DC: American Bar Association.

Boruch, R.F. and W. Wothke (1985) "Seven Kinds of Randomization Plans for Designing Field Experiments." In R.F. Boruch and W. Wothke (eds.), *Randomization and Field Experimentation*, pp. 95-113. San Francisco: Jossey-Bass.

Carrington, F., and E.E. Younger (1979) "Victims of Crime Deserve More Than Pity." *Human Rights* 8:10-15.

Clark, T., J. Housner, J. Hernon, E. Wish and C. Zelinski (1984) "Evaluation of the Structured Plea Negotiation Project." Report of the Institute for Law and Social Research to the National Institute of Justice.

Davis, R.C. (1985) "First Year Evaluation of the Victim Impact Demonstration Project." Unpublished report, Victim Services Agency, New York.

Davis, R.C., P. Fischer, A. Paykin (1985) "Victim Impact Statements: The Experience of State Probation Officers." *Journal of Probation and Parole* 16:18-20.

Davis, R.C. and M. Henley (1990) "Victim Service Programs." In A. Lurigio, W. Skogan, and R. Davis (eds.), *Victims in the Criminal Justice System*, pp. 157-171. Beverly Hills: Sage.

Davis, R.C., F. Kunreuther, and E. Connick (1984) "Expanding the Victim's Role in the Criminal Court Dispositional Process: The Results of an Experiment." *Journal of Criminal Law and Criminology* 2:491-505.

Dubow, F. and T. Becker (1976) "Patterns of Victim Advocacy." In W.F. McDonald (ed.), *Criminal Justice and the Victim*, pp. 147-164. Beverly Hills: Sage.

Erez, E. and P. Tontodonato (1990) "The Effect of Victim Participation in Sentencing on Sentence Outcome." *Criminology* 28:451-74.

Goldstein, A.S. (1982) "Defining the Role of the Victim in Criminal Prosecution." *Mississippi Law Journal* 52:515-61.

Henderson, L.N. (1985) "The Wrongs of Victims' Rights." *Stanford Law Review* 37:937-1021.

Hernon, J.C. and B. Forst (1984) "The Criminal Justice Response to Victim Harm." Report of the Institute for Law and Social Research to the National Institute of Justice.

Hudson, P.S. (1984) "The Crime Victim and the Criminal Justice System: Time for a Change." *Pepperdine Law Review* 11:23.

Kelly, D.P. (1987) "Victims." *Wayne Law Review* 34(1):69-86.

——— (1990) "Victim Participation in the Criminal Justice System." In A. Lurigio, W. Skogan, and R. Davis (eds.), *Victims and the Criminal Justice System*, pp. 172-187. Beverly Hills: Sage.

Kerstetter, W.A. and A.M. Heinz (1979) "Pretrial Settlement Conference: An Evaluation." Report of the University of Chicago Law School to the National Institute of Justice.

McLeod, M. (1988) *The Authorization and Implementation of Victim Impact Statements*. Washington, DC: National Institute of Justice.

Rosett, A. and D. Cressey (1976) *Justice by Consent: Plea Bargains in the American Courthouse*. New York: Lippincott.

Rubel, M.C. (1986) "Victim Participation in Sentencing Proceedings." *Criminal Law Quarterly* 28:226-50.

Talbert, P. (1988) "The Relevance of Victim Impact Statements to the Criminal Sentencing Decision." *UCLA Law Review* 36:199-202.

## CASES CITED

*Booth v. Maryland*, 482 U.S. 496 (1987).

*Payne v. Tennessee*, 111 S. Ct. 2597, 115 L. Ed. 2d 720 (1991).

*S. Carolina v. Gathers*, 490 U.S. 805 (1989).

# JUVENILE VICTIMIZATION
# AND DELINQUENCY

FINN-AAGE ESBENSEN
DAVID HUIZINGA
University of Colorado

**The study of crime victims** has witnessed a steady increase in popularity among both criminologists and the general public during the past 2 decades. The victim's rights movement has no doubt spurred public interest in the study of victims, primarily as it relates to demographic characteristics and the likelihood and fear of victimization. For criminologists, the surge in interest may be attributable, in part, to the development of large-scale victimization surveys in the early 1970s (e.g., the United States' National Crime Survey and Great Britain's British Crime Survey). Prior to these surveys, relatively little systematic information was available concerning victims of crime. These surveys improved the level of methodological sophistication necessary for examination of key issues associated with victimization and have paved the way for other researchers to undertake their own specific research projects.

AUTHORS' NOTE: *The research reported here was funded by the Office of Juvenile Justice and Delinquency Prevention (#86-JN-CX-006) and the National Institute of Drug Abuse (#DA-05183). Points of view or opinions expressed in this article do not necessarily represent the official position or policies of these agencies. The authors would like to thank research assistants Linda Cunningham, Meg Dyer, Judy Perry, and Judy Laurie for their assistance in the collection of these data; Amanda Elliott and Anne Weiher for their assistance in the preparation of the data for this analysis; and Scott Menard and an anonymous reviewer for their comments on an earlier draft. An earlier version of this article was presented at the annual meeting of the Academy of Criminal Justice Sciences in Nashville, TN, March 1991.*

YOUTH & SOCIETY, Vol. 23 No. 2, December 1991 202-228

During its relatively short history, victimization research has branched into a number of diverse areas of interest. Among these have been (a) the descriptive study of demographic characteristics of victims (e.g., Baker, Mednick, & Carothers, 1989; Singer, 1981), (b) examination of census characteristics associated with victimization (e.g., Booth, Johnson, & Choldin, 1977; Decker, Schichor, & O'Brien, 1982; Sampson, 1983, 1985; Sampson & Wooldredge, 1987; Schichor, Decker, & O'Brien, 1979; Skogan, 1989; Smith & Jarjoura, 1988), (c) investigation of the relationship between victimization and the fear of crime (e.g., Garofalo, 1979; Menard & Covey, 1987; Stafford & Galle, 1984), and (d) development of a life-style/routine activities theoretical perspective (e.g., Cohen & Felson, 1979; Cohen, Kluegel, & Land, 1981; Garofalo, 1987; Gottfredson, 1986; Hindelang, Gottfredson, & Garofalo, 1978; Jensen & Brownfield, 1986; Lasley & Rosenbaum, 1988; Massey, Krohn, & Bonati, 1989; Maxfield, 1987; Miethe, Stafford, & Long, 1987; Sampson & Lauritsen, 1990).

Traditionally, crime and victimization have been studied as if they were two separate domains, unrelated except for the fact that they represented opposite sides of the crime situation. Indicative of this position is the fact that most studies of the crime situation have focused on the offender, attempting to describe the typical criminal and to explain the etiology of crime. Others, on the other hand, have made the victim the object of attention. These victimization studies have proceeded with a similar emphasis on providing descriptive information about crime victims and the effects of crime on individuals. One early exception to this approach of divorcing criminal activity from victimization is the work of Thornberry and Figlio (1974) who examined the relationship between victimization and both self-reported delinquency and arrest data. Although they did not find a temporal relationship between the type of offending and the type of victimization, they suggested that the juvenile years may well be characterized by a general behavioral pattern "typified by both commission of and victimization by various kinds of mild assaults and property offenses" (p. 109). More recently, Jensen and Brownfield (1986) commented that "for personal victimization, those most likely to be victims of crime are those who have been most involved in crime" (p. 97). In a recent publication using the British Crime Survey, which is limited to respondents 16 years of age and older, Sampson and Lauritsen (1990) reported findings similar to those reported for juveniles. More specifically, they found that "offense activity . . . directly increases the risk of personal victimization" (p. 110).

Since the seminal works by Hindelang et al. (1978) and Cohen and Felson (1979), proponents of the routine activities/life-style perspective have sought to explain an individual's increased risk of victimization as an artifact of their own behavioral patterns. A primary assumption of the routine activities approach proposed by Hindelang et al. (1978) is that demographic characteristics, although not part of the causal chain, do influence intervening or mediating variables (e.g., social constraints, life-style, and associations) associated with victimization. Thus along with examination of life-style variables, it is helpful to determine the demographic distribution of victims.

The majority of victimization research has examined adult victims, and little research has focused specifically on the relationship between victimization and offending. Knowledge of adolescent victimization historically has been limited by the scarcity of research focusing on this age group. Recent research efforts, however, have addressed this shortcoming and have improved our understanding of victimizations among juveniles (e.g., Ageton, 1981; Baker et al., 1989; Jensen & Brownfield, 1986; Singer, 1981; Toby, 1986). In one of the earlier studies to investigate adolescent victimization, Mawby (1979) accounted for the paucity of information, writing that although "juvenile victimization would be exposed in a household survey, most incidents, perhaps because they are minor or because they are not known by the adult respondent, are apt to be missed in a survey directed initially at adults" (p. 99). The primary objective of the analyses presented in this article is to examine the notion that adolescent behavioral patterns (e.g., involvement in delinquent activities) are associated with an increased risk of victimization.

A more basic objective is to provide a description of adolescent victims. That is, who is most likely to be a victim of crime? Several individual characteristics appear to be related to the likelihood of being victimized. Females are less likely to be victims of crime than are males, especially for violent offenses (Feyerherm & Hindelang, 1974; Gottfredson, 1986; Mawby, 1979; Miethe et al., 1987). In general populations, age has also been found to have a distinct relationship with victimization, but contrary to popular perception, the elderly have a low probability of victimization. General survey samples have found young people to have the highest likelihood of becoming the victims of crime (Gottfredson, 1986; Miethe et al., 1987). Among adolescent samples, however, there have been inconsistent results. Whereas some studies reported lower rates for younger adolescents (e.g., Baker et al., 1989), others reported different results (e.g., Blyth, Thiel, Bush, & Simmons, 1980). This, however, appears to be more of a definitional problem than a substantive issue associated with a particular sample. Instead of referring to actual age distributions of victimizations, authors discuss older and younger victims relative to the sample. Baker et al. (1989), for example, using a high school sample, found that the youngest age group (under 17 years of age) in their study experienced the lowest victimization rates for property offenses, whereas Blyth et al. (1980) found that the seventh graders in their junior high school sample had a higher risk of victimization than did the seventh graders in a K-8 school configuration. This latter finding, in conjunction with the fact that "junior high schools are found to be more victimizing environments than senior high schools in the Safe School Study" (cited in Baker et al., 1989, p. 331), highlights not only the difficulty of assessing the relationship between age and victimization in an adolescent sample but the importance of contextual factors.

Another characteristic commonly associated with victimization is ethnic status. Non-Whites are generally reported to have higher victimization rates than Whites (e.g., Gottfredson, 1986; Singer, 1981; Thornberry & Figlio, 1974). Miethe et al. (1987), however, failed to replicate this finding of a relationship between victimization and ethnicity. In Baker et al. (1989), White victimization rates were found to be associated with their status within schools; Whites experienced lower rates when they were in the majority, so again, a contextual effect may be operating. Similarly, there appears to be a lack of consensus with regard to the relationship between community factors and victimization rates. Although Mawby (1979) found no community contextual differences in his study of British youths, others reported that victimization varied by neighborhood contextual factors (e.g., Decker et al., 1982; Sampson & Lauritsen, 1990; Sampson & Wooldredge, 1987; Singer, 1981). Sampson and Wooldredge (1987), for example, found victimization rates to be highest in communities characterized by high rates of unemployment and high building density.

Family structure is another demographic correlate of victimization that has been examined through the use of both census and survey data. Results indicate that single people and people living alone have higher rates of victimization than do people living in traditional family contexts (Gottfredson, 1986; Miethe et al., 1987).

In this article, we examine a probability sample of youths aged 11-15 years residing in high-risk neighborhoods and avoid problems associated with reliance on school samples.[1] Interview data provide self-reported measures of victimization and delinquency to allow investigation of the possible relationship between these two characteristics of the crime situation. Additionally, census data permit an examination of the potential effect of neighborhood descriptors on victimization rates.

## METHOD

### SAMPLE SELECTION

The research reported here is part of a longitudinal study investigating the causes and correlates of delinquency.[2] Census and police data were used to identify "high risk" neighborhoods in a large midwestern city. As part of a multiple cohort sequential design, a random sample of households in these neighborhoods was selected, and interviews were conducted with 1,530 children and youths aged 7, 9, 11, 13, and 15 and one of their parents. This report focuses on the 877 youths between the ages of 11 and 15.[3]

Individual-level data were obtained during face-to-face hour-long interviews conducted in a private setting in the respondent's home. A fuller description of the sampling design and respondent selection criteria can be found in Esbensen and Huizinga (1990).

## MEASUREMENTS

The measures used in this analysis included: (a) self-reported victimization; (b) self-reported delinquency; (c) demographic data including birth year, race, family structure, and gender; and (d) census descriptors of neighborhoods.

### Self-Reported Victimization

Self-reported victimization is a composite measure of six items asked of youth respondents. Measures of *lifetime prevalence* (ever during one's lifetime) as well as *last year prevalence* (ever during the past year) and *frequency of victimization* during the past year were obtained from respondents. For victimizations during the past year, detailed follow-up questions were asked to determine the extent of loss or injury as well as to gain information about the offender. Lifetime prevalence of victimization provides a description of a larger sample of victims than either of the past year measures because numerous studies (not to mention common sense) have indicated that only a subset of all victims are victimized in a given year. Last year prevalence and frequency of victimization are important to examine in order to assess the relationship between current behavior and victimization.

Items included in the victimization indices are listed here. Analyses examine both Personal and Property Victimization scales as well as Total Victimization, a composite measure of the two specific subscales.

Personal Victimization Scale:
1. Have you ever had someone use a weapon, force, or strong-arm methods to get money or things from you?
2. Have you ever been hit by someone trying to hurt you? (A follow-up question asked if the victim was hurt. If the response to this

question was no, the item was considered as a trivial response and eliminated.)
3. Have you ever been attacked by someone with a weapon or by someone trying to seriously hurt or kill you?
4. Have you ever been physically hurt or threatened to be hurt by someone trying to have sex with you?

Property Victimization Scale:
1. Have you ever had your pocket picked or your purse or wallet snatched, or an attempt made to do so?
2. Have you ever had some of your things, other than a wallet or purse, stolen from you?

Last year frequency of victimization was obtained in separate items by asking "How many times in the last year from Christmas a year ago to the Christmas just past have you . . . ?" Detailed follow-up questions were asked for the most recent of the reported victimization during the past year.

## Self-Reported Delinquency

The self-report delinquency measure includes information about involvement in 39 delinquent acts. As with the victimization data, detailed follow-up questions were asked of delinquency reported during the past year. Analyses include ever prevalence, last year prevalence, and last year frequency reports. Seven different behavior specific indices that comprise the General Delinquency Scale are used for analysis purposes: (a) involvement in drug sales, (b) minor theft, (c) felony theft, (d) minor assault, (e) felony assault, (f) alcohol use, and (g) marijuana use. We dichotomized assault and theft items into minor and felony categories in order to better examine the relationship of victimization with serious delinquent involvement. Felony theft included only thefts of merchandise worth more than $50 or motor vehicle theft. Felony assault included only those items in which more extreme forms of physical force were used against another person. Items included in these self-reported delinquency indices are presented in the appendix.

### Demographic Data

Self-reported age, race, family living arrangement, and gender were collected from each of the respondents. In the case of age, all reports were verified and validated with parent reports of birthdate. Race is also a self-reported measure in which respondents could identify themselves as belonging to one of nine specific ethnic/racial groupings. For this analysis, these categories were collapsed to represent Anglo, Black, Hispanic, and other. Family living arrangement was categorized as (a) intact home with both parents present, (b) single-parent families, (c) recombined families (e.g., presence of stepparent in household), and (d) other living arrangement (usually living with other relatives). Gender is based on interviewer observation and parent report.

A fifth demographic characteristic included in the analysis involves a categorization of the level and type of social disorganization of the community in which the respondent lived. This measure is based on a social ecology analysis using census data. Three different types of disorganized neighborhoods were identified: (a) traditional (i.e., representative of the archetypical Shaw and McKay [1942] type of disorganization, ethnic diversity, poverty and unemployment, high density, and mobility)[4]; (b) dense (characterized primarily by high density, high rates of mobility, and high concentration of single people); and (c) Black (characterized by a high proportion of Blacks, high concentration of single-parent families, and high density per household).[5]

## RESULTS

### DEMOGRAPHIC CHARACTERISTICS

Lifetime prevalence of victimization by demographic characteristics is summarized in Table 1. Although the percentage of individuals victimized did vary somewhat by ethnicity, these differences were not statistically significant. This was the case for both personal and property types of victimizations. As in other studies

TABLE 1
### Epidemiology of Victimization: Ever Prevalence

| Victimization Type | Ethnicity | | | | |
| --- | --- | --- | --- | --- | --- |
| | Anglo | Black | Hispanic | Other | Total |
| Personal | 41.4 | 43.0 | 35.6 | 47.5 | 39.8 |
| Property | 57.1 | 51.6 | 44.3 | 48.1 | 48.2 |
| Total | 68.6 | 65.9 | 59.8 | 70.0 | 63.6 |

| | Living Arrangement | | | | |
| --- | --- | --- | --- | --- | --- |
| | Intact | Single Parent | Recombined Families | Other | Total |
| Personal* | 33.4 | 44.7 | 41.2 | 38.2 | 39.8 |
| Property* | 44.5 | 51.6 | 53.3 | 38.2 | 48.2 |
| Total | 59.2 | 67.8 | 64.7 | 57.9 | 63.6 |

| | Neighborhood Type | | | |
| --- | --- | --- | --- | --- |
| | Traditional | Dense | Black | Total |
| Personal* | 36.4 | 47.7 | 44.7 | 39.8 |
| Property | 45.7 | 54.7 | 51.9 | 48.2 |
| Total** | 59.9 | 77.9 | 66.8 | 63.6 |

| | Age | | | |
| --- | --- | --- | --- | --- |
| | 15 | 13 | 11 | Total |
| Personal*** | 45.5 | 43.1 | 31.2 | 39.8 |
| Property** | 52.0 | 52.3 | 40.7 | 48.2 |
| Total*** | 67.9 | 68.4 | 54.7 | 63.6 |

| | Gender | | |
| --- | --- | --- | --- |
| | Male | Female | Total |
| Personal*** | 46.5 | 32.2 | 39.8 |
| Property* | 51.5 | 44.6 | 48.2 |
| Total** | 67.6 | 59.0 | 63.6 |

$*p < .05$; $**p < .01$; $***p < .001$; significance level indicated by a chi-square test of independence.

(e.g., Feyerherm & Hindelang, 1974; Gottfredson, 1986; Mawby, 1979; Miethe et al., 1987), the rate of victimization varied significantly by gender. Approximately half of all males reported being victims of both personal (46.5%) and property (51.5%) crimes at some time during their lives, compared to 32% and 45% of females, respectively.

Significant differences were also found by age, family living arrangement, and type of neighborhood disorganization. Members of the youngest cohort (11-year-olds) were the least likely to report both personal and property victimizations. Children residing in intact families reported the lowest rates of personal victimizations, and those in single-parent households reported the highest. For property crimes, children in recombined and single-parent families had similarly high rates of victimization. With respect to neighborhood type, residents of the traditionally disorganized communities indicated the lowest rates of victimization for both personal and property types of crime. Black neighborhoods had the highest rates of personal victimization, and dense neighborhoods had the highest rates of property victimization.

Further analyses of victimization and demographic characteristics examined last year prevalence and the average number of victimizations per victim during the preceding year. It is not surprising that the annual prevalence rates are lower than lifetime rates. As Sparks (1981) indicated, "Victimization surveys over the past fifteen years have found that the great majority of the surveyed population report that none of the incidents they were asked about had happened to them during the period covered" (p. 762). This comment makes good intuitive sense in that whereas many people may be victimized some time in their lifetime, only a few are the victims of crime in a specific year. Unlike the lifetime prevalence findings, only four of the relationships for last year prevalence of person or property victimizations proved to be statistically significant (see Table 2). Three of the demographic characteristics that had significant relationships with last year total victimization were living arrangement, neighborhood type, and age. As with lifetime prevalence, the 11-year-olds reported the lowest rate of victimization in the past year, and no differences were found for ethnicity. Males reported more personal victimizations, but no difference was found for property offenses. For family living arrangement, youths living in single-parent or recombined families reported the high-

**TABLE 2**
**Epidemiology of Victimization: Last Year Prevalence**

| Victimization Type | Ethnicity | | | | |
| --- | --- | --- | --- | --- | --- |
| | Anglo | Black | Hispanic | Other | Total |
| Personal | 20.0 | 18.3 | 15.1 | 17.7 | 16.9 |
| Property | 50.0 | 45.7 | 40.5 | 46.9 | 43.7 |
| Total | 55.7 | 52.2 | 48.1 | 50.6 | 50.3 |

| | Living Arrangement | | | | |
| --- | --- | --- | --- | --- | --- |
| | Intact | Single Parent | Recombined Families | Other | Total |
| Personal | 14.4 | 19.0 | 17.7 | 14.7 | 16.9 |
| Property** | 37.5 | 48.4 | 48.3 | 36.8 | 43.7 |
| Total* | 45.3 | 54.8 | 53.8 | 42.7 | 50.3 |

| | Neighborhood Type | | | |
| --- | --- | --- | --- | --- |
| | Traditional | Dense | Black | Total |
| Personal | 15.1 | 18.6 | 20.4 | 16.9 |
| Property | 41.5 | 50.0 | 46.4 | 43.7 |
| Total** | 47.1 | 60.5 | 54.0 | 50.3 |

| | Age | | | |
| --- | --- | --- | --- | --- |
| | 15 | 13 | 11 | Total |
| Personal* | 19.9 | 18.8 | 12.2 | 16.9 |
| Property | 46.1 | 47.4 | 37.8 | 43.7 |
| Total** | 54.1 | 54.0 | 43.2 | 50.3 |

| | Gender | | |
| --- | --- | --- | --- |
| | Male | Female | Total |
| Personal** | 20.7 | 12.7 | 16.9 |
| Property | 45.6 | 41.5 | 43.7 |
| Total | 52.3 | 48.2 | 50.3 |

$*p < .05$; $**p < .01$; significance level based on a chi-square test of independence.

est rates of victimization for both personal and property offenses, although only the latter was statistically significant.

The frequency of victimization per victim is of interest much for the same reason that lambda (the rate of offending within the offending population) has become a common descriptor of criminal activity (see Blumstein, Cohen, & Farrington, 1988). Whereas prevalence refers to the proportion of the population who are victims during some time period, frequency or lambda refers to an average rate of victimizations *among those victimized*. This is an especially relevant statistic for evaluating the routine activities perspective which stipulates that certain types of individuals are more likely to be victimized because of demographic characteristics or because of their life-styles. Within this study sample, however, individual characteristics did not help much in differentiating the frequency of victimization among those victimized during the past year. Only one of the relationships between demographic characteristics and frequency of victimization achieved statistical significance. Despite the finding reported earlier that the ever prevalence rate for personal victimizations was *lowest* in the traditional neighborhoods, the mean number of reported victimizations of personal crimes was substantially *greater* for residents of these very neighborhoods. Contrary to most prior research, no gender or age differences were found. Analysis by ethnicity indicated that Anglos have lower mean rates of victimization than do other groups, although these observed differences lacked statistical significance. Overall, as seen in Table 3, there were only small differences in the annual frequency of victimization by race, sex, age, neighborhood, or family type, with victims reporting roughly an average of from two to three personal and from two to three property victimizations per year.

### VICTIMIZATION AND SELF-REPORTED DELINQUENCY

According to the routine activities/life-style perspective, one would expect to discover a relationship between involvement in delinquent activities and the risk of victimization. Likewise, the use of alcohol and other illegal drugs would also be expected to be associated with a life-style conducive to exposure to crime situations. The results presented in Tables 4, 5, and 6 lend support to this approach to the study of victimization. A focus on involvement in different kinds of behaviors was emphasized using variety-scored

TABLE 3
## Epidemiology of Victimization:
## Average Last Year Frequency of Victimization Per Victim

| Victimization Type | Ethnicity | | | | |
| --- | --- | --- | --- | --- | --- |
| | Anglo | Black | Hispanic | Other | Total |
| Personal | 2.07 | 2.31 | 2.95 | 2.57 | 2.59 |
| Property | 1.97 | 2.31 | 2.15 | 2.50 | 2.23 |
| Total | 2.51 | 2.60 | 2.60 | 2.70 | 2.60 |

| | Living Arrangement | | | | |
| --- | --- | --- | --- | --- | --- |
| | Intact | Single Parent | Recombined Families | Other | Total |
| Personal | 2.23 | 2.96 | 2.00 | 2.73 | 2.59 |
| Property | 2.09 | 2.29 | 2.16 | 2.50 | 2.23 |
| Total | 2.35 | 2.83 | 2.44 | 2.53 | 2.60 |

| | Neighborhood Type | | | |
| --- | --- | --- | --- | --- |
| | Traditional | Dense | Black | Total |
| Personal* | 3.12 | 1.88 | 1.92 | 2.59 |
| Property | 2.13 | 1.98 | 2.52 | 2.23 |
| Total | 2.66 | 2.21 | 2.64 | 2.60 |

| | Age | | | |
| --- | --- | --- | --- | --- |
| | 15 | 13 | 11 | Total |
| Personal | 2.34 | 2.81 | 2.61 | 2.59 |
| Property | 2.31 | 2.06 | 2.35 | 2.23 |
| Total | 2.56 | 2.62 | 2.62 | 2.60 |

| | Gender | | |
| --- | --- | --- | --- |
| | Male | Female | Total |
| Personal | 2.69 | 2.40 | 2.59 |
| Property | 2.26 | 2.19 | 2.23 |
| Total | 2.76 | 2.41 | 2.60 |

a. The upper end of these scales was truncated so that all frequencies > 10 were recoded to 10. This was done to reduce the possibility that one or two extreme outliers would artificially inflate the mean frequencies.
*$p < .05$; significance level based on an equal variance $t$ test because heteroscedasticity precluded use of ANOVA techniques.

delinquency scales. These analyses found lifetime personal victimizations to be associated with lifetime reports of all seven types of delinquent behavior as well as with the general delinquency measure. The likelihood of having been victimized increased with the number of different types of delinquent acts committed within each specific scale.[6]

The overall relationship between the variety of delinquent involvement and the likelihood of victimization was remarkably strong. Even in the instances in which the findings failed to achieve statistical significance, the relationship was in the expected direction. In all instances, those juveniles reporting no involvement in delinquent behavior also reported the lowest level of victimization.

It should be carefully noted what this finding means. The results suggest that the probability of being victimized is substantially greater if one engages in delinquent behavior. This does not mean that nondelinquents are not victimized. With respect to lifetime prevalence rates, for example, 49% of the 307 youths reporting no delinquency did report at least one lifetime victimization. This rate, however, is substantially lower than the rate of 86% of the 91 youths who had reported involvement in six or more different types of delinquency. Whether lifetime prevalence data, last year prevalence, or last year frequency of victimization and offending were used, the pattern remained the same: Nonoffenders reported the lowest probability of victimization.

Given a general increased risk for victimization among delinquents, the question arises, does the type of delinquency have any relationship to the type of victimization experienced by juveniles? Here, we find further support for the routine activities perspective. Most pronounced is the finding for adolescents involved in assaultive behavior. Although those youths who reported never having committed a felony assault had a lifetime prevalence of personal victimization of 37%, 86% of those who reported having committed two or more different types of felony assaults during their lives indicated that they had experienced at least one personal victimization (see Table 4). Similar results were found for involvement in minor assaultive behavior and being victimized of assault. The relationship between commission of theft and property victimiza-

TABLE 4
### Prevalence of Lifetime Victimization, by Lifetime Prevalence of Delinquent Behavior[a]

| Offense Type[b] | | Lifetime Personal Victimization | Lifetime Property Victimization | Lifetime Victimization | n |
|---|---|---|---|---|---|
| Drug sales | 0 | 39 | 48 | 63* | 843 |
|  | 1 | 56 | 63 | 85 | 27 |
| Alcohol use | 0 | 31*** | 41*** | 56*** | 474 |
|  | 1 | 43 | 52 | 68 | 194 |
|  | 2 | 52 | 57 | 72 | 111 |
|  | 3 | 63 | 70 | 85 | 91 |
| Marijuana use | 0 | 36*** | 45*** | 60*** | 724 |
|  | 1 | 59 | 65 | 80 | 146 |
| Theft | 0 | 39** | 48 | 63* | 826 |
|  | 1 | 58 | 56 | 79 | 43 |
| Minor theft | 0 | 34*** | 41*** | 58*** | 610 |
|  | 1 | 48 | 64 | 77* | 164 |
|  | 2 | 60 | 65 | 78 | 95 |
| Assault | 0 | 37*** | 47** | 62*** | 783 |
|  | 1 | 60 | 65 | 78 | 72 |
|  | 2 | 86 | 50 | 93 | 14 |
| Minor assault | 0 | 29*** | 40*** | 54*** | 554 |
|  | 1 | 57 | 62 | 79 | 242 |
|  | 2 | 70 | 66 | 88 | 73 |
| Total delinquency | 0 | 24*** | 35*** | 49*** | 307 |
|  | 1 | 37 | 44 | 62 | 183 |
|  | 2 | 45 | 48 | 67 | 113 |
|  | 3-5 | 51 | 67 | 78 | 174 |
|  | ≥ 6 | 68 | 68 | 86 | 91 |

a. See appendix for identification of items included in the delinquency scales.
b. Categories refer to variety scores (i.e., the number of items in the scale to which a respondent admitted being involved).
$*p < .05$; $**p < .01$; $***p < .001$; significance level indicated by a chi-square test of independence.

tion was not as pronounced. Those juveniles who reported involvement in thievery were only slightly more likely to experience theft of their own personal property than were youths who reported no such delinquent activity. They were, however, almost twice as likely to be the victims of assaultive behavior (only 34% of those reporting no involvement in minor theft over their lifetimes reported being victims of assault compared to 60% of those who had committed at least two types of minor theft). It is interesting to note that contrary to what would be expected given prior research in the routine activities perspective, no relationship was found between involvement in drug sales and victimization. Although the lifetime prevalence rates of victimizations were higher for those reporting drug sale activity, it failed to achieve statistical significance for the two subtypes of victimizations.

Examination of last year prevalence data revealed results comparable to those for lifetime prevalence of victimization. In this analysis, however, a statistically significant relationship was found for drug sales and victimization of crimes against the person. For this more finite time period, it is interesting to note that there appears to be only a small difference in the probability of victimization depending on whether an adolescent has committed no delinquency as opposed to only one type of delinquent act (e.g., 41% of nonoffenders versus 46% of those committing only one delinquent type). The increased risk of victimization becomes more noticeable when the youth has committed two or more different types of delinquency. This suggests the possibility that infrequent or casual delinquent behavior has little effect on victimization. It is those youths involved in delinquency on a more regular basis for whom the risk of victimization is increased. Separate analyses not presented in tabular form supported this interpretation. Focusing on the number of delinquent acts rather than on a variety score as in Tables 4 and 5, these analyses showed that those committing a high volume of offenses were those most likely to report being victims of crime.

Findings similar to those reported by Gottfredson (1986) were found with respect to adolescent drinking of alcohol and use of marijuana. Those youths refraining from use of these substances had significantly lower rates of both types of victimization than did youths involved in one or more types of drinking or in the use of marijuana. For example, whereas only 31% of youths reporting no use of alcohol had been victims of assaultive behavior, twice as many (63%) using beer, wine, and hard liquor reported such victimizations. The same pattern maintained for the relationship between substance use and lifetime property victimizations.

TABLE 5
## Last Year Prevalence of Victimization,
## by Last Year Prevalence of Delinquent Behavior[a]

| Offense Type[b] | | Last Year Property | Last Year Personal | Last Year Victimization | n |
|---|---|---|---|---|---|
| Drug sales | 0 | 43 | 16** | 50* | 839 |
| | 1 | 64 | 41 | 73 | 22 |
| Alcohol use | 0 | 39*** | 14*** | 46*** | 549 |
| | 1 | 44 | 17 | 49 | 161 |
| | 2 | 53 | 24 | 63 | 88 |
| | 3 | 71 | 37 | 79 | 63 |
| Marijuana use | 0 | 41*** | 15*** | 47*** | 747 |
| | 1 | 64 | 31 | 71 | 113 |
| Theft | 0 | 44 | 16*** | 50* | 823 |
| | 1 | 48 | 48 | 70 | 27 |
| Minor theft | 0 | 39*** | 14*** | 46*** | 704 |
| | 1 | 61 | 25 | 65 | 113 |
| | 2 | 67 | 40 | 83 | 42 |
| Assault | 0 | 42* | 14*** | 49** | 796 |
| | 1 | 63 | 43 | 68 | 56 |
| | 2 | 56 | 78 | 89 | 9 |
| Minor assault | 0 | 39*** | 13*** | 46*** | 664 |
| | 1 | 61 | 26 | 67 | 162 |
| | 2 | 48 | 42 | 65 | 31 |
| Total delinquency | 0 | 35*** | 12*** | 41*** | 417 |
| | 1 | 39 | 14 | 46 | 174 |
| | 2 | 54 | 17 | 61 | 94 |
| | 3-5 | 67 | 23 | 69 | 123 |
| | ≥ 6 | 60 | 53 | 79 | 47 |

a. See appendix for identification of items included in the delinquency scales.
b. Categories refer to variety scores (i.e., the number of items in the scale to which a respondent admitted being involved).
*$p < .05$; **$p < .01$; ***$p < .001$; significance level indicated by a chi-square test of independence.

The previously discussed results addressed the association between demographic characteristics and victimization and the relationship between both lifetime victimization and last year prevalence rates and various forms of self-reported delinquency. To assess the legitimacy of the life-style/routine activities approach, however, it was necessary to examine current behavior and current victimization. Table 6 shows the mean rates of victimizations experienced in the past year for youths with no self-reported

TABLE 6

**Mean Frequency of Last Year Victimization,
by Last Year Involvement in Delinquency**

| Offense Type[a] | Personal Victimization Frequency[b] | | Property Victimization Frequency | | Total Victimization Frequency | |
|---|---|---|---|---|---|---|
| | Mean | n | Mean | n | Mean | n |
| Drug sales | | | | | | |
| No | 2.47* | 137 | 2.18 | 364 | 2.56* | 418 |
| Yes | 4.33 | 9 | 2.86 | 14 | 3.88 | 16 |
| Alcohol | | | | | | |
| No | 2.15* | 75 | 2.00** | 216 | 2.27*** | 250 |
| Yes | 3.06 | 71 | 2.52 | 164 | 3.05 | 184 |
| Marijuana use | | | | | | |
| No | 2.45 | 110 | 2.07*** | 305 | 2.37*** | 353 |
| Yes | 3.03 | 35 | 2.89 | 74 | 3.59 | 80 |
| Theft | | | | | | |
| No | 2.35*** | 133 | 2.15** | 365 | 2.49*** | 415 |
| Yes | 5.00 | 13 | 3.69 | 13 | 4.95 | 19 |
| Minor theft | | | | | | |
| No | 2.38 | 100 | 1.98*** | 279 | 2.31*** | 324 |
| Yes | 2.89 | 45 | 2.79 | 98 | 3.40 | 109 |
| Assault | | | | | | |
| No | 2.28** | 115 | 2.15 | 338 | 2.41*** | 388 |
| Yes | 3.74 | 31 | 2.63 | 40 | 4.24 | 46 |
| Minor assault | | | | | | |
| No | 1.82*** | 89 | 2.12 | 262 | 2.28*** | 303 |
| Yes | 3.87 | 55 | 2.38 | 114 | 3.33 | 129 |
| Total delinquency | | | | | | |
| No | 1.74** | 50 | 1.95* | 146 | 2.10*** | 172 |
| Yes | 3.03 | 96 | 2.40 | 234 | 2.93 | 262 |

a. See appendix for identification of items included in delinquency scales.
b. The upper end of the three victimization scales were truncated so that all frequencies > 10 were recoded to 10. This was done to reduce the possibility that one or two extreme outliers would artificially inflate the mean frequencies.
*$p < .05$; **$p < .01$; ***$p < .001$; significance levels based on unequal variance $t$ tests because heteroscedasticity precluded use of ANOVA techniques.

delinquency and for youths who indicated commission of at least one offense within the delinquency subtypes. It is important to remember that only those youths reporting one or more victimizations in the past year were included in this particular analysis.

In general, victimized youths who reported some involvement in delinquency had significantly higher mean rates of victimizations. Of those who were victims of assaultive behavior in the preceding year, for example, the mean rate of victimization was 1.82 for those youths who did not report having committed a minor assault in the past year. The comparable mean was 3.87 for those who reported having committed at least one minor assault. Given the interactive nature of assault, it is not surprising that such a relationship was found. Theft, however, does not require physical contact between victim and offender, yet among victims, the mean frequency of victimizations is significantly higher for youths who had committed at least one minor theft (2.79) than it was for those reporting no minor thefts (1.98). Although the analyses reported in Table 6 treated self-reported delinquency as a last year prevalence rate, a similar analysis using last year frequency of offending produced similar results: Youths with higher self-reported levels of delinquency also had higher mean rates of victimization during the past year.

Several of the specific analyses presented in Table 6 involved so few subjects that the tests of statistical significance should be viewed with caution. With only 9 victims of personal crime reporting involvement in drug sales during the preceding year, for example, the lambda may have been unduly inflated by 1 or 2 individuals. The same can be said of the serious theft analysis. We felt it important, however, to present the results for consistency and to show that the direction of the relationship remains constant, despite sample size.

## DISCUSSION

In this article, we set out to examine the demographic characteristics of juvenile victims of crime and to partially investigate the potential relationship between victimization and self-reported delinquency. Research to date has provided inconsistent data with regard to the distribution of several demographic characteristics of victims (e.g., age, ethnicity, and neighborhood contextual factors). Because of the finding reported by Sparks (1981) that people tend not to report victimizations for a finite period being studied, the relationship between both demographic characteristics and self-reported delinquency and victimization for both lifetime prevalence and last year prevalence, as well as frequency of victimization were examined. The findings lend support to the notion that people do report different levels of victimization depending on the time frame for which they are reporting.

With respect to reports of lifetime victimization, our analyses provided mixed results. As was found in prior research (e.g., Feyerherm & Hindelang, 1974; Gottfredson, 1986; Mawby, 1979; Miethe et al., 1987), females in this sample experienced lower rates of victimization than did males, although the difference was not as pronounced for property offenses as for crimes against persons. Also consistent with previous publications (e.g., Gottfredson, 1986; Miethe et al., 1987), family structure was found to be related to victimization rates. Juveniles living in intact families tended to be victimized less than did youths residing in single-parent or recombined families. As has been the case with respect to self-report studies of delinquency (e.g., Elliott, Huizinga, & Ageton, 1985; Huizinga & Elliott, 1987), few ethnic differences in lifetime prevalence of victimization were uncovered. Given the discrepancy in earlier studies using National Crime Survey data (i.e., Gottfredson, 1986, reported higher rates for Blacks, whereas Miethe et al., 1987, found no ethnic differences), these results only confirm the need for further investigation of this issue. Part of the confusion clearly stems from the use of noncomparable samples in the different studies.

Although earlier studies of victimization found both positive and inverse relationships between age and victimization, the differential findings were confounded by a reliance on school-based samples. The neighborhood sample used in this report provided support for a positive relationship between age and victimization. For crimes against person and property, the younger youths (11-year-olds) had considerably lower rates of victimization than did the older ones (15-year-olds).

Included in the analysis of the demographic characteristic, neighborhood descriptors stemmed from the social disorganization perspective advanced by Shaw and McKay (1942) and recently revived in the criminological arena (e.g., Bursick, 1986; Esbensen &

Huizinga, 1990; Sampson, 1983, 1985; Sampson & Wooldredge, 1987; Schichor et al., 1979). As has been noted in the studies cited, rates of victimization varied by the type of community contextual factors. Although all three areas described in this article represented "high risk" neighborhoods, the underlying characteristics reflected different types of social disorganization with different rates of victimization. Those neighborhoods with higher concentrations of single-parent families and those with higher unit-density rates exhibited the highest levels of victimization. Each of these characteristics may be mediated by more proximate causes of behavior; that is, both of these structural variables may reflect a lower level of parental supervision of children and therefore greater risk of exposure to criminal behavior as both victim and offender. This possibility has been pursued by delinquency researchers during the past decade (e.g., Johnstone, 1983; Sampson & Groves, 1989; Simcha-Fagan & Schwartz, 1986) and suggests further work to explore this possible relationship.

In every instance save one, significant differences by demographic characteristics disappeared when the level of analysis shifted to the mean number of victimizations per victim during the past year. The only significant finding was that the traditional areas of social disorganization had the highest rate (frequency) of victimization despite having the overall lowest rate of ever prevalence. For advocates of the routine activities approach who have suggested that demographic variables influence intervening or mediating variables (e.g., Hindelang et al., 1978), this finding suggests that further specification is needed.

Another proposition espoused by the routine activities perspective suggests that an individual's involvement in delinquent behavior is associated with a higher level of exposure to potential victimization and will subsequently result in more self-reported victimization than individuals not involved in a criminal life-style. Similar to the recent findings reported by Sampson and Lauritsen (1990), who studied adults in the British Crime Survey, we found that adolescents involved in criminal activity indicated that they also experienced a higher rate of victimization. This is consistent with the early finding of a positive relationship between self-reported delinquent behavior and victimization reported by Thornberry and Figlio (1974) and the more recently reported finding of a relationship between offense type and the type of victimization (Jensen & Brownfield, 1986). The lifetime victimization prevalence rates for youths involved in all types of delinquency were higher than those of youths reporting no delinquent activity, and the prevalence increased with higher levels of involvement in delinquency.

Further examination of this relationship, however, is essential if one wants to adequately test the routine activities perspective. The analysis of last year frequency of victimization and offending allows for a better test of the relationship between these two sides of the crime situation. Although lifetime victimization rates may be descriptive, it is somewhat misleading to suggest that a criminal offense at age 12, for example, is indicative of a criminal life-style at age 15 and accountable for the theft of one's bicycle while eating at the local fast food restaurant at age 10. The routine activities/ life-style perspective would lead us to believe that victims of crime are more likely to engage in risky behavior or to be found in situations where the risk of victimization is enhanced than are nonvictims. The analysis of last year victims, both prevalence and frequency rates, lends further support to the routine activities approach. Of those youths victimized during the past year, the rate of victimization was substantially greater for those involved in any type of delinquent activity, and the probability of victimization increased with both the variety and frequency of involvement in delinquent behavior, thus suggesting that for this group of victims, their own behavior may contribute to their high rate of victimization.

An obvious question of vital importance is raised by these data: What is the temporal relationship, if any, between victimization and delinquent activity? Because of the cross-sectional nature of the current data, this question could not be addressed here, but it is clearly an issue for future research.

## APPENDIX

---

Drug sales
   1. Sold marijuana or hashish
   2. Sold hard drugs such as heroin, cocaine, and LSD
Minor theft
   1. Stole less than $5
   2. Stole more than $5 but less than $50
   3. Joyriding
Felony theft
   1. Stole more than $50 but less than $100
   2. Stole more than $100
   3. Motor vehicle theft
Minor assault
   1. Hit someone with the idea of hurting them
   2. Thrown objects such as rocks or bottles at people
   3. Had or tried to have sexual relations with someone against their will
Felony assault
   1. Attacked someone with a weapon or with the idea of seriously hurting
      or killing them
   2. Been involved in gang fights
   3. Physically hurt or threatened to hurt someone to get them to have sex
      with you
Alcohol use
   1. Drank beer
   2. Drank wine
   3. Drank hard liquor
Marijuana use
   1. Used marijuana or hashish

---

## NOTES

1. Among the numerous problems raised with relying on school samples are (a) representativeness of the schools selected and/or agreeing to participate; (b) the exclusion of youths not attending school (a major problem for delinquency research given the relationship between delinquency and dropout; e.g., Elliott & Voss, 1974; Thornberry, Moore, & Christenson, 1985); (c) the exclusion of youths attending private schools; and (d) the exclusion of youths not in attendance on the day of survey administration.

2. The research reported in this article is part of a collaborative effort known as the Program of Research on the Causes and Correlates of Delinquency funded by the Office of

Juvenile Justice and Delinquency Prevention. The three collaborating projects include studies conducted by the University at Albany, the University of Colorado, and the University of Pittsburgh.

3. The child data were not included in this analysis for two reasons. First, the measures of delinquency for the child respondents differed from those used for the youths, and only four of the six victimization items were asked of the two younger cohorts. These measurement differences did not permit comparable analyses to be conducted. A second reason for excluding the younger cohorts concerned the developmental differences between 7- and 9-year-olds and 11- to 15-year-olds. We felt that these differences were of such a magnitude that the younger cohorts should be analyzed separately and reported in a separate article. Sample characteristics of the three remaining cohorts included the following: ethnicity — 8% White, 35% Black, 48% Hispanic, and 9% other; family living arrangement — 34% intact families, 43% single-parent families, 14% recombined families, and 9% other; neighborhood type — 63% traditional, 10% dense, and 27% Black; age — 31% age 15 years, 35% age 13 years, and 35% age 11 years; and gender — 53% male and 47% female.

4. Shaw and McKay (1942) indicated that juvenile delinquency was an artifact of social disorganization and social values found in specific types of communities. Census descriptors associated with high levels of social disorganization include, among others, ethnic diversity, unemployment, high density, high percentage of renters, and high rates of poverty.

5. On the basis of earlier studies, we selected 35 variables from the 1980 census data representing seven conceptual areas: family structure, ethnicity, socioeconomic status, housing, mobility, marital status, and age composition. A factor analysis (principal components with varimax rotation) of variables within each of these seven conceptual domains resulted in the identification of 11 distinct factors (eigenvalues greater than 1.0 and scree criteria were used in determining the number of factors). A cluster analysis ($K$ means with iterative relocation) was subsequently run to combine and identify similar block groups of the city. Seven distinct clusters emerged, three of which were the socially disorganized areas referred to in the text (for further discussion of this method of classifying neighborhood types, consult Esbensen & Huizinga, 1990).

6. Given the montonically increasing relationship between juvenile delinquency and age (e.g., Hirschi & Gottfredson, 1983) and the positive relationship reported in this article between victimization and age, is the relationship between victimization and self-reported offending a purely spurious one? To test for this possibility, separate analyses controlling for age were conducted. It does not appear that the reported relationship is spurious, as the relationship between offending and victimization reported for the general sample was also present when we controlled for age.

# REFERENCES

Ageton, S. S. (1981). *The relationship between delinquency and victimization in a national panel*. Boulder, CO: Behavioral Research Institute.

Baker, R. L., Mednick, R., & Carothers, L. (1989). Association of age, gender, and ethnicity with juvenile victimization in and out of school. *Youth & Society, 20*, 320-341.

Blumstein, A., Cohen, J., & Farrington, D. P. (1988). Criminal career research: Its value for criminology. *Criminology, 26*, 1-35.

Blyth, D. A., Thiel, K. S., Bush, D. M., & Simmons, R. G. (1980). Another look at school crime: Student as victim. *Youth & Society, 11*, 369-388.

Booth, A., Johnson, D. R., Choldin, H. M. (1977). Correlates of city crime rates: Victimization surveys versus official statistics. *Social Problems, 25*, 187-197.

Bursick, R. J., Jr. (1986). Ecological stability and the dynamics of delinquency. In A. J. Reiss & M. H. Tonry (Eds.), *Crime and community* (pp. 35-66). Chicago: University of Chicago Press.

Cohen, L. E., Felson, M. (1979). Social change and crime rate trends: A routine activities approach. *American Sociological Review, 44*, 588-608.

Cohen, L. E., Kluegel, J. & Land, K. (1981). Social inequality and predatory criminal victimization: An exposition and test of a formal theory. *American Sociological Review, 46*, 505-524.

Decker, D. L., Schichor, D., & O'Brien, R. M. (1982). *Urban structure and victimization.* Lexington, MA: Lexington Books.

Elliott, D. S., Huizinga, D., & Ageton, S. S. (1985). *Explaining delinquency and drug use.* Beverly Hills, CA: Sage.

Elliott, D. S., & Voss, H. (1974). *Delinquency and dropout.* Lexington, MA: Lexington Books.

Esbensen, F. A., & Huizinga, D. (1990). Community structure and drug use: From a social disorganization perspective. *Justice Quarterly, 7*, 691-709.

Feyerherm, W. H., & Hindelang, M. J. (1974). On the victimization of juveniles: Some preliminary results. *Journal of Research in Crime and Delinquency, 11*, 40-50.

Garofalo, J. (1979). Victimization and the fear of crime. *Journal of Research in Crime and Delinquency, 16*, 80-97.

Garofalo, J. (1987). Reassessing the lifestyle model of criminal victimization. In M. R. Gottfredson & T. Hirschi (Eds.), *Positive criminology* (pp. 23-42). Beverly Hills, CA: Sage.

Gottfredson, M. R. (1986). Substantive contributions of victimization surveys. In M. Tonry & N. Morris (Eds.), *Crime and justice: An annual review of research* (pp. 251-287). Chicago: University of Chicago Press.

Hindelang, M. J., Gottfredson, M. R., & Garofalo, J. (1978). *Victims of personal crime: An empirical foundation for a theory of personal victimization.* Cambridge, MA: Ballinger.

Hirschi, T., & Gottfredson, M. (1983). Age and the explanation of crime. *American Journal of Sociology, 89*, 552-584.

Huizinga, D., & Elliott, D. S. (1987). Juvenile offenders: Prevalence, offender incidence, and arrest rates by race. *Crime & Delinquency, 33*, 206-223.

Jensen, G., & Brownfield, D. (1986). Gender, lifestyles, and victimization: Beyond routine activity. *Violence and Victims, 1*, 85-99.

Johnstone, J.W.C. (1983). Recruitment to a youth gang. *Youth & Society, 14*, 281-300.

Lasley, J. R., & Rosenbaum, J. L. (1988). Routine activities and multiple personal victimization. *Sociology and Social Research, 73*, 47-49.

Massey, J. L., Krohn, M. D., & Bonati, L. M. (1989). property crime and the routine activities of individuals. *Journal of Research in Crime and Delinquency, 26*, 378-400.

Mawby, R. I. (1979). The victimization of juveniles: A comparative study of three areas of publicly owned housing in Sheffield. *Journal of Research in Crime and Delinquency, 16*, 98-113.

Maxfield, M. G. (1987). Lifestyle and routine activity theories of crime: Empirical studies of victimization, delinquency, and offender decision-making. *Journal of Quantitative Criminology, 3*, 275-284.

Menard, S., & Covey, H. C. (1987). Patterns of victimization, fear of crime, and crime precautions in non-metropolitan New Mexico. *Journal of Crime and Justice, 10*, 71-100.

Miethe, T. D., Stafford, M. C., & Long, J. S. (1987). Social differentiation in criminal victimization: A test of routine activities/lifestyle theories. *American Sociological Review, 52*, 184-194.

O'Brien, R. M. (1985). *Crime and victimization data.* Beverly Hills, CA: Sage.

Sampson, R. J. (1983). Structural density and criminal victimization. *Criminology, 21*, 276-293.

Sampson, R. J. (1985). Neighborhood and crime: The structural determinants of personal victimization. *Journal of Research in Crime and Delinquency, 22*, 7-40.

Sampson, R. J., & Groves, W. B. (1989). Community structure and crime: Testing social disorganization theory. *American Journal of Sociology, 94*, 774-802.

Sampson, R. J., & Lauritsen, J. L. (1990). Deviant lifestyles, proximity to crime, and the offender-victim link in personal violence. *Journal of Research in Crime and Delinquency, 27*, 110-139.

Sampson, R. J., & Wooldredge, J. D. (1987). Linking the micro- and macro-level dimensions of lifestyle-routine activity and opportunity models of predatory victimization. *Journal of Quantitative Criminology, 3*, 371-393.

Schichor, D., Decker, D. L., & O'Brien, R. M. (1979). Population density and criminal victimization. *Criminology, 17*, 184-193.

Shaw, C. R., & McKay, H. D. (1942). *Juvenile delinquency and urban areas.* Chicago: University of Chicago Press.

Simcha-Fagan, O., & Schwartz, J. E. (1986). Neighborhood and delinquency: An assessment of contextual effects. *Criminology, 24*, 667-699.

Singer, S. I. (1981). Homogeneous victim-offender populations: A review and some research implications. *Journal of Criminal Law and Criminology, 72*, 779-788.

Skogan, W. G. (1989). Communities, crime, and neighborhood organization. *Crime & Delinquency, 35*, 437-457.

Smith, D. A., & Jarjoura, G. R. (1988). Social structure and criminal victimization. *Journal of Research in Crime and Delinquency, 25*, 27-52.

Sparks, R. F. (1981). Multiple victimization: Evidence, theory and future research. *Journal of Criminal Law and Criminology, 72*, 762-778.

Stafford, M. C., & Galle, O. R. (1984). Victimization rates, exposure to risk, and fear of crime. *Criminology, 22*, 173-185.

Thornberry, T. P., & Figlio, R. M. (1974). Victimization and criminal behavior in a birth cohort. In T. P. Thornberry & E. Sagarin (Eds.), *Images of crime: Offenders and victims* (pp. 102-112). New York: Praeger.

Thornberry, T. P., Moore, M., & Christenson, R. L. (1985). The effect of dropping out of high school on subsequent criminal behavior. *Criminology, 23*, 3-18.

Toby, J. (1986). The victims of school crime. In T. F. Hartnagel & R. A. Silverman (Eds.), *Critique and explanation: Essays in honor of Gwynne Nettler* (pp. 171-184). New Brunswick, NJ: Transaction Books.

*Finn-Aage Esbensen is a research associate at the Institute of Behavioral Science at the University of Colorado. His current interests revolve around the causes and correlates of delinquency and drug use. Recent publications have appeared in Justice*

Quarterly, Quality and Quantity, *and* American Journal of Police. *He recently coauthored* Criminology: Explaining Crime and Its Context *(with S. Brown and G. Geis).*

*David Huizinga is a research associate at the Institute of Behavioral Science at the University of Colorado, where he is involved in several longitudinal studies of social problems. Recent publications have appeared in* Criminology, Justice Quarterly, Journal of Research in Crime and Delinquency, *and* Social Science Research. *He recently coauthored* Multiple Problem Youth *(with D. Elliott and S. Menard).*

# From Crime Policy to Victim Policy
# The Need for a Fundamental
# Policy change*

by Ezzat A. FATTAH, Professor of Criminology
Simon Fraser University
Vancouver, Canada

Recent years have witnessed great strides in applied victimology. During the 1980s legislation was passed, services were created, programs were set up, all aimed at helping crime victims and improving their unhappy lot. One of the most important developments was the formal approval of the UN declaration of basic principles of justice for victims of crime and abuse of power by the General Assembly on November 11, 1985 (1). In adopting it, the General Assembly of the United Nations stated that it was "*Cognizant* that millions of people throughout the world suffer harm as a result of crime and the abuse of power and that the rights of these victims have not been adequately recognized" (See Joutsen, 1987, p. 68). All this signals the dawning of the promised golden age of the victim.

What is remarkable about the developments of the last decade is the ease and smoothness with which the legislative changes were introduced and passed. Not only was there no opposition to the proposed initiatives but they were also not preceded by the usual impact studies to assess the effects they were likely to have on the criminal justice system and on the larger society. Even more surprising was the fact that the changes were introduced in the absence of clear empirical evidence indicating that they do represent what crime victims really want. It is therefore time to critically assess these victim initiative and to see how successful they have been in alleviating the plight of the victims of crime.

This paper will attempt to show that despite the fanfare with which the new measures were introduced, they have not tangibly improved the lot of crime victims. The paper will show that what is necessary to achieve this goal is a new criminal justice policy, a new penal and sentencing philosophy that places the emphasis not on punishment and retaliation but on reparation, mediation and conciliation. In most instances these two sets of goals (retributive/distributive are functionally incompatible. Parallel to this change, there needs to be another fundamental change in the

---

* International Workshop on Victimology and Victim's Rights Thammasat University - Bangkok, April 2-4, 1991.
(1) The history of the UN declaration and the dynamics involved are outlined by Joutsen (1987), pp. 55-69.

traditional views on crime. The offence should cease to be regarded as an affront to the state and be viewed as an offence against the individual victim, not as a violation of an abstract law but a violation of the rights of the victim.

The argument I am advancing is that if we genuinely care about crime victims and truly want to substantially improve their lot then we will need much more than hollow slogans (justice for victims), symbolic gestures (victim impact statements), punitive measures (fine victim surcharge), and political palliatives and placebos (victim compensation schemes).

# THE LEGAL STATUS OF CRIME VICTIMS

Protection of, and assistance to, victims will have to become part of the core values of society. Social commitment to victims will have to be deeply rooted in the general belief system. It is important, therefore, to establish the legal sources of the rights of victims. If action and policies are to be guided by more than just humanitarian concern for the victims and their plight, it is necessary to identify the legal as well as the social bases for both society's obligation and the offender's responsibility to the victim.

In the 1950s and the 1960s, when Margery Fry and others called for state compensation to victims of crime, there were serious attempts to determine the legal and philosophical foundations on which such compensation is to be based. Among the theories advanced at the time, were the legal tort theory, the social contract theory, the utilitarian theory, and the social solidarity theory, to mention but a few. Current concern for, and discussions of victims other rights have not been accompanied by any similar attempt. Probably the reason is that the emergence and enactment of Victims' Bills of Rights was the outcome of political and grass root initiatives rather than legal or juridical initiatives.

Since in law rights originate from and are closely linked to the person's status, to establish the rights to which victims of crime are entitled it is necessary to define their legal status. This is all the more important since in many jurisdictions, at present, victims seem to have no legal status. Prior to the amendments made to the Criminal Code of Canada in 1988, (2) this was made abundantely clear by court

---

(2) To remedy the situation, Bill C-89 "An Act to amend the Criminal Code" (assented to on 21st July, 1988) added to Section 662 of the Canadian Criminal Code the following subsection among others :

For the purpose of determining the sentence to be imposed on an offender or whether the offender should be discharged pursuant to section 662.1 in respect of any offence, the court may consider a statement, prepared in accordance with subsection (1.2), of a victim of the offence describing the harm done to, or loss suffered by, the victim arising from the commission of the offence.

76

rulings in Ontario and British Columbia. In november 1987, in a criminal case of dangerous driving resulting in the death of a 16 year old youth, a Supreme Court judge in the province of British Columbia denied the prosecutor's request to submit a statement by the family of the victim. He quoted from a judgement of the High Court of Ontario in which the sentencing judge declared that "the principles of sentencing establish guidelines for judges and do not include consideration of the effects of the tragic death upon the survivors". (The Vancouver Sun, Nov. 1987). This judicial statement suggests that the victim of crime (or his survivors in the case of death) does not enjoy any legal status and cannot, therefore, become legal party to the proceedings. It highlights the need to fundamentally change the way society looks upon crime and punishment if the victim is to become a full party in judicial proceedings and if she is to recover their lost status in the criminal process. In other words, what is urgently needeed is a new paradigm of criminal justice. In this new paradigm, which in reality is a very old one, crime will no longer be viewed as a wrongful, sinful act that needs to be punished. It will be regarded as a harmful behavior that needs to be redressed in the present and prevented in the future.

Victims were better off when there was no differentiation between civil law and criminal law, when all harmful actions were civil torts. Victims were the principal protagonists when prosecutions were private, handled not by the Crown but by the person who suffered or his representative. The reduction of the victim to an inconsequential figure coincided with the emergence of the public prosecutor. (Gallaway and Hudson, 1981). But the real decline started with the emergence of a criminal law which viewed the criminal act not as an offence against the victim but as an offence against the sovereign and later the state. Gradually, the victim who used to be the cental figure, in whose name and on whose behalf the proceedings were conducted, was reduced to the status of a witness used to buttress the Crown's case and abused if he refused to cooperate or to testify. Once the state monopolized the right to criminal prosecution and converted the "wergeld" or the composition paid to the victim into a fine destined for the king's coffers, the victim became the forgotten man, a legal nonentity.

The historical decline of the victim is traced by the Law Reform Commission of Canada (1974) to the emergence of the criminal law. The Commission describes the process as follows :

> In Anglo-Saxon England there was no criminal law as we know it. Disputes were dealt with by a process greatly resembling our civil law. When an individual felt that he had suffered damage because of another's wrongful conduct he was permitted either to settle the matter by agreement or to proceed before a tribunal. Restitution was the order of the day and other sanctions, including imprisonment, were rarely used.

---

Another subsection defines the victim as "the person to whom harm is done or who suffers physical or emotional loss as a result of the commission of the offence" and adds that where the victim is dead, ill or otherwise incapable of making the statement, the definition would include "the spouse or any relative of that person, anyone who has in law or in fact the custody of that person or is responsible for the care or support of that person or any dependent of that person".

*As the common law developed, criminal law became a distinct branch of law. Numerous antisocial acts were seen to be "offenses against the state" or "crimes" rather than personal wrongs or torts. This tendency to characterize some wrongs as "crimes" was encouraged by the practice under which the lands and property of convicted persons were forfeited to the king or feudal lord; fines, as well, became payable to feudal lords and not to the victim. The natural practice of compensating the victim or his relatives was discouraged by making it an offense to conceal the commission of a felony or convert the crime into a source of profit. In time, fines and property that would have gone in satisfaction of the victim's claims were diverted to the state. Compounding an offense (that is, accepting an economic benefit in satisfaction of the wrong done without the consent of the court or in a manner that is contrary to the public interest) still remains a crime under the Canadian Criminal Code and discourages private settlement or restitution.*

*It would now seem that historical developments, however well intentioned, effectively removed the victim from sentencing policy and obscured the view that crime was social conflict. (1974 : 4-5).*

This historical development leaves no doubt that it was political ruse by which the legitimate rights of the victims were usurped by the rulers to the latters' benefit. It is this usurpation that Christie (1977) refers to when he states that conflicts have been stolen from the parties directly involved and thereby have either disappeared or become other people's property. It is also a historical fact that with the passage of time the criminal law became a powerful tool of subjugation used by governments and by rulers to consolidate their grip over the population and it is not a coincidence that many criminal codes begin with the section dealing with offenses against the state.

At present, the administration of criminal justice emphasizes the roles played by professional, specialized third parties : judges, prosecutors, defense lawyers, experts, and so on. While these third parties have assumed an increasingly important place in the criminal justice system, the victim's role has become largely peripheral and the victim has been treated by the system as largely irrelevant (see Galaway and Hudson, 1981 : 229). Christie (1978) believes that the root problem of the administration of justice is that conflicts have become the property of professionals rather than people. He adds that by taking over the ownership of disputes between people, professionals have taken the community's opportunity to learn from individual disputes and develop structures for improving the situation.

# THE OLD AND NEW PARADIGMS OF CRIMINAL JUSTICE

Victim's current plight stems from the fact that crime is no longer regarded as a conflict between two individuals, two human beings, but as a conflict between the offender and society. Viewed as such, crime generates not an obligation to the victim, but a debt to society, and once the criminal is punished the debt is paid. In this scenario, there is no place for the victim, no part for him to play. The recent report of the Canadian Sentencing Commission leads to the painful realization that despite all the current talk about victims of crime, their rights and their plight, this basic outlook has not changed. Instead of stating that the primary goal of sentencing is to repair the harm done to the victim by the offence and to prevent future harm, the Sentencing Commission (1987) regrettably declared that :

> ...the fundamental purpose of sentencing is to preserve the authority of, and pro-mote respect for, the law through the imposition of just sanctions (1987 : 151).

Such abstract goals are responsible for the depersonalization and dehumaniza-tion of the justice system, for the reification of both the offender and the victim. In an era meant to become the golden age of the victim, there seems to be a growing obsession with punishment, euphemistically called "just deserts". And yet, having punishment as the central focus of the criminal justice system is neither morally legitimate nor practically effective. It can only act to the detriment of the victim. Dispute-settlement, mediation, reconciliation, arbitration, reparation, are concepts foreign to a system centered on punishment, a system which regards the crime not as a human action but as a legal infraction. Such a system acts to intensify the conflict rather than settling it. And instead of bringing the feuding parties closer to one another, it widens the gap that separates them. The obsession with punishment leads to an unwarranted differentiation between criminal victimization and other type of victimization and results in grave injustices to those who offend and those who suffer.

In the new paradigm of criminal justice, the primary purpose of the criminal law would be to heal the injury, repair the harm, compensate the loss and prevent further victimization. This requires among other things a rethinking and a reexami-nation of the artifical boundaries which have been erected over the years between civil and criminal law, between civil and criminal courts, as well as the artificial distinction between crimes and torts. This artificial distinction, which seemingly is taken for granted, is detrimental to the victims and their interests. The greatest majority of criminal offences brought to trial end in a sentence to a fine. Civil cases end in the payment of damages. Thus, the only actual difference in outcome be-tween a civil and a criminal case is that in the former the damages are paid to the person who suffered the loss whereas in the latter it is the state that benefits at the expense of the victim. And this is what has to change.

The band-aid remedies that were adopted by any countries in the past ten years ignore the roots of the present plight of crime victims. The philosophical, deonto-logical and theological ideas and the political interests that led to the emergence of the notions of crime and punishment are responsible for the decline of the victim. The constructive practices of reparation, composition, reconciliation gave way to punishments supposedly aimed at achieving expiation and atonement. Improving the victim's lot requires that the notion of crime be taken back to its sociological origins. Sociologically, crime is not a sin, it is not an immoral behavior, it is a harmful, injurious act. Since crime is an inevitable feature of social life, it is only logical that it be considered in a secular, technological society as a social risk, as a hazard of modern life, not very different from other risks to which people are daily exposed. The way society responds to other social risks to minimize their occurrence and their effects should guide the action against crime. Crime is as much a fact of life as are natural disasters, traffic accidents, disease and death. But while other social risks are covered, in the welfare state, by some form of insurance or another, the risk of becoming victim of crime is not adequately covered. Victim compensation schemes have done little to remedy or to improve this situation. Insufficient funding, inadequate information and stringent eligibility requirements have meant that the overwhelming majority of victims are excluded from the realm of compensation (3). Because the funds allocated to these programs are severely limited, more publicity and more applications can only result in lower awards and a higher rate of rejection. As to restitution by the offender, it remains, for obvious reasons, a seldom used and largely ineffective means of redress. The only potential restitution has is to be used instead of, and not in addition to, incarceration. In the present punitive climate, this is not a very attractive proposition.

The reluctance of governments to go beyond symbolic gestures, political palliatives and placebos, to improve the plight of crime victims is quite evident in victim legislation introduced in several countries.

In 1987, for example, the Canadian government, following the steps of some American states, introduced in the federal Parliament a Bill (see note no. 2) aimed, among other things, at imposing a victim fine surcharge not exceeding 15% of any fine that is imposed on the offender, or where no fine is imposed for the offence, ten thousand dollars. Instead of returning the fines to their original and legitimate owners by placing them in a fund earmarked for victim compensation, or using them to finance a comprehensive insurance scheme for crime victims, the new legislation is a clear attempt to finance the present compensation programs by imposing an *additional* penalty on the offender. The fine surcharge concept is neither practical nor fair. Most offenders, particularly those charged with violent crimes, are unable bo pay whatever fines they are sentenced to and have to spend additional time in prison for default. What the fine surcharge really does is to make an already bad situation much worse. The idea is also unfair because it penalizes all offenders and not only those who should be responsible for compensation. Most victimless crimes are punished by a fine. People convicted ot these offences will be paying extra to make up for the stinginess of the government. Drug offenders and non-violent offenders would be charged what should have been paid by those who commit crimes of violence.

# VICTIMS NEEDS AND VICTIMS SERVICES

The question of how crime victims are currently treated and how the *should* be treated by criminal justice personnel is an administrative issue. It has to do with the

---

(3) For a detailed analysis of victim compensation programs in Canada see Fattah (1988).

attitudes, the policies, the practices of the system and the interactions between those working in it and their clientele. As mentioned in chapter one, all users of the system have to be treated with courtesy, sensitivity, understanding, compassion as well as respect for their dignity. This should be the case regardless of their role or charateristics, whether complainants or suspects, victims or offenders, young or old, male or female, rich or poor, white or black. Improving the general attitudes of those in the system to its users is both essential and beneficial. The training of criminal justice personnel should be designed to sensitize them to the needs and plight of their clients. Special training is necessary for those who will be called upon to deal with special categories or specific types of clients. Special training should also be required for those whose activites dictate that they intervene in certain conflict situations such as family violence.

What are the needs of crime victims and how could these needs be met? (4) These are research issues. Some of the needs may be obvious, others are less evident. There are general needs and there are needs that are specific to certain categories or types of victims. Once the needs are properly identified the question is : what existing services should cater to these needs? What services have to be created or strengthened to adequately satisfy them? This requires full assessements of existing services. Then political decisions will have to be made. Implementation of the declaration's provisions in this area is problematic because of the financial costs involved. As commitments by politicians do not usually match their rhetoric, it would be rather naive to expect, especially in times of economic restraint, that there will be massive infusion of funds into victim services. This, however, is the area where society can show the extent of its real commitment to victims.

Before embarking on the creation of large scale victim services it is also nec-essary to assess some of the dangers involved (5). Social services in the welfare state, whether run by professionals or volunteers, have a tendency to develop de-pendency among their clients and even to extract those clients from their social networks. In the long run, these networks, composed of relatives, neighbors, friends, peers and so on, are weakened as their members are freed from their social obliga-tions. The professionalization of victim services presents yet another danger. The personalized care of the victim's social network is replaced by the depersonalized care of the state. The victim, who within his family, neighborhood or small com-munity, is treated as a person and who in such setting feels and acts as an individual

---

(4) The greatest and primary need of crime victims seems to be the need for information. The Canadian Federal-Provincial Task Force on Justice for Victims of Crime (1983) concluded that "the most frequently expressed need by the great majority of victims interviewed is the need for information. To meet this need, it is not new services which are required, but a firm commitment on the part of the various criminal justice officials to let the victims know what is happening to "their" case (p. 150)... the key words are concern, consideration and commu-nication" (p. 152). The South Australian Committee of Inquiry on Victims of Crimes conclu-ded that the primary needs of crime victims were for social support and information.
(5) For a discussion of some of the visible and hidden dangers of victim movemnts, see Fattah (1986).

is converted into a "client" or a "recipient of services" (6). He/she has to suffer the dehumanization of being transformed from a person to a number. The psychological support and regeneration the victim feels when cared for by family or friends is replaced by the confusion and humiliation of having been placed within the hands of strangers who have to deal daily with dozens of other victims.

In addition to the dangers outlined above, there are the general dangers of intervention. In providing the care, help and support victims need, caution have to be exercised to avoid causing greater harm to the victim. Intensive and/or excessive intervention can delay the natural healing process. It can prolong the agony and the trauma resulting from the offence, create undue anxieties about the crime situation and the risks of victimization, and nurture attitudes of mistrust or distrust among actual and potential victims. There are reasons to suspect that there might be a link between the new interventionist strategies and techniques with victims and the growing pains of victimization. This raises the question of whether the heightened fear of victimization, reported in recent years, is in any way related to the increasing attention and publicity being given to crime victims. Do policies of intervention prolong rather than shorten the traumatic effects of victimization? These are all questions worthy of serious exploration. The zeal to help and assist crime victims should not blind us to the potential dangers of our action (see Fattah, 1986).

The consistent talk about victim services in recent years has already created or heightened expectations among crime victims. Such expectations, if not met, can only lead to various levels of insatisfaction and frustration with the CJS and the greater society. The history of victim services, as brief as it may be, is one of unfulfilled promises and unmet expectations. There is ample empirical evidence of the inadequacy of the services and the frustrations that ensue. In England, Shapland (1986) detected a mismatch between victim expectations of the system and the system's assumptions about victim needs. Consequently, she warns that public statements about the worth of victims, which are later shown to be hollow, may rebound on any who set up such ineffective schemes. This is confirmed by her finding that by the end of police and court processes, there was a significant decline in victim's satisfaction with the police handling of the case and also a decline in attribution of positive qualities to the police generally. In the U.S., Elias (1983) found considerable disenchantement and even some evidence of greater discontent among appli-

---

(6) In her critical analysis of the bureaucratization and professionalization of the shelter movement, Morgan (1981) shows how the victim, in this instance the battered wife, is transformed into a program client. Morgan identifies other dangers as well. She explains, for example, how social control devices are masked under the cloak of modern professionalized services, how the requirements for evaluation and reporting can seriously compromise client confidentiality and how some clients get trapped as a result for welfare fraud, drug problems, or parole violations. Morgan insists that the growth of the interventionist state has meant the growth of bureaucratic and professionalized forms penetrating into everyday life. She also quotes an early shelter organizer, Betsy Warrior, who warned against the "exploitation by well off professionals and bureaucrats who fund themselves with the money obtained, rather than letting it benefit the people whom it was secured for".

cants to victim compensation : delays, inconveniences, poor information, inability to participate, restrictive eligibility requirements, denial of awards in many cases, unrealistic ceilings and so on.

# THE ROLE OF THE VICTIM IN THE CRIMINAL JUSTICE PROCESS

The United Nations declaration calls for "allowing the views and concerns of victims to be presented and considered at appropriate stages of the proceedings where their personal interests are affected...". This provision raises fundamental questions about the victims' legal standing and their role in the criminal justice process, whether they should have a say in bail hearings, plea-bargaining, sentencing, parole hearings or parole decision-making and so on and form such input should take (7).

A brief review of the initiatives taken in recent years to ensure victims' participation in the justice process suggests that the changes have been hastily introduced without a full assessment of their potential effects, nor concern for whether or not they are compatible with existing policies and philosophies. The review also provides unmistakeable clues to the real intentions behind victim legislation.

Thus a dispassionate analysis of the so-called victims Bills of Rights inevitably leads to the conclusion that such a legislation is not meant to improve the lot of crime victims but to toughen an already harsh system of punishment. For example, Attorney General George Deukmejian's (who later became the State's governor) comments on California's Proposition 8, "The Victims Bill of Rights" leave no doubt as to the real objectives underlying the legislation. Writing in a voters' brochure, Deukmejian said :

*There is absolutely no question that the passage of this proposition will result in more criminal convictions, more criminals being sentenced to state prison, and more protection of the law-abiding citizenry (Quoted after Paltrow, 1982, p. 1)*

The statement is very revealing of what seems to be the hidden agenda of those who are willing to exploit the noble cause of crime victims to bring about more punishment.

---

(7) Rossini (1987) points out that giving victims legal standing could allow them to initiale criminal proceedings, contest a prosecutor's decision by means of an appeal to the court, examine evidence in the course of a court trial, and to make submissions regarding sentencing and parole. Reffering to the disparity which characterizes the existing system of sentencing and parole, Grabosky (1985) suggests that to inject another element, particularly one so variable by virtue of its dependence upon the resiliency, vindictiveness or other personality attributes of a victim, is to invite further inconsistency, a situation which the criminal justice system could ill afford.

California's proposition 8, the Victims Bill of Rights is certainly one of the strongest attempts to formalize the victim's role in the judicial process. The Bill gives the victims the right of allocution, that is the right to appear and be heard at felony sentencing hearings. A 1986 study by the McGeorge School of Law, of the implementation of this right by state and local agencies revealed that less than three percent of the eligible victims appeared at sentencing hearings. Another interesting finding is that the majority of judges and chief probation officers viewed allocution at sentencing as unnecessary while the majority of distict attorneys viewed it favorably and were more confident than judges that it affected sentencing.

Obviously, the overwhelming majority of crime victims are unwilling, for one reason or another, to exercise whatever rights they may be given. Thus, one might question the practical value and returns of granting victims such rights despite strong objections from many quarters (8).


# VICTIM-IMPACT STATEMENTS

Do victim-impact statements and victim allocution have on impact on sentencing? If they do *not* influence the sentence, then they are bound, at least in the long run, to alienate the victims who in good faith exercise this right believing that it will have an impact on the court's decision. In case they *do* have an impact, one might question their effects on the principles of fairness and equality. The tiny minority of offenders in whose cases the right is exercised will receive harsher sanctions than others who had committed identical offences. In other words, if victim-impact statements have no impact on sentencing they can only heighten the victim's sense of irrelevance, if they do, they can only aggravate the problem of sentencing disparity.

Despite all these problems with victim-impact statements, at no time was there any serious challenge to the proposed Canadian legislation (Bill C-89) and only few voices were heard opposing the suggested procedural change.

In his testimony before the legislative Committee of the Canadian House of Commons on Bill C-89 (An Act to amend the Criminal Code -Victims of Crime), a distinguished Ontario lawyer, Mr. Paul Calarco (Feb. 9, 1988) criticized the Bill for being seriously flawed and for its failure to recognize the right of an accused

---

(8) Evidence from the U.S., Australia, and the U.K. suggests that where the right to appear is accorded to victims only a very small minority of victims take up the opportunity. Walker (1985) notes that Arizona, Connecticut and California already have laws giving the victim a voice in criminal proceedings. He suggests that the evidence indicates that in fact victims do not want an active role. He refers to judge Lois Forer of Philadelphia who routinely extends an invitation to victims but only few bother to appear. And in Connecticut, where the victim's right to participate has become law, victims appear at only about 3 % of all sentencings. The percentage is strikingly similar to the one reported by Neto et al. (1986) for California.

person to a fair trial and the right of that accused person to test the Crown's case. He also predicted that once passed, the Bill will lead to longer trials, more appeals, greater legal costs, both to an accused person and to the public in terms of Crown attorneys and legal aid costs, as well as a greater court backlog. He added that the Bill may indeed lead to illegal sentences, depending of course on the constitutional challenges, and an improper deprivation of the liberty of the subject (House of Commons, Issue no. 7, p. 5).

Addressing the specific issue of victim-impact statements, Mr. Calarco said :

*Finally, the victim impact statement is, in my respectful submission, completely inappropriate. The principles of sentencing do not look and should not look at how an individual offence has affected and individual complainant. If an individual complainant has perhaps been emotionally shattered by an experience, instead of perhaps a six-month sentence, are we to say that the devastating effect on that victim would bring the sentence up to 12 or 18 months or more? Conversely, are we to say that if this complainant has forgiven the offender totally, or not had any adverse effect from the offence, that offender should then receive a suspended sentence rather than the six months society says should be imposed? (1988-7:9)*

Calarco's statements before the House of Commons legislative Committee echoed those made by other lawyers. Earl Levy, president of the Criminal Lawyers Association of Ontario was quoted in the Globe and Mail (April 11, 1984) as saying "(Victims impact statement) injects an air of emotionalism in the sentencing procedure... I feel there are enough problems now with the disparity of sentencing". Levy added that victim-impact statements will only compound that problem because with human nature being what it is, judges are bound to be affected by this air of emotionalism. Another lawyer, Richard Peck, who at the time was clairing the criminal justice section of the Canadian Bar Association, declared to the Vancouver Sun (Sept. 21, 1983, p. A3) that judges are expected to act dispassionately and that the justice system relies on impartial judges handing down sentences based on a well-tried set of criteria. He insisted that "there is no place for vengeance in a dispassionate, logical sentencing process", and that victims "should never directly influence the length of sentence".

The same article (Still, 1983) quoted another Vancouver lawyer, Michael Bolton, who deplored the fact that the government appeared to be responding to pressure groups (the victim lobby) and expressed the opinion that organized groups, though serving a useful function in helping to alleviate the anguish felt by many crime victims, should not be involved in procedural reforms.

Political considerations overrode legal objections and the Bill was passed with an astounding majority and very little change. Victim-impact statements became, despite the reservations articulated by legal practitioners, part of the criminal code of Canada. It is still too early to assess the impact of this procedural change and to establish whether any of the predictions made by those who argued against the statements did in fact materialize. A recent development in the United States is worth noting, namely the fact that some courts have ruled that victim-impact statements are unconstitutional in capital cases (Sharman, 1988). There is also some evidence suggesting that at least some of the provisions contained in victim legislation under the guise of helping the victim may backfire. For example, one of the California Bill of Rights (Proposition 8) provisions is "Truth in Evidence". Originally this provision was intended as a way of eliminating the exclusionary rule, a rule that renders illegally obtained evidence inadmissible in court. This particular section of the California Bill stipulates that "relevant evidence shall not be excluded in any criminal proceedings". It turned out that such a provision is in fact a double-edged sword. Paltrow (1982) reports that under this new provision it became possible for lawyers in rape cases to have victims examined by psychiatrists or to question the victim about sexual activity she had engaged in shortly prior to the alleged rape.

There are several additional problems with victim-impact statements and the right of allocution. It has been pointed out (Neto, 1986, p. 7) that victims' interests are usually well enough represented by prosecutors and that victim intervention would add little that is useful to most cases and would impose upon an already overburdened system irrelevant information and requests.

It is also suggested that allowing the victim to play a direct role in the sentencing process injects an emotional element in what is meant to be a dispassionate and logical process (see above). Mention is also made that lengthy trials would become even longer because the accused will have to be given the right to challenge the victim's statement and to require the Crown to prove it (9).

And with the overcrowding of prisons a wide use of this right may worsen an already intolerable situation since judges may mete out longer sentences or become reluctant to use alternatives to incarceration.

More important still, is that if we allow the victim to play a direct role in sentencing and to ask more punishment, then logically we will have to give the victim also the right to demand an acquittal or no punishment! Are we willing to substitute the victim's wish for what we currently believe is society's right? Or are we willing to follow the victim's desire only if the call is for more pnishment? And what about the right to appeal? Should the victim be given the right to appeal if he/she is not satisfied with the sentence?

---

(9) Rossini (1987) highlights some of the problems associated with greater victim participation in the criminal justice process. She notes that there are many reasons why victims may choose to participate only occasionally which would make the criminal process arbitrary. The cost of separate legal representation for a victim would be prohititive for the majority. Use of Government funds for this purpose (eg. through legal aid) would add enormous financial coast to the State. The alternative of using Crown Prosecutors to act on a victim's behalf could lead to a conflict of interest, particularly where the issue in question is the prosecution of a lesser charge or a decision not to continue with the case. She also discusses the problem of determining at what stage the victim should appear (p. 16).

After reviewing the arguments for and against victim statements, and after noting that many victims do not wish to be involved by giving evidence on the impact of offences on their lives, the Victorian Sentencing Committee (Australia) concluded that the case against the introduction of victim-impact statements is more compelling than the case for them. Consequently, the Committee (1988) recommended that victim-impact statements not be adopted in Victoria (p. 545).

According to popular estimates (Ranish and Schichor, 1985), about 90 % of the criminal cases in the U.S. are disposed of through plea bargaining. This means that victims involvement in the plea bargaining phase is even more important than at the sentencing stage. The growing trend to resort to determinate sentences means that whatever input the victim might be allowed, will have to be made at the stage of plea bargaining. The Canadian Sentencing Commission (1987) examined the issue and rejected the idea of victims becoming independent parties in plea negotiations. The Commission believed that this would be inconsistent with the ultimate responsibility of the Attorney General in each province for the prosecution of criminal code offences. The Commission added that such concept could potentially precipitate an adversarial relationship between Crown council and victims and that such provision may render victims vulnerable to pressure from either the crown prosecutor or defence council respecting a plea bargain.

Ranish and Shichor (1985) conclude that the evidence is clear, the two procedures they examined : victim's appearance at sentencing hearing and before parole board panels, have not had any dramatic impact on the way in which sentencing and parole decisions are rendered. After examining victim recommendations and offender sentences in sexual assault cases in a metropolitan Ohio county during the years 1980 through 1983, Walsh (1986) concluded that requiring a victim-impact statement and recommendation as part of the presentence report is a mere genuflection to ritualistic legalism. Walsh further detected a marked disregard for the preferences of victims of incestuous sexual assault.

These are by no means the only criticisms made of the new victim initiatives. Another authority, Elias (1990), is critical of victim policy for its explicit or implicit assumption that defendants have too many rights and for emphasizing a contest between victim and offender rights as if the former have to be at the expense of the latter. Elias finds many of the resulting changes disturbing : mandatory and increased imprisonment, longer sentences, and eliminating parole. These "reforms", he suggests, seem to be a new dose of historically unsuccessful, get-tough policies that probably dont't satisfy victim needs, including not being victimized in the first place. Elias passes a harsh judgement on the new victim initiatives. He writes :

*Yet for all the new initiatives, victims have gotten far less than promised. Rights have often been unenforced or unenforcable, participation sporadic or ill-advised, services precarious and underfunded, victim needs unsatisfied if not further jeopardized, and victimization increased, if not in court, then certainly in the streets. (1990.242)*

# CONCLUSION

Many initiatives in the area of victims rights seem to have been introduced without any serious assessment of their likely impact on the criminal justice system and the larger society. Post facto evaluations, on the other hand, are available. The picture they paint of the impact such new initiatives have had is far from rosy and is clearly negative. This is neither a criticism nor an indictment of the principles underlying these new measures or some of the humanitarian intentions behind them. It is simply another reminder that within the current structure of our criminal justice system, band-aid measures are not likely to work or to have their desired effects. Some contribute to the further alienation of the victim while others highten the victim's sense of irrelevance.

The reasons why many of these new initiatives do not work are not too difficult to comprehend. Some were conceived and set up for political and administrative purposes that had nothing to do with helping victims. This is particularly true of victim compensation schemes which have been called, and rightly so, political placebos (Chappell, 1973) or political palliatives (Burns, 1980). Many of these programs, though propagated as a means of alleviating the suffering of the victim, were actually designed to increase victim reporting to the police and to improve victim cooperation with the Criminal Justice System. The primary benefits were seen as enhancing victim participation and collaboration, thus increasing the efficiency and effectiveness of the system.

The same can be said of victim assistance programs. The major guiding influence is not compassionate or humanitarian considerations for victims, but the administrative goals of the agency. The Calgary Victim Services Program, one of the first of its kind in Canada (started in 1977), is just one example of many. The program is described in a document published by the Solicitor General Departement in Ottawa. The document makes no secret of the fact that the objective of the program "is to develop a good working relationship with victims of crime in order to encourage their future cooperation with the police in crime prevention". This statement tells a great deal about victim service programs which were set up by various police departments in Canada as in other countries. It explains the distinct preference to have these programs housed in police departments or in public prosecutor's offices, rather than in the community. The hidden danger of many of these programs is that they allow the police to have more control over the victim and for long periods of time.

Last but not least, some of the new rules on victim partcipation in criminal justice and parole processes do not meet the evidentiary standards required by the fundamental principle of due process. They risk to heighten an already recognized disparity in sentencing and to inject an element of emotionality in what should otherwise be an impartial and unemotional process. Furthermore, as Ranish and Schichor (1985) point out, some of these initiatives are clearly designed to intimidate judges and parole board members and to influence these professionals in one specific policy direction —toward harsher punishment or denial of parole. The drastic results of such a policy to an already punitive justice system and an over-crowded prison system are not too difficult to figure out.

If victims of crime are to regain their lost status, if they are to have a real say in the justice system and to play a direct (not symbolic) role, then we will have to move from retribution to restitution, from a punitive justice to a distributive justice. In other words what is needed is a new criminal justice paradigm, a fundamental change in criminal policy.

# BIBLIOGRAPHY

Australia, *Report of the Committee of Inquiry on Victims of Crime*, South Australia, 1981.

Australia, *Victims Past, Victims Future : A South Australian Police Perspective*, South Australia Police Department, 1986.

Australia, Victorian Sentencing Committee : *Final Report*, Melbourne : Government Printing Office, 1988.

BASSIOUNI, Ch., *Introduction to the United Nations Resolution and Declaration of Basic Principles of Justice for Victims of Crime and abuse of Power*, Chicago : De Paul University, 1987.

BASSIOUNI, C., *International Protection of Victims*, Association Internationale de Droit Penal, Toulouse : ERES, 1988.

BURNS, P., *Criminal Injuries Compensation : Social Remedy or Political Palliative for Victims of Crime*, Toronto : Butterworths, 1980.

Canada, House of Commons-Minutes of Proceedings and Evidence of the Legislative Committee on Bill C-89, An Act to amend the Criminal Code (Victims of Crime) Ottawa : House of Commons, 1988.

Canada, Canadian Sentencing Commission : *Final Report*, Ottawa : Ministry of Supply and Services, 1987.

Canada, Canadian Federal-Provincial Task Force on Justice for Victims of Crime : *Report*, Ottawa : Ministry of Supply and Services, 1983.

Canada, Law Reform Commission of Canada : *Restitution and Compensation - Fines*, Working papers 5 and 6, Ottawa : Information Canada, 1974.

CHAPPELL, D., Providing for the Victim of Crime : Political Placebos or Progressive Programs?, *Adelaide Law Review*, vol. 4, no. 2, pp. 294-306, 1972.

CHRISTIE, N., Conflicts as Property, *British J. of Criminology*, vol. 17, no. 1, pp. 1-19.

Council of Europe, *The Position of the Victim in the Framework of Criminal Law and Procedure*, Strasbourg, 1985.

DAMASKA, M., *Some Remarks on the Status of the Victim in Continental and Anglo-American Administration of Justice*, Paper presented at the 5th International Symposium on Victimology, Zagreb, Yugoslavia, August, 1985.

DOLLIVER, J.-M., Victims' Rights Constitutional Amendment : A Bad Idea Whose Time Should Not Come, *The Wayne Law Review*, 34 (1) : 87-93, 1987.

ELIAS, R., *Victims of the System*, New Brunswick, N.J. : Transaction Books, 1983.

ELIAS, R., Community Control, Criminal Justice and Victim Services. In Ezzat A. FATTAH (ed.), *From Crime Policy to Victim Policy*, London : MacMillan, 1986.

ELIAS, R., The symbolic Politics of Victim Compensation, *Victimology*, vol. 8, no. 1-2, pp. 213-224, 1983.

ELIAS, R.,Which Victim Movement? The Politics of Victim Policy. In A.J. Lurigio, W.G. Skogan, and R.C. Davis (eds.), *Victims of Crime : Problems, Policies and Programs*, California : Sage Publications, 1990.

FATTAH, E.A., On some visible and hidden dangers of victim movements, in E.A. Fattah (ed.), *From Crime Policy to Victim Policy : Reorienting the Justice System*, London : MacMillan, 1986.

FATTAH, E.A., *The Impact of Crime Prevention and Offender Rehabilitation Programs on the Costs of Victim Compensation - A Methodological Approach*, Unpublished report prepared under contract with the Ministry of Justice in Ottawa, 1988.

FORER, L.G., *Criminals and Victims : A trial judge reflects on crime and punishment*, N.Y. : W.W. Norton and Company, 1980.

GALAWAY, B. and HUDSON, J., *Perspectives on Crime Victims*, St. Louis : The C.V. Mosby Company, 1981.

GALAWAY, B., Restitution as Innovation or Unfilled Promise, *Federal Probation*, 51, pp. 3-14, 1988.

GITTLER, J., Expanding the Role of the Victim in a Criminal Action : An Overview of Issues and Problems, *Pepperdine Law Review*, vol. 11, pp. 117-182, 1984.

GRABOSKY, P.N., *Crime Victims in Australia*, Canberra : Australian Institute of Criminology, 1985.

HENDERSON, L.N., The Wrongs of Victim's Rights, *Stanford Law Review*, vol. 37 (April), pp. 937-1021, 1985.

JOUTSEN, M., *The Role of the Victim of Crime in European Criminal Justice Systems*, Helsinki : Heuni, 1987.

MACDONALD, W.F., Expanding the Victim's Role in the Disposition Decision : Reform in Search of a Rationale, in Gallaway, B. and Hudson, J. (eds.), *Offender Restitution in Theory and Action*, Mass. : Lexington Books, pp. 101-104, 1978.

MALAREK, V., Voice-for-Victim Trend disturbs Lawyers, *The Globe and Mail*, April 11, 1984.

MARSHALL, T.F., *Reparation, Conciliation and Mediation*, London : Home Office Research and Planning Unit, Paper no. 27, 1984.

McLEOD, M., *Beyond the Law : An Examination of Policies and Procedures governing the Nature of Victim Involvement at Parole*, Paper presented at the ASC meeting, Montreal, November, 1987.

MORGAN, P., From Battered Wife to Program Client : The state's Shaping of Social Problems, *Kapitalistate*, 9, pp. 17-39, 1981.

NETO, V. et al., *Victims Appearances at Sentencing Hearings Under the California Victims' Bill of Rights*, Sacramento : Center for Research, McGeorge School of Law, 1986.

PALTROW, S.J., Opposite Effects : New Anti-Crime Law in California is helping Some Accused Felons, *The Wall Street Journal*, Nov. 26, 1982.

RANISH, D.R. and SCHICHOR, D., The Victim's Role in the Penal Process : Recent Developments in California, *Federal Probation*, vol. 49 (1), March, pp. 50-57, 1985.

ROSSINI, G., *Victims and the Criminal Justice System in South Australia*, Paper presented at the third annual conference of the Australian and New Zealand Society of Criminology, 1987.

RUBEL, H.C., Victim Participation in Sentencing Proceedings, *Criminal Law Quarterly*, 28, pp. 226-250, 1986.

SHAPLAND, J., WILLMORE, J. and DUFF, P., *Victims in the Criminal Justice system*, London : Gower Publishing Company Limited, 1985.

SHAPLAND, J., Victims and the Criminal Justice System, in E.A. Fattah (ed.), *From Crime Policy to Victim Policy*, London : MacMillan, 1986.

SHAPLAND, J., Victim Assistance and the Criminal Justice System : the Victim's Perspective, in E.A. Fattah (ed.), *From Crime Policy to Victim Policy, London : MacMillan, 1986.*

SHARMAN, J.R., Constitutional Law : Victim Impact Statements and the 8th Amendment, *Harvard Journal of Law and Public Policy*, 11 (Spring), 583-593, 1988.

TALBERT, P.A., The Relevance of Victim Impact Statements to the Criminal Sentencing Decision, *UCLA Law Review*, 36, pp. 199-232, 1988.

STILL, L., Victim Say in Sentencing Just Vengeance : Lawyers, *The Vancouver sun*, Sept. 21, 1983, p. A3.

United Nations, *Declaration of Basic Principles of Justice for Victims of Crime and Abuse of Power*, N.Y. : United Nations Department of Public Information, 1985.

United States, President's Task Force on Victims of Crime : *Final Report*, Washington, D.C. : U.S. Government Printing Office, 1982.

WALKER, S., *Sense and Nonsence about Crime : A policy Guide*, Monterey, California : Brooks/Cole Publishing Company, 1985.

WALSH, A., Placebo Justice : Victim Recommendations and Offender Sentences in Sexual Assault Cases, *The Journal of Criminal Law and Criminology*, vol. 77, no. 4, pp. 1126-1141, 1986.

WELLING, S.N., Victim Participation in Plea Bargains, *Washington University Law Quarterly*, vol. 65, pp. 301-356, 1987.

WELLING, S.N., Victims in the Criminal Process : A Utilitarian Analysis of Victim Participation in the Charging Decision, *Arizona Law Review*, 30 : 85-117, 1988.

# SUMMARY

Recent years have witnessed great strides in applied victimology. During the 1980s legislation was passed, services were created, programs were set up, all aimed at helping crime victims and improving their unhappy lot. What is remarkable about these developments is the ease with which the legislative changes were introduced and approved. Not only was there no opposition but they were also not preceded by the usual impact studies to assess the effects they were likely to have on the CJS and the larger society. Even more surprising is that they were introduced in the absence of clear empirical evidence indicating that they do represent what crime victims really want.

The paper is an attempt to show that despite the fanfare with which the new measures were introduced, they have not tangibly improved the lot of crime victims. It claims that what is necessary to achieve this goal is a new criminal justice policy, a new penal and sentencing philosophy that places the emphasis not on punishment and retaliation but on reparation, mediation and conciliation. In most instances these two sets of goals are functionally incompatible. Parallel to this change, there needs to be another fundamental change in the traditional views on crime. The offense should cease to be regarded as an affront to the State and be viewed as an offense against the individual victim, not as a violation of an abstract law but a violation of the rights of the victim.

# RESUME

La victimologie appliquée a fait de grands progrès dans les années '80. L'auteur s'étonne de la facilité avec laquelle les législations créant des services ou lançant des programmes en faveur des victimes ont été votées. Elles n'ont pas été précédées des habituelles études d'impact sur le système pénal et la société, ni de recherches empiriques sur les souhaits des victimes.

Malgré la fanfare avec laquelle ces modifications ont été introduites, elles n'ont pas changé de façon tangible la situation des victimes de crimes. Ce qu'il faudrait pour atteindre cet objectif, c'est une nouvelle politique criminelle axée non sur la punition et les représailles, mais sur la réparation, la médiation et la conciliation. L'infraction ne devrait plus être vue comme un affront à l'Etat et à sa loi abstraite, mais comme une atteinte à une victime individuelle et à ses droits.

# RESUMEN

La victimología aplicada ha hecho grandes progresos en los años '80. El autor se asombra de la facilidad con la cual han sido votadas las legislaciones que han creado servicios y han lanzado programas en favor de las víctimas. Estas no se han visto precedidas de los habituales «estudios de impacto» sobre el sistema penal y la sociedad, ni de investigaciones empíricas sobre las aspiraciones de las víctimas.

A pesar de publicidad con la cual estas modificaciones han sido introducidas, éstas no han cambiado de manera tangible la situación de las víctimas de crímenes. Lo que se necesita para alcanzar este objetivo es de una nueva política en materia criminal, centrada no sobre la pena y las represalias, sino sobre la reparación, la mediación y la conciliación. La infracción ne debería ser nunca más considerada como un atentado al estado y a su ley abstracta, sino que como un atentado a una víctima individual y a sus derechos.

*The goals of this investigation were to examine the prevalence of Post-Traumatic Stress Disorder (PTSD) and victim service utilization among crime victims and family members recently involved in the criminal justice system (N = 251). About one half of the participants met PTSD diagnostic criteria during their lifetime. Females were overrepresented in the more violent crimes (e.g., homicide and sexual assault). Victims of more violent crimes—who sustained physical injuries, who perceived that they would be seriously injured, and who perceived their lives were threatened—were more likely to suffer from PTSD than victims who did not have these characteristics. Most participants believed the criminal justice system should provide a range of victim services. However, most participants reported inadequate access to services. Also, receipt of psychological counseling and diagnostic status were significantly associated with crime type. Results imply that crime victims involved in the criminal justice system are at risk for developing PTSD, which often never is addressed by a mental health professional due to inadequate access to health care services.*

# The Psychological Adjustment of Recent Crime Victims in the Criminal Justice System

JOHN R. FREEDY
HEIDI S. RESNICK
DEAN G. KILPATRICK
BONNIE S. DANSKY
RITCHIE P. TIDWELL
*Medical University of South Carolina*

## The Scope of Traumatic Events

Traumatic events are a tragic reality within American society. General population surveys estimate that between 40 and 70% of adults will experience at least one traumatic event during their life (Breslau, Davis, Andreski, & Peterson, 1991; Norris, 1992). Equally alarming are estimates that 21% of adults experienced a traumatic event within one year prior to an assessment (Norris, 1992).

Authors' Note: This research was supported by the Justice Assistance Act Grant No. 86-024 from the Division of Public Safety Program, Office of the Governor of the State of South Carolina.

JOURNAL OF INTERPERSONAL VIOLENCE, Vol. 9 No. 4, December 1994 450-468

This study focuses on violent crime as one class of traumatic events that can impact the lives of victims and their families. Similar to other traumatic events, the lifetime prevalence of crime is alarmingly high. For example, one national probability sample of 4,008 adult women found that approximately 23% of women surveyed had been the victim of either completed rape (12.7%) or physical assault (10.3%) during their lifetime (Resnick, Kilpatrick, Dansky, Saunders, & Best, 1993).

## The Impact of Violent Crime

Violent crime may affect victims and their families in both objective and subjective ways. Objectively, violent crime has both a physical and financial impact. Regarding the physical impact of violent crime, the Department of Justice estimates that rapes, robberies, and assaults account for 2.2 million injuries and more than 700,000 hospital days annually (Harlow, 1989). The financial costs associated with violent crime are substantial. Cohen, Miller, and Rossman (1993) estimated annual costs associated with Department of Justice prevalence estimates of rape, robbery, and assaults. Annual costs (1987 dollars) due to medical bills, mental health bills, and lost productivity were estimated to exceed $6.1 billion.

The impact of violent crime also can be defined in more subjective terms. For example, violent crime appears to impact social attitudes and behavior. One study surveyed a household probability sample of 1,000 American adults concerning the social impact of violent crime (Kilpatrick, Seymour, & Boyle, 1991). Respondents expressed some fear of attack or robbery in a range of situations, including when traveling (72%), out alone at night in their own neighborhood (61%), and in their own residence (60%). Respondents also reported restrictions in activities due to fear of crime, including limiting where you go alone (60%), limiting the places or times when you go shopping (32%), and limiting places of employment (22%). In general, women were more fearful of crime and restricted activities more than men.

Adverse mental health consequences are another subjective cost frequently associated with violent crime. Consensus has emerged regarding a positive association between the number of traumatic events experienced and adverse mental health consequences (Breslau et al., 1991; Norris, 1992). Several risk indicators of the following negative mental health outcomes have been documented following violent crime: Post-Traumatic Stress Disorder (PTSD), substance abuse, suicidality, and increased usage of mental health services (Kilpatrick et al., 1985; Resnick et al., 1993).

### Violent Crime and Post-Traumatic Stress Disorder (PTSD)

PTSD is a diagnostic entity that appears well suited for capturing the essence of adverse mental health functioning following traumatic life events (APA, 1987). PTSD is a debilitating anxiety disorder that may develop following experience with highly traumatic events, such as violent crime. Symptoms include: reexperiencing (e.g., memories, flashbacks, dreams); avoidance (e.g., of thoughts, feelings, or other reminders); and arousal (e.g., sleep problems, hypervigilance) (APA, 1987). It is generally believed that the symptoms of PTSD wax and wane across time, depending on experiencing reminders of a traumatic event as well as individual resiliency (Horowitz, 1986). Although symptoms of PTSD may remit, a chronic and debilitating course of symptomatology is not unusual (Kilpatrick et al., 1985; Kilpatrick, Saunders, Veronen, Best, & Von, 1987).

A recent study underscores a linkage between victimization by crime and the development of PTSD. Resnick et al. (1993) estimated that the lifetime PTSD prevalence rate for a representative national sample of adult women was approximately 12%. The lifetime prevalence rate of PTSD increased dramatically for women who had experienced violent crimes. For example, lifetime PTSD prevalence rates were more than 30% for sexual assault victims and almost 40% for physical assault victims.

A combination of objective (e.g., physical injury) and subjective (e.g., perception of threat to life) factors are believed to be responsible for negative mental health outcomes (Green, 1990). Researchers have found that crime factors such as physical injury and perceived life threat are strongly associated with the development of PTSD (Kilpatrick et al., 1989). Moreover, studies have demonstrated that indirect victims such as loved ones of criminal and vehicular homicide victims are at an increased risk for developing PTSD (Amick-McMullan, Kilpatrick, Veronen, & Smith, 1989).

### The Role of the Criminal Justice System

Attitudes regarding the criminal justice system are challenged following violent crime experiences. Victims and family members may find understanding and influencing legal procedures to be extremely difficult. Interacting with criminal justice representatives may become a reminder of painful, sometimes humiliating, experiences (Kilpatrick & Otto, 1987). If the perpetrator of the crime is known to the victim (typically the case following sexual assault), the victim may fear revenge being sought if charges are pursued (Kilpatrick, Best, Saunders, & Veronen, 1988). Victims often fear social stigma associated with reporting, being believed (or not), and having temporarily lost personal control. Even when victims decide to press charges, ideal images of swift justice can be quickly dashed as legal proceedings drag out for months (or years) (Kilpatrick & Otto, 1987).

A movement promoting the establishment of rights for crime victims has developed during the last 2 decades (Kelly, 1990). This movement has developed in the context of a substantial gap between desires for ideal protection for crime victims and the harsh reality that is often faced. The success of the criminal justice system in prosecuting criminals might be substantially improved by offering more sensitive and humane treatment to the victims of crime. The crime victim who believes he or she will be listened to, believed, protected, guided, and offered needed services (including mental health services) may be more likely to cooperate with the criminal justice system (Kelly, 1990; Kilpatrick & Otto, 1987).

### Research Focus

This study focused on mental health status and service utilization among recent crime victims and their families. The examined areas included: (1) prevalence of PTSD; (2) the relationship between PTSD, demographic characteristics, type of crime, and crime characteristics; and (3) access to and utilization of crime victim services.

## METHOD

### Subjects

Potential participants were identified in two ways. One pool of potential participants was generated through a file review of consecutive court cases adjudicated in the year prior to September 1988 in four circuit courts within South Carolina (three metropolitan circuits and one rural circuit). A second pool of potential participants was obtained from a South Carolina Department of Corrections list of violent crime victims or family members of victims from cases resulting in conviction and incarceration (same time period).

A pool of 591 potential participants was identified. The following information was available: name, most recent address, most recent telephone number, next of kin, and crime type. Extensive efforts were made to locate all potential participants (both direct crime victims and the family members listed in reviewed documents). Outdated telephone numbers were followed by manual searches of directory listings. When manual searches were unsuccessful, a letter was sent explaining the purpose of the study and asking the potential participant to contact a toll-free number to provide a correct telephone number. Despite extensive efforts, 40.8% ($n$ = 244) of the potential participants could not be located. In addition, when contacted 6.6% ($n$ = 39) reported that no one in the household had recently been a crime victim.

Based upon the above process, 309 eligible participants were located (i.e., using telephone and acknowledged victimization). Of the 309 eligible participants, 81.2% completed a structured telephone interview that averaged 34 minutes in length ($n$ = 251). A small percentage of eligible participants refused participation (13.9%; $n$ = 43). A few eligible participants began the telephone interview, but terminated prior to completion (4.9%; $n$ = 15).

Of the 251 participants, 51.0% had been the direct victim of a crime. Direct crime victims suffered the following crimes: 37.5% physical assault, 12.5% criminal sexual conduct, 17.2% robbery, and 32.8% burglary. Almost one half of the participants (49.0%) were family members (indirect victims) of a crime victim. The family members (indirect victims) suffered these crimes: 50.4% murder/vehicular homicide, 34.1% criminal sexual conduct, 13.0% physical assault, 1.6% robbery, and 0.8% burglary. Among the indirect victims, 52.0% were stepchildren, 15.4% were siblings, 10.5% were spouses, 10.6% were "other relatives," 9.8% were parents, and 1.6% were grandchildren. Most index crimes had occurred recently with regard to study participation (89.7% within three years).

The demographic characteristics of participants are generally representative of the communities from where the sample was drawn. The mean age was 38.2 years ($SD$ = 12.8, range = 17 to 75). Most of the sample were female (63.3%). Most of the sample (62.5%) were Caucasian (35.5% African American). Many participants were married (49.4%) with the remaining respondents identifying themselves as single/never married (21.1%), widowed (10.0%), divorced (14.7%), or separated (4.8%). Although 28.7% of the participants never completed high school, 35.1% were high school graduates, 23.9% earned some college credits, 7.2% received a bachelor's degree, and 4.2% completed a postgraduate program. The modal yearly family income was between $15,001 and $25,000 (20.3%) with equal percentages in the lowest and highest income groups (14.3% earned below $5,000 and 14.8% earned more than $35,000).

### Assessment Instrument

The assessment instrument was a structured telephone interview developed for this study. To ensure reliability, the interview consisted of carefully worded, closed-ended questions. (e.g., "Did you recognize the person or persons who committed the crime?"). The interview represents a script that was followed *verbatim* when interviewing participants.

The following areas were included in the interview: (1) introduction, (2) crime characteristics, (3) perceptions of and experience with the criminal justice system, (4) symptoms of Post-Traumatic Stress Disorder, and (5) demographic characteristics.

*Introduction.* Telephone interviews began with the following introduction:

> Hello, I'm _____ from SRBI, the national survey research organization. We are conducting a study for the State of South Carolina concerning crime and the criminal justice system. The purpose of the study is to help evaluate the adequacy of the justice system in meeting the needs of crime victims.
>
> In order to really know what kinds of problems occur within the system and what kinds of assistance crime victims and their families currently receive, we are interviewing a representative sample of persons who have been involved as victims or relatives of victims in criminal cases.
>
> We would like to ask you some questions about your experience with the police, courts, and legal system, so that the state can better plan for the needs of other crime victims and their families in the future.

*Crime Characteristics.* Participants answered questions about whether they were a direct or indirect (family member of a victim) victim, the relationship between the victim and the perpetrator, the type of crime committed, whether the crime involved life threat or threat of serious injury (direct victims only), and the extent of physical injuries sustained.

*Experiences with the Criminal Justice System.* While several areas were covered in this section, this report focuses on questions concerning perceptions of crime victim services. Participants were asked if they "feel that the justice system should be responsible for seeing that crime victims and their families get . . . " the following services: psychological counseling, information on case status, personal protection, legal assistance, information for social service referrals, or assistance in dealing with police or courts. Next, participants were asked the following with regard to each listed service: "While the case was going on, did you and your family have adequate access to. . . . "

*Mental Health.* PTSD symptoms were assessed using standardized questions. Although the symptom questions were adapted from the Diagnostic Interview Schedule (DIS; Robins, Helzer, Croughan, & Ratcliff, 1981), respondents were not required to link symptoms specifically to traumatic events (requiring insight that a respondent may or may not possess). It was required that individual symptoms have at least a one-week duration. Participants were asked about age of symptom onset, recency of symptoms, and the content of appropriate symptoms (e.g., "What were those bad dreams about?"). This approach has been used in previous studies and yields PTSD prevalence rates that are similar to structured in-person interviews and other standardized assessment procedures (Resnick et al., 1993).

Both lifetime and current PTSD prevalence rates were determined. A positive lifetime diagnosis was assigned if a respondent met the *DSM-III-R* criteria (APA, 1987) by endorsing the necessary number of PTSD symptoms (one reexperiencing, three avoidance, and two increased arousal symptoms). A positive current PTSD diagnosis was assigned if the respondent reported the presence of the necessary symptoms within the 6 months of the interview.

## Procedure

All structured interviews were conducted by professional telephone interviewers employed by Schulman, Ronca, and Bucuvalas, Inc. (SRBI), a national survey research firm. All telephone surveys were conducted from SRBI's telephone research center in New York City. This center maintains a staff of professional telephone interviewers and supervisory staff. Only interviewers with prior experience in conducting sensitive topic interviews (e.g., impact of violent crime) were used.

The field period of this study was 4 weeks. Interviewers attempted numerous phone calls (up to 25 in some cases) to reach eligible participants. The days and times of calls were rotated to maximize the chance of contact. When necessary (to ensure privacy or convenience), interviews were scheduled for a more appropriate day and time. Hesitant participants were offered a toll-free number to allow verification of survey authenticity. Confidentiality of the data was maintained because personal identifiers were removed and destroyed by SRBI staff prior to coding data for statistical analysis. Interviewers were silently monitored at least twice during each interviewing shift. Feedback that reinforced adherence to training standards was provided following monitoring.

## RESULTS

### Prevalence of PTSD

At the time of the interview, 25.5% ($N = 64$) of the respondents met diagnostic criteria for PTSD ("Current PTSD"). Another 25.9% ($N = 65$) of the participants had developed PTSD at one time but did not endorse enough symptoms to meet the criteria for PTSD at the time of the interview ("Previous PTSD"). *The remaining 48.6% (n = 122) of the sample had never developed PTSD (negative lifetime prevalence of PTSD). Chi-square statistics were calculated to test for significant differences between the two PTSD positive groups. There were no differences detected for demographic variables, crime type, or other crime characteristics. Therefore, the two PTSD positive groups were collapsed into a single group ("Positive Lifetime PTSD"; n =* 128) for all remaining analyses.

### The Relationship Between PTSD, Demographic Characteristics, Type of Crime, and Crime Characteristics

A series of analyses compared the Positive Lifetime PTSD group with the Negative Lifetime PTSD group on demographics, crime type, and crime characteristics. Since the variables were categorical, the chi-square statistic was employed and a Bonferroni correction was used to reduce the likelihood of Type I errors. Among the demographic variables, only gender yielded a significant association with PTSD prevalence; the prevalence of Lifetime PTSD was not significantly associated with age (divided into three groups), marital status, employment, education, race, or yearly income.

Regarding the significant gender difference detected, female crime victims were almost two times more likely than male crime victims to have a lifetime prevalence of PTSD ($\chi^2$ = 19.35, $p$ < .001). However, this association is likely due to the significant relationship between gender and crime type (see Table 1). Women were overrepresented among crime types typically associated with an increased risk for developing PTSD (i.e., sexual assault, homicide of a family member, and physical assault).

The relationship between crime type and PTSD prevalence was found to be significant (see Table 1). The relationship between crime type and PTSD was strongest for violent and sexual crimes. The positive lifetime prevalence of PTSD for respondents who were (indirect) victims because of the homicide death of a family member was 71.1%, although a majority (59.4%) of the victims of physical assault also were in the Positive Lifetime PTSD group. Similarly, more than one half of the sexual assault victims scored positively for lifetime prevalence of PTSD (55.2%). In contrast, fewer of the (direct and indirect) victims of the typically less violent crimes (robbery and burglary) reported symptoms that met the criteria for Lifetime PTSD.

Both objective and subjective crime characteristics across all crime types also were associated with the prevalence of PTSD (see Table 2). The results

101

TABLE 1:    Gender and PTSD as a Function of Crime Type (in percentages)

| | Gender[a] | | PTSD Prevalence[b] | |
| --- | --- | --- | --- | --- |
| Crime Type | Male | Female | Negative Lifetime PTSD | Positive Lifetime PTSD |
| All crimes ($N = 251$) | 36.7 | 63.3 | 48.6 | 51.4 |
| Homicide ($n = 62$) | 32.3 | 67.7 | 29.0 | 71.0 |
| Physical assault ($n = 64$) | 40.6 | 59.4 | 40.6 | 59.4 |
| Robbery ($n = 24$) | 79.2 | 20.8 | 70.8 | 29.2 |
| Burglary ($n = 43$) | 46.5 | 53.5 | 81.4 | 18.6 |
| Sexual assault ($n = 58$) | 12.1 | 87.9 | 44.8 | 55.2 |

a. $\chi^2 = 34.73, p < .001$.
b. $\chi^2 = 34.73, p < .001$.

of the chi-square analysis for one objective crime characteristic, victim status (direct vs. indirect), indicated that indirect victims were significantly more likely to be classified in the Positive Lifetime PTSD group than direct victims ($\chi^2 = 11.26, p < .001$).

The second objective crime characteristic, physical injury, was found to be significantly associated with PTSD prevalence in that injured crime victims were more likely than uninjured crime victims to be classified in the Positive Lifetime PTSD group ($\chi^2 = 15.14, p < .001$; see Table 2). As with the two objective crime characteristics, both of the subjective factors were significantly associated with PTSD prevalence (see Table 2; only direct victims were asked to provide information about subjective factors). Victims who feared injury were more than three times as likely as those without such fears to be in the Positive Lifetime PTSD group ($\chi^2 = 17.09, p < .001$). Similarly, victims who feared death were more than three times more likely than respondents who did not fear death to have experienced PTSD during their lifetime ($\chi^2 = 14.15, p < .001$).

The association between victim status (direct vs. indirect) and PTSD prevalence is likely due to the significant relationship between victim status and crime type ($\chi^2 = 145.37, p < .001$). Indirect crime victims were over-represented among two more violent crime types: homicide and sexual assault. All respondents who reported a homicide (100%) were family members of the deceased, and almost two thirds of the participants in the sexual assault group were family members (indirect victims) of the sexual assault victim. In contrast, direct victims outnumbered indirect victims for all other crime types (physical assault, robbery, and burglary).

A three-way chi-square analysis was conducted to assess the relationship between victim status (direct vs. indirect) and Lifetime PTSD prevalence

TABLE 2:    Prevalence of PTSD as a Function of Crime Characteristics (in percentages)

| | PTSD Prevalence | |
| | Negative | Positive |
| Crime Variables | Lifetime Prevalence | Lifetime Prevalence |
|---|---|---|
| Direct victims ($n = 128$)[a] | 59.4 | 40.6 |
| Indirect victims ($n = 123$)[a] | 37.4 | 62.6 |
| Injured ($n = 140$)[b] | 37.1 | 62.9 |
| Not injured ($n = 140$)[b] | 62.7 | 37.3 |
| Feared injury ($n = 88$)[c] | 45.5 | 54.5 |
| Did not fear injury ($n = 45$)[c] | 84.4 | 15.6 |
| Fear death ($n = 88$)[d] | 46.6 | 53.4 |
| Did not fear death ($n = 45$)[d] | 82.2 | 17.8 |

a. $\chi^2 = 11.26, p < .001$.
b. $\chi^2 = 15.14, p < .001$.
c. $\chi^2 = 17.09, p < .001$.
d. $\chi^2 = 14.15, p < .001$.

controlling for the effect of crime type. These results were nonsignificant ($p > .05$), indicating that victim status is not related to Lifetime PTSD prevalence when the type of crime is statistically controlled.

To test the relationship between PTSD and crime type while controlling for the effect of victim status (direct vs. indirect), another three-way chi-square analysis was calculated (see Table 3). For direct victims, type of crime was significantly associated with Lifetime PTSD prevalence ($\chi^2 = 23.11, p < .001$). However, among indirect crime victims type of crime was not significantly associated with Lifetime PTSD prevalence ($\chi^2 = 4.70, p < .096$).

A hierarchical logistical regression was computed to assess the relative contributions of objective and subjective crime characteristics and crime type for predicting Lifetime PTSD prevalence. Since subjective crime characteristics were only available for direct crime victims, no indirect crime victims were included in the analysis.

Based upon previous research findings (e.g., Kilpatrick et al., 1989), the predictor variables were entered in three steps. The first variable entered into the logistic regression was a variable in which the two subjective crime characteristics (Fear of Death and Fear of Injury) were combined. If participants indicated that they had *either* feared for their life (Fear of Death) *or* feared that they would be seriously injured (Fear of Injury) during the crime, they were classified as positive on the new variable referred to as Fear of Death or Serious Injury. The second step entered the variable concerning

TABLE 3:    Chi-Square Analyses for Crime Type and PTSD Controlling for Victim Status
(in percentages)

| Direct Victims[a] | Negative Lifetime PTSD | Positive Lifetime PTSD |
|---|---|---|
| Crime type | | |
| Physical assault ($n = 48$) | 41.7% | 58.3% |
| | ($n = 20$) | ($n = 28$) |
| Robbery ($n = 22$) | 72.7% | 27.3% |
| | ($n = 16$) | ($n = 6$) |
| Burglary ($n = 42$) | 83.3% | 16.7% |
| | ($n = 35$) | ($n = 7$) |
| Sexual assault ($n = 16$) | 31.3% | 68.8% |
| | ($n = 5$) | ($n = 11$) |

| Indirect Victims[b,c] | Negative Lifetime PTSD | Positive Lifetime PTSD |
|---|---|---|
| Crime type | | |
| Murder ($n = 62$) | 29.0% | 71.0% |
| | ($n = 18$) | ($n = 44$) |
| Physical assault ($n = 16$) | 37.5% | 62.5% |
| | ($n = 6$) | ($n = 10$) |
| Sexual assault ($n = 42$) | 50.0% | 50.0% |
| | ($n = 21$) | ($n = 21$) |

a. $\chi^2 = 23.11, p < .001$.
b. $\chi^2 = 4.70, p < .096$.
c. This chi-square analysis did not include robbery victims ($n = 2$) or burglary victims ($n = 1$) due to the insufficient cell counts.

whether the participants had experienced any actual physical injury as a result of the victimization. The final step included the crime type variable, which consisted of the following crimes: robbery, physical assault, burglary, and sexual assault with robbery serving as the reference category.

The model goodness-of-fit $\chi^2$ was 123.107 ($df = 122, p = 0.455$), which indicated that the "perfect" or predicted model was not significantly different from the observed data. On the final step of the regression, the addition of the crime-type variable significantly added to the predictive power, because the model chi-square improvement value was 8.43 ($p = 0.04$) for the final step. Examination of the odds ratios indicated that the odds of Lifetime PTSD among victims who feared death or serious injury were 3.2 times the odds of PTSD among victims who did not have such a fear, controlling for actual physical injury experienced and type of crime (see Table 4). In addition, the odds of Lifetime PTSD among physical assault victims were 3.3 times the odds among robbery victims, adjusting for fear of death or serious injury and

TABLE 4:   Logistic Regression Testing the Relationship Between Crime Characteristics, Crime Type, and PTSD

| Interval | Odds Ratio | Confidence Interval (95%) |
|---|---|---|
| Step 1 | | |
| Fear of death and/or serious injury | 3.21 | 1.09-9.49 |
| Step 2 | | |
| Physical injury | 0.88 | 0.32-2.44 |
| Step 3 | | |
| Type of assault | | |
| Physical assault | 3.28 | 1.00-10.70 |
| Burglary | 0.83 | 0.21-3.26 |
| Sexual assault | 4.50 | 1.07-18.98 |

Goodness-of-Fit $\chi^2 = 123.11$, $p = 0.455$.
NOTE: Robbery victims served as the reference group.

actual injury experienced. Finally, as compared to robbery victims, the odds of PTSD among sexual assault victims were 4.5 times greater, controlling for fear of death or serious injury and actual physical injury experienced (see Table 4). A 95% confidence interval was calculated for each odds ratio.

### Availability and Access to Crime Victim Services

Crime victims' opinions concerning their needs for and access to services in the criminal justice system are depicted in Table 5. More than 90% of all victims believed that the criminal justice system should be responsible for providing a broad range of services, including psychological counseling, information about case status, personal protection, legal assistance, social service referral information, and assistance in dealing with police or court. Reported access to such desired services fell below victims' expectations with the lowest proportion of victims receiving access to psychological counseling and the highest proportion receiving access to assistance in dealing with police or court.

It is possible that access to needed services might change across time. Accordingly, the relationship between time elapsed since index crime and *adequate access* to services was assessed. Time elapsed since index crime was divided into these three categories: within the last year ($n = 120$), one to two years ($n = 91$), and two years or more ($n = 39$). Six $3 \times 2$ (time elapsed by service access) chi-square analyses were conducted. No contrast was significant ($p > .05$), indicating that adequate service access did not change as a function of time elapsed since victimization.

TABLE 5: Opinions About the Provision of and Access to Services Provided by the Criminal Justice System (CJS) (in percentages)

| Type of Service | Think CJS Should Provide Services | Received Adequate Access to Services |
|---|---|---|
| Psychological counseling | 91.2 | 39.4 |
| Case status information | 98.9 | 59.7 |
| Personal protection | 95.8 | 44.1 |
| Legal assistance | 94.4 | 58.3 |
| Social service referral information | 93.4 | 43.8 |
| Assistance in dealing with police or courts | 98.3 | 60.4 |

The relationship between time elapsed since index crime and the belief that the criminal justice system should provide services was not examined. This decision was made because more than 90% of respondents believed that the criminal justice system should provide a range of services (see Table 5). The extreme skew in responses mitigates against the likelihood of changes (particularly increases) in this belief over time. Thus this trend analysis would be of minimal value.

Because lifetime PTSD prevalence varied across crime type, it was of interest to explore receipt of psychological counseling as a function of crime type and diagnostic status (positive or negative PTSD prevalence; see Table 6). A significant relationship between crime type and the receipt of psychological counseling was obtained ($\chi^2 = 52.03, p < .001$). More than one half of all sexual assault victims received psychological counseling, although less than one quarter of the victims of the two other violent crimes—homicide and physical assault—received counseling. Victims of less violent crimes such as burglary and robbery rarely obtained psychological services (14.3% and 4.2%, respectively) in reference to their victimization experience. Across all crime types, only 27.0% of the victims had been involved in psychological counseling relevant to their crime experience.

The association between diagnostic status and the receipt of psychological counseling was significant ($\chi^2 = 11.63, p < .001$; see Table 6). Crime victims in the Positive Lifetime PTSD group were two times more likely to receive crime-related psychological services than crime victims in the Negative Lifetime PTSD group (36.7% vs. 16.7%). It should be noted that the minority of victims suffering from PTSD (36.7%) received psychological counseling.

TABLE 6:    Receipt of Psychological Counseling as a Function of Crime Type and Diagnostic Status (in percentages)

| Crime Type[a] | Received Psychological Counseling | Received No Psychological Counseling |
|---|---|---|
| All crime ($n = 251$) | 27.0 | 73.0 |
| Homicide ($n = 62$) | 16.1 | 83.9 |
| Physical assault ($n = 63$) | 22.2 | 77.8 |
| Robbery ($n = 24$) | 4.2 | 95.8 |
| Burglary ($n = 42$) | 14.3 | 85.7 |
| Sexual assault ($n = 57$) | 63.2 | 36.8 |
| *Diagnostic Status*[b] | | |
| Negative Lifetime PTSD prevalence ($n = 120$) | 16.7 | 83.3 |
| Positive Lifetime PTSD prevalence ($n = 128$) | 36.7 | 63.3 |

a. $\chi^2 = 52.03, p < 0.001$.
b. $\chi^2 = 11.63, p < 0.001$.

## DISCUSSION

### Mental Health Findings

About one half of the sample met *DSM-III-R* diagnostic criteria for PTSD during their life span (APA, 1987). In addition, one quarter of the sample scored positively for PTSD at the time of the interview. These prevalence rates suggest that PTSD may represent a substantial mental health concern for crime victims and family members involved with the criminal justice system. Furthermore, when the lifetime PTSD prevalence rate for this sample is compared to a lifetime PTSD prevalence rate from a national household probability sample of adult female crime victims (51.4% vs. 25.8%), it supports the assertion that PTSD prevalence for victims involved in the criminal justice system may be substantially higher than that of crime victims in general (Resnick et al., 1993).

There are several possible explanations for the substantial PTSD rates found in the sample. First, it may be that crimes involving criminal prosecution are more likely to be violent crimes, involving life threat and injury. Such violence was found to be significantly associated with the development of PTSD. A second explanation is that crime victims involved in the criminal justice system repeatedly encounter trauma-related stimuli that may trigger symptomatic responses (Kilpatrick & Otto, 1987). A final possibility is that the crime victims in this study were interviewed relatively soon (within 3 years) following their victimization. Some studies have indicated that the recency of criminal victimization is positively associated with the presence of PTSD symptoms (Resnick, Veronen, & Saunders, 1988; Rothbaum, Foa, Riggs, Murdock, & Walsh, 1991).

In addition to finding that the lifetime prevalence of PTSD was substantially elevated in the present sample of crime victims, it was found that direct and indirect crime victims who were most likely to develop PTSD were those participants whose victimization can be classified as due to "violent crimes" such as homicide, physical assault, or sexual assault, who sustained physical injuries, or who feared death or serious injury during the crime incident. These findings highlight the importance of careful screening to obtain specific details about the crime that can be used to identify victims who are particularly at risk for experiencing psychological difficulties. Crime victims who have experienced the indicated risk factors for PTSD development should be referred to a mental health professional for further evaluation and services.

## Experiences with the Criminal Justice System

The final set of results demonstrates that although victims had a strong expectation that they should be provided with victim services, receipt of services through the criminal justice system appeared to be limited. Furthermore, victims who were involved with the criminal justice system for longer periods of time did not report more access to services. Although financial constraints may limit service provision by the criminal justice system, some crucial services may involve minimal costs. Examples are educational information about how the judicial process works, referrals to community agencies, and follow-up telephone calls to report on case status. Such low-cost services might encourage victims to feel that the justice system is invested in their welfare. More important, better coordination between criminal justice system professionals and outside agencies may facilitate victims receiving the services that they desire, yet seldom receive.

Only a majority of sexual assault victims reported that they had received psychological counseling; overall, less than one third of the victims reported having received any psychological services related to their victimization. Over the last 20 years, the rape crisis movement has provided a model for how advocacy can lead to increased awareness about the service needs of sexual assault victims. The current study suggests the need for similar advocacy efforts on behalf of the victims of other violent crimes.

The importance of advocacy efforts for crime victims and their families deserves careful consideration in light of the objective and subjective costs associated with crime. Here, we are thinking of the potential to limit suffering and costs to victims, their families, and to society. As mentioned in the introduction, costs can be physical (injuries requiring medical attention), financial, social (fearful attitudes and restrictions of activities), and psychological (increased risk for PTSD). Based on our clinical experiences with crime victims, we believe that the humane treatment of victims and their families can foster optimum cooperation with the criminal justice system. Such cooperation may be the key to minimizing the varied and tragic costs associated with violent crime because it may facilitate an increase in the number of crimes being reported and enable victims to optimally manage the difficulties involved in cooperating with criminal justice representatives.

### Limitations

As with any study, there are certain limits on quality. For example, unmeasured variables, such as additional mental health problems, could have produced informative results if assessed. As another example, we did not assess for history of prior traumatic events. Thus we do not know what impact prior trauma experience may have upon PTSD prevalence or attitudes regarding the criminal justice system. The existence of prior traumatic experiences would increase the likelihood of developing PTSD (Norris, 1992; Resnick et al., 1993). However, the fact remains that substantial numbers of recent crime victims and their family members will suffer from PTSD.

An additional limitation concerns the issue of sample selection. Some eligible participants could not be located, although a few refused participation or withdrew. Thus some unknown selection bias may exist. Although extensive recruitment efforts minimize potential bias, we suggest modest caution in interpreting results.

A final study limitation concerns the cross-sectional design and use of retrospective measures. Based on this methodology, the results are subject to certain memory biases (e.g., negative response set, selective memory). Although many studies of traumatic stress use a similar methodology, replication based on a prospective design would lessen these concerns.

109

## CONCLUSIONS

Crime victims and their family members who participate in the criminal justice system appear vulnerable to experience PTSD. Violent crimes (homicide, physical assault, and sexual assault) and experiencing a physical injury or a fear of death or serious injury appear to be associated with PTSD prevalence. Despite the high prevalence of PTSD in the entire sample, most participants reported inadequate access to victim services, including mental health services. Because recent crime victims and family members appear at risk for psychological difficulties, it is essential that agents of the criminal justice system be willing to provide information and referrals regarding mental health and other services. The consistent provision of needed services would benefit victims, their families, and agents of the criminal justice system. Based on mutual cooperation, it would be possible to make American society safer and more humane for all citizens.

## REFERENCES

American Psychiatric Association. (1987). *Diagnostic and statistical manual of mental disorders* (3rd ed. revised). Washington, DC: Author.

Amick-McMullan, A., Kilpatrick, D. G., Veronen, L. J., & Smith, S. (1989). Family survivors of homicide victims: Theoretical perspectives and an exploratory study. *Journal of Traumatic Stress, 2*, 21-35.

Breslau, N., Davis, G. C., Andreski, P., & Peterson, E. (1991). Traumatic events and posttraumatic stress disorder in an urban population of young adults. *Archives of General Psychiatry 48*, 216-222.

Cohen, M. A., Miller, T. R., & Rossman, S. B. (1994). The costs and consequences of violent behavior in the United States. In A. J. Reiss & J. A. Roth (Eds.), *Understanding and preventing violence: Vol. 1. Consequences and control* (pp. 67-166). Washington, DC: National Academy Press.

Green, B. L. (1990). Defining trauma: Terminology and generic stressor dimensions. *Journal of Applied Social Psychology, 20*, 1632-1642.

Harlow, C. W. (1989). *Injuries from crime*. Bureau of Justice Statistics Special Report NCJ-116811. Washington, DC: U.S. Department of Justice.

Horowitz, M. J. (1986). *Stress response syndrome* (2nd ed.). Northvale, NJ: Jason Aronson.

Kelly, D. (1990). Victim participation in the criminal justice system. In A. J. Lurigio, W. G. Skogan, & R. C. Davis (Eds.), *Victims of crime: Problems, policies, & programs* (pp. 172-187). Sage Criminal Justice System Annuals, *25*. Newbury Park, CA: Sage.

Kilpatrick, D. G., Best, C. L., Saunders, B. E., & Veronen, L. J. (1988). Rape in marriage and dating relationships: How bad is it for mental health? *Annals of the New York Academy of Sciences, 528*, 335-344.

Kilpatrick, D. G., Best, C. L., Veronen, L. J., Amick, A. E., Villeponteaux, L. A., & Ruff, G. A. (1985). Mental health correlates of criminal victimization: A random community sample. *Journal of Consulting and Clinical Psychology, 53*, 866-873.

Kilpatrick, D. G., & Otto, R. K. (1987). Constitutionally guaranteed participation in criminal proceedings for victims: Potential effects on psychological functioning. *The Wayne Law Review, 34,* 7-28.

Kilpatrick, D. G., Saunders, B. E., Amick-McMullan, A., Best, C. L., Veronen, L. J., & Resnick, H. S. (1989). Victim and crime factors associated with the development of crime-related Post-traumatic Stress Disorder. *Behavior Therapy, 20,* 199-214.

Kilpatrick, D. G., Saunders, B. E., Veronen, L. J., Best, C. L., & Von, J. M. (1987). Criminal victimization: Lifetime prevalence, reporting to police, and psychological impact. *Crime and Delinquency, 33,* 479-489.

Kilpatrick, D. G., Seymour, A. K., & Boyle, J. (1991). *America speaks out: Citizens' attitudes about victims' rights and violence.* Arlington, VA: National Victim Center.

Norris, F. H. (1992). The epidemiology of trauma: Frequency and impact of different potentially traumatic events on different demographic groups. *Journal of Consulting and Clinical Psychology, 60,* 409-418.

Resnick, H. S., Veronen, L. J., & Saunders, B. E. (1988, October). *Symptoms of post-traumatic stress disorder in rape victims and their partners: A behavioral formulation.* Paper presented at the Fourth Annual Meeting of the Society for Traumatic Stress Studies, Dallas, TX.

Resnick, H. S., Kilpatrick, D. G., Dansky, B. S., Saunders, B. E., & Best, C. L. (1993). Prevalence of civilian trauma and posttraumatic stress disorder in a representative national sample of women. *Journal of Consulting and Clinical Psychology, 61*(6), 984-991.

Robins, L. N., Helzer, J. D., Croughan, J., & Ratcliff, K. S. (1981). The NIMH diagnostic interview schedule: Its history, characteristics, and validity. *Archives of General Psychiatry, 38,* 381-389.

Rothbaum, B. O., Foa, E. B., Riggs, D. S., Murdock, T., & Walsh, W. (1991). A prospective examination of post-traumatic stress disorder in rape victims. *Journal of Traumatic Stress, 5,* 455-475.

*John R. Freedy is an assistant professor of clinical psychology at the National Crime Victims Research and Treatment Center (NCVC) in Charleston, South Carolina. The NCVC is a division of the Department of Psychiatry and Behavioral Sciences at the Medical University of South Carolina in Charleston. Dr. Freedy received his B.A. from the University of North Carolina-Chapel Hill in 1984 and Ph.D. in clinical psychology from Kent State University in 1990. He has published and presented papers concerning occupational stress, crime-related stress, and disaster-related stress. Dr. Freedy's clinical activities involve direct service provision and clinical supervision of a range of traumatic stress cases. His teaching activities involve lectures to the following audiences: psychology interns, psychiatry residents, medical students, undergraduate students, and the general public.*

*Heidi S. Resnick is an associate professor of clinical psychology at the National Crime Victims Research and Treatment Center (NCVC). Dr. Resnick received her B.A. from the University of Wisconsin–Madison in 1980 and Ph.D. in clinical psychology from Indiana University in 1987. Her major research interest is the study of factors involved in the development of post-traumatic stress following civilian trauma. Recent research has included the study of rape victims' immediate postrape biological and psychological response profiles in association with specific assault characteristics and as predictors of long-term PTSD outcome. In addition, she is studying rape victims' concerns about*

111

*their physical health following rape, and development of appropriate medical care and health care counseling for rape victims.*

*Dean G. Kilpatrick is professor of clinical psychology and director of the National Crime Victims Research and Treatment Center at the Medical University of South Carolina in Charleston. For the last 20 years, he has been involved in the crime victims' rights movement, having served as a founding member of South Carolina's first rape crisis center in 1974 and of the South Carolina Victim Assistance Network in 1984. He was appointed by Governor Richard Riley in 1984 to the South Carolina Crime Victims Advisory Board and reappointed by Governor Carroll Campbell to a second term in 1991. Dr. Kilpatrick and his colleagues have received several grants from the National Institute of Mental Health, National Institute of Justice, and the National Institute of Drug Abuse supporting their research on the scope of violent crime and its psychological impact on victims. His work has been published in scientific and professional journals, and he has made presentations to numerous state, national, and international groups. In 1985 he was given the National Organization of Victim Assistance Stephen Schafer Award for Outstanding Contributions to Victims Research. In 1990, President George Bush presented Dr. Kilpatrick with the U.S. Justice Department Award for Outstanding Contributions on Behalf of Victims of Crime. Dr. Kilpatrick has testified about crime victim issues at hearings held by the South Carolina General Assembly, the United States House of Representatives, and the United States Senate.*

*Bonnie S. Dansky is an assistant professor of clinical psychology at the National Crime Victims Research and Treatment Center (NCVC) and at the Consultation/Liaison Service in the Department of Psychiatry and Behavioral Sciences of the Medical University of South Carolina. Dr. Dansky received her B.A. from the University of Albany–State University of New York and her M.A. and Ph.D. in clinical psychology from Duke University. She completed a clinical internship and postdoctoral fellowship at the Medical University of South Carolina. Dr. Dansky's primary research interests involve examining psychological responses to criminal victimization and comorbidity of Post-traumatic Stress Disorder with substance abuse and eating disorders. Dr. Dansky is a co-principal investigator for a National Institute of Drug Abuse-funded grant concerning the prevalence of victimization and PTSD in patients with substance use disorders. She has published in professional journals and made numerous presentations to local and national groups on these topics, and has an active clinical practice.*

*Ritchie P. Tidwell holds a B.S. degree in journalism from the University of Florida and an M.S. degree in criminology from Florida State University. Mr. Tidwell has served as director of the Division of Public Safety Programs in the South Carolina's Governor's Office with responsibility for criminal/juvenile justice, highway safety, and crime prevention programs. He concurrently served as co-director of the Governor's Children's Coordinating Cabinet and as a member of the South Carolina Sentencing Guidelines Commission. Mr. Tidwell has been instrumental in a wide range of legislative accomplishments in the criminal, juvenile justice, victim's rights, and health and rehabilitative service fields.*

# The Hate Crime Statistics Act of 1990

## By James B. Jacobs* and Barry Eisler**

*In contrast with the highly visible controversy over the constitutionality of new substantive hate crime laws and enhanced punishments, the significance of the Hate Crime Statistics Act of 1990 seems to have been virtually ignored by criminal lawyers and criminologists. This is probably due to the fact that the Act does not affect criminal cases, although it does have implications for police policy. However, the Act's greatest significance is its potential impact on how we think about crime and intergroup relations in American society. The Act recognizes hate crime as a new type of criminal offense, and in effect, establishes a new societal indicator of certain types of prejudice. This article explicates the new law and explains how difficult it will be to implement it reliably. The larger issue the article seeks to raise is what kind of contribution this newly minted indicator of hate crime will make to our understanding of crime and certain odious prejudices that blight American society.*

The Hate Crime Statistics Act of 1990[1] (the Act) calls for federal compilation and reporting of "hate crime" statistics.[2] It mandates data acquisition beginning in 1990 and publication of an annual summary, but the first report (for 1990) had not

---

* Professor of Law and Director, Center for Research in Crime & Justice, New York University School of Law, New York, N.Y.

** Third-year law student, New York University School of Law, New York, N.Y.

[1] Hate Crime Statistics Act, Pub. L. No. 100-275, 104 Stat. 140 (1990).

[2] In R.A.V. v. City of St. Paul, Minnesota, 112 S. Ct. 2538 (1991), the U.S. Supreme Court struck down a hate crime statute that focused on "fighting words" and not just motivation. Nevertheless, the majority showed itself hostile to the idea of criminalizing and punishing some motivations and not others. Since *R.A.V.*, the Wisconsin Supreme Court has struck down a hate crime statute that makes it a special aggragated crime to commit one of a number of predicate offenses because of an enumerated prejudice. Wisconsin v. Mitchell, 169 Wis. 2d 153, 485 N.W.2d 807 (1992) *cert. granted*, 1992 U.S. LEXIS 8000. The Oregon Supreme Court distinguished *R.A.V.* and upheld an intimidation statute making it a "crime for two or more persons to intentionally, knowingly or recklessly cause physical injury to another because of their perception of that person's race, color, religion, national origin or sexual orientation." Oregon v. Plowman, 314 Or. 157, 838 P.2d 558 (1992). The Hate Crime Statistics Act, of course, is not vulnerable to constitutional attack since it does not impose punishments or regulation on anyone.

appeared as of December 1992.[3] The Act directs the attorney general to collect data on eight predicate "crimes [where there is] manifest evidence of prejudice based on race, religion, sexual orientation, or ethinicity."[4] It instructs the attorney general to "establish guidelines" for data collection and to determine the "necessary evidence and criteria that must be present for a finding of manifest evidence [of the enumerated prejudices]."[5] In an apparent non sequitur, Section 2 expresses congressional approval of "American family life," and disclaims any intent to promote homosexuality.[6]

Religious, gay and lesbian, racial and ethnic advocacy, and civil rights groups were chiefly responsible for the Act's passage. Some of these groups, to a greater or lesser extent, had been collecting their own statistics for years. B'nai B'rith's Anti-Defamation League's annual Audit of Anti-Semitic Incidents,[7] (published since 1979) is the most systematic private effort to monitor hate crime.[8] Other groups that collected hate crime data prior to the passage of the Act include the Southern Poverty Law Center's Klanwatch Project, which, since 1981, has distributed

---

[3] In April 1992, the UCR Section, note 23 *infra*, stated that the first report on hate crime is "some time off." Telephone interview with Bernie Dryden, Training Instructor, Uniform Crime Reports Section, Federal Bureau of Investigation (Apr. 1, 1992).

*Editor's Note*: As this article was going to press, the FBI released preliminary data on hate crimes for 1991. (The Bureau decided that it was unable to produce a report for 1990.) Law enforcement agencies in only 32 states provided any data at all. Of these agencies, 83 percent reported no hate crimes. For the entire state of California only 5 hate crimes were reported. Intimidation and vandalism accounted for 61 percent of the total 4,755 hate crimes reported by all agencies.

[4] Hate Crime Statistics Act at § (b)(1).

[5] Hate Crime Statistics Act at § (b)(2).

[6] Hate Crime Statistics Act at § 2.

[7] Hate Crime Statistics Act of 1988; Hearing before the Subcommittee on the Constitution of the Senate Committee on the Judiciary, 100th Cong., 2d Sess. 38 (1988) (Prepared Statement on behalf of the Anti-Defamation League of B'nai B'rith) (hereinafter Senate Hearings).

[8] The ADL Audit served as an important resource for the influential Abt Associates' report commissioned by the National Institute of Justice. Finn & McNeil, "Bias Crime and the Criminal Justice Response," Abt Associates Inc., May 1988 at 5, (hereinafter Abt Report). This report was based on interviews with forty respondents, including representatives from the criminal justice system, interest groups, and researchers. It also relied on research conducted by the National Organization of Black Law Enforcement Executives (NOBLE). The report was included, in its entirely, in the record of the hearings before the Senate, see Senate Hearings, note 7 *supra* at 175, and was cited prominently in the Judiciary Committee Report. See S. Rep. No. 21, 101st Cong., 1st Sess. 4 (1989).

a bi-monthly newsletter listing hate crime incidents,[9] and the National Gay and Lesbian Task Force, which established an Anti-Violence Project in 1982 and a data collection effort in 1985.[10] These groups and others argued that bias crimes[11] have been increasing dramatically[12] and urged Congress to begin collecting and reporting official national statistics on hate crimes.

The Hate Crime Statistics Act of 1990 began life in the Ninety-Ninth Congress.[13] In the One Hundred-First Congress,

---

[9] Senate Hearings, note 7 *supra*, at 66 (prepared Statement on behalf of the Southern Poverty Law Center's Klanwatch Project). The Klanwatch Project newsletters are based on newspaper clippings and informal reports from law enforcement agencies.

[10] Recent Developments, "Bringing Hate Crime Into Focus," 26 Harv. C.R.-C.L. L. Rev. 261, 271 (1991).

[11] The terms "bias crime" and "hate crime" are used interchangeably throughout this article. The UCR Program, note 23 *infra*, also equates these terms. Uniform Crime Reporting, *Training Guide for Hate Crime Data Collection*, Fed. Bureau of Investigation, U.S. Dep't of Justice, at 14, 15 [hereinafter *Training Guide*].

[12] See, e.g., Senate Hearings, note 7 *supra*, at 66 (prepared Statement on behalf of the Southern Poverty Law Center's Klanwatch Project) ("For the past seven years we have been collecting newspaper clippings and informal reports from law enforcement around the country, and we have noticed what appears to be a significant increase in crimes motivated by racial, ethnic, religious, or sexual orientation bias."); *Id*. at 74 (prepared statement of John C. Weiss, Executive Director, National Institute Against Prejudice and Violence) ("Over the last eight years, many of us have become aware of the increase in reported crimes based on prejudice."); *Id*. at 87 (Testimony of the Japanese American Citizens League) (referring to the rise in anti-Asian sentiment in the 1980s); *Id*. at 96 (prepared statement of Kevin Berrill, Director, Anti-Violence Project, National Gay and Lesbian Task Force) ("Reports to the National Gay and Lesbian Task Force of harassment, assault, arson, vandalism, homicide and other crimes against lesbian and gay people have increased dramatically in recent years."); Racially Motivated Violence, Hearings Before the Subcommittee on Criminal Justice of the House Committee on the Judiciary, 100th Cong., 2d Sess. 14 (1988) (Statement of the Rev. C.T. Vivian, Chairman of the Board, Center for Democratic Renewal) ("Not since the days when the Klan regularly lynched people at the turn of the century—and some 4,129 people were lynched in that twenty-six year period—have we had anything like we have today.").

[13] The House Judiciary Committee favorably reported H.R. 2455, which called for the collection of data on specific crimes "committed to manifestly express racial, ethnic, or religious prejudice." H.R. Rep. No. 208, 99th Cong., 1st Sess. (1985). H.R. 2455 was the end product of a process that began with the introduction of two bills, H.R. 775, and H.R. 1171. The bill passed in the House, but died in the Senate. See H.R. Rep 575, 100th Cong., 2d. Sess. 2 (1988). In the One-hundredth Congress, the House passed H.R. 3193 in May 1988. See S. Rep. 514, 100th Cong., 2d Sess. 2 (1988). H.R. 3193, as eventually passed, was similar to its predecessor, but it included "homosexuality or heterosexuality" along with racial, ethnic, or religious violence, and most of the debate over the bill involved this change. Five Judiciary Committee members had strongly objected to the inclusion of sexual orientation in the bill. See H.R. Rep. No. 575, 100th Cong., 2d Sess. 12 (1988) (dissenting views of Mr. Gekas, Mr. McCollum, Mr. Coble, Mr. Dannemeyer, and Mr. Smith to

the House Committee on the Judiciary favorably reported H.R. 1048,[14] and the full House passed it.[15] In the Senate, the Judiciary Committee favorably reported S. 419,[16] which engendered extensive floor debate, largely due to Senator Jesse Helms's[17] opposition to the inclusion of sexual orientation as a hate crime category. To quell Helms's claim that the bill promoted homosexuality, proponents added a statement of support for the traditional family (thus, the apparent non sequitor).[18] The Senate passed the Act by a vote of 92-4;[19] the House amended H.R. 1048 to conform to the Senate's changes and passed it by a vote of 368-47.[20] On April 23, 1990, in a public ceremony, President George Bush signed the Hate Crime Statistics Act of 1990 into law.[21]

## The UCR Guidelines

The Hate Crime Statistics Act delegated implementing authority to the attorney general. The attorney general assigned the

---

H.R. 3193). Nonetheless, the Committee ordered the bill reported favorably by a vote of 21–13. *Id.* at 6.

The Subcommittee on the Constitution of the Senate Judiciary Committee held hearings on three different hate crimes statistics acts in June 1988. Senate Hearings, note 7 *supra.* The three bills were S. 702, 100th Cong., 1st Sess. (1987); S. 797, 100th Cong., 1st Sess. (1987); and, S. 2000, 100th Cong., 2d Sess. (1988). By this time, the race, ethnic, religious, and sexual orientation advocacy groups had the full backing of certain congressmen and some representatives of the law enforcement community, such as NOBLE. Recent Developments, "Bringing Hate Crime into Focus," 26 Harv. C.R.-C.L. L. Rev. 261, 274 (1991). The Senate Judiciary Committee favorably reported S. 702, S. Rep. No. 514, 100th Cong., 2d Sess. (1988), a bill almost identical to the Hate Crime Statistics Act of 1990, but it died when the One-hundredth Congress adjourned. S. Rep. No. 21, 101st Cong., 1st Sess. 3 (1989).

[14] H.R. Rep. No. 109, 101st Cong., 1st Sess. (1989).

[15] 135 Cong. Rec. H3238 (1989).

[16] S. Rep. No. 21, 101st Cong., 1st Sess. (1989).

[17] Toner, "Senate, 92 to 4, Wants U.S. Data on Crimes That Spring From Hate," N.Y. Times, Feb. 9, 1990 at A17, Col. 3.

[18] For a complete discussion of the debate leading to the inclusion of Section 2 of the Act, see Recent Developments, "Bring Hate Crime into Focus," 26 Harv. C.R.-C.L. L. Rev. 261, 276–281 (1991).

[19] 136 Cong. Rec. S1092 (1990).

[20] 136 Cong. Rec. H1460 (1990).

[21] Rosenthal, "President Signs Law for Study of Hate Crimes," N.Y. Times, Apr. 24, 1990, at B6, col. 5. While passage of the Act was a victory for all the interest groups involved, the public ceremony was regarded as especially significant for gay and lesbian rights advocates because it marked their first participation in such a ceremony.

responsibility to the Federal Bureau of Investigation (FBI).[22] The FBI passed the assignment along to its Uniform Crime Reports (UCR) Section,[23] which had already conducted a preliminary feasibility study.[24]

The Act provided little guidance on what specific data should be acquired or how the data should be collected. In devising its plan, the UCR Section surveyed twelve states and a number of cities with hate crime reporting laws,[25] and turned to pri-

---

[22] 28 C.F.R. § 0.85(m) (1990).

[23] As a result of an initiative undertaken by the International Association of Chiefs of Police in the 1920s, Congress authorized the FBI to establish the Uniform Crime Reporting Program in 1930. The UCR Program is managed by the FBI's UCR Section. The Summary Reporting System (SRS) facilitates the collection of data on occurrences of eight crimes. For most other crimes, arrest data are collected. Participating agencies—city, county, and state law enforcement programs—voluntarily submit aggregate monthly reports. In states that have developed state UCR Programs, data are first cleared through a state agency before their submission to the UCR Section.

In the 1980s, the UCR section launched an effort to revamp the old system. The result was the National Incident-Based Reporting System (NIBRS), which is currently being phased in throughout the nation. The NIBRS is more comprehensive and more detailed than the SRS. "In NIBRS, law enforcement agencies collect detailed data regarding individual crime incidents and arrests and submit them in separate 'reports' using prescribed data elements and data values to describe each incident and arrest." See Fed. Bureau of Investigation, Uniform Crime Reporting Handbook, U.S. Dep't of Justice (1984); Uniform Crime Reporting, *National Incident-Based Reporting System, Volume 1 Data Collection Guidelines*, Fed. Bureau of Investigation, U.S. Dep't of Justice (July 1, 1988). Because NIBRS is not yet widely in use, this article focuses on the collection of hate crime data within the SRS framework.

[24] Earlier versions of H.R. 2455 had specifically mandated that hate crime data be included in the UCR Program, H.R. Rep. No. 208, 99th Cong., 1st Sess. 2 (1985), and it was generally assumed in Congress that the UCR Program would be used to implement the Act. S. Rep. No. 21, 101st Cong., 1st Sess. 4 (1989) ("While S.419 does not require the Attorney General to use the UCR to collect the data on hate crimes, the committee believes that the updated UCR [NIBRS] would enable the Justice Department to easily implement S.419. Whether or not the UCR is the vehicle to record hate crimes, the categories of crimes listed in the act correspond with those in the new UCR and should expedite implementation of the bill, as the FBI has already developed uniform offense definitions for these categories."); see also, H.R. Rep. No. 109, 101st Cong., 1st Sess. 3 (1989) ("While the legislation does not require that the Justice Department use the Uniform Crime Report (UCR), the Committee believes that the UCR is particularly adaptable to collecting hate crime statistics."). The UCR Section began studying the problems in implementing the Act two years before it was passed. Telephone interview with Harper Wilson, FBI (Nov. 1991), (hereinafter Wilson interview).

[25] Wilson interview, note 24 *supra*.

vate groups for input.[26] After a national conference in August 1990,[27] the guidelines were drafted.

The guidelines define a hate crime as, "[a] criminal offense committed against a person or property, which is motivated, in whole or in part, by the offender's bias against a race, religion, ethnic/national origin group, or sexual orientation group."[28] This definition has three elements: predicate crimes, types of prejudice, and motivation.

### Predicate Crimes

The Act enumerates eight predicate crimes;[29] "murder; non-negligent manslaughter; forcible rape; aggravated assault; simple assault; intimidation; arson; and destruction, damage or vandalism of property,"[30] which, if they are motivated by one of the enumerated prejudices, should be counted as hate crimes. It also gives the attorney general discretion to add to or delete from this list. Congress apparently enumerated the eight predicate crimes in order to facilitate the acquisition of hate crime data through the UCR, not because these crimes are more likely than others to be motivated by certain undesirable prejudices.[31] The attorney

---

[26] *Training Guide*, note 11 *supra*, at 2. The Training Guide lists the following as "organizations which had expressed interest in seeing a national hate crime statistical program established": the National Institute Against Prejudice & Violence, the Anti-Defamation League of B'nai B'rith, and the National Association for the Advancement of Colored People.

[27] Wilson interview, note 24 *supra*; see Uniform Crime Reporting, *Hate Crime Data Collecting Guidelines*, Fed. Bureau of Investigation, U.S. Dep't of Justice [hereinafter *Guidelines*].

[28] *Guidelines*, note 27 *supra* at 4.

[29] By use of the word "crime," Congress indicated that only incidents that violate a provision in the criminal code ought to be reported and recorded. This approach is followed by the UCR Section. This is not, however, the only plausible approach. Under Maryland's hate incident data collection program, the police attempt to catalogue all bias-motivated "incidents," whether or not criminal offenses. For example, in one incident, antiblack racist flyers were placed on automobile windshields outside a predominantly black church during Sunday mass. Even though no crime was committed, the police included the incident in their statistics. See note 69 *infra*. Telephone interview with Col. Leonard Supinski, Baltimore County Police Department (Apr. 16, 1992).

[30] Hate Crime Statistics Act § (b)(1) (emphasis added).

[31] As the Senate Judiciary Committee explained, "[t]he Committee included those crimes that correspond with crimes that are included in the updated UCR, as these crimes have been given a uniform definition and this will facilitate implementation. As the new UCR collects comprehensive information on all the listed crimes, including race, age, ethnicity, and gender of the victim and perpetrator, information on whether the crime was motivated by hate could be easily incorporated." S. Rep. No. 21, 101st Cong., 1st Sess. 6 (1989).

general exercised his discretion by adding robbery, burglary, and motor vehicle theft.[32] The UCR already contains uniform definitions[33] of these offenses,[34] but the same could be said of many other offenses that are not on the list. Why, for example, should not kidnapping, if motivated by one of the enumerated biases, be classified as a hate crime? Perhaps, if the Act is considered a success in the short run, it will be amended so that *any offense*, if motivated by certain prejudices, will count as a hate crime.

### Types of Prejudice

The Act specifies four categories of prejudice that transform an ordinary crime into a hate crime: those based on race, religion, sexual orientation, and ethnicity. Ethnic prejudice is defined as "[a] preformed negative opinion or attitude toward a group of persons of the same race or national origin who share common or similar traits, languages, customs, and traditions (e.g., Arabs, Hispanics, etc.)."[35] On its face, it could include prejudice between national origin groups that belong to the same racial group, e.g., Italians against Irish or Haitians against Nigerians. Sexual orientation is defined in the Act as "consensual homosexuality or heterosexuality."

The reasoning that supports the effort to count crimes moti-

---

[32] *Guidelines*, note 27 *supra*, at 8. Those law enforcement agencies participating in UCR and using the SRS (all UCR participants that are not yet using the NIBRS, and NIBRS participants that are not yet prepared to add the hate crime data element to their data submissions) must submit quarterly hate crime reports containing summary statistics on these eleven predicate crimes. In NIBRS, data are submitted on computer tapes. Agencies that are part of NIBRS and have the appropriate facilities will add a hate crime data element to their UCR submissions. In contrast to the thirteen crimes included in SRS hate crime reports, NIBRS data encompasses forty-six different offenses, grouped into twenty-two categories.

[33] For example, "robbery" is defined for SRS purposes as, "the taking or attempting to take anything of value from the care, custody, or control of a person or persons by force or threat of force or violence and/or by putting the victim in fear."

[34] Several SRS offense definitions have been revised for use in NIBRS. For example, rape is defined in the SRS as "carnal knowledge of a female forcibly and against her will," while in NIBRS rape is defined as "the carnal knowledge of a person, forcibly and/or against that person's will; or, not forcibly or against the person's will where the victim is incapable of giving consent because of his/her temporary or permanent mental or physical incapacity." Uniform Crime Reporting, *National Incident-Based Reporting System, Volume 1 Data Collection Guidelines*, Fed. Bureau of Investigation, U.S. Dep't of Justice at 12 (July 1, 1988).

[35] *Guidelines*, note 27 *supra*, at 5.

vated in whole or in part by race, ethnicity, religion, and sexual orientation applies equally well to other types of prejudice. Many women will likely think it perverse that rape will not be counted as a hate crime unless the offender was motivated by racial, ethnic, or religious prejudices. Some members of the elderly, disabled, homeless, and other groups will no doubt feel that the Hate Crime Statistics Act ought to recognize offenses motivated by prejudice against them as warranting inclusion under the hate crime umbrella. At least eight congressmen found the Act deficient because it did not cover union-related violence.[36] They argued that violence committed by and against union members is a serious nationwide problem, and that statistics on pro- and antiunion crimes would aid federal law enforcement efforts. The UCR Section recognized that these categories do not exhaust the types of prejudice that motivate crime:

> There are, of course, many kinds of bias. Some of the more common kinds are those against race, religion, ethnicity/national origin, or sexual orientation. But, there are also biases against rich people, poor people, men who wear long hair and/or beards, people who dress oddly, smokers, drinkers, people with diseases such as AIDS, motorcycle gangs, "rock" musicians, etc. The types of bias to be reported to the FBI's UCR Section are limited to those mandated by the enabling Act.[37]

It is possible that if the implementation of the Act proves successful, some or all of these other groups will lobby to have their victimization included under the definition of hate crime. The guideline's rather flaccid definition of "prejudice" ("preformed negative opinion") seems quite different than the popular understanding of hate crimes as offenses perpetrated by rabid racists, antisemites, homophobes, and so forth. On its face at least, the guidelines would count as hate crimes car thefts committed by persons who believe Jews are too stingy, blacks are too noisy, and gays too promiscuous. This demonstrates the excrutiatingly difficult problem of actually defining (1) what we mean by "prejudice," and (2) what kind (degree, intensity, consciousness) of prejudice, when motivating an offender, are enough to classify a crime as a "hate crime."

---

[36] Congressmen Henry J. Hyde, D. French Slaughter, Jr., Larkin Smith, Craig T. James, Bill McCollum, Howard Coble, Lamar S. Smith, and Chuck Douglas expressed their disappointment with H.R. 1048 in the Report of the Committee on the Judiciary. H.R. Rep. 109, 101st Cong., 1st Sess. 7 (1989).

[37] *Guidelines*, note 27 *supra* at 1.

**Determining Motivation**

Many of the problems associated with classifying incidents as hate crimes flow from the difficult task of assessing motivation.[38] This is also what sets hate crime data collection apart from the collection of statistics on other crimes. Unlike other crimes, hate crimes are defined by the *motivation* of their perpetrators: A predicate crime becomes a hate crime if it is motivated in whole or in part by certain enumerated prejudices.

Congress mandated collection of data on "crimes that *manifest evidence* of prejudice."[39] How much prejudice (in absolute or proportional terms) is necessary to qualify a crime as a hate crime was left to the attorney general. The guidelines instruct police officers to label a crime as a suspected bias incident when there is some evidence that the offender was in part motivated by wrongful prejudice. One might, of course, believe that there is some (conscious or unconscious) prejudice at work in all crimes committed by members of one group against another and therefore label all such crimes hate crimes, or at least create a presumption that would have to be overcome by strong evidence that prejudice in no way was a factor. But, if one is not willing to make such an assumption or presumption, one will be left with the formidable challenge of making inferences about offenders' motivations in all offenses where the perpetrator and victim are members of different groups.

The guidelines provide that crimes that are motivated, in whole or in part, by bias, should be reported as hate crimes.[40] Because it could be said that practically everyone's behavior is "in part" motivated by prejudice, all intergroup crimes could be potential hate crimes. Consider a Protestant mugger who assaults a Jewish merchant, a white rapist who victimizes a black woman, or a black robber who holds up a Korean-owned grocery.[41] In each of these cases, animosity toward the race or

---

[38] See O'Kelly, "Motivation," 10 Int'l Encyclopedia of the Soc. Sci. 507–513 (1968).

[39] Hate Crime Statistics Act at § (b)(1) (emphasis added).

[40] See *Training Guide*, note 11 *supra*, at 18.

[41] Consider the following vignette from the Hate Crime Data Collection Guidelines: "Example (2): A white juvenile male snatched a Jewish woman's purse, and in doing so, knocked her down and called her by a well known and recognized epithet used against Jews. The offender's identity is not known. Although the offender used an epithet for Jews, it is not known whether he belongs to another religious group or whether his motive was anything more than robbery. Because the

ethnicity of the victim *may be a factor* in the offender's target selection. The dominant motive however, may be money, sex, thrill-seeking, or peer approval, or the crime may simply be the product of an antisocial personality. Categorizing incidents in which prejudice is a minor or submerged factor as hate crimes could expand the classification to practically all incidents in which the victim and offender are members of different groups.[42]

How will it be determined whether a crime was motivated, in whole or in part, by a bad prejudice? In its *Training Guide for Hate Crime Data Collection*, the UCR Section prescribes a two-step decision-making process for local law enforcement.[43] The officer who responds to a potential bias crime should classify the crime as a suspected bias incident if there is *"any indication* that the offender was motivated by bias."[44] The *Training Guide* lists the following factors the responding officer should consider in determining whether a crime qualifies as a suspected bias incident; it requires that discretion should be exercised in favor of a broad and inclusive definition of hate crime:[45]

- Is the motivation of the alleged offender known?
- Was the incident known to have been motivated by racial, religious, ethnic, or sexual orientation bias?
- Does the victim perceive the action of the offender to have been motivated by bias?
- Is there no clear other motivation for the incident?
- Were any racial, religious, ethnic, or sexual orientation bias remarks made by the offender?

---

facts are ambiguous, agencies should not report this incident as bias motivated." *Guidelines*, note 27 *supra*, at 6. This conclusion seems inconsistent with the UCR Section's instruction that incidents motivated "in whole or in part, by bias" be coded as hate crimes.

[42] See note, "Combatting Racial Violence: A Legislative Proposal," 101 Harv. L. Rev. 1270 (1988); Note, 'Teeth for a Paper Tiger: A Proposal to Add Enforceability to Florida's Hate Crimes Act," 17 Fla. St. U.L. Rev. 697 (1990). These two articles suggest that criminal civil rights laws should create a presumption of bias motivation in intergroup crimes when the defendant is white and the victim is nonwhite. Defendants would be allowed to assert an affirmative defense that their crime was not motivated by prejudice.

[43] *Training Guide*, note 11 *supra*, at 16. See also, S. Rep. No. 21, 101st Cong., 1st Sess. 4 (1989) ("The committee recommends that any guidelines include verification and follow-up procedures to ensure the accuracy of the data.")

[44] *Training Guide*, note 11 *supra*, at 16 (emphasis added).

[45] *Id*. at 17–18.

- Were there any offensive symbols, words, or acts that are known to represent a hate group or other evidence of bias against the victim's group?
- Did the incident occur on a holiday or other day of significance to the victim's or the offender's group?
- What do the demographics of the area tell you about the incident?[46]

It is apparent that these bias incident indicators, although not intended to be exhaustive, hardly provide an accurate and reliable means for identifying hate crimes. The first two questions merely restate the issue: Was the offense motivated by one of the enumerated prejudices? The third factor, the victim's perception of the offender's motivation, although obviously important, ought not be determinative; indeed, the victim himself may be biased. The other questions also are problematic. Many incidents have "no clear other motivation," but does that justify an inference, much less a finding, of bias? Much human conduct has no apparent logical motivation, especially when it is self-destructive and antisocial. Many incidents involve language that could be construed as reflecting racial, religious, or sexual orientation bias. Are some or all of them to be classified as hate crimes? The *Training Guide* specifically cautions against reliance on "the mere utterance of a racial epithet."[47] Other factors would permit an inference of bias if the crime occurred on a "day of significance," or in an area with particular, but unspecified, "demographic composition." How should a police officer or bias unit interpret this? Which neighborhoods or whole cities are demographically suspect? Is a robbery of a white person in Harlem presumptively a hate crime? These problems suggest that identification of hate crimes will be fraught with subjectivity. And, it should be emphasized, that a hate crime "finding" does not come after a trial, but after a limited police investigation of the crime scene or incident.

The second step in the labeling process involves a review officer's (or unit's) analysis of those offenses identified as suspected hate crimes in the first step. The *Training Guide* instructs the reviewing officer or unit to classify an incident as a

---

[46] *Id.*

[47] *Id.* at 18.

hate crime only if there exists sufficient objective facts "to lead a reasonable and prudent person to conclude that the offender's actions were motivated, in whole or in part, by bias."[48] How is that to be determined? What is known about a reasonable and prudent person's perceptions of prejudice? The *Training Guide* provides a second list of questions that should be considered by the reviewing officer; in some cases, the authors of this article have inserted in brackets some difficulties perceived in interpreting and answering these questions.[49]

> The Second Level Judgment Officer/Unit should seek answers to the following types of questions before making the final determination of whether an incident was motivated by bias:
>
> • Is the victim a member of a target, racial, religious, ethnic/national origin, or sexual orientation group? *[Are all ethnic groups "target" groups? Do "whites" count as a "target racial group"? Do all religious groups?]*
>
> • Were the offender and the victim of different racial, religious, ethnic/national origin, or sexual orientation groups? For example, the victim was black and the offenders were white. *[What if one of the offenders is from the same group as the victim?]*
>
> • Would the incident have taken place if the victim and offender were of the same race, religion, ethnic group, or sexual orientation?
>
> • Were biased oral comments, written statements, or gestures made by the offender which indicate his/her bias? For example, the offender shouted a racial epithet at the victim. *[Suppose if this was a response to bias statements or gestures by the victim?]*
>
> • Were bias-related drawings, markings, symbols, or graffiti left at the crime scene? For example, a swastika was painted on the door of a synagogue.
>
> • Were certain objects, items, or things which indicate bias used (e.g., the offenders wore white sheets with hoods covering their faces) or left behind by the offender(s) (e.g., a burning cross was left in front of the victim's residence)?
>
> • Is the victim a member of a racial, religious, ethnic/national origin, or sexual orientation group which is overwhelmingly outnumbered by members of another group in the neighborhood where the victim lives and the incident took place? This factor loses significance with the passage of time, i.e., it is most significant when the victim first moved into the neighborhood and becomes less significant as time passes without incident.

---

[48] *Id.*

[49] *Id.* at 19–20.

- Was the victim visiting a neighborhood where previous hate crimes had been committed against other members of his/her racial, religious, ethnic/national origin, or sexual orientation group and where tensions remain high against his/her group? *[This seems to call for historical data and sociological assessments that would be very difficult to make reliably. Is there any neighborhood where a previous hate crime has never taken place?]*

- Have several incidents occurred in the same locality at or about the same time, and are the victims all of the same racial, religious, ethnic/national origin, or sexual orientation group?

- Does a substantial portion of the community where the crime occurred perceive that the incident was motivated by bias? *[How could the police make such a determination?]*

- Was the victim engaged in activities promoting his/her racial, religious, ethnic/national origin, or sexual orientation group? For example, the victim is a member of the NAACP, participates in gay rights demonstrations, etc.

- Did the incident coincide with a holiday relating to, or a date of particular significance to, a racial, religious, or ethnic/national origin group (e.g., Martin Luther King Day, Rosh Hashanah, etc.)?

- Was the offender previously involved in a similar hate crime or is he/she a member of a hate group? *[Searching out the defendant's organizational memberships and magazine subscriptions will set off First Amendment alarms.]*

- Were there indications that a hate group was involved? For example, a hate group claimed responsibility for the crime or was active in the neighborhood.

- Does a historically established animosity exist between the victim's group and the offender's group? *[How shall we answer such questions as whether there is historic animosity between blacks and whites, blacks and latinos, whites and latinos, Jews and gentiles, and so forth? Does historic animosity exist between all racial, ethnic, and religious groups or is it more complicated than that?]*

- Is this incident similar to other known and documented cases of bias, particularly in this area? Does it fit a similar modus operandi to these other incidents?

- Has this victim been previously involved in similar situations?

- Are there other explanations for the incident, such as a childish prank, unrelated vandalism, etc? *[Won't many young hate crime offenders wish to characterize their conduct as a prank?]*

- Did the offender have some understanding of the impact his/her actions would have on the victim? *[Won't this be difficult to determine, especially if the offender is not apprehended or does not make a statement?]*

The *Training Guide* does not state how many of the preceding questions must be answered affirmatively in order to confirm a hate crime. As indicated by the comments following some questions, it is dubious that affirmative answers, at least to several of the questions by themselves, ought to justify a hate crime label. For example, how much weight should be accorded biased utterances or the community's perception of the incident (assuming "community" could be defined and its "perception" reliably determined)? Should a hate crime be predicated on the review officer's guess as to whether the crime *would have taken place* if the offender and victim were members of the same racial, religious, or sexual orientation group? Would a police department be correct in assuming that there is historic animosity between all national origin, racial, and sexual orientation groups? Interestingly, the operating definition of a hate crime depends on the perpetrator's motivation, not on the victim's actual identity. Thus, the guidelines take the position that a crime is a hate crime even if the biased perpetrator mistakenly victimizes someone *who is not a member* of the intended target group, in effect, an attempted hate crime.[50]

## Problems in Implementing the Act

The UCR depends on local law enforcement being ready, willing, and able to follow the guidelines. After many years of operation, almost all police departments contribute data to the UCR, but it is not certain that all departments will choose to collect and report hate crime statistics. Those that decide to do so will face some challenges. Attributing motivation to criminal acts is an inherently subjective task. Senator Gordon Humphrey, in the Senate Judiciary Committee report, warned of the dangers posed by the subjective nature of hate crime data collection: "[I]t will be impossible to prevent the inclusion of distorted, mistaken, exaggerated or simply fraudulent crime reports, because the mere reporting of a crime is not subject to the standards of credibility or evidence that apply in the subsequent stages of the criminal process."[51] Political and community pressures may affect which and how many crimes are reported as hate crimes.

---

[50] *Guidelines*, note 27 *supra*, at 4.

[51] S. Rep. No. 21, 101st Cong., 1st Sess. 13 (1989) (Additional views of Mr. Humphrey).

Consider the mind-boggling question of determining how many hate crimes were committed during the Los Angeles riots, or how the aggregate number of hate crimes will be affected by a police department's decision whether to count bias-related graffiti (if it rises to the level of "vandalism") a predicate offense under the Act. Moreover, definitional differences between the federal program and parallel state or local hate crime statistics programs can overburden or confuse the police who collect, interpret, and report the data.

### Political Pressure and False Reporting

It is not unlikely that police departments will find themselves under pressure to exercise their hate crime reporting discretion narrowly or broadly. Some political leaders and police officials will no doubt be interested in minimizing the perception that their community has a hate crime problem.[52] For example, local political leaders, fearing that hate crime data may portray their city as "the most bigoted city in America," may pressure the police to operate with a presumption against confirming hate crimes. This could be accomplished easily by not labeling ambiguous, minor, or less serious crimes as bias-related.

Conversely, advocacy groups, which are monitoring police departments with increasing vigilance, may try to influence police in the other direction. If the police refuse to label a hate crime or to make what is perceived as an adequate effort to apprehend a perpetrator, they may be excoriated in the press, on radio, and on television, and be the targets of protests and demonstrations. Under such circumstances, the police might understandably be quick to label borderline incidents as hate crimes. Thus, when national hate crime statistics finally appear, we will have to be very careful in making intercity comparisons.

In addition to inaccurately reported incidents, the hate crime data collection effort is also vulnerable to false and fraudulent reporting.[53] All crime data are subject to false reporting, but

---

[52] The Abt report characterized this problem as, "[c]oncern that collecting data on hate violence will be used against the department and against public officials either to damage the community's image, or to document a serious problem which responsible authorities will be accused of having neglected." Abt Report, note 8 *supra*, at 16.

[53] The New York Times reported that of sixty-one bias crimes reported to the New York City Bias Crime Unit in January 1992, two were classified as hoaxes. "One was perpetrated by a twenty-five-year-old black man from Brooklyn who claimed he was beaten by five white men and told, 'You aren't going to rape any

ordinarily there is relatively little incentive to falsify crime reports. However, inflated hate crime statistics can serve ideological purposes. Interest groups that seek greater attention, access to funds, and political support from their own community and the larger society may perceive a benefit from the exaggeration of their victimization.[54]

### Federal-State Variation in Defining and Reporting Hate Crimes

Differences between state and local hate crime data collection guidelines and the federal guidelines may confuse the federal data collection efforts. At least seventeen states have enacted legislation mandating the collection of hate crime statistics.[55] These statutes, and the programs that implement them, are far from uniform. State statutes differ widely with respect to types of bias and predicate crimes. For instance, Oregon's statute defines hate crimes much more broadly than federal law:

> All law enforcement agencies shall report to the Executive Department statistics concerning crimes: . . . (c) Motivated by prejudice based on the perceived race, color, religion, national origin, sexual orientation, marital status, political affiliation or beliefs, membership or activity in or on behalf of a labor organization or against a labor organization, physical or mental handicap, age, economic or social status, or citizenship of the victim.[56]

While Oregon's statute has a broader definition of hate crime than the federal act, it also requires compliance with the FBI's uniform crime reporting system.[57] Thus, local law enforcement

---

more white women.' He later confessed to the police that he had lied 'to get attention from his family.' '' Richardson, "61 Acts of Bias: One Fuse Lights Many Different Explosions," N.Y. Times, Jan. 28, 1992, at B6, col. 2. This account illustrates the difficulty involved in verifying actual bias incidents. The infamous Tawana Brawley incident demonstrates the incendiary effect false hate crime reports can have.

[54] See Epstein, The Joys of Victimhood, N.Y. Times July 2, 1989 (Magazine) at 20.

[55] See, Hate Crime Statutes: A 1991 Status Report, ADL Law Report, Anti-Defamation League, App. b (1991). Because of delay in the implementation of hate crime data collection procedures, the UCR Section is partially dependent on information gathered under state and local programs. Telephone interview with Ashton Flemings, FBI (Jan. 16, 1992); Telephone interview with Bernie Dryden, Training Instructor, Uniform Crime Report Section, Fed. Bureau of Investigation (Apr. 1, 1992).

[56] Or. Rev. Stat. § 181.550(1) (1989).

[57] "All law enforcement agencies shall report to the Executive Department statistics concerning crimes: . . . (b) As directed by the Executive Department, for purposes of the Uniform Crime Reporting System of the Federal Bureau of Investigation;" id.

agencies in Oregon must scrutinize crimes twice, once to see if they are hate crimes under the state statute, and again to see if they are federal hate crimes. For instance, if prolife activists assault prochoice demonstrators in Oregon (or vice versa), local police ought to classify the incident as a hate crime for state reporting purposes but not for federal purposes. To take another example, Virginia's reporting statute mandates "the collection and analysis of information on terrorist acts and groups and individuals carrying out such acts."[58] Terrorist acts are defined as:

> (i) a criminal act committed against a person or his property with the specific intent of instilling fear or intimidation in the individual against whom the act is perpetrated because of race, religion or ethnic origin or which is committed for the purpose of restraining that person from exercising his rights under the Constitution or laws of this Common-wealth or of the United States, (ii) any illegal act directed against any persons or their property because of those persons' race, religion or national origin, and (iii) all other incidents, as determined by law-enforcement authorities, intended to intimidate or harass any individual or group because of race, religion, or national origin.[59]

In Virginia, "gay-bashing" is a hate crime for federal reporting purposes, but not for state reporting purposes. Local bias crime investigation units acting pursuant to city and county ordinances or departmental regulations, such as those in Baltimore, New York City, and Los Angeles, proliferate the problems of police reporting.

State and local law enforcement agencies are trained in the laws of their jurisdictions and, although the FBI has a program for training local law enforcement agents, it may be too much to expect police officers to become familiar with the elements of, and subtle differences between, federal, state, and local hate crime statutes. If local law enforcement agencies and officers are not capable or willing to follow the federal guidelines, the UCR Section will end up aggregating apples and oranges.[60]

---

[58] Va. Code Ann. § 52-8.5A (1991).

[59] Va. Code Ann. § 52-8.5C (1991).

[60] The federal guidelines use this definition of intimidation: "To unlawfully place another person in reasonable fear of bodily harm through the use of threatening words and/or conduct, but without displaying a weapon or subjecting the victim to actual physical attack." *Guidelines*, note 27 *supra*, at 9. However, a uniform federal definition does not fully address the problem because state or local law enforcement may define intimidation differently, thereby requiring the local police to use different definitions for different purposes.

## What Can Be Expected From Hate Crime Statistics?

The Act's potential impact should be assessed in light of its stated goals: 1) to help law enforcement more effectively combat hate crimes; 2) to help policy makers develop strategies to fight hate crimes; and 3) to demonstrate the nation's concern for the victimized groups. Even if the reporting system established to acquire hate crime data operates reasonably effectively, the Act will do little to help law enforcement officials or policymakers solve or prevent hate crimes (goals 1 and 2). Official abhorrence of hate crime (goal 3) was expressed by passage of the Act.

### Aggregating and Reporting Hate Crimes

Aggregate statistics are created by adding up reported incidents in both the Summary Reporting System (SRS) and the National Incident-Based Reporting System (NIBRS). Police officers will complete a one-page Hate Crime Incident Report form[61] for use in the SRS[62] for each bias incident. One section of the form has boxes for the eleven offenses on which data will be gathered. Another section lists the codes for twenty-five different locations, such as "Bar/Night Club," "Construction Site," or "Lake/Waterway." A third section asks the officer to explain the type of bias motivation displayed by the offender. There are twenty different choices, including "Anti-Black," "Anti-Hispanic," "Anti-Catholic," and "Anti-Female Homosexual." A fourth section includes a set of questions on type of victim (individual, business, society, and so forth). The only offender-based questions are number of offenders involved and race. The only other information reflected on the Incident Report is the incident number, the agency identifier, and the date of the incident.

Local police departments are asked to submit their Incident Reports quarterly to the UCR Section along with a Quarterly Hate Crime Report.[63] The Quarterly Report aggregates the individual Incident Reports and provides police agencies an opportunity to delete previously reported incidents subsequently determined not

---

[61] See *id.* at Appendix.

[62] Agencies participating in the NIBRS will submit basically the same bias motivation information, but in a different format. See note 23 *supra*.

[63] *Guidelines*, note 27 *supra*, at Appendix.

to be hate crimes. The UCR Section simply tabulates the data it receives, although it does check for aberrant figures, usually the result of clerical errors.[64]

### Usefulness of Hate Crime Data for More Effective Law Enforcement

Advocacy groups and some law enforcement officials urged Congress to pass the Act on the ground that the data could be used to help reduce the occurrence of bias crimes. The Abt report stated, "One of the most pressing considerations related to bias crime is the need for adequate data."[65] The Senate Judiciary Committee report on S.419 states, "This information can help law enforcement agencies and local communities combat hate crimes more effectively by identifying their frequency, location, and other patterns over time."[66] The House Committee on the Judiciary reiterated this prediction and added, "The nine states which collect hate crime data have found such information *indispensable* to their law enforcement efforts."[67]

There is, however, reason to question this claim and the Act's potential to aid law enforcement significantly. Although proponents claimed that hate crime statistics aid police in allocating resources,[68] they did not document or explain how. No figures were provided to permit before and after comparisons of hate crimes in the states with hate crime reporting laws. One law enforcement official told Congress that "a problem defined is a

---

[64] Telephone interview with Bernie Dryden, Training Instructor, Uniform Crime Report Section, Fed. Bureau of Investigation (Apr. 1, 1992).

[65] Abt Report, note 8 *supra*, at 12.

[66] S. Rep. No. 21, 101st Cong., 1st Sess. 2 (1989). The Committee report refers to the Abt Report, a 1988 resolution of the U.S. Commission on Civil Rights, and the experience of the Baltimore County Police Department for the proposition that hate crime data can be an effective law enforcement tool, but does not explain how. See also, Senate Hearings, note 7 *supra*, at 175, 210, 217.

[67] H.R. Rep. No. 109, 101st Congs., 1st Sess. 3 (1989) (parenthetical omitted) (emphasis added).

[68] See, e.g., Senate Hearings, note 7 *supra*, at 16 (prepared Statement of Rep. John Conyers, Jr.) ("Nationwide hate crimes data can be very useful to law enforcement agencies seeking to combat these offenses."); *id*, at 93 (testimony of the Japanese American Citizens League) ("More information about hate crimes including where they occur, the groups they are perpetrated against, and the types of crime could focus the efforts of law enforcement officials in identifying areas requiring greater law enforcement attention."); see also, Abt Report, note 8 *supra*, at 12 ("With improved data collection, law enforcement officials and prosecutors will be better able to make appropriate resource allocation decisions and to target specific neighborhoods or organizations for special attention.").

problem half solved.''[69] However, the logic of this observation is far from obvious. Moreover, its empirical validity is belied by the fact that crimes like murder, robbery, and burlary are not "half solved" despite the existence of national statistics on their occurrence for half a century.

The strategic value of crime statistics, especially hate crime statistics, seems small. The Hate Crime Statistics Act will provide information on the type of location of an incident, not the geographic location. An example best illustrates the weak connection between the data acquired and its use by law enforcement agencies to reduce hate crime. Suppose the UCR Section determines that there were nationwide 1,000 "anti-Arab" motivated burglaries committed by "American Indian/Alaskan Natives" at "rental storage facilities." It is not clear how this type of information could aid law enforcement. Is this a large or small number? In answering that question, does it matter that altogether there were 1,000 or 10,000, or 100,000 burglaries of rental storage facilities? Or, consider a finding of 5,000 "antimale homosexual" simple assaults at a "highway/road/alley/street," a more realistic profile of a hate crime. What does this statistic imply for preventive or investigative police strategies?

Admittedly, the actual geographic location of hate crimes will be known to each local police agency. However, it is still not clear whether, and if so, how local police could use such information. If hate crimes follow a geographic pattern, it might be possible to increase patrols, but the relation between patrol and crime rate is not great, if it exists at all. Furthermore, hate crimes, however defined, are still relatively rare events compared with the far more numerous intraracial and intragroup offenses. Moreover, in cities, where vulnerable minority groups (like gays and lesbians) are, to some extent, clustered in certain neighborhoods, this fact is already well known to police authori-

---

[69] Senate Hearings, note 7 *supra*, at 213 (1988). According to Col. Leonard Supinsky, who developed Baltimore County's hate crime data collection program, data collection is only one leg of a comprehensive approach to the hate crime problem. In Baltimore County, law enforcement goes beyond the traditional police role of "fighting crime." Police in Maryland are trained to participate in an integrated approach aimed at comforting victims of hate crimes, diffusing (even arbitrating) tense situations, easing community fear, demonstrating official concern, and so forth. The police work with school administrators, social workers, and other community leaders towards these goals. Telephone interview with Col. Leonard Supinski, Baltimore County Police Department (Apr. 16, 1992).

ties. Would knowing that 100 out of 200 or out of 2,000 assaults in such a neighborhood were motivated by homophobic prejudice have strategic significance for the police?

The offender-based data that will be collected under the Act is also unlikely to have any application to the design and implementation of practical law enforcement strategies. Oddly, no information about the offender's religion, ethnicity, national origin, or sexual orientation will even be coded. Only the number of offenders and their races will be reported.

We have been arguing that it is not at all obvious that police departments can come up with specialized responses to hate crime, and that even if they could, the number or rate of such crimes is probably not an important precondition. It must also be asked whether police would choose to redeploy resources to deter and solve hate crimes if this were possible. The Abt report noted that police administrators may be "[d]isinclin[ed] to divert resources from other law enforcement responsibilities—that is, competing priorities."[70] Very few police departments would choose, as New York City has, to create a specialized bias crime unit[71] and resources for particular types of police anticrime initiatives are unlikely to be made available. In 1991, the New York City Bias Unit recorded 540 bias crimes, of which 146 were assaults and three were murders.[72] However, there are almost that many asssaults and twice as many murders every day in New York City. Thus, how much priority should be given to hate crimes?[73]

While the New York City Police Department, the country's

---

[70] The other reasons police might be recalcitrant were:

Concern that collecting data on hate violence will be used against the department and against public officials either to damage the community's image, or to document a serious community problem which responsible authorities will be accused of having neglected; reluctance to saddle officers with increased paperwork, and; recognition of the complexities in determining motivation.

Abt Report, note 8 *supra*, at 15, 16.

[71] See Jacobs, "Rethinking the War on Hate Crime: A New York City Perspective," 11 J. Crim. Just. Ethics 55 (Summer/Fall 1992).

[72] N.Y. Times, Jan. 27, 1992, at B2, col. 1.

[73] It could be argued that bias crimes are more culpable and personally and socially damaging than other crimes, but a full discussion of these arguments is beyond the scope of this article. See Jacobs, "The Emergence and Implications of American Hate Crime Jurisprudence," 22 Israel Yearbook on Human Rights 39 (1992).

largest, has the resources to staff a specialized bias unit, most police departments could not afford to fashion such a specialized response.[74] In any event, hate crimes will likely be investigated the same way that other crimes are investigated, indeed the same way they would be investigated if they were dealt with as homicides, rapes, or robberies rather than as homicides, rapes, or robberies motivated by prejudice.

### The Use of Hate Crime Data by Policy Makers

The Senate Judiciary Committee Report on the Act stated that "[s]ystematic data about hate crimes would be useful . . . to policy makers at every level of government to better gauge the extent of the problem, and to local/community groups to direct their educational and similar efforts."[75] Representative John Conyers, Jr., testified before the Senate Subcommittee on the Constitution saying, "Public policy makers will find the data useful as it can provide them the basis for the development of educational programs designed to promote the understanding and tolerance of different races, cultures, and beliefs. The data can also provide the basis for enactment of new or enhanced criminal sanctions."[76]

For the reasons already discussed, the hate crime statistics generated by the Act will not be of much help in gauging the extent of the problem. Identifying hate crimes will be a highly subjective undertaking. This will probably result in severe undercounting, perhaps even far more severe than for other offenses. But even if, somehow, an accurate number of hate crimes could be determined, we would still not have a clue about how to evaluate "the extent of the problem." For hate crime to be considered a "big problem," how many would there have to be? The groups that pressured passage of the Act would probably respond that any hate crimes represent a serious problem. In a sense, that is true. But the question is whether national hate crime statistics will tell us something useful and important about American society.

---

[74] Law enforcement agencies considering implementing a specialized unit to handle hate crimes may be discouraged by the results in New York City that show that despite a special bias unit, "the number of bias cases in New York City has remained fairly steady over the last four years." N.Y. Times, Jan. 27, 1992, at B2, col. 1.

[75] S. Rep. No. 21, 101st Cong., 1st Sess. 3 (1989).

[76] Senate Hearings, note 7 *supra*, at 17.

The Act may serve the purpose of providing statistics that will impress legislatures with the gravity of the hate crime problem. (Of course, there is the possibility that the number of confirmed hate crimes will turn out to be smaller than the advocacy groups claimed.) However, Congress and the majority of state legislatures have already accepted the problem's existence.[77] Moreover, it is unclear how national hate crime data will aid the development of educational programs. The myriad and intractible problems of prejudice, hate, and intergroup relations are far too complex to be captured by hate crime statistics.[78] In addition to *hate crimes*, discrimination, hatred, prejudice, and intolerance are extremely serious problems, corrosive of the social and political order, and in need of farsighted, creative, and vigorous remediation.

### The Act's Symbolic Role

Perhaps the most important goal of the Hate Crime Statistics Act was to demonstrate government's concern over hate crimes. Thus, the Senate report states:

> The enactment of a Federal law requiring the systematic collection of hate crime data is a significant step. The very effort by the legislative branch to require the Justice Department to collect this information would send an additional important signal to victimized groups everywhere that the U.S. Government is concerned about this kind of crime.[79]

Interest groups for many religious, racial, ethnic, and sexual orientation blocs considered the Act a victory because it evinced congressional concern for their interests. The Act does not criminalize any hate activity, lead to any bias crime arrests, or extend the sentence of any offenders. Moreover, it does not set out a strategy for reducing hate and intolerance and for improving intergroup relations. The Act mandates the reporting and recording of hate crime incidents, but there is no likelihood that it

---

[77] At the state level, "almost every state in the nation has some form of hate crimes legislation." Hate Crime Statutes: A 1991 Status Report, ADL Law Report, Anti-Defamation League, at 1, 1991.

[78] See Jacobs, "The Emergence and Implications of American Hate Crime Jurisprudence," 22 Israel Yearbook on Human Rights 39 (1992) (discussing hate crime legislation since 1980, and examining the rationales for substantive hate crime laws). See also, Jacobs, The New Wave of American Hate Crime Legislation, 12 Inst. for Phil. & Pub. Policy 9 (1992).

[79] S. Rep. No. 21, 101st Cong., 1st Sess. 3 (1989).

will generate anything like an accurate picture of this species of conduct, even assuming that it has been satisfactorily defined. Congress could just as easily have demonstrated concern by passing a resolution condemning certain types of prejudice, or by establishing a national hate crime recognition week. Hate crimes are reprehensible and condemnable regardless of the frequency with which they occur.

## Conclusion

Crimes motivated by prejudice on the basis of religion, race, and sexual orientation are, like all crime, reprehensible and socially damaging. The Hate Crime Statistics Act, however, will add little, if anything, to preventing or solving this species of crime because of the tenuous relationships between crime statistics and law enforcement strategies, and between law enforcement strategies and crime rates. Even as an information gathering tool, the Act, though well-intentioned, has many deficiencies. Hate crimes defined in terms of motivation will be extremely difficult to identify and count reliably. Furthermore, the Act arbitrarily limits the covered hate motivations to those based on racial, ethnic, religious, and sexual orientation bias; many others, especially age, gender, and handicap, could easily be added to this list. Acquisition of accurate data will also be frustrated by inaccurate definitions of hate crimes, and by conflicting national, state, and local definitions of hate crimes. These problems make it certain that the Act will fail to produce an accurate or comprehensive picture of hate crime in America.

The House Judiciary Committee report on the Act stated, "[b]ecause exact data on such crimes is unavailable, we do not know whether there are geographical patterns to these crimes, who the main perpetrators are, or what individuals are most susceptible to attack."[80] The data collected under the Act will do little to answer these questions. Perhaps Congress's main goal in passing the Act was to demonstrate support for certain advocacy groups. The Act clearly serves that goal.[81] In that case, the

---

[80] H.R. Rep. No. 109. 101st Cong., 1st Sess. 3 (1989)

[81] Although Congress authorized the allocation of money for this effort, the UCR Section did not receive any additional funding or staffing specifically for hate crime data acquisition. Telephone interview with Bernie Dryden, Training Instructor, Uniform Crime Report Section, Fed. Bureau of Investigation (Apr. 1, 1992).

function of the Act was accurately summed up by Senator Chuck Grassley, who said, "This is part of a larger, and most disturbing trend in the legislative branch. We pass many bills calculated to make us 'feel good,' but without any standards or guidance to the Executive about how to execute them, or to the judiciary about how to interpret them."[82]

---

[82] S. Rep. No. 21, 101st Cong., 1st. Sess. 12 (1989).

# ECOLOGICAL AND BEHAVIORAL INFLUENCES ON PROPERTY VICTIMIZATION AT HOME: IMPLICATIONS FOR OPPORTUNITY THEORY

## JAMES P. LYNCH
## DAVID CANTOR

*The purpose of this article is to test criminal opportunity theories of victimization for the crimes of burglary and household larceny. Using the National Crime Survey and the Victim Risk Supplement, this test includes direct behavioral and ecological measures of concepts central to the theory. Ecological concepts are measured at several different levels of aggregation. Of particular importance is the introduction of a control for the dangerousness of the block in which the housing unit is located. Other ecological variables include (a) the environmental design of the housing unit (location, protective practices, single family versus other), (b) the degree of social disorganization in the neighborhood, (c) the location of commercial establishments in the neighborhood, and (d) the perceived dangerousness of the neighborhood. Measures of key behavioral concepts include (a) time spent in the house during the day, and (b) time spent in the house during the evening. None of the environmental design variables have a significant effect on victimization. The significance of the other ecological and behavioral measures differ by type of crime. These results are discussed in light of the importance of refining opportunity concepts, especially with respect to how they apply to different types of crime.*

For decades, the study of crime has focused almost exclusively on explaining criminal motivation. More recently, criminologists have shifted their focus to understanding why criminal events occur. This approach to the

This was truly a joint effort. The order in which the authors' names appear in this article was determined by the flip of a coin. This article was written under Grant 86-IJ-CX-0085 from the National Institute of Justice. The opinions expressed in this article are solely those of the authors and do not reflect the policy of NIJ. The data used in this article were made available by the Interuniversity Consortium for Political and Social Research. The NCS and VRS data were collected by

JOURNAL OF RESEARCH IN CRIME AND DELINQUENCY, Vol. 29 No. 3, August 1992 335-362
© 1992 Sage Publications, Inc.

study of crime has emphasized the identification of factors that afford the *opportunity* for criminal acts (Cohen and Felson 1979; Hindelang, Gottfredson, and Garafalo 1978; Clarke 1983; Cornish and Clarke 1986).

One of the principal attractions of opportunity theory is its potential to provide more practical guidance for crime control strategies than theories of offender motivation do. The former suggests that crime can be prevented by changing the victim or the target rather than by changing the behavior of the offender. On its face, opportunity seems more amenable to change than motivation.

Despite this practical and intuitive appeal, the theory remains too general and ill-defined to link particular behaviors with opportunity concepts. This lack of specificity is due largely to the limitations of empirical tests of the theory. Specifically, most empirical tests of opportunity theory have focused on the social structural correlates of victimization without taking into account the ecological contexts[1] in which these crimes occur and the behavior of the victim. More recently, work has been done that incorporates ecological context and specific behaviors into opportunity models (Sampson 1986; Hough 1987). The limitations of these models, however, still leave open the question of whether observed relationships between the sociodemographic characteristics of victims and victimization could be due to the behavior of the victim or to the ecological contexts in which they occur. Specifically, these models have often included only one ecological unit when several different levels may be required. This unit is often large and internally heterogeneous with respect to crime and opportunity. Moreover, the measures used to characterize areal units and persons with respect to opportunity are often only indirectly related to the concept. All of these limitations can result in misspecifying opportunity models.

In addition, empirical tests of opportunity theory have been used to predict the incidence of broad crime classes such as "violent crime" or "property crime" that include very heterogeneous events. It is unlikely that a single opportunity model can explain or predict these internally heterogeneous classes of crime. Variables that correlate with one component of the crime class may be negatively related to another. This will result in quantitative

the Census Bureau under the sponsorship of the Bureau of Justice Statistics (BJS). The sponsor, the collector, and the Consortium bear no responsibility for the analyses or the interpretations presented here. The authors would like to thank Richard Titus for his useful comments on earlier drafts of this article, Vicki Schneider for her help with the ICPSR data, David Naden for his assistance in preparing the segment-level files, and Norma Chapman for her general assistance throughout. Three anonymous reviewers provided very detailed and helpful comments.

models that are misspecified and have low explanatory power (Lynch 1987; Lynch and Biderman 1984). Constructing crime-specific models for explaining more narrowly defined classes of crime could improve our ability to predict and to understand victimization risk (Cornish and Clarke 1987).

This article attempts to refine opportunity theory further by building on previous models that included both measures of ecological context and behavioral measures of opportunity concepts. Specifically, several different levels of ecological context are included in the models tested here. Moreover, a new and particularly stringent control for the "dangerousness" of the ecological context is used in this model in order to provide a more conservative test of the effects of behavioral variables net of ecological context. Finally, separate analyses are done for burglary and household larceny to see if different opportunity models predict the occurrence of different subclasses of property crime. This approach to multilevel analysis is not necessarily superior to those that have been taken heretofore, it complements them. If our findings differ substantially from those of previous work in the area, then we will know that the limitations of previous multilevel models affect substantive results. If our findings do not differ from those of earlier multilevel models, then the appropriateness of these models will be confirmed.

## THE OPPORTUNITY MODEL

Opportunity theories are rooted in the work of urban geographers (Jacobs 1961; Newman 1972) who contend that environmental-design factors may deter or prevent offenders from choosing particular targets for crime. This tradition later developed into what is now known as "environmental criminology" (Brantingham and Brantingham 1981; Jeffery 1977). The opportunity perspective was not integrated into a comprehensive theory of crime causation, however, until the late 1970s, when several different groups of researchers began analyzing victimization data in the United States and other countries (Hindelang et al. 1978; Cohen and Felson 1979; Cohen, Kluegel, and Land 1981; Sparks, Genn, and Dodd 1977; Van Dijk and Steinmetz 1983).

Cohen and Felson (1979) presented a formal version of this theory to explain the occurrence of criminal events. The basic assumption of their model was that these events depend on the coincidence of: (a) a motivated offender, (b) a suitable crime target, and (c) absence of a capable guardian. Cohen et al. (1981) went a bit further in refining the concept of target suitability by dividing it into four dimensions:

1.  Target exposure—The visibility and physical accessibility of the target.
2.  Guardianship—The ability of persons or objects to prevent crime from occurring.
3.  Target attractiveness—The material or symbolic value of persons or property.
4.  Proximity—The physical distance between potential targets and populations of potential offenders.

The first generation of empirical tests of opportunity theory were designed to test the plausibility of the general approach to understanding the occurrence of crime. Sociodemographic characteristics of respondents and gross activity measures such as labor force participation, were used to measure opportunity concepts (Cohen and Cantor 1981; Cohen et al. 1981; Hindelang et al. 1978). The second generation of empirical tests used more direct behavioral measures of opportunity concepts (Lynch 1987; Hough 1987; Gottfredson 1984). Questions were asked about respondents' behaviors that placed them in situations rather than inferring behavior and situations from social status. Although both of these traditions seemed to support the general utility of the opportunity approach, they did not include extensive measures of ecological context.[2]

Some question was raised about the relative importance of behavioral determinants of opportunity and ecological contexts by comparative case studies of communities and neighborhoods. In these studies, behavioral measures of opportunity concepts such as time out of the home had little or no effect on victimization when area was held constant (Greenberg et al. 1982). However, the small number of people interviewed in each community and the atypical areas chosen raised some doubts about the accuracy and generalizability of these results.

More recently, tests of opportunity theory that include both behavioral measures of opportunity concepts and ecological context have been done with large, nationally representative samples of persons (Cantor and Lynch 1988; Sampson and Wooldredge 1987; Hough 1987; McDowell, Loftin, and Wersima 1989).[3] They suggest that both ecological context and behavioral variables affect risk of victimization.

Although these multilevel opportunity models are useful, only a very few studies have employed such models. The problems inherent in obtaining both ecological- and individual-level data inhibit the broad-based use of this approach. Moreover, the particular strengths and weaknesses of the available data on individuals and areas raise some questions about the utility of these models for assessing the relative affect of opportunity variables on risk. The specific problems with previous models incorporating ecological context are discussed in the following section.

## ESTIMATING MODELS OF VICTIMIZATION WITH ECOLOGICAL CONTEXT

Models of victimization risk that have included ecological variables have two major problems that limit their utility in refining opportunity theory. The first involves the quality of the data on ecological units. Most models use only one areal unit when there is good reason to suspect that opportunity dimensions, including proximity, may be affected by factors operating at different levels of aggregation, for example, block, neighborhood, and community (Taylor and Gottfredson 1986). Moreover, the ecological units used have been large and often internally heterogeneous with respect to opportunity dimensions. This lessens the accuracy of the data as a descriptor of the particular area. The second problem involves the quality of the measures of opportunity dimensions at the household or individual level. The information used to measure concepts such as exposure or guardianship is often not directly related to the behavior or conditions included under that concept. To the extent that inadequate measurement has affected empirical tests of opportunity theory, the influence of opportunity variables may not be properly identified.

### Choosing One Ecological Unit

There is considerable debate over the appropriate ecological unit for the study of crime. Ecological studies of offender residences have used communities, "natural areas," census tracts, and blocks (Shannon with McKim, Curry, and Haffner 1988; Bursik and Webb 1982; Schuerman and Kobrin 1983). It is not surprising that such debates rage given that many of the factors known to be related to crime can be expected to vary across different ecological units. Physical design features such as access to the residence, amount of through traffic, building structure, proximity to commercial areas, and population density vary by block and subblock areas. Some aspects of the social organization of areas vary at the neighborhood level. The level of economic resources tends to vary by neighborhood units as does the level of political organization (Hunter 1974) and neighborhood image (Taub, Taylor, and Dunham 1984; Stark 1987). Given this variation then, no one level of ecology should be entirely adequate for use in models predicting victimization risk.

*Size and Heterogeneity of the Areal Unit Chosen*

A number of studies have included two levels of aggregation in analyzing household victimization risk—neighborhood and household. One important problem in prior research has been the size and variable operational definition of neighborhood. In analyses using the National Crime Survey (NCS) data, neighborhoods were defined as four contiguous enumeration districts (Sampson, Castellano, and Laub 1981; Cohen et al. 1981). In some cases this could be an area consistent with the concept of neighborhood, whereas in others it could be much larger and more heterogeneous. Because crimes vary substantially across small areas, the size (and variability) of the census's definition of "neighborhood" could be a real impediment to the use of these data in multilevel models. Aggregating data into a unit consisting of four contiguous enumeration districts may mask areal differences at the neighborhood level and lead to a misspecification of neighborhood effects. Analyses done with the British Crime Survey (BCS) clustered observations within "electoral wards" of approximately 5,000 people, including about 50 respondents within each ward (Sampson and Wooldredge 1987). Although this definition of an ecological unit does not vary, as in the NCS, it may be too large to characterize neighborhoods adequately.

Smith and Janjoura (1989) conducted an analysis of burglary victimization using 57 neighborhoods in three different SMSAs. Their definition of a neighborhood comes the closest to capturing ecological variation that is specifically linked to a theoretically meaningful unit.[4] As with the two studies cited above, however, the unit chosen may be too heterogeneous to capture variation at lower levels of aggregation. The average size of a neighborhood was 1.5 square miles. This is extremely large in light of the substantial variation in crime rates at the block or block group level.

*Using Structural Attributes to Measure*
*Opportunity Concepts at the Areal Level*

The ecological units used in empirical models are often characterized by aggregated social structural characteristics of their residents (Hough 1987; Sampson and Wooldredge 1987; Smith and Janjoura 1989). The density of motivated offenders in an area, for example, may be measured by the proportion of the adult population that is unemployed. Although this indicator of the density of motivated offenders makes sense, it does not completely measure the concept. Generally, social structural attributes of persons are not highly correlated with offending. Aggregating these attributes of persons to

144

characterize areas will not produce good ecological measures of proximity. The same general argument can be made for other opportunity concepts such as attractiveness or guardianship.

Using aggregated sociodemographic characteristics of residents to describe the level and type of criminal opportunity in areas can be more or less damaging depending on the purpose of the analysis. If the intent is to determine which attributes of areas affect the opportunity for victimization, then the incompleteness of these measures may not be a problem. If the errors in measurement are reasonably random then the relative effects of areal characteristics on victimization risk may not be affected. If, however, the intent is to test the effects of individual-level factors after all of the effects of ecological factors are held constant, then the incompleteness of the measures can be a more substantial problem. To the extent that the effects of ecological factors are understated due to measurement error, the effects of individual level variables can be overstated.

### Limited Range of Opportunity Variables
### at the Household and Individual Level

The number and variety of behavioral measures of opportunity concepts have also inhibited the testing of opportunity theory. The social roles or statuses of respondents are often used to measure key opportunity concepts. Exposure, for example, is measured by a person's major activity. Persons working are considered higher on exposure than persons who keep house (Cohen et al. 1981). This distinction does not completely differentiate the exposed from the unexposed. We know that there is considerable variation in exposure within the work force, such that persons with certain jobs are more exposed than those with others (Block, Felson, and Block 1984; Lynch 1987; Collins, Cox, and Langan 1986). Moreover, the use of social roles and statuses as measures of opportunity concepts is also unsatisfying because these indicators lack the specificity necessary to interpret the relationships observed. Although major activity has been interpreted as an indicator of time outside of the home on the job, it could as easily be interpreted as a measure of the vitality of a person's social life and therefore the exposure of a person or a measure of the volume of goods that a person has and therefore the attractiveness of a person as a crime target.

More recent tests of opportunity theory, including some multilevel models, have used more direct and specific measures of opportunity concepts (Maxfield 1987; Sampson and Wooldredge 1987; Miethe, Stafford, and Long 1987; Gottfredson 1984). While this movement to greater directness and specificity in measuring opportunity concepts is a step in the right direction, it has been quite modest. At most, four or five survey questions have been used to measure several major opportunity concepts. Given the complexity and variety of routine activities and social contexts that can affect opportunity, much more information would be required to claim that we have adequately measured this variety. Moreover, some factors affecting opportunity such as the physical design of structures and areas have been routinely excluded from models altogether.[5] To the extent that opportunity concepts are poorly or incompletely measured at the individual level, the resulting multilevel models may overestimate the effect of ecological factors on the risk of victimization.

### Predicting Broad Crime Classes

Empirical tests of opportunity theories have been complicated by the need to balance precision in measurement with considerations of sampling error and sample size. Defining very narrow classes of crime will increase the internal homogeneity of crime categories and thereby reduce measurement error. This, in turn, will improve the predictive power of empirical models. Empirical tests of opportunity models, however, have often used broad crime classes such as "property" or "violent" crime. This has been done to increase the number of crime incidents available for analysis. Crime is a rare event and even large-scale victimization surveys like the NCS and the BCS identify a relatively small number. To further reduce this number by defining narrow, but more internally homogeneous, classes of crime severely limits our ability to conduct multivariate analyses.

Some compromise must be reached between the requirements of good measurement and of multivariate analysis. One approach would involve testing crime-specific opportunity models using crime classifications somewhat narrower than property crime and violent crime. If these tests are conducted using the same data, then comparisons of the result would indicate whether the same opportunity models predict specific crime classes equally well. If that is the case, there is no need to distinguish these crime classes in subsequent analyses.

### Summary

The foregoing should not be interpreted as an indictment of previous empirical tests of opportunity theory that involve multilevel models. However, the issues noted raise legitimate doubts about the findings of previous research. Many of these doubts may be unfounded or unresolvable, but the only way to remove these doubts is to conduct analyses that examine previous results using somewhat different approaches to the problems outlined above. This is the intent of this analysis.

## DATA AND METHOD

The following analysis takes a different approach to including ecological context in opportunity models than those used heretofore. Specifically, this analysis incorporates a number of different levels of geography into the model, including municipality, neighborhood, block, and housing unit levels. As part of this strategy, the model includes measures of opportunity concepts and "dangerousness" at a very small level of geography. This is done by taking advantage of the cluster design of the NCS to generate indicators at the block or "segment level." Segments are clusters of four housing units that serve as the ultimate sampling unit in the NCS sample. In addition, the models estimated here draw on the Victim Risk Supplement (VRS) to provide many more specific measures of opportunity dimensions than previous multilevel models. These innovations should provide useful tests of (a) the affects of attributes of areas of different sizes on opportunity and (b) the relative affects of ecological context and individual behavioral measures of opportunity concepts on victimization risk. Finally, opportunity models are used to predict two subclasses of property crime—burglary and household larceny. The results are compared and similarities and differences are highlighted.

### Data Base and Logic of Analysis

The analysis is based on data from a supplement to the NCS.[6] The VRS was a special supplement to the NCS conducted in February of 1984. As part of this supplement, approximately 10,000 housing units were interviewed. The purpose of the supplement was to collect detailed information on factors commonly thought to influence the probability of victimization.

Logistic regression was used to test the hypotheses that are supported in previous research (see Table 1). This statistical method was used because of the skewed distribution of household victimization in the sample. Even though the VRS contains approximately 10,000 responding households, the infrequent nature of household victimization does not yield a large number of incidents to analyze.

Given the small number of victimizations available for analysis, the multilevel models were estimated with several restrictions in order to pre-

**TABLE 1:    Summary of Hypotheses Supported in Previous Empirical Tests**

1. The greater the distance from the central city, the lower the risk of household victimization.
2. Risk of household victimization is directly related to the disorderly appearance of the neighborhood that the unit is in.
3. The greater the amount of commercial activity in the area, the higher the probability of household victimization.
4. The greater the frequency that neighbors watch each other's housing units, the lower the risk of household victimization.
5. The closer the unit is to the residences of potential offenders, the higher the risk of household victimization.
6. The number of units in a structure should be inversely related to risk of household victimization, especially household larceny.
7. The greater the visibility of the unit, the greater the risk of household victimization.
8. The more security measures taken in a housing unit, the less the risk of household victimization.
9. The amount of time the unit is occupied is inversely related to risk of household victimization.

serve statistical power. First, all higher-order interactions were assumed to be zero. Second, equations were estimated in three different stages. The first equation was a bivariate model that included the opportunity variable that is hypothesized to affect the dependent variable. The second equation introduced household-level sociodemographic controls (i.e., age, race, and marital status of head of household). By comparing the results of this to the bivariate model, the importance of opportunity variables could be assessed after individual characteristics are taken into account. The third equation added the control for dangerousness of the block as described in the following section.

*Measuring Variables in the Model*

DANGEROUSNESS OF THE AREA

To create the measure of dangerousness, we formed a five-category typology using crime rates from the VRS segments. This typology included five categories of area types:

1.   urban areas with high violence and property crime rates
2.   urban areas with high property crime rates

148

3.  urban areas with low crime rates
4.  rural areas
5.  other areas

The distinctions between urban (categories 1-3), rural (category 4), and other (category 5) areas reflect procedural differences in the construction of segments in the NCS. Urban segments are formed on the basis of grouping four contiguous housing units in an urban area. Units within a rural segment may be adjacent but not proximate to each other. Other segments represent a residual category that includes units that have been built since the 1970 census and "special places" (rooming houses, group quarters). The units within this last category are not likely to be proximate or adjacent.

These differences in the structure of segments are important for two reasons. First, they make necessary substantive distinctions between urban and rural segments. In rural areas the meaning of neighborhood or "block" is not as clear as it is for urban areas. In addition, the rural segments are not designed to necessarily include households that are in the same small area. Rather, they are structured to include all housing units that are on the same large area of land. Second, the "other" segments represent a mix of units that does not constitute a homogeneous category. For both of these reasons, it was important to treat both rural and "other" segments as different from urban segments in the typology.[7]

The three categories of urban segments were formed using the following procedure:

1.  NCS data from 1979 through 1983 were used to aggregate victimization reports for the entire 3.5 years that each segment was in sample.
2.  The aggregated victimization rates were used to construct four different crime rates for the segment: serious violent crime, personal theft away from home, burglary, and household larceny.[8]
3.  The rates computed in step 2 above were dichotomized at the median. These variables were entered in to a latent class analysis (McCutcheon 1987) that produced three "types" of urban segments.[9]
4.  Victimization rates were computed using the VRS segments by aggregating all data for the entire time period that the segment was in sample (excluding the month when the VRS was actually conducted).
5.  Using the typology from the latent class analysis computed with the 1979-1983 data, the VRS segments[10] were classified into the three types computed in step 3.[11]

The three urban classes created from the latent class analysis are viewed as representing three distinct area types. The first are areas with extremely high crime rates, including serious violent crime. Individuals living in this area are those who are most proximate to offenders. This is based on the assumption that violent crimes tend to be clustered within a relatively short distance from the offender's home. The second type represents an area with extremely high property crime rates. This is interpreted as an area with either property that was attractive to steal or where there was high exposure and/or low guardianship of property. The third (and most prevalent) type is composed of the segments with relatively low crime rates.

### MEASURES OF CRIMINAL OPPORTUNITY

The measures of criminal opportunity were divided into four different levels of analysis: (a) municipal, (b) neighborhood, (c) segment, and (d) unit.

*Municipality*. Municipality was used to supplement the segment typology by indicating whether or not the unit is located in a central city (hypothesis 1). Because the typology has an urban-rural break, the introduction of municipality further distinguishes between the suburbs and central city.

*Neighborhood characteristics*. The neighborhood indicators are based on a series of items from the VRS that pertain to the 2-3 block area around the respondent's home. Three measures were created for the analysis at this level. The first is a measure of residential proximity of offenders to the housing unit (hypothesis 5). It is based on a VRS item that asked each respondent, age 16 years or older, whether crime in the area was committed largely by persons within or outside the area (VRS-3, question 24). Those claiming that there was no crime in the neighborhood or that crime in the area was committed by outsiders received a score of 1, those claiming that half of the crimes were committed by residents received a score of 2, and those claiming all the crime was committed by residents were given a score of 3. A mean of this score was taken across all respondents in the segment. This mean was used in the analysis.

The second variable provides an indicator of the amount of commercial activity in the area (hypothesis 3). This was measured by using the item that asked whether there were any convenience stores, grocery stores, bars, fast food restaurants or liquor stores in the neighborhood (VRS-3, question 20a). The total number of such places was computed for each respondent answering the question. A mean of this sum was then computed for all persons interviewed in the segment.

The third neighborhood variable is an indicator of the degree of "disorderly appearance" (hypothesis 2). It was measured by interviewer observation of the presence of litter or trash. Because it was measured by observation, it is available only for housing units where a personal interview was administered. This constitutes about half of the sample.[12]

*Segment level.* In addition to the primary control at the segment level, that is, the segment typology, a second indicator was created that measures the amount of guardianship exerted by immediate neighbors (hypothesis 4). The VRS contained an item that asked one respondent in each household whether "neighbors watch one another's place when no-one is at home" (VRS-3, item 23). This variable was scored a 2 if the answer to this question was "yes," a 1 if it was "sometimes," and 0 if it was "no." The mean of this variable across all units in the segment was then used to represent guardianship by neighbors within the block.

*Housing-unit characteristics.* The third level of aggregation is for characteristics of the housing unit. The model included two characteristics of the housing unit—the physical structure of the unit and the activities of the members of the household. Three different measures of the physical structure were used. The first is whether the structure is a single-family residence or not (hypotheses 6 and 7).

The second measure was a combination of several VRS items that examined the exposure of the structure from the street (hypothesis 7). Interviewers were asked to report on: (a) the distance from the road to the unit, (b) whether the unit was visible from the road and (c) the speed limit of the nearest road (VRS-4, items 9, 10, and 12). These variables were all measured on ordinal scales. The distance and speed-limit scales ranged from 1 to 4. The visibility scale ranged from 1 to 3. To form the variable used in the analysis, the mean of these three scales was taken for each housing unit.[13]

The third measure was whether the household had taken any security measures to protect the unit or valuables (hypothesis 9). These included whether there was a burglar alarm, guard dog, guns/firearms, or valuables that had been marked (VRS-3, items 21a, 21b, 21c, and 21d). The mean number of measures in each housing unit was used in the analysis.[14]

Two different activity variables were constructed (hypothesis 10). The first represented the amount of time household members spent outside of the home during the day. This was measured using VRS items that separately asked about work, school, and shopping activities for all persons that were at least 16 years old (VRS-1, item 32c; VRS-3, items 16a, 16c, and 18a). Each of these employed a scale that ranged from 1 to 5.[15] The mean of each of these variables was taken across all persons in the household. The sum of these means for each activity measure was then computed for each household and used in the analysis. A second scale measured occupancy during the evening. This was constructed in a similar way using the number of times each household member 16 years of age or older worked at night, went to school at night, or engaged in leisure activities at night (VRS-3 15d, 16g, 17a).[16] The variable used in the analysis was the mean of these variables over all persons in the household.

### DEMOGRAPHICS OF HOUSEHOLD

The demographic characteristics include: (a) age of the head of the household, (b) whether the head of the household is married, and (c) whether the head of the household is White.[17] All three of these variables have been used in previous analyses as proxies for different types of opportunity structures (Cohen et al. 1981; Cohen and Cantor 1981; Hindelang et al. 1978). Households with heads who are young, unmarried, and non-White should have a higher probability of being victimized.

### DEPENDENT VARIABLES

Burglary and household larceny are the two dependent variables. Larceny involves theft from both around and inside the home. Burglary requires that the theft be from the home (or a building on the property) and involve unlawful entry. These types of crime were chosen because they are prevalent and because they occur at or near the home where the NCS provides useful measures of the social context of victimization. For purposes of the analysis, these two variables were dichotomized into two categories: (a) no crime reported for the 6-month reference period and (b) at least one crime reported for the 6-month reference period.

## RESULTS

The means, standard deviations, and sample sizes for all variables in the models are displayed in Table 2. The results of the logistic regressions for burglary and home larceny are displayed in Tables 3 and 4, respectively. In Tables 3 and 4, each column represents one of the three equations estimated for each of the opportunity variables included in the model. Column 1 provides estimates for the bivariate equation that only includes the opportunity variable listed in the table. Column 2 is for the equation that includes the opportunity variable and the sociodemographic controls. Column 3 provides the full model with the opportunity variable, the sociodemographics and the segment-level typology.

152

**TABLE 2: Descriptive Statistics for Variables Included in Logistic Regression Equations**

| | N | Percentage in Category | Minimum | Maximum | Mean | Standard Deviation |
|---|---|---|---|---|---|---|
| **Controls** | | | | | | |
| Age of head of household | 9,553[a] | — | 15 | 99[a] | 47.7 | 17.7 |
| Marital status of head of household | | | | | | |
| Married | 5,541[a] | 58 | — | — | — | — |
| Not married | 4,012 | 42 | — | — | — | — |
| Residential location | | | | | | |
| Urban, high violent crime rate | 478[a] | 5 | — | — | — | — |
| Urban, high property crime rate | 1,337 | 14 | — | — | — | — |
| Urban, low crime rate | 3,248 | 34 | — | — | — | — |
| Rural | 2,484 | 26 | — | — | — | — |
| Other | 2,006 | 21 | — | — | — | — |
| **Opportunity** | | | | | | |
| City type | | | | | | |
| Central city | 2,768 | 29 | — | — | — | — |
| Not central city | 6,778 | 71 | — | — | — | — |
| Trash and litter | 7,493 | — | 0 | 1 | 0.28 | 0.40 |
| Commercial establishment | 9,553 | — | 1 | 5 | 2.02 | 1.44 |
| Offender within neighborhood | 9,341 | — | 0 | 3 | 1.32 | 0.61 |

*(continued)*

**TABLE 2 Continued**

| | N | Percentage in Category | Minimum | Maximum | Mean | Standard Deviation |
|---|---|---|---|---|---|---|
| Neighbors watch house | 9,552 | — | 0 | 3 | 2.39 | 0.63 |
| Unit type | | | | | | |
| Multiple-unit structure | 3,243 | 34 | — | — | — | — |
| Single-family structure | 6,294 | 66 | — | — | — | — |
| Visibility from street | 5,657 | — | 3 | 11 | 6.11 | 1.60 |
| Internal security | 9,471 | — | 0 | 36 | 2.84 | 7.65 |
| Occupancy during day | 9,233 | — | −5.81 | 7.68 | 0.03 | 1.87 |
| Occupancy during night | 9,242 | — | −3.46 | 10.25 | 0.05 | 1.98 |
| Dependent | | | | | | |
| Burglary victimization | | | | | | |
| Not victim | 9,259[a] | 97 | — | — | — | — |
| Victim | 294 | 3 | — | — | — | — |
| Household larceny victimization | | | | | | |
| Not victim | 9,101 | 95 | — | — | — | — |
| Victim | 452[a] | 5 | — | — | — | — |

a. Sample size computed using the maximum number of cases available for analysis (N = 9,553). The number used to estimate equations depends on the opportunity variable included in the model.

154

TABLE 3:    Unstandardized Logistic Effect Parameters for Selected Opportunity
            Variables on Burglary by Whether Demographic and Residential
            Controls Are in the Model

| | Controls Introduced | | | |
| | None | Demographics[a] | Segment Danger[b] | N[c] |
|---|---|---|---|---|
| Municipal | | | | |
|   Central city | .45* | .37* | .11 | 9,546 |
| Neighborhood | | | | |
|   Trash and litter | .66* | .53* | .30* | 7,493 |
|   Commercial establishments | .17* | .11* | .05 | 9,553 |
|   Offender within neighborhood | .36* | .26* | .16*** | 9,341 |
| Segment (immediate neighbors) | | | | |
|   Neighbors watch houses | −.24* | −.15*** | −.10 | 9,552 |
| Housing unit | | | | |
|   Single-family structure | −.32* | .04 | .09 | 9,537 |
|   Visibility from street | −.04 | −.13 | −.03 | 5,657 |
|   Internal security | .0 | .0 | .0 | 9,471 |
|   Occupancy during day | .07** | −.01 | .01 | 9,233 |
|   Occupancy during night | .14* | .07** | .08* | 9,242 |

a. Includes age of head and marital status of head.
b. Also includes age and marital status.
c. Represents sample size with opportunity, demographics, and residential location variables in the equation.
*$p < .01$; **$p < .05$; ***$p < .10$.

The results for each of the opportunity variables is discussed by level of aggregation. Only the coefficients for the opportunity variables are discussed. Unless specifically mentioned, the effects of the sociodemographic controls and the segment typology remained significant and in the expected direction for all of the equations displayed in Tables 3 and 4.

### Municipal and Neighborhood Level

The results for central city are similar for both burglary and household larceny. The effect of central city is significant and positive in both the bivariate model and when the sociodemographics are included. It drops to insignificance, however, once the segment typology is introduced.

The effects of neighborhood disorganization (trash and litter) differ slightly for burglary and household larceny. In both cases, this variable is positively related to risk in the bivariate model and after sociodemographic variables are controlled. This relationship is substantially reduced, however,

TABLE 4:    Unstandardized Logistic Effect Parameters for Selected Opportunity
Variables on Household Larceny by Whether Demographic and
Residential Controls Are in the Model

| | Controls Introduced | | | |
|---|---|---|---|---|
| | None | Demographics[a] | Segment Danger[b] | N[c] |
| **Municipal** | | | | |
| Central city | .36* | .31* | .01 | 9,546 |
| **Neighborhood** | | | | |
| Trash and litter | .47* | .39* | .17 | 7,493 |
| Commercial establishments | .18* | .15* | .07** | 9,553 |
| Offender within neighborhood | .38* | .30* | .20* | 9,341 |
| **Segment (immediate neighbors)** | | | | |
| Neighbors watch houses | −.03 | .05 | .09 | 9,552 |
| **Housing unit** | | | | |
| Single-family structure | −.25* | −.01 | .00 | 9,537 |
| Visibility from street | −.06*** | −.05 | −.02 | 5,657 |
| Internal security | −.01 | −.01 | −.01 | 9,471 |
| Occupancy during day | .13* | .05*** | .06 | 9,233 |
| Occupancy during night | .09* | 0 | −.01 | 9,242 |

a. Includes age of head and marital status of head.
b. Also includes age and marital status.
c. Represents sample size with opportunity, demographics, and residential location variables in the equation.
*$p < .01$; **$p < .05$; ***$p < .10$.

once the segment typology is introduced. For burglary, neighborhood disorganization remains significant across all three equations estimated. For household larceny, however, this variable drops to insignificance after the segment typology is introduced.

The effect of commercial activity in the neighborhood also differs across each type of crime. For both crimes, this variable is significantly positive in the bivariate case and when the demographics are introduced into the equation. For burglary, the effect drops to insignificance once the typology is introduced. For household larceny, it remains significant after the typology is introduced.

The final neighborhood-level variable, the source of offenders, is significant for both types of crimes. This result provides evidence that segments or blocks may be too small as units to measure the proximity to potential offenders. Larger areas, at least as large as a 2- to 3-block area, may be necessary to measure the influence of living proximate to residences of motivated offenders.[18]

*Segment Level*

The extent to which neighbors watch each other's homes does have a significant effect on burglary, but not household larceny. For burglary, this variable is significant after controlling for the demographic characteristics of household. Not surprisingly, it completely drops out of the model when the segment typology is introduced. This suggests that guardianship at the block level is related to risk of burglary. This variable has no effect on household larceny, however. The bivariate relationship is not significant and this does not change after introducing the other controls.

It is difficult to interpret the effects of introducing the segment typology on the relationship between neighbors watching houses and burglary victimization because the temporal order of the variables is ambiguous. If we assume that the dangerousness of the area (as indicated by the segment typology) occurs in time prior to current watching practices, then the fact that the relationship between watching and victimization decreases when the segment typology is introduced suggests that the effect of watching is spurious. The level of watching has no effect on victimization risk. High levels of watching occur in safe areas, but watching itself has no effect on risk. If, however, we assume that the current level of watching in a block is a function of longer term patterns of surveillance, then we cannot say that persistent patterns of risk in a block occur before current surveillance practices. If this is the case, then we cannot say that the level of watching does not affect burglary risk. Rather, it would be more plausible to interpret these findings as indicating that high levels of surveillance are one of the attributes of low crime areas that keeps crime low.

*Housing-Unit Characteristics*

The variables at the housing-unit level provide mixed support for several basic-opportunity hypotheses. None of the environmental-design variables seem to be significant after introducing the demographic controls. This is the case for both burglary and household larceny. The number of units in the structure has a significant bivariate relationship indicating that multiunit dwellings have higher rates of victimization than single unit dwellings. After controlling for demographic variables, however, this drops to insignificance. It stays insignificant when the segment typology is introduced. Similarly, the accessibility of the unit to the street drops to insignificance when the typology is introduced into the model. The relationships found prior to controlling for the typology seem to be due to the fact that housing units with these characteristics are generally located in dangerous areas. After controlling for this fact with the residential typology, the effects disappear.

The effects of internal security measures are insignificant in the bivariate as well as in the multivariate models. Taking one or more of the security measures tested here does not have statistically significant effects on victimization risk.

The opportunity variables that measure the amount of activity out of the home by unit residents indicate different effects for each type of crime. For burglary, occupancy during the day has a significant bivariate relationship with victimization. This drops to insignificance, however, after introducing the demographic controls. The extent that the unit is occupied during the evening does have a significant effect on risk even after the segment typology is introduced. The opposite pattern occurs for household larceny. Daytime occupancy has a significant effect on risk, while that of nighttime occupancy has no effect at all.

## DISCUSSION

This analysis has a number of implications for refining opportunity theories of victimization. First, it suggests that ecological factors that affect the risk of household property crime operate at different levels of aggregation. Some elements of opportunity are a function of neighborhood, for example, whereas others are functions of blocks. Second, a number of the hypothesized relationships between victimization and opportunity variables measured at the unit level persist even after strict controls are employed for the dangerousness of the social context at the segment level. Perhaps just as importantly, several of the hypotheses were not significant. Third, different opportunity models predict burglary and household larceny.

### The Need for Multiple Levels of Geography

Because the foregoing analyses included several levels of geography, it was possible to assess the effect of factors at one level while holding constant the characteristics of larger or smaller areas. The fact that the effect of central city residence (hypothesis 1) becomes insignificant when the dangerousness of the block is held constant supports the belief that victimization risk varies substantially within central cities. This calls into question the utility of using units as large as a city in modeling risk at the household level. Several attributes of neighborhoods—the level of community disorganization (hypothesis 2), the presence of establishments that attract outsiders (hypothesis 3), and whether offenders are from the neighborhood (hypothesis 5)—have a significant effect on the risk of burglary and larceny even when the dangerousness of the block is held constant. This suggests that neighborhoods affect the degree of guardianship exercised, the degree to which residents are exposed and the proximity to offenders, independently of factors that may be operating at the block level.

These results are consistent with models of hierarchical target selection outlined by Taylor and Gottfredson (1986). This perspective contends that offenders choose targets by selecting smaller areas within larger areas in a sequential fashion until they ultimately choose a particular household. A particular area of the city will be chosen, for example, and then a neighborhood, and within a neighborhood, a block. The fact that attributes of neighborhoods and blocks have independent effects on the risk of property victimization at home is consistent with a selection process that considers multiple levels of geography. Because our sample was not large enough to support tests of interactions between levels of geography, we could not explicitly test the hierarchical nature of the selection process.

### The Importance of Opportunity Variables

These results support the contention that opportunity variables other than proximity affect risk of victimization. Significant effects on victimization were found for occupancy (guardianship; hypothesis 10), the presence of establishments (exposure and guardianship; hypothesis 3) and community disorganization (guardianship; hypothesis 2).[19] The fact that the effects of these variables are not reduced to zero when the segment level typology is introduced, provides solid support for opportunity theory in general. The segment typology is a particularly conservative control for the dangerousness of the immediate social context. Because indicators of guardianship, exposure, and attractiveness at the unit level still have an effect on victimization when this conservative measure of proximity is used, we cannot say that opportunity is a function of social context. The behaviors of individuals that influence their exposure, guardianship, and attractiveness affect their risk of victimization.

The results provide no support for the selected environmental-design hypotheses tested. Building structure, the accessibility of the unit, and internal security measures have no effect on either type of crime (hypotheses 6, 7, and 8). When simply examining the bivariate models, multiple unit dwellings have higher rates of crime than single units. Once the demographics are introduced, however, the effect goes to zero. This suggests that it is the distribution of persons across types of housing that produces the relationship between housing structure and risk.

Taking one or more steps to increase the security of your unit, such as having locks or alarms, does not seem to affect the risk of burglary (hypothesis 9). These results must be treated with some caution, however. It may be that scaling security measures in the way we did combined effective and ineffective security measures in a way that masked the effect of a particular device or action. Also, having security devices is quite different from *using* these devices (Scarr 1973). There can also be qualitative differences in security devices, such as locks, that could explain the fact that these measures have no affect on the risk of burglary. Although all of these factors could explain the observed results, our analyses contribute to a growing literature that finds no effect of security measures on the risk of burglary. This suggests that the burden of proof must shift from demonstrating that these actions have no effect to showing empirically that they do.

### Need for Separate Models for Burglary and Household Larceny

These results also provide important information on differences in the effects of criminal opportunities on the incidence of burglary and household larceny. Our findings suggest that household larceny is largely a function of exposure, whereas burglary is more a function of guardianship.

For household larceny, the presence of establishments in the neighborhood (exposure) is significant, but the level of disorganization (guardianship) is not. The extent to which neighbors on the block watch each other's homes (guardianship) does not affect risk of household larceny. Daytime occupancy (guardianship) reduces the risk of household larceny, but nighttime occupancy (guardianship) does not. All of these results support the notion that larceny is more dependent on simple exposure and less dependent on the other dimensions of opportunity such as guardianship.

Guardianship is a more important factor in determining the risk of burglary than it is for household larceny. For burglary, the level of social disorganization in the community (guardianship) affects the risk of victimization, but the presence of commercial establishments (exposure) does not. The extent to which neighbors on the block watch each other's homes (guardianship) does affect the risk of burglary but not the risk of larceny. Although occupancy during the day (guardianship) does not influence the risk of burglary, occupancy during the night (guardianship) does reduce risk.

The image that emerges from these results is that household larceny is the quintessential crime of opportunity, whereas burglary is somewhat more planned or complex. The more people who pass by household property (the greater the exposure) the greater the chance of it being stolen. Because household larceny involves theft of property outside the home, potential offenders are more likely to be exposed to potential targets during the day, when it can be plainly seen. If household members are present during the day, they can clarify ambiguities in ownership and supervise people who pass by during the course of their routine activities. Burglary is less dependent on simple exposure because the potential targets are generally concealed within a housing unit. The sheer number of persons passing by therefore does not substantially increase exposure. In addition, guardianship can be exerted by watchful neighbors because of the unambiguous nature of the crime. Unlike larceny, where ownership of goods laying about in semipublic places may be ambiguous, forcible entry is rarely ambiguous. This type of intrusion must be more covert and therefore takes place more frequently at night. Hence, the deterrent affect of night time occupancy on burglary.

## LIMITATIONS AND FUTURE RESEARCH

The foregoing analysis is limited by a number of measurement problems. First, the analysis was restricted by the relatively artificial method used to operationalize different levels of analysis. The segment typology, although an improvement in many ways over previous small-area indicators, measures the "dangerousness" of the block. The effects of different attributes of the block that may influence opportunity cannot be distinguished. The segment is representative of an extremely small area that was created for sampling purposes and not analysis purposes.

A second limitation relates to the method used to perform the multilevel analysis. For multilevel analyses, samples should be drawn such that smaller ecological units are chosen from within larger units. Differences across neighborhoods within the same community and blocks within the same community could then be examined. This would insure that all factors operating at the higher level of geography would truly be held constant as the effects of factors at the lower level of aggregation are estimated. In this and most other multilevel analyses, "similar" neighborhoods are represented on the basis of certain attributes. To the extent that the characteristics introduced in the analysis capture all attributes of areas that are relevant for crime, then the lack of a true multilevel analysis is not a problem. If these characteristics do not capture all relevant variables, the results could be due to an omitted variable.

The only solution to this problem is to design a survey with a sample explicitly designed to estimate multilevel effects. This is not practical for surveys such as the NCS and BCS, which have the primary goal of generating national-level estimates. Clustering within areas, such as required for a multilevel design, reduces the overall statistical efficiency for estimating national-level crime rates. It is only through a study that is specifically designed to examine the causal mechanisms discussed above that such multilevel models could be estimated.

Other limitations of this study are due to both the small sample size and measures used on the VRS. The models employed in this analysis are very simple. The effect of one measure of an opportunity concept is assessed when sociodemographic characteristics of respondents and the segment typology are held constant. More complex models that include more indicators of opportunity concepts and interactions among indicators at different levels of aggregation would be preferable. Estimating such models could indicate that many of the effects of opportunity variables are quite different from those observed here. More complex models can only be estimated with larger samples. This could be achieved in this instance if BJS increased the size of the VRS. Alternatively, several administrations of the VRS could be combined to form a larger sample that could be used for analytical purposes.

As this article has discussed, understanding the affect of opportunity on criminal events involves a very complex set of theoretical arguments. It is only by attempting to collect information that captures this complexity, both with respect to multilevel processes and to different types of criminal events, that both the potential and the limitations of opportunity theories of crime can be realized.

## NOTES

1. For purposes of this analysis, ecological context refers to the social and physical aspects of locations.

2. Several analyses of household property crime did include whether or not the residence was located in the central city. See Cohen and Cantor (1981).

3. There have been other multilevel analyses of victimization risk that include good measures of ecological context, but no behavioral measures of opportunity concepts at the person or household level. For an important study of this type see Smith and Janjoura (1989).

4. They were formed to represent "residential neighborhoods" and were defined using a combination of census block groups, enumeration districts, and police beat boundaries.

5. A number of studies exploring community crime prevention have included data on the physical design of housing units, but these studies employed very small samples and very little information on the routine activity of respondents (Skogan and Maxfield 1981; Greenberg et al. 1982; Fowler and Mangione 1981).

6. The NCS is a victimization survey used to measure the amount of crime in the United States and to understand the causes and consequences of crime from a victim's perspective. It is sponsored by the Bureau of Justice Statistics and administered by the U.S. Census Bureau. The survey is structured as a rotating panel design of housing units. Interviewers visit these units every 6 months for a total of seven visits over a 3-year period. At each visit, every person age 12 and over is interviewed.

7. The analyses presented here include urban segments as well as rural and other segments. Because rural and other segments may not conform as well to the concept of "block" as do urban segments, we conducted the analyses first including all segments, and then with rural and other segments excluded. The results do not change when the analysis is restricted to urban segments.

8. Because the VRS was administered to one panel of the NCS sample, the households included in the VRS should be representative of the larger NCS sample and the U.S. population as a whole. There should be no systematic differences, therefore, between the households included in the segment aggregation and the VRS subsample.

9. These variables were dichotomized rather than used in their more continuous form because of the need to use latent structure analysis rather than cluster analysis in creating the typology. There were two problems in using cluster analysis with the segment crime rates. First, the distribution of crime rates was very different across types of crimes. The rates for certain crimes approached a normal distribution, whereas others were highly skewed. This makes it difficult to uniformly scale crime rates in a cluster analysis. Second, given the potentially high sampling error of the segment crime rates the use of these data at an interval level was not clearly justified. Latent structure analysis does not impose any restrictions on the distribution of the variables used. In addition, making the crime rates ordinal is a more conservative approach with respect to sampling error.

10. The segments that were in the incoming rotation group at the time of the VRS (i.e., February, 1984) could not be included in the analysis because they had no historical data to use in the typology. Because the incoming rotation is a random sample of the entire NCS sample, the exclusion of the data should not introduce any bias to the sample.

11. To test whether the VRS segments conformed to the same typology found with the 1979-1983 data, a *restricted* latent structure analysis was performed. This analysis assumed the area types using the 1979-1983 data were "correct" and tested whether the VRS segments conformed to the same typology. The results of this test confirmed this assumption.

12. Telephone interviews are conducted for all units where this is acceptable at the second, fourth, and sixth visits that the interviewer makes to a sampled housing unit.

13. The measures of signs of disorder in the neighborhood and of visibility of the unit were both obtained from interviewer observation. The difference in sample $N$s between the two items—7,493 versus 5,657—is due largely to missing values on the items used to construct the visibility scale and the different levels at which the variables were aggregated. The signs of disorder variable was aggregated at the segment level. The responses to this item were aggregated across households within the segment and the sum divided by the number of households responding. The segment received a score on this variable if any household in the segment responded. This seemed appropriate because the interviewer was asked to report on the area around the unit. In contrast, the visibility variable was measured at the housing-unit level. If the

interviewer did not answer any of the items used to construct the scale, the household was deleted from the analysis.

14. It may have been more informative to treat each type of safety measure individually rather than combining them in a scale. Unfortunately this was not practical because so few housing units employed any given device. Combining these measures improved the variance, although it complicates the interpretation of results.

15. The work variable was divided according to the number of hours worked during the week: 1 = 0 hours, 2 = 1-29 hours, 3 = 30-39 hours, 4 = 40-49 hours, and 5 = 50+ hours. The school attendance variable was scored a 1 if no school was attended, a 3 if attendance was part-time, and 5 if attendance was full-time. The shopping variable was an ordinal scale ranging from 1 to 5 with the categories ranging from high to low of *every day, at least once a week, at least once a month, less often*, and *never*.

16. This was: *every day, at least once a week, at least once a month, less often*, and *never*.

17. Race of the head of household was included in the initial models tested, but was excluded from the models presented in Tables 2 through 4. This was done because this variable had no significant relationship to the risk of burglary and it was highly collinear with the segment cluster measure of the dangerousness of the residential area.

18. When only including urban segments in the analysis, the significance of the source of offenders variable drops to zero.

19. Signs of disorder in the neighborhood are interpreted here as indicators of guardianship. This follows the usage of Taylor and Gottfredson (1986, p. 393) who argue that the presence of signs of disorder indicate that residents do not feel strong attachments to the area. Given this lack of attachment, residents do not feel responsible for the maintenance of the area. They will not, therefore, intervene to fix vandalism or pick up litter. This same unwillingness to intervene extends to intervening to prevent or interrupt crime incidents.

## *REFERENCES*

Block, R., M. Felson, and C. R. Block. 1984. "Crime Victimization and the United States Occupational Structure: Victimization Risk of the Civilian Labor Force." Paper presented at the Annual Meetings of the American Society of Criminology, Cincinnati, OH, November.

Brantingham, P. J. and P. L. Brantingham. 1981. *Environmental Criminology*. Beverly Hills, CA: Sage.

Bursik, Robert J., Jr., and Jim Webb. 1982. "Community Change and Patterns of Delinquency." *American Journal of Sociology* 88:24-42.

Cantor, David and James P. Lynch. 1988. "Empirical Test of Opportunity Theories of Victimization: Multi-level and Domain-Specific Models." Draft Final Report submitted to National Institute of Justice, Washington, DC.

Clarke, R. V. 1983. "Situational Crime Prevention: Its Theoretical Basis and Practical Scope." Pp. 225-56 in *Crime and Justice, An Annual Review of Research*, edited by M. Tonry and A. Reiss. Chicago: University of Chicago Press.

Cohen, Lawrence and David Cantor. 1981. "Residential Burglary in the United States: Life-style and Demographic Factors Associated with the Probability of Victimization." *Journal of Research in Crime and Delinquency* 18:113-27.

Cohen, Lawrence and Marcus Felson. 1979. "Social Change and Crime Rate Trends: A Routine Activity Approach." *American Sociological Review* 44:588-608.

Cohen, Lawrence, J. R. Kluegel, and Kenneth Land. 1981. "Social Inequality and Predatory Criminal Victimization: An Exposition and Test of a Formal Theory." *American Sociological Review* 46:505-24.

Collins, James J., Brenda Cox, and P. A. Langan. 1986. "Job Activities and Personal Victimization: Implications for Theory." *Social Science Research* 16:345-60.

Cornish, Derek B. and Ronald V. Clarke. 1986. *The Reasoning Criminal: Rational Choice Perspectives on Offending*. New York: Springer-Verlag.

———. 1987. "Understanding Crime Displacement: An Application of Rational Choice Theory." *Criminology* 25:4.

Fowler, F. G. and T. W. Mangione. 1981. "An Experimental Effort to Reduce Crime and Fear of Crime in an Urban Residential Neighborhood: Re-evaluation of the Hartford Neighborhood Crime Prevention Program." Draft executive summary. Cambridge: Harvard/MIT Center for Survey Research.

Gottfredson, Michael. 1984. *Victims of Crime: The Dimensions of Risk*. London: Her Majesty's Stationery Office.

Greenberg, Stephanie, William Rohe, and J. R. Williams. 1982. *Safe and Secure Neighborhoods: Physical Characteristics and Informal Territorial Control in High and Low Crime Neighborhoods*. Washington, DC: National Institute of Justice.

Hindelang, Michael, Michael Gottfredson, and James Garafalo. 1978. *Victims of Personal Crime: An Empirical Formulation For a Theory of Personal Victimization*. Cambridge, MA: Ballinger.

Hough, Michael. 1987. "Offenders' Choice of Targets: Findings from the Victims Survey." *Journal of Quantitative Criminology* 3:355-69.

Hunter, Albert. 1974. *Symbolic Communities: The Persistence and Change of Chicago's Local Communities*. Chicago: University of Chicago Press.

Jacobs, Jane. 1961. *The Life and Death of Great American Cities*. New York: Vintage.

Jeffery, C. R. 1977. *Crime Prevention Through Environmental Design*. Beverly Hills, CA: Sage.

Lynch, James P. 1987. "Routine Activities and Victimization at Work." *Journal of Quantitative Criminology* 3:283-300.

Lynch, James P. and Albert D. Biderman. 1984. "Cars, Crime and Crime Classification: What the UCR Does Not Tell Us That it Should." Paper delivered at the Annual Meetings of the American Society of Criminology, Cincinnati, OH, November.

Maxfield, Michael. 1987. "Household Composition, Routine Activity and Victimization: A Comparative Analysis." *Journal of Quantitative Criminology* 3:301-20.

McCutcheon, A. L. 1987. *Latent Structure Analysis*. Newbury Park, CA: Sage.

McDowell, David, Colin Loftin, and Brian Wersima. 1989. "Multi-level Risk Factors for Burglary Victimization." Paper presented at the Annual Meetings of the American Society of Criminology, Reno, NV, November.

Miethe, Terance D., Mark Stafford, and J. Scott Long. 1987. "Social Differentiation in Victimization: An Application of Routine Activity/Lifestyle Theory Using Panel Data." *American Sociological Review* 52:184-94.

Newman, Oscar. 1972. *Defensible Space*. New York: Collier Books.

Sampson, R. A. 1986. "Neighborhood Family Structure and the Risk of Criminal Victimization." Pp. 25-46 in *The Social Ecology of Crime*, edited by J. Byrne and R. Sampson. New York: Springer-Verlag.

Sampson, R. A., Thomas Castellano, and John Laub. 1981. *Analysis of National Crime Survey Data to Study Serious Delinquent Behavior: Volume 5. Juvenile Delinquency Behavior and*

*Its Relation to Neighborhood Characteristics*. Washington, DC: U.S. Government Printing Office.

Sampson, R. A. and J. D. Wooldredge. 1987. "Linking the Micro and Macro-level Dimensions of Lifestyle, Routine Activity and Opportunity Models of Predatory Victimization." *Journal of Quantitative Criminology* 3:371-94.

Scarr, Harry A. with J. L. Pinsky and Deborah S. Wyatt. 1973. *Patterns of Burglary*. Washington, DC: U.S. Government Printing Office.

Schuerman, Leo A. and Solomon Kobrin. 1983. "Crime and Urban Ecological Processes: Implications for Public Policy." Paper presented at the Annual Meetings of the American Society of Criminology, Denver, CO, November.

Shannon, Lyle W. with Judith L. McKim, James P. Curry, and Lawrence J. Haffner. 1988. *Criminal Career Continuity: Its Social Context*. New York: Human Sciences Press.

Skogan, Wesley and Michael Maxfield. 1981. *Coping With Crime*. Beverly Hills, CA: Sage.

Smith, D. and G. R. Janjoura. 1989. "Household Characteristics, Neighborhood Composition and Victimization Risk." *Social Forces* 68:621-40.

Sparks, Richard F., Hazel G. Genn, and David J. Dodd. 1977. *Surveying Victims: A Study of the Measurement of Criminal Victimization, Perceptions of Crime, and Attitudes to Criminal Justice*. New York: Wiley.

Stark, Rodney. 1987. "Deviant Places: A Theory of the Ecology of Crime." *Criminology* 25: 893-909.

Taub, Richard, D. Garth Taylor, and J. D. Dunham. 1984. *Paths of Neighborhood Change: Race and Crime in Urban America*. Chicago: University of Chicago Press.

Taylor, Ralph and Stephen Gottfredson. 1986. "Environmental Design, Crime and Prevention: Examination of Community Dynamics." Pp. 387-416 in *Communities and Crime*, edited by M. Tonry and A. Reiss. Chicago: University of Chicago Press.

Van Dijk, J. J. and C. Steinmetz. 1983. "Victimization Surveys: Beyond Measuring the Volume of Crime." *Victimology* 8:291-301.

*Although many victims of crime apparently remain passive during criminal victimization, some choose to respond with force. In this article, the authors have used National Crime Survey data to examine this type of response to victimization. Using the NCS data, the authors have described three groups of victims: (a) those who use a gun in self-defense, (b) those who use a weapon other than a gun, and (c) those who use no weapon but fight back by kicking, hitting, or biting. Further, the authors have described some of the key aspect characteristics of the victimization incident for each of these three victim-response groups in an effort to identify differences between them.*

# A Portrait of Crime
# Victims Who Fight Back

### CHRIS E. MARSHALL
### VINCENT J. WEBB
*University of Nebraska at Omaha*

*Goode's 1972 presidential address* to the American Sociological Association provided an important incentive to the research community. Goode suggested that the humanistic tradition in social science has blinded many to the role of force in modern societies; force plays an integral role in democracies, as it does in tyrannies. Goode stated: "in any civil society . . . everyone is subject to force. All are engaged in it daily, not alone as victims but as perpetrators as well. . . . We are all potentially dangerous to one another" (p. 510).

Many victims of crime apparently remain passive during incidents of personal victimization. However, many others take measures to protect themselves: They respond with force. In the present article, we use data from the National Crime Survey (NCS) (U.S. Department of Justice, 1990) to examine those victims who use various forceful measures in self-defense. We focus on three victim groups: (a) those who use a gun in self-defense, (b) those who use a weapon other than a gun, and (c) those who use no weapon but fight back by kicking, hitting, or biting. In addition to describing these three victim groups, we examine the characteristics of the victim and the incident for factors that might generate various responses by victims. The central research question is: What influences a victim to use one particular form of force in self-defense (e.g., fire a gun) instead of another (e.g., kick or bite)?

JOURNAL OF INTERPERSONAL VIOLENCE, Vol. 9 No. 1, March 1994 45-74
© 1994 Sage Publications, Inc.

The present research differs from other work on victim responses based on the NCS (e.g., Marshall & Webb, 1987; Webb & Marshall, 1989) in that its focus is on the most *atypical* response to criminal victimization. It is, in fact, a fairly small group of victims of crime who actually physically fight back through shooting, knifing, beating, or kicking. In the current study, we do not attempt to describe how victims who take strong self-protective action differ from their counterparts who are passive; rather, we explore differences between those in that small group who fire a gun, use another weapon, or fight back in other ways.

## CONCEPTUAL AND RESEARCH FOUNDATIONS

Considerable research effort has been made in describing and understanding the offender who uses a firearm in the commission of a criminal act (e.g., Wright, Rossi, & Daly, 1983), but there has been relatively little examination of the victims who choose to use guns and other weapons in their own defense. Survey findings indicate that between 2% and 6% of the American public has brandished or fired a handgun in self-protection (Wright et al., 1983, pp. 142-145).

Kleck (1988) reports the results of a 1981 Peter D. Hart Research Associates' poll of 1,228 registered voters. In this poll, 6% of the adults polled responded "yes" to the question: "Within the past five years, have you yourself or another member of your household used a handgun, even if it was not fired, for self-protection or for the protection of property at home, work, or elsewhere, excluding military service or police work?" (p. 2). Of the total sample, 2% were protecting against an animal rather than a person; the remaining 4% of the sample reported gun use against a person by someone in their household.

In a related study, Kleck (1986) reports the relatively frequent use of guns by civilians against criminals. He states

> Civilians shoot many criminals—more than the police do. Unpublished data from the FBI indicate that 490 justifiable homicides by civilians were reported to the police in 1981, 422 of which were committed with guns. . . . These figures underestimate defensive shootings, however, since the FBI does not count most self-defense killings by civilians as justifiable homicides, but rather as excusable homicides. . . . If it is conservatively assumed that there are twice as many civilian excusable self-defense killings nationally as there are civilian justifiable homicides, this yields an estimate of 1,266 excusable self-defense or justifiable homicides by civilians with guns in 1981. . . . The magnitude of these figures can be judged from the fact that police officers in the United States killed only 388 felons during the same period. (pp. 43-44)

Accordingly, civilians in the early 1980s were shooting and killing criminals at a rate nearly four times that of the police.

Whitehead and Langworthy (1989) identified several controversies or issues arising out of research on gun ownership. These include (a) the role of fear as a determinant of gun ownership, (b) the confounding effects of sport versus protective gun ownership, (c) the importance of gender in gun ownership and related research, (d) the confounding of household ownership with personal ownership, (e) research issues arising out of the subculture of violence hypothesis, and (f) the relationship of collective security to gun ownership. Whitehead and Langworthy examined the data from a 1982 ABC News Poll of Public Opinion on Crime in order to determine which of these variables influence the self-reported willingness of a person to shoot a hypothetical burglar. The sample included 1,100 persons who had a gun or revolver in the home; of that 1,100 persons, about 70% claimed a willingness to shoot a nighttime intruder (p. 268).

In Whitehead and Langworthy's (1989) analysis, the main sets of variables thought to have an impact upon the willingness to shoot a burglar were (a) *ascriptive variables*, including age, race, and sex; (b) *experiential variables*, including education, income, and victimization; (c) *attitudinal variables*, including liberalism, fear of victimization, evaluation of police, and neighborhood crime trend; and (d) *contextual variables*, including proximity of Blacks, size of community, and region. These authors found that fear of crime and gender have an important influence upon the willingness to shoot. Also, the region—specifically, being southern—is especially important in explaining both the presence of a gun in the home and the willingness to use one (pp. 279-280).

In the present study, we follow the lead of Whitehead and Langworthy's (1989) classification of variables inasmuch as the data allows. Whitehead and Langworthy focused on willingness to use a weapon; we expand that focus to also include willingness to hit, kick, or bite without using a weapon. An important difference between our work and that of Whitehead and Langworthy is the prospective/hypothetical event nature of their data versus the retrospective/actual event nature of the data used in our analysis. The ABC poll reports on gun owners who report that they would or would not be willing to use a weapon—a prospective/hypothetical event. Alternatively, we use NCS data on victims who report that they actually used weapons—a retrospective/actual event. In theory, the findings from our analysis, when compared with those of Whitehead and Langworthy, should enable us to determine if the same variables can be used to predict what people say they will do with weapons and what they actually do with weapons.

Our data do not include all of the variables used by Whitehead and Langworthy. For instance, we lack a regional indicator; this variable would have enabled us to reach some conclusions about the important notion of the Southern Culture of Violence Hypothesis (Gastil, 1971). In the present report, we have, in adapting to the character of the NCS data, chosen to focus on microcontextual variables—the Incident Environment and Offender Environment factors—as distinguished from Whitehead and Langworthy's (1989) macrocontextual variables which, for them, include proximity of Blacks, size of community, and region. We introduce a fifth set of variables: Victim Insecurity factors. We speculate that a person's feelings of insecurity will influence the way she or he will respond in a threatening situation. Specifically, it is reasonable to expect that factors such as being close to home, having lived in the same area for a long time, or having experienced repeated victimization in the recent past will have some impact on a victim's response. The present study identifies the following five sets of factors as being involved in determining the type of physical action victims take for self-protection:

1.  Ascriptive factors, including age, race, and sex of victim
2.  Achievement factors, including family income and education of victim
3.  Victim Insecurity factors, including number of moves in the last 5 years, series victimization, and distance from home when incident occurs
4.  Incident Environment factors, including amount of light, time of incident, and presence of household members
5.  Offender Environment factors, including offender(s) in possession of a weapon, offender(s) hit or attacked victim, offender(s) threatened victim, offender(s) known to the victim, and offender(s) race.

## METHOD

We use NCS data (U.S. Department of Justice, 1990) on criminal incidents. The data cover the period from the first quarter of 1987 through the second quarter of 1990. These data were made available through the Inter-University Consortium for Political and Social Research (ICPSR) of the University of Michigan.

One of the questions asked of the respondents in the NCS is, "Was there anything you did or tried to do about the incident while it was going on?" The response framework included "yes," "no/took no action/kept still."[1] Of the total 56,442 incidents reported over the period from the first quarter of 1987 through the second quarter of 1990, 7,507 (13.3%) answered yes to the question; 6,152 (10.9%) answered no to the question; and the remaining

42,783 cases (75.8%) consisted of cases where the question was not applicable (because incident did not involve a face-to-face situation) or the respondents did not answer.

Further excluded from the present description are those victims who answered that they did try to do something about the incident while it was going on by threatening or verbally fighting back—by far the most common self-protective response ($n = 6,234$; 83.1%). Thereby we focus only on those incidents where the victim actually physically fought back by using a gun or other weapon or kicking, biting, and so on. The present focus on this relatively rare victim response—only 16.9% of those who took any self-protective action actually were physically aggressive toward the offender— further reduced our sample to 1,273 cases.

A full description of the measurement of the key variables[2] is provided in the appendix. Simple univariate and bivariate techniques best serve the purpose of the present study: to describe the three victim groups in terms of the five sets of variables—Ascriptive, Achievement, Insecurity, Incident, and Offender. We also examine the bivariate relationships controlling for the sex and race of the victim. Sex and race are among the most consistent correlates of both offending and victimization. At this point, we lack sufficient theoretical grounds to formulate hypotheses specifying the exact nature of the relationships. Simple descriptive approaches will help us search for basic insights into the patterns working in the data set. In addition, the small sample size in one of the groups ($n = 29$) makes reliable estimates from multivariate procedures problematic.

## FINDINGS

We have mentioned that only a small proportion of all victims take any self-defensive action; an even smaller percentage of the victims actually physically fight back. Table 1 presents the frequency distributions of the variable sets for the three response groups: (a) those victims who fire a gun ($n = 29$), (b) those victims who fight back with a weapon other than a gun ($n = 106$), and (c) those victims who fight back without a weapon ($n = 1,138$). Table 1 shows that the distribution of physical responses to criminal victimization is highly skewed: Almost 90% of the physically aggressive responses to victimization consisted of hitting, kicking, biting, and so on, without the use of a weapon. Not surprisingly, using a gun is very uncommon: Only in a little over 2% of those cases where the victim put up physical resistance did the victim actually fire a gun.

171

**TABLE 1: Frequency Distributions by Victim Response Group**

| | Victim Response Groups | | | | | |
| | Group 1: Fired Gun | | Group 2: Hit With Weapon | | Group 3: Hit Without Weapon | |
| Overall | n[a] 29 | Percentage 2.4 | n 106 | Percentage 8.3 | n 1,138 | Percentage 89.4 |
|---|---|---|---|---|---|---|
| **Ascriptive variable** | | | | | | |
| Age | | | | | | |
| 12-18 | 3 | 11.1 | 26* | 25.7 | 360** | 33.2 |
| 19-26 | 5 | 18.5 | 32 | 31.7 | 361 | 33.3 |
| 27-45 | 12 | 44.4 | 30 | 29.7 | 305 | 28.1 |
| 46 and over | 7 | 25.9 | 13 | 12.9 | 59 | 5.4 |
| Race | | | | | | |
| White | 19* | 70.4 | 75** | 74.3 | 908*** | 83.9 |
| Non-White | 8 | 29.6 | 26 | 25.7 | 174 | 16.1 |
| Sex | | | | | | |
| Male | 21* | 77.8 | 63* | 62.4 | 722** | 66.5 |
| Female | 6 | 22.2 | 38 | 37.6 | 363 | 33.5 |
| **Achievement variable** | | | | | | |
| Education | | | | | | |
| K through 11 | 9 | 33.3 | 38 | 37.6 | 400* | 36.7 |
| High school degree | 9 | 33.3 | 36 | 35.6 | 351 | 32.3 |
| College work | 9 | 33.3 | 27 | 26.7 | 334 | 30.8 |
| Family income | | | | | | |
| Less than $9,999 | 8 | 32.0 | 26* | 28.6 | 276** | 28.3 |
| $10,000-$17,499 | 3 | 12.0 | 21 | 23.1 | 209 | 21.4 |
| $17,500-$29,999 | 5 | 20.0 | 25 | 27.5 | 212 | 21.7 |
| $30,000-$49,999 | 6 | 24.0 | 14 | 15.4 | 196 | 20.1 |
| $50,000 and over | 3 | 12.0 | 5 | 5.5 | 82 | 8.4 |

| Insecurity variable | | | | | | |
|---|---|---|---|---|---|---|
| **Number of moves in last 5 years** | | | | | | |
| No moves | 15* | 55.6 | 29** | 28.7 | 303** | 27.9 |
| One move | 4 | 14.8 | 16 | 15.8 | 195 | 18.0 |
| Two moves | 4 | 14.8 | 13 | 12.9 | 138 | 12.7 |
| Three or more moves | 4 | 14.8 | 43 | 42.6 | 449 | 41.4 |
| **Series victimization** | | | | | | |
| Yes | 1** | 3.7 | 6** | 5.9 | 68** | 6.3 |
| No | 26 | 96.3 | 95 | 94.1 | 1,017 | 93.7 |
| **Distance from home** | | | | | | |
| At home, near building | 5 | 22.7 | 7** | 9.6 | 89*** | 9.5 |
| Mile or less | 3 | 13.6 | 19 | 26.0 | 246 | 26.4 |
| 5 miles or less | 3 | 13.6 | 22 | 30.1 | 268 | 28.7 |
| 50 miles or less | 9 | 40.9 | 21 | 28.8 | 280 | 30.0 |
| More than 50 miles | 2 | 9.1 | 4 | 5.5 | 50 | 5.4 |
| Incident variable | | | | | | |
| **Amount of light** | | | | | | |
| Light | 5** | 18.5 | 37** | 36.6 | 443** | 40.9 |
| Dawn or dusk | 2 | 7.4 | 4 | 4.0 | 35 | 3.2 |
| Dark | 20 | 74.1 | 60 | 59.4 | 604 | 55.8 |
| **Time of incident** | | | | | | |
| 6 a.m. to noon | 4* | 14.8 | 15** | 15.0 | 112** | 10.4 |
| Noon to 6 p.m. | 1 | 3.7 | 25 | 25.0 | 327 | 30.3 |
| 6 p.m. to 12 a.m. | 13 | 48.1 | 36 | 36.0 | 462 | 42.8 |
| After midnight | 9 | 33.3 | 24 | 24.0 | 178 | 16.5 |
| **Household member present** | | | | | | |
| Yes | 4*** | 14.8 | 24** | 23.8 | 177** | 16.3 |
| No | 23 | 85.2 | 77 | 76.2 | 906 | 83.7 |

*(Continued)*

51

173

TABLE 1: Continued

| | Victim Response Groups | | | | | |
|---|---|---|---|---|---|---|
| | Group 1: Fired Gun | | Group 2: Hit With Weapon | | Group 3: Hit Without Weapon | |
| Overall | n[a] 29 | Percentage 2.4 | n 106 | Percentage 8.3 | n 1,138 | Percentage 89.4 |
| Offender variable | | | | | | |
| Offender had weapon | | | | | | |
| Yes | 18 | 66.7 | 46 | 45.5 | 328** | 30.2 |
| No | 9 | 33.3 | 55 | 54.5 | 757 | 69.8 |
| Offender hit or attacked | | | | | | |
| Yes | 7* | 25.9 | 62* | 61.4 | 878** | 80.9 |
| No | 20 | 74.1 | 39 | 38.6 | 207 | 19.1 |
| Offender threatened | | | | | | |
| Yes | 15 | 55.6 | 29** | 28.7 | 161** | 14.8 |
| No | 12 | 44.4 | 72 | 71.3 | 924 | 85.2 |
| Offender known to victim | | | | | | |
| Yes | 6* | 22.2 | 41 | 40.6 | 485** | 42.2 |
| No | 21 | 77.8 | 60 | 59.4 | 627 | 57.8 |
| Race of offender(s) | | | | | | |
| White | 15 | 60.0 | 42 | 41.6 | 343** | 32.2 |
| Non-White | 10 | 40.0 | 58 | 58.4 | 723 | 67.8 |

a. There will be some variation in the total $ns$ within the response groups due to missing information.
*Differences across categories are statistically significant at the $p < 0.05$ level using a single-sample $\chi^2$ test.
**Differences across categories are statistically significant at the $p < 0.001$ level using a single-sample $\chi^2$ test.

In the following section, we provide a tentative description of the members of each of the three focal groups. In addition to frequencies and percentages, Table 1 also reports the results of single sample chi-square tests. This particular chi-square test simply indicates whether the observed cell frequencies differ significantly from expected or chance cell frequencies for a single group. It does not serve to reflect differences between groups, as does the more familiar chi-square test of independence used in contingency table analyses.[3]

## Group Descriptions

### Group 1: Those Victims Who Fight Back by Firing a Gun

Table 1 suggests that those victims who fired a gun tend to be White males in the 27-45 age category. This group does not seem to fall into any distinct educational or income category. It appears that those who shot back at the attacker typically had not moved within the last 5 years (55.6%). The incident is not part of a series victimization (96.3%). The results of the chi-square test suggest that victims were not more likely to respond with gunfire at any particular distance from home, although very few of the incidents (9.1%) took place more than 50 miles from home.

The incident was most likely to occur in the period from 6 p.m. to midnight (48.1%), primarily in the dark hours (74.1%). In most of the incidents where the victim fired a gun, no other household members were present (85.2%).

Regarding the qualities of the offender(s), Table 1 suggests that in incidents where victims actually use a gun, the victim and the offender typically do not know each other (77.8%). In about two thirds of these incidents, the offender did have a weapon (note, however, that the chi-square test indicates a lack of statistical significance). In slightly over half of the incidents (55.6%), the offender apparently threatened the victim; and in one fourth of the cases, the offender actually was said to have hit or attacked the victim. Of the incidents where the victim fired a gun, 40% involved a non-White offender.

### Group 2: Those Victims Who Fight Back by
### Using a Weapon Other Than a Gun

As was previously noted, use of a gun by crime victims is a fairly rare event. Victims are more likely to report that they fought back with the use of a weapon other than a gun (e.g., knife or club). In the present study, a total of 101 victims fit in this category (8.3% of the total group of victims who indicated a physical response to their victimization). Table 1 suggests that this group consists predominantly of White males, but that unlike Group 1, they tend to be younger (57.4% were younger than 26 years). Over one third of those who fought back using a weapon other than a gun were female. This group appears not to be characterized by a particular educational level, but the reported family income is disproportionately in the lower- to middle-income ranges.

Unlike Group 1, this group has moved around a lot over the last 5 years: 42.6% reported three or more moves. Slightly more than one fourth of these victims reported no recent moves, however. Most of these incidents did not involve a series victimization (94.1%). Victims were least likely to use a weapon other than a gun in or near home or more than 50 miles away from home.

The incident was most likely to occur when it was dark (59.4%). Still, over one third of the cases (36.6%) where the victim used a weapon other than a gun took place in broad daylight. These incidents were least likely to happen in the morning (15.0%). Typically, no other household members were present during the incident.

Table 1 further shows that slightly more than one fourth of these victims (28.7%) reported that they had been threatened by their attacker, and the majority of victims who fought back with a weapon other than a gun (61.4%) reported that the offender had actually hit or attacked them. It is interesting that the group which fired a gun—Group 1—is less likely to have been hit or attacked during the incident while this reverses for the group that fights back with some other weapon—Group 2. In almost half of these incidents (45.5%), the offender reportedly did have a weapon. Although the results of the chi-square test indicate a lack of statistical significance, it appears that in the majority of these incidents, the offender was non-White (58.4%) and that the offender and the victim did not know each other (59.4%).

*Group 3: Those Victims Who Fight Back but Use No Weapon*

Using a gun or any other weapon is the least common way of physically resisting criminal attack. In almost 90% of the incidents, the victim reportedly fought back without any weapons, using feet, fists, or other body parts. Table 1 shows that those victims who fight back using no weapons tend to be younger, White, and male. Still, one third of the victims who reported physical resistance without a weapon were female. Only 16.1% of this group were non-White. The members of this group tend to be less educated and fall into lower- and middle-income categories.

A large portion of this group (41.4%) reportedly moved at least three times over the past 5 years (similar to Group 2). Only a very small proportion of these incidents involved series victimization (6.3%). Physically resisting the attacker without weapon use is least likely to occur at home or more than 50 miles from home.

The incident was most likely to occur in the period from 6 p.m. to midnight (42.8%) and when it was dark (55.8%). In only a small proportion of these incidents (16.3%) was another household member present during the attack.

Table 1 further shows that in the majority of these incidents, the offender was not reported to have threatened the victim (85.2%), but did actually hit or attack him or her (80.9%). The offender did have a weapon in almost one third of the incidents (30.2%). In slightly over half of the cases (57.8%), the victim and the offender did not know each other. The race of the offender appears important in this context; over two thirds of the incidents where the victim reported physical resistance without a weapon involved a non-White offender.

## Bivariate Results

In the foregoing section, we have provided a preliminary description of the three victim response groups. We will now examine the influence of selected factors upon the type of response chosen by the victim. The summary results are given in Table 2, which provides bivariate results for the Ascriptive factors, Achievement factors, Insecurity factors, Incident factors, and Offender factors; additionally, the tables present the character of the relationships controlled for sex. Table 3 repeats the bivariate results for the key influence variables but, this time, the relationships are controlled for race.

### Relationship Between Ascriptive Variables and Victim Response

*Age.* It appears age does significantly influence the type of victim response. Specifically, older citizens are more likely to fire a gun and hit an offender with a weapon in response to victimization than younger ones; younger persons are more likely to hit, kick, or bite the offender.

Although the gamma value (-0.29) indicates a low degree of overall association between the variables, it seems as though the largest shift in type of victim response occurred between the 27- to 45-year-old age group and those 46 and over. Fairly obvious interpretation of this would include the lessened confidence in the physical capacity to fight back by use of simple

*(Text continues on page 64)*

**TABLE 2:** Percentage Distribution of Victim Responses by Selected Factors (includes control for sex)

| | Total | | | | Male | | | | Female | | | |
|---|---|---|---|---|---|---|---|---|---|---|---|---|
| | Victim Response | | | | Victim Response | | | | Victim Response | | | |
| | Fired Gun | Hit With Weapon | Hit Without Weapon | Statistics[a] | Fired Gun | Hit With Weapon | Hit Without Weapon | Statistics | Fired Gun | Hit With Weapon | Hit Without Weapon | Statistics |
| **Ascriptive variable** | | | | | | | | | | | | |
| **Age** | | | | | | | | | | | | |
| 12-18 | .7 | 6.4 | 92.8 | 39.28** | .7 | 7.8 | 91.5 | 24.32** | .8 | 3.3 | 95.9 | 26.83**[b] |
| 19-26 | 1.2 | 8.3 | 90.5 | .12 | 1.4 | 7.8 | 90.8 | .12 | .7 | 9.4 | 89.9 | .18 |
| 27-45 | 3.6 | 8.7 | 87.7 | -.29 | 5.0 | 7.2 | 87.8 | -.21 | 1.4 | 11.2 | 87.4 | -.44 |
| 46 and over | 9.8 | 15.9 | 74.4 | | 10.5 | 10.5 | 78.9 | | 8.3 | 29.2 | 62.5 | |
| **Race** | | | | | | | | | | | | |
| White | 2.0 | 7.5 | 90.5 | 7.54* | 2.2 | 8.0 | 89.8 | 4.41 | 1.5 | 6.6 | 91.9 | 13.61**[b] |
| Non-White | 3.6 | 12.2 | 84.2 | .08 | 5.5 | 7.1 | 87.4 | .07 | 1.1 | 19.1 | 79.8 | .18 |
| | | | | -.27 | | | | -.13 | | | | -.47 |
| **Sex** | | | | | | | | | | | | |
| Male | 2.7 | 7.8 | 89.4 | 2.98 | | | | Not applicable | | | | |
| Female | 1.4 | 9.4 | 89.2 | .05 | | | | Not applicable | | | | |
| | | | | .00 | | | | | | | | |
| **Achievement variable** | | | | | | | | | | | | |
| **Family income** | | | | | | | | | | | | |
| Less than $9,999 | 2.4 | 9.1 | 88.5 | 5.89 | 3.2 | 7.9 | 88.9 | 4.18 | 1.4 | 10.7 | 87.9 | 3.75[b] |
| $10,000-$17,499 | 1.2 | 8.6 | 90.2 | .05 | 1.3 | 9.2 | 89.5 | .05 | 1.1 | 7.6 | 91.3 | .07 |
| $17,500-$29,999 | 1.9 | 10.1 | 87.9 | .04 | 2.1 | 9.3 | 88.6 | .01 | 1.6 | 12.5 | 85.9 | .13 |
| $30,000-$49,999 | 3.1 | 6.3 | 90.6 | | 3.7 | 6.8 | 89.4 | | 1.7 | 5.0 | 93.3 | |
| $50,000 and over | 3.3 | 5.4 | 91.3 | | 4.2 | 5.6 | 90.1 | | .0 | 4.8 | 95.2 | |

| | | | | | | | | | | | | |
|---|---|---|---|---|---|---|---|---|---|---|---|---|
| **Education** | | | | | | | | | | | | |
| K through 11 | 2.2 | 8.4 | 89.5 | .80 | 2.3 | 9.0 | 88.7 | 1.37 | 1.8 | 7.4 | 90.8 | 2.31[b] |
| High school degree | 2.1 | 9.0 | 88.9 | .02 | 2.6 | 7.4 | 90.0 | .03 | 1.3 | 11.8 | 86.8 | .05 |
| College work | 2.6 | 7.5 | 89.9 | .01 | 3.3 | 7.0 | 89.7 | .03 | .9 | 8.9 | 90.2 | -.04 |
| | | | | | | | | | | | | |
| **Insecurity variable** | | | | | | | | | | | | |
| **Number of moves in last 5 years** | | | | | | | | | | | | |
| No moves | 4.5 | 8.4 | 87.2 | 14.10* | 4.7 | 7.4 | 87.9 | 10.46 | 4.0 | 10.0 | 85.1 | 11.68[b] |
| One move | 1.8 | 7.6 | 90.7 | .07 | 2.0 | 6.0 | 91.9 | .08 | 1.3 | 10.5 | 88.2 | .12 |
| Two moves | 3.1 | 8.0 | 89.0 | .11 | 3.4 | 5.2 | 91.4 | .02 | 2.1 | 14.9 | 83.0 | .27 |
| Three or more moves | .8 | 8.7 | 90.5 | | 1.2 | 10.0 | 88.8 | | .0 | 6.9 | 93.1 | |
| **Series crime** | | | | | | | | | | | | |
| Yes | 1.2 | 7.1 | 91.7 | .67 | .0 | 7.8 | 92.2 | 1.53[b] | 3.0 | 6.1 | 90.9 | 1.10[b] |
| No | 2.4 | 8.4 | 89.2 | .02 | 2.9 | 7.8 | 89.3 | .04 | 1.3 | 9.6 | 89.1 | .05 |
| | | | | -.14 | | | | -.18 | | | | -.09 |
| | | | | | | | | | | | | |
| **Distance from home** | | | | | | | | | | | | |
| At home, near building | 4.5 | 6.4 | 89.1 | 7.05 | 6.0 | 9.0 | 85.1 | 8.87 | 2.4 | 2.4 | 95.2 | 3.05[b] |
| Mile or less | 1.4 | 6.8 | 91.8 | .06 | 1.5 | 7.3 | 91.3 | .07 | 1.4 | 5.6 | 93.1 | .07 |
| 5 miles or less | 1.0 | 7.9 | 91.1 | -.02 | .9 | 9.1 | 90.0 | -.01 | 1.2 | 4.9 | 93.9 | .00 |
| 50 miles or less | 2.8 | 7.2 | 90.0 | | 3.7 | 7.3 | 89.0 | | .0 | 6.7 | 93.3 | |
| More than 50 miles | 3.3 | 6.7 | 90.0 | | 3.8 | 7.5 | 88.7 | | .0 | .0 | 100.0 | |
| | | | | | | | | | | | | |
| **Incident variables** | | | | | | | | | | | | |
| **Amount of light** | | | | | | | | | | | | |
| Light | 1.0 | 7.5 | 91.5 | 8.20[b] | 1.3 | 6.8 | 92.0 | 5.00[b] | .5 | 8.7 | 90.8 | 5.38 |
| Dawn or dusk | 4.5 | 11.4 | 84.1 | .06 | 3.3 | 10.0 | 86.7 | .05 | 7.1 | 14.3 | 78.6 | .08 |
| Dark | 3.1 | 8.8 | 88.2 | -.16 | 3.6 | 8.4 | 88.0 | -.20 | 1.8 | 9.7 | 88.5 | -.11 |

*(Continued)*

57

179

**TABLE 2:  Continued**

| | Total | | | | Male | | | | Female | | | |
|---|---|---|---|---|---|---|---|---|---|---|---|---|
| | Victim Response | | | | Victim Response | | | | Victim Response | | | |
| | Fired Gun | Hit With Weapon | Hit Without Weapon | Statistics[a] | Fired Gun | Hit With Weapon | Hit Without Weapon | Statistics | Fired Gun | Hit With Weapon | Hit Without Weapon | Statistics |
| **Incident variables** | | | | | | | | | | | | |
| Time of incident | | | | | | | | | | | | |
| 6 a.m. to noon | 3.0 | 11.1 | 85.9 | 19.06* | 3.6 | 8.4 | 88.0 | 8.52 | 2.0 | 15.7 | 82.4 | 16.91*[b] |
| Noon to 6 p.m. | .3 | 7.3 | 92.5 | .09 | .4 | 7.0 | 92.6 | .07 | .0 | 7.7 | 92.3 | .14 |
| 6 p.m. to 12 a.m. | 2.6 | 6.9 | 90.4 | -.12 | 3.0 | 7.7 | 89.3 | -.13 | 1.8 | 5.4 | 92.8 | -.10 |
| After midnight | 4.5 | 11.6 | 83.9 | | 5.0 | 8.7 | 86.3 | | 3.2 | 19.0 | 77.8 | |
| Household members present | | | | | | | | | | | | |
| Yes | 1.8 | 11.5 | 86.6 | 3.60 | 2.9 | 8.8 | 88.2 | .17 | .9 | 14.0 | 85.1 | 4.22[b] |
| No | 2.4 | 7.7 | 89.9 | .05 | 2.7 | 7.7 | 89.6 | .01 | 1.6 | 7.7 | 90.7 | .10 |
| | | | | -.15 | | | | -.07 | | | | -.25 |
| **Offender variable** | | | | | | | | | | | | |
| Offender had weapon | | | | | | | | | | | | |
| Yes | 4.5 | 11.6 | 83.8 | 24.25** | 5.5 | 12.8 | 81.7 | 35.88** | 1.1 | 7.5 | 92.4 | .58[b] |
| No | 1.2 | 6.7 | 92.1 | .14 | 1.0 | 4.7 | 94.4 | .21 | 1.5 | 9.9 | 88.6 | .04 |
| | | | | .39 | | | | .58 | | | | -.15 |
| Offender hit or attacked | | | | | | | | | | | | |
| Yes | .8 | 6.5 | 92.7 | 66.32** | 1.1 | 6.1 | 92.8 | 35.01** | 8.6 | 17.1 | 74.3 | 17.35** |
| No | 7.4 | 14.8 | 77.7 | .23 | 7.3 | 12.8 | 79.9 | .20 | 7.8 | 21.9 | 70.3 | .30 |
| | | | | -.57 | | | | -.53 | | | | -.68 |

58

| | | | | | | | | | | | | |
|---|---|---|---|---|---|---|---|---|---|---|---|---|
| **Offender threatened** | | | | | | | | | | | | |
| Yes | 6.9 | 14.7 | 78.4 | 40.74** .18 .50 | | 6.6 | 14.2 | 79.2 | 27.43** .18 .51 | | 8.6 | 17.1 | 74.3 | 17.35**[b] .20 .54 |
| No | 1.3 | 7.0 | 91.7 | | | 1.7 | 6.1 | 92.3 | | | .8 | 8.7 | 90.6 | |
| **Offender known to victim** | | | | | | | | | | | | |
| Yes | .8 | 8.3 | 90.8 | 16.40** .11 .18 | | 1.0 | 8.3 | 90.7 | 9.25* .10 .14 | | .6 | 8.4 | 90.9 | 7.13*[b] .13 .31 |
| No | 4.2 | 8.3 | 87.5 | | | 4.4 | 7.4 | 88.3 | | | 3.7 | 12.1 | 84.1 | |
| **Race of offender(s)** | | | | | | | | | | | | |
| White | 3.8 | 10.3 | 85.9 | 11.98* .10 .27 | | 4.8 | 9.2 | 86.0 | 8.47* .10 .26 | | 2.1 | 12.5 | 85.4 | 4.16[b] .10 .30 |
| Non-White | 1.3 | 7.3 | 91.3 | | | 1.6 | 7.2 | 91.2 | | | .7 | 7.7 | 91.6 | |

a. Summary statistics are provided in the following order: $\chi^2$; Cramer's V; and Gamma.
b. More than 20% of the cells have less than five expected frequencies.
$*p < .05$; $**p < .001$.

TABLE 3: Percentage Distribution of Victim Responses by Selected Factors (includes control for race)

| | Total | | | | White | | | | Non-White | | | |
|---|---|---|---|---|---|---|---|---|---|---|---|---|
| | Victim Response | | | | Victim Response | | | | Victim Response | | | |
| | Fired Gun | Hit With Weapon | Hit Without Weapon | Statistics[a] | Fired Gun | Hit With Weapon | Hit Without Weapon | Statistics | Fired Gun | Hit With Weapon | Hit Without Weapon | Statistics |
| **Ascriptive variable** | | | | | | | | | | | | |
| Age | | | | | | | | | | | | |
| 12-18 | .7 | 6.4 | 92.8 | 39.28** | .3 | 6.0 | 93.7 | 38.68** | 2.9 | 8.7 | 88.4 | 18.04*[b] |
| 19-26 | 1.2 | 8.3 | 90.5 | .12 | .9 | 6.6 | 92.6 | .14 | 2.8 | 16.7 | 80.6 | .20 |
| 27-45 | 3.6 | 8.7 | 87.7 | -.29 | 3.4 | 9.5 | 87.1 | -.33 | 4.3 | 5.7 | 90.0 | -.16 |
| 46 and over | 9.8 | 15.9 | 74.4 | | 10.0 | 11.4 | 78.6 | | 9.1 | 45.5 | 45.5 | |
| Race | | | | | | | | | | | | |
| White | 2.0 | 7.5 | 90.5 | 7.54* | | | | Not applicable | | | | |
| Non-White | 3.6 | 12.2 | 84.2 | .08 | | | | Not applicable | | | | |
| | | | | -.27 | | | | | | | | |
| Sex | | | | | | | | | | | | |
| Male | 2.7 | 7.8 | 89.4 | 2.98 | 2.2 | 8.0 | 89.8 | 1.29 | 5.5 | 7.1 | 87.4 | 9.76*[b] |
| Female | 1.4 | 9.4 | 89.2 | .05 | 1.5 | 6.6 | 91.9 | .04 | 1.1 | 19.1 | 79.8 | .21 |
| | | | | .00 | | | | .13 | | | | -.23 |
| **Achievement variable** | | | | | | | | | | | | |
| Family income | | | | | | | | | | | | |
| Less than $9,999 | 2.4 | 9.1 | 88.5 | 5.89 | 1.6 | 8.2 | 90.1 | 4.02[b] | 4.6 | 11.5 | 83.9 | 4.96[b] |
| $10,000-$17,499 | 1.2 | 8.6 | 90.2 | .05 | 1.0 | 8.7 | 90.4 | .05 | 2.8 | 8.3 | 88.9 | .11 |
| $17,500-$29,999 | 1.9 | 10.1 | 87.9 | .04 | 1.9 | 8.9 | 89.2 | .01 | 2.3 | 15.9 | 81.8 | .06 |
| $30,000-$49,999 | 3.1 | 6.3 | 90.6 | | 2.5 | 6.6 | 90.9 | | 8.7 | 4.3 | 87.0 | |
| $50,000 and over | 3.3 | 5.4 | 91.3 | | 3.4 | 5.7 | 90.8 | | .0 | .0 | 100.0 | |

|  | | | | | | | | | | | | |
|---|---|---|---|---|---|---|---|---|---|---|---|---|
| **Education** | | | | | | | | | | | | |
| K through 11 | 2.2 | 8.4 | 89.5 | .80 | 1.9 | 7.0 | 91.2 | .99 | 3.3 | 14.1 | 82.6 | .87[b] |
| High school diploma | 2.1 | 9.0 | 88.9 | .02 | 1.7 | 8.4 | 89.9 | .02 | 4.0 | 12.0 | 84.0 | .04 |
| College work | 2.6 | 7.5 | 89.9 | .01 | 2.4 | 7.3 | 90.2 | -.04 | 3.6 | 9.1 | 87.3 | .10 |
| **Insecurity variable** | | | | | | | | | | | | |
| **Number of moves in last 5 years** | | | | | | | | | | | | |
| No moves | 4.5 | 8.4 | 87.2 | 14.10* | 4.0 | 7.4 | 88.6 | 11.38 | 6.6 | 13.1 | 80.3 | 6.53[b] |
| One move | 1.8 | 7.6 | 90.7 | .07 | .6 | 7.4 | 92.0 | .07 | 6.0 | 8.0 | 86.0 | .12 |
| Two moves | 3.1 | 8.0 | 89.0 | .11 | 2.9 | 7.3 | 89.8 | .09 | 3.8 | 11.5 | 84.6 | .13 |
| Three or more moves | .8 | 8.7 | 90.5 | -.14 | .9 | 7.7 | 91.3 | -.13 | .0 | 14.1 | 85.9 | -.23 |
| **Series crime** | | | | | | | | | | | | |
| Yes | 1.2 | 7.1 | 91.7 | .67 | 1.5 | 6.1 | 92.4 | .32[b] | .0 | 11.1 | 88.9 | .77[b] |
| No | 2.4 | 8.4 | 89.2 | .02 | 2.0 | 7.6 | 90.3 | .02 | 3.9 | 12.3 | 83.8 | .06 |
| **Distance from home** | | | | | | | | | | | | |
| At home, near building | 4.5 | 6.4 | 89.1 | 7.05 | 4.8 | 6.0 | 89.2 | 8.24[b] | 3.7 | 7.4 | 88.9 | 5.54[b] |
| Mile or less | 1.4 | 6.8 | 91.8 | .06 | .9 | 6.7 | 92.4 | .07 | 3.8 | 7.5 | 88.7 | .12 |
| 5 miles or less | 1.0 | 7.9 | 91.1 | -.02 | .8 | 8.0 | 91.2 | .00 | 1.9 | 7.5 | 90.6 | -.15 |
| 50 miles or less | 2.8 | 7.2 | 90.0 | | 2.5 | 6.8 | 90.7 | | 5.0 | 10.0 | 85.0 | |
| More than 50 miles | 3.3 | 6.7 | 90.0 | | 1.8 | 5.5 | 92.7 | | 20.0 | 20.0 | 60.0 | |
| **Incident variables** | | | | | | | | | | | | |
| **Amount of light** | | | | | | | | | | | | |
| Light | 1.0 | 7.5 | 91.5 | 8.20[b] | 1.0 | 6.2 | 92.8 | 5.69[b] | 1.0 | 12.9 | 86.1 | 6.07[b] |
| Dawn or dusk | 4.5 | 11.4 | 84.1 | .06 | 2.6 | 10.5 | 86.8 | .05 | 16.7 | 16.7 | 66.7 | .12 |
| Dark | 3.1 | 8.8 | 88.2 | -.16 | 2.6 | 8.3 | 89.1 | -.20 | 5.3 | 11.4 | 83.3 | -.11 |

*(Continued)*

183

61

**TABLE 3: Continued**

| | Total | | | | White | | | | Non-White | | | |
|---|---|---|---|---|---|---|---|---|---|---|---|---|
| | Victim Response | | | | Victim Response | | | | Victim Response | | | |
| | Fired Gun | Hit With Weapon | Hit Without Weapon | Statistics[a] | Fired Gun | Hit With Weapon | Hit Without Weapon | Statistics | Fired Gun | Hit With Weapon | Hit Without Weapon | Statistics |
| **Incident variables** | | | | | | | | | | | | |
| **Time of incident** | | | | | | | | | | | | |
| 6 a.m. to noon | 3.0 | 11.1 | 85.9 | 19.06* | 3.9 | 7.8 | 88.3 | 16.47* | .0 | 22.6 | 77.4 | 9.42[b] |
| Noon to 6 p.m. | .3 | 7.3 | 92.5 | .09 | .0 | 6.4 | 93.6 | .09 | 1.4 | 11.1 | 87.5 | .15 |
| 6 p.m. to 12 a.m. | 2.6 | 6.9 | 90.4 | -.12 | 2.2 | 6.5 | 91.2 | -.17 | 4.6 | 9.2 | 86.2 | -.04 |
| After midnight | 4.5 | 11.6 | 83.9 | | 3.6 | 11.4 | 85.0 | | 9.7 | 12.9 | 77.4 | |
| **Household members present** | | | | | | | | | | | | |
| Yes | 1.8 | 11.5 | 86.6 | 3.60 | 1.7 | 11.5 | 86.8 | 4.67 | 2.4 | 11.9 | 85.7 | .23 |
| No | 2.4 | 7.7 | 89.9 | .05 | 2.1 | 6.8 | 91.2 | .07 | 3.9 | 12.2 | 83.9 | .03 |
| | | | | -.15 | | | | -.21 | | | | .08 |
| **Offender variable** | | | | | | | | | | | | |
| **Offender had weapon** | | | | | | | | | | | | |
| Yes | 4.5 | 11.6 | 83.8 | 24.25** | 3.6 | 11.6 | 84.8 | 18.66** | 8.3 | 11.9 | 79.8 | 8.72*[b] |
| No | 1.2 | 6.7 | 92.1 | .14 | 1.3 | 5.6 | 93.1 | .13 | .7 | 12.3 | 87.0 | .20 |
| | | | | .39 | | | | .41 | | | | .28 |
| **Offender hit or attacked** | | | | | | | | | | | | |
| Yes | .8 | 6.5 | 92.7 | 66.32** | .7 | 5.7 | 93.5 | 46.41** | 1.1 | 9.9 | 89.0 | 24.61**[b] |
| No | 7.4 | 14.8 | 77.7 | .23 | 6.2 | 13.6 | 80.2 | .21 | 15.0 | 22.5 | 62.5 | .33 |
| | | | | -.57 | | | | -.56 | | | | -.66 |

| | | | | | | | | | | | | |
|---|---|---|---|---|---|---|---|---|---|---|---|---|
| **Offender threatened** | | | | | | | | | | | | |
| Yes | 6.9 | 14.7 | 78.4 | 40.74** | 5.4 | 13.0 | 81.6 | 23.71** | 15.2 | 24.2 | 60.6 | 21.56**[b] |
| No | 1.3 | 7.0 | 91.7 | .18 | 1.3 | 6.4 | 92.4 | .15 | 1.6 | 10.1 | 88.4 | .31 |
| | | | | .50 | | | | .46 | | | | .66 |
| **Offender known to victim** | | | | | | | | | | | | |
| Yes | .8 | 8.3 | 90.8 | 16.40** | .5 | 7.0 | 92.5 | 14.82** | 1.9 | 13.5 | 84.6 | 4.85 |
| No | 4.2 | 8.3 | 87.5 | .11 | 3.8 | 8.2 | 88.0 | .12 | 7.6 | 9.1 | 83.3 | .15 |
| | | | | .18 | | | | .26 | | | | .08 |
| **Race of offender(s)** | | | | | | | | | | | | |
| White | 3.8 | 10.3 | 85.9 | 11.98* | 4.1 | 8.2 | 87.7 | 9.40* | 3.5 | 13.3 | 83.2 | .65 |
| Non-White | 1.3 | 7.3 | 91.3 | .10 | 1.1 | 7.3 | 91.6 | .10 | 4.5 | 9.1 | 86.4 | .05 |
| | | | | .27 | | | | .22 | | | | .11 |

a. Summary statistics are provided in the following order: $\chi^2$; Cramer's V; Gamma.
b. More than 20% of the cells have less than five expected frequencies.
* $p < .05$; ** $p < .001$.

63

185

physical means among this older group and consequent increased reliance upon other "tools" for self-defense.

Table 2 also presents the age-response relationship, controlled for sex. We find virtually no change in this relationship for males. However, for women the level of association increases (gamma = –0.44). It appears that women in the 46-and-over group are much less likely to fight back without a weapon than their younger counterparts, but they are more likely than younger women to use a weapon other than a gun when resisting attack.

Table 3 shows the age-victim response relationship, controlled for race. There is little difference from the overall sample for Whites. However, for non-White victims, there does seem to be a smaller impact of age upon the type of response (gamma = –0.16) than that for Whites (gamma = –0.33). Older non-Whites appear much less likely to fight back without a weapon than older Whites (45.5% vs. 78.6%).

*Race.* Table 2 shows that race does have a statistically significant impact upon the type of response, but there is only a low degree of association (Cramer's V = 0.08). Non-Whites are somewhat more likely to use a gun or other weapon than their White counterparts. None of the percentage differences reaches close to the 10% difference rule of thumb for percentage tables.

Table 2 further shows that the racial effect changes when controlling for sex. For males race is not statistically significantly related to type of response. However, for females the initially noted racial difference increases under controlled conditions. Specifically, female non-White victims are much more likely to use a weapon other than a gun against the offender (19.1%) than White females (6.6%); White female victims are more likely to fight back with their fists, feet, and so on (91.9%) than their non-White counterparts (79.8%). There is virtually no difference between non-White and White female victims in their use of a gun to resist attack.

*Sex.* Contrary to expectations, Table 2 fails to show that sex is strongly related to type of physical victim response. Male victims were slightly more likely to fire a gun (2.7%) than female victims (1.4%); females were somewhat more likely to use a weapon other than a gun (9.4% vs. 7.8%), but these differences are not statistically significant.

The sex-victim response relationship changes, however, when controlling for race (see Table 3): For non-White victims, sex does appear to be weakly related to type of victim response (Cramer's V = 0.21). Non-White females are more likely than their non-White male counterparts to have used a weapon other than a gun to resist the attack (19.1% vs. 7.1%); non-White females were less likely to have fired a gun (1.1%) as compared to their male counterparts (5.5%). Note, however, that White and non-White females were about equally as likely to have fired a gun (1.5% vs. 1.1%).

### Relationship Between Achievement Variables and Victim Response

*Family income.* The family income of the victim seems to be an insignificant factor in the type of victim response. There is no effect for the total group, for the Whites, for non-Whites, for males, or for females.

*Education.* The level of education of the victim has no apparent effect upon the type of response. Again, there exists no relationship for the total group, for the Whites, for non-Whites, for males, or for females.

### Relationship Between Insecurity Variables and Victim Response

*Number of moves in the last 5 years.* Table 2 shows that there exists a significant relationship between the number of moves variable and the type of response. The relationship is a weak one (gamma = 0.11): It seems that, generally, the more moves a victim makes, the more likely she or he will fight back without the use of a weapon; alternatively, the less the number of moves, the more likely the victim will use a gun. There is little that can be drawn from the remaining analyses of Tables 2 and 3 for this variable, except that the use of race and sex as control variables reduces the initially noted weak association to the level of statistical insignificance.

*Series victimization.* Again, Tables 2 and 3 demonstrate that the fact that the incident was a series victimization had no clear effect upon type of victim response. There exists no relationship for the total group, for Whites, for non-Whites, for males, or for females.

*Distance from home.* Tables 2 and 3 show that the distance from home has no effect upon the victim's response. Moreover, there exists no relationship for the total group, for Whites, for non-Whites, for males, or for females.

### Relationship Between Incident Variables and Victim Response

*Amount of light.* Tables 2 and 3 demonstrate that the amount of light at the time of the victimization had no effect upon the type of victim response. There exists no relationship for the total group, for Whites, for non-Whites, for males, or for females.

187

*Time of incident.* Table 2 indicates that the time of incident has a weak influence on the type of self-defensive response the victim takes (gamma = −0.12). It appears that it is very unlikely that a victim will discharge a gun in the afternoon hours (0.3%); a more likely victim response during that time period consists of physical fight without a weapon (92.5%). Using a gun in self-defense appears most likely in the period between midnight and 6 a.m.—during that time period, 4.5% of those victims who put up physical resistance actually used a gun, 11.6% used another weapon, and 83.9% fought back without the use of a weapon. It is notable that for males, females, and Whites, this relationship holds. However, for non-White respondents, Table 3 enables us to tentatively conclude the time of day has no significant bearing upon the type of victim response.

*Household members present.* The presence of household members appears to have no influence upon the type of self-defense response a victim uses. There exists no relationship for the total group, for Whites, for non-Whites, for males, or for females.

### Relationship Between Offender Characteristics and Victim Response

*Offender had weapon.* Tables 2 and 3 demonstrate that victims were most likely to kick, bite, hit, and so on when confronted with an offender who did not have a weapon (92.1%). In those incidents where the offender did have a weapon, the victim more likely responded by firing a gun (4.5%) or using another weapon (11.6%). It is notable that for the males, this relationship holds; however, for females, the presence of a weapon appears to make no difference.

Controlling for race does not seem to have a significant impact on the originally noted relationship between presence of weapon and type of victim response. A notable fact for the non-White group is that the presence of a weapon makes the person about 12 times more likely to fire a gun than if the offender had no weapon; for Whites, the presence of a gun increases the chance of the victim firing a gun only threefold.

*Offender(s) hit or attacked.* Victims were more likely to fight back using their hands, feet, and so on (without a weapon) if the offender had hit or attacked them (92.7%) than in those cases where the offender had not hit or attacked them (77.7%). Somewhat surprising is the observation that victims were more inclined to fire a gun (7.4%) or use another weapon (14.8%) when the offender had not hit or attacked them; only .8% responded by firing a gun, and 6.5% responded by using another weapon when the offender had actually hit or attacked them. Tables 2 and 3 indicate that this relationship is not very strong (Cramer's V = 0.23), but it holds for males, females, Whites, and non-Whites. For non-Whites, however, the relationship increases in strength; specifically, non-White victims are much more likely than White victims to fire a gun or hit the offender with a weapon in the instance in which the offender has not hit or attacked.

*Offender(s) threatened.* Whether or not the victim was threatened by the offender(s) results in differences in victim responses (Cramer's V = 0.18). In situations where the offender(s) threatened, the victim was more likely to use a gun (6.9%) or other weapon (14.7%) against the offender than in the incidents where no threat was made (1.3% fired a gun; 7.0% used another weapon).

For males, females, and Whites, the relationship holds at about the same level of significance and degree. For non-White respondents, however, the degree of relationship as measured by Cramer's V (0.33) is greater for non-White victims. Specifically, if the offender threatens the victim, non-White persons are about three times more likely to fire a gun at the offender than are White victims and are about twice as likely as White victims to use another weapon against the offender.

*Offender(s) known to the victim.* In cases where the offender is known to the victim, the victim is less likely to fire a gun as a means of self-defense (0.8%) than in cases where the victim and the offender do not know each other (4.2%). Conversely, when victim and offender know each other, the victim response is somewhat more likely to consist of fighting back through hitting, kicking, and so on (90.8% vs. 87.5% for cases where victim and offender do not know each other). There are no differences in likelihood of using a weapon other than a gun between the two groups (8.3% for both incidents involving strangers and incidents involving people known to each other).

Tables 2 and 3 show that the relationship remains virtually unchanged for males, females, and Whites. However, controlled analysis suggests that for non-Whites, there is no longer a significant difference in victim response depending upon knowing the offender(s). It is noteworthy that non-White victims were twice as likely as White victims to fire a gun in incidents where they did not know the offender (7.6% vs. 3.8%).

*Race of offender(s).* Tables 2 and 3 indicate that White offenders are more likely than non-White offenders to elicit a response of gun (3.8% vs. 1.3%) or weapon (10.3% vs. 7.3%) attack from a victim. This relationship is weak

(Cramer's $V = 0.1$), however. Controlled analysis shows that males are 3 times more likely to fire a gun at a White offender (4.8%) than at a non-White offender (1.6%). The initial relationship between offender's race and type of response fails to reach statistical significance when focusing on females only; yet the general pattern of increased likelihood to fight back without any weapons when the offender is non-White persists (91.6% for non-White offenders; 85.4% for White offenders) for females.

## CONCLUSIONS

Wolfgang's (1958) groundbreaking work in *Patterns in Criminal Homicide* was the first to focus on the importance of the victim in violent crime. Wolfgang's approach was based on the premise that the criminal act is not a simple, one-directional one originating in the character and qualities and attitudes of the perpetrator. Rather, the violent criminal incident is a complex interaction of factors of the offender(s), the victim, and environmental aspects of the situation itself. Our report follows this lead by focusing on factors which distinguish between different types of response to criminal victimization, including offender, victim, and incident characteristics. We must note that using NCS data limits our analysis of the victim-offender interaction by not providing adequate information; also, NCS provides no information to help understand the temporal character of the events constituting a criminal victimization.

Using a weapon in self-defense is a relatively rare occurrence. Most crime victims either do not actively resist their attacker, or use yelling, talking, or some other form of evasive action (Webb & Marshall, 1989). The present research report focuses on a relatively atypical response to criminal victimization: victims who reportedly used some form of physical resistance when attacked. The NCS data used in the present report indicate, not surprisingly, that the most common form of physical resistance is hitting, biting, kicking, or pushing—not firing a gun or using a knife or other weapon.

The typical crime victim, particularly of crimes involving violence, is male, young, and White (Johnson & DeBerry, 1989). Consistent with the sociodemographic characteristics of the most victimized groups, we found that the majority of the victims who reportedly defended themselves physically during the criminal incident were male, White, and young. Also consistent with the well-documented disproportionate victimization rate among Blacks (Whitaker, 1990), our data showed a slight overrepresentation of non-White victims among all three response groups (29.6% of those who

190

fired a gun; 25.7% of those who used another weapon; 16.1% of those who fought back without a weapon).

When describing the characteristics of the three groups, we noted that the frequency distributions of Group 2 and Group 3 were rather similar and quite different from the victims who used a gun (Group 1). Comparisons of the distribution of the variables for the three response groups suggest that the group who fired a gun differs from the two other response groups in several ways. Specifically, those who fired a gun were somewhat less likely to be young, poorly educated, or poor than those victims who used another weapon or fought back through kicking, hitting, and so on. Furthermore, the victims who used a gun tended to have lived in the same residence for a longer time period; conversely, victims who used another weapon or their hands tended to have moved quite frequently during the past several years.

The descriptions also suggest important differences in characteristics of the offender, distinguishing those who use a gun from the other two response groups. A gun was used more frequently in incidents where the victim was faced by an armed White stranger; other physical responses (either another weapon or fists or feet) more typically involved an unarmed, non-White offender (often known to the victim) where the victim reported being hit or attacked by the offender.

The descriptions presented in the first part of the article suggest both differences and similarities between the three response groups. In order to be able to better specify the interrelationships between the focal variables and type of victim response, the second part of the article presented the results of cross-tabular analysis, controlling for race and sex of the victim. Generally speaking, we found that the clusters of Achievement factors (family income, education), Victim Insecurity factors (number of moves in the last 5 years, series victimization, distance from home when incident occurs), and Incident Environment factors (amount of light, time of incident, and presence of household members) were relatively insignificant in determining type of physical victim response.

On the other hand, the actions and characteristics of the offender (Offender Environment factors), as well as the victim characteristics of age, race, and sex (Ascriptive factors), appear to definitely be of importance in determining victim response. Our initial analysis suggests some kind of interaction between race of both victim and offender, sex of victim, presence of weapon, prior relationship between victim and offender, and type of physical victim response. In view of the paramount importance of race and sex as correlates of both criminal offending and criminal victimization, our findings are hardly surprising. For example, Blacks are more likely to be the victim of a violent crime than Whites; violent crimes against Blacks tend to be more serious than against Whites; Black victims are more likely to face an armed offender; Black victims are more likely to be physically attacked and injured than Whites (Whitaker, 1990). Differential involvement in both offending and victimization of males, females, Blacks, and Whites reflects structural and cultural differences. Similarly, differential responses to criminal victimization are likely to reflect the different cultural and social backdrop for the different race/sex/age categories in U.S. society.

In this analysis, we have only begun to delineate some of the variables which seem to belong in the mix of victim characteristics, offender characteristics and actions, and incident variables. Although our simple analytic approach is valuable for uncovering interesting and thought-provoking relationships, a more complete understanding of the use of self-defensive measures in the event of criminal victimization surely calls for more complicated multivariate approaches. These multivariate approaches should be built upon suitable theoretical foundations: Our study is meant to contribute this end.

## APPENDIX
### Measurement of Key Variables

*Dependent Variables*

1. Fired gun at offender(s): This is a computed 2-value (yes/no) variable composed of the responses to the following item: "Attacked offender with gun; fired gun?"
2. Used other weapon: This is a computed 2-value (yes/no) variable composed of the responses to the following item: "Attacked offender with other weapon?"
3. Hit offender(s) without weapon: This is a computed 2-value (yes/no) variable composed of the responses to the following item: "Attacked offender without weapon (hit, kick, etc.)?"

*Ascriptive Factors*

1. Age: This variable reflects the response to the question: "Age last birthday?"
2. Race: The variable reflects the respondent's designation of his or her racial category. The choices were White, Black, American Indian/Aleutian/Eskimo, Asian/Pacific Islander. In the present analysis, the data was grouped into White and non-White.
3. Sex: This reflects the interviewer's recording of the respondent's gender.

*Achievement Factors*

1. Education: Response to the question, "What is the highest grade or year of regular school you have ever attended?" We employed three categories: K through 11th grade, high school diploma, and college work.
2. Family income: The respondent was provided with 14 income categories which were recoded into 5 categories (see Table 1).

*Insecurity Factors*

1. Number of moves in the last 5 years: This variable reflects the response to the question, "Altogether, how many times have you moved in last 5 years?" (see Table 1).
2. Series victimization: This variable reflects the interviewer's response on the question, "Is this incident report for a series crime?" This label is applied to victimizations if the incidents are very similar in detail, there are at least three incidents in the series, and the respondent is not able to recall dates and other details well enough to report them.
3. Distance from home when incident occurs: The variable reflects the response to the question, "How far away from home did this [incident] happen?" (see Table 1 for categories employed).

*Incident Environment Factors*

1. Amount of light: The variable reflects the response to the question, "Was it daylight or dark outside when (this/the most recent) incident happened?"
2. Time of incident: The variable reflects the response to the question "About what time did (this/the most recent) incident happen?" (see Table 1).
3. Household members present: This variable represents the response to the question, "Which household members were present [at the time of the incident]?"

*Offender Environment Factors*

1. Offender had weapon?: This variable reflects the yes/no response to the question, "Did the offender(s) have a weapon such as a gun or knife, or something to use as a weapon, such as a bottle or wrench?"
2. Offender hit or attacked: This variable represented the yes/no response to the question, "Did the offender(s) hit you, knock you down, or actually attack you in any way?"

*(Continued)*

**APPENDIX Continued**

3.  Offender threatened: This variable represents the response to the question, "Did the offender(s) threaten you with harm in any way?"
4.  Offender known to victim: This variable is a computed 2-value variable based upon responses to two items:
    Item Number 1: (single offender) Was the offender someone you knew or a stranger you had never seen before?
    Item Number 2: (multiple offenders) Were any of the offenders known to you or were they all strangers you had never seen before?
5.  Race of offender(s): This variable is a computed 2-value variable based upon responses to two items:
    Item Number 1: (single offender) Was the offender White, Black, or some other race?
    Item Number 2: (multiple offenders) Were the offenders White, Black, or some other race?

## NOTES

1. Earlier versions of the NCS questionnaire posed the question: "Did you do anything to protect yourself or your property during the incident?" If the respondent answers "yes," he or she is asked to describe the details of the action taken. The response categories are coded: (1) *used or brandished gun or knife*; (2) *used/tried physical force*; (3) *tried to get help, attract attention, scare offender away*; (4) *threatened, argued, or reasoned with offender*; and (5) *resisted without force, used evasive action*. Since 1987, the question has been revised to segregate those who use a gun in self-defense and those who use another type of weapon in self-defense. This change makes possible the specific analysis of gun users, weapon users, and those who use physical force.

2. The present article does not include a direct measure of the seriousness of the offense; however, variables such as the presence of a weapon, offender hit or attacked, and offender threat may be seen as indirect reflection of the nature of the incident.

3. Caution must be used in the interpretation of this statistic because this univariate description does not take into account the nonrandom distribution of characteristics of the total population of crime victims. For instance, Table 1 indicates that 70.4% of the victims who fired a gun are White; the table does not provide any information on whether this percentage is different from the percentage of all crime victims who are White—only that there is a significant difference between the number of Whites and non-Whites in this particular group. Thus Table 1 simply provides a description of each of the three response groups without providing data that would allow us to make any inferences about the differences or similarities of these subgroups with victims who did not respond physically to their victimization.

194

## REFERENCES

Bankston, W. B., & Thompson, C. Y. (1989). Carrying firearms for protection: A causal model. *Sociological Inquiry, 59*(1), 75-87.

Claster, D. S., & David, D. S. (1981). The resisting victim: Extending the concept of victim responsibility. In B. Galaway & J. Hudson (Eds.), *Perspectives on crime victims* (pp. 183-188). St. Louis: C. V. Mosby.

Cook, P. J. (1982). The role of firearms in violent crime: An interpretive review of the literature. In M. E. Wolfgang & N. A. Weiner (Eds.), *Criminal violence* (pp. 236-291). Beverly Hills, CA: Sage.

Gastil, R. D. (1971). Homicide and a regional culture of violence. *American Sociological Review, 36*, 412-427.

Goode, W. J. (1972). Presidential address: The place of force in human society. *American Sociological Review, 37*, 507-519.

Hill, G. D., Howell, F. M., & Driver, E. T. (1985). Gender, fear, and protective handgun ownership. *Criminology, 23*(3), 541-552.

Johnson, J. M., & DeBerry, M. M., Jr. (1989). *Bureau of Justice statistics bulletin: A national crime survey report—Criminal victimization 1989.* Washington, DC: U.S. Department of Justice.

Kleck, G. (1986). Policy lessons from recent gun control research. *Law and Contemporary Problems, 49*(1), 35-62.

Kleck, G. (1988). Crime control through the private use of armed force. *Social Problems, 35*(1), 1-21.

Marshall, C. E., & Webb, V. J. (1988). *A descriptive analysis of crime victims who use guns in self-defense.* Presented at the annual meeting of the Academy of Criminal Justice Sciences, San Francisco.

Marshall, I. H., & Webb, V. J. (1987). Fighting back: A test of the subculture of violence. *Criminal Justice Policy Review, 2*(4), 325-336.

Polsby, D. D. (1986). Reflections on violence, guns, and the defensive use of lethal force. *Law and Contemporary Problems, 49*(1), 89-111.

U.S. Department of Justice, Bureau of Justice Statistics. (1990). *National crime surveys: National sample, 1987-1989* (near-term data). Ann Arbor, MI: Inter-University Consortium for Political and Social Research.

Webb, V. J., & Marshall, I. H. (1989). Response to criminal victimization by older Americans. *Criminal Justice and Behavior, 16*, 239-258.

Whitaker, C. J. (1990). *Bureau of Justice statistics special report: Black victims.* Washington, DC: U.S. Department of Justice.

Whitehead, J. T., & Langworthy, R. H. (1989). Gun ownership and willingness to shoot: A clarification of current controversies. *Justice Quarterly, 6*, 263-282.

Wolfgang, M. E. (1958). *Patterns in criminal homicide.* Philadelphia: University of Pennsylvania Press.

Wright, J. D., Rossi, P. H., & Daly, K., with the assistance of Weber-Burdin, L. (1983). *Under the gun: Weapons, crime and violence in America.* New York: Aldine.

Young, R. L., McDowall, D., & Loftin, C. (1987). Collective security and the ownership of firearms for protection. *Criminology, 25*(1), 47-81.

*Chris E. Marshall, Ph.D., is an assistant professor in the Department of Criminal Justice at the University of Nebraska at Omaha. His research interests include fear of crime, self-protective measures used by victims of crime, the use of weapons by crime victims in self-defense, and the factors influencing the choice to report incidents of victimization.*

*Vincent J. Webb, Ph.D., is a professor and chairman of the Department of Criminal Justice at the University of Nebraska at Omaha. During the past few years, his research has focused on victim responses to victimization, violence, especially homicide, and drugs and crime. He also is a coinvestigator of the U.S. component of the International Self-Report Delinquency Project.*

*INTERNATIONAL JOURNAL OF COMPARATIVE AND APPLIED CRIMINAL JUSTICE*
*FALL 1994, VOL. 18, NO. 2*

# United States Crime Victim Assistance: History, Organization and Evaluation

### ROBERT J. MC CORMACK
### Trenton State College

Segments of this article originally were written and presented to an international audience at the meetings of The World Society of Victimology, held in Jerusalem in 1988; other parts of the paper are new. The early material has been expanded and updated to reflect recent changes in assistance to crime victims. The first part of the paper presents a brief history of the victim assistance movement in the United States from the 1960s to the 1990s. The second part discusses the organization and operations of the victim assistance system at the federal, state, and local levels; the final section provides suggestions for evaluation, and perhaps change, in policy and procedure.

Over the past several decades, as a result of dramatic increases in violent crime, concern for the victims of crime has been growing in the United States. A general anxiety about the government's ability to provide a basic level of safety for its citizens has contributed significantly to this concern.

The heightened awareness of crime and victims has been ascribed to several major factors. First was the sheer number of individuals affected by crime during the 1960s, and the apparent inability of the criminal justice system to respond effectively. Second was the initiation of the National Crime Surveys in 1972 by the Law Enforcement Assistance Administration. These surveys showed that the official FBI data significantly underestimated actual levels of victimization, and thus increased citizen anxiety. A third factor was the simultaneous resurgence of the feminist movement and its advocacy for the increasing number of female crime victims. The movement highlighted the particular vulnerability of women as a social group to violent crimes such as rape, battering, and other forms of domestic abuse (Schwendinger and Schwendinger, 1983). A final factor was the determination and eventual success of victims' advocates in placing financial responsibility for victim compensation on state governments (Young, 1987:9). I discuss each of these factors briefly.

## Crime in America

The beginning of the baby boom in the late 1940s and the concomitant increase in crime in the United States are related to the circumstances surrounding the conclusion of World War II. More than 16 million Americans served in the armed forces from 1940 through 1945. When the war ended, Americans were eager to resume their previous lives. One of the fruits of victory was a return to familism. This traditional orientation was particularly strong during the postwar years; home life had been threatened so seriously that most women (and men) wanted more than anything else to marry and have families (Hunt, 1970:95). During the ensuing years, 1946 through 1964, 76 million Americans were born. In 1946, the year immediately following the end of hostilities, the birth rate was the highest ever for Americans — more than 30 births per 1,000 of the population (Time, 1986:22).

By the mid-1960s an unanticipated by-product of the baby boom developed: the unprecedented increase in teenagers was accompanied by a corresponding increase in the volume of crime. "The crime rate skyrocketed between 1960, when about 3.3 million crimes were reported to police agencies, and 1981, when 13.4 million crimes were recorded" (Seigel and Senna, 1991:28). Concern about crime victims grew steadily during this period. Law-and-order groups began to call for tougher measures against offenders. They criticized civil rights and civil liberties groups for their efforts to control government responses to the crisis, and began to champion a victim-oriented criminal justice system (Karmen, 1990:36).

For the first time in this century, victims began to be included in the criminal justice process in a meaningful way. In the 1970s, prosecutors began to consider their concerns seriously in plea bargains; "impact statements" from victims and/or survivors became a part of the courts' sentencing process; probation and parole conditions included restitution more frequently than in the past. By the mid-1980s, well over half the states had passed victims' rights legislation. By the later part of the decade at least 10 states had introduced legislation to amend the Sixth Amendment to the U.S. Constitution to guarantee that "the victim, in every prosecution, has the right to be present and to be heard at all critical stages of judicial proceedings" (Task Force Report on Victims of Crime, 1982).

More recently, court decisions at the federal level have supported crime victims and survivors, In June 1991, for example, the United States Supreme Court overruled a state court decision (*Payne v. Tennessee*) that prohibited impact statements in death penalty hearings. Chief Justice William H. Rehnquist found that those prior rulings turned the victim into a "faceless stranger." He concluded that allowing the family and friends of a convicted murderer to testify to a sentencing jury on the offender's behalf while silencing the victim's family "unfairly weighted the scales" of justice.

People still harbor serious doubts about the ability of government or the criminal justice system to significantly reduce current levels of personal violence and property crime, even though the increase in the crime rate has slowed since the early 1980s and the prison and probation populations have doubled.

### Crime Reporting and the National Crime Surveys

Although fear of crime has affected the quality of life in the United States since the early 1960s, the true extent of victimization was not known until the National Crime Surveys were initiated in 1972. Before that time, the American public relied on the Uniform Crime Reports (UCR) of the Federal Bureau of

Investigation for their information. The accuracy of the UCR had been the subject of much discussion since the creation of the system by Congress in 1930. The data came from local police agencies throughout the country and included only reported crimes. Further, in the early years, the types, numbers, and clearance rates for crimes were false in many cases, and were intended to make police agencies appear more effective than they were.

Many of these reporting problems were corrected over the years as police departments became more professional and crime analysis techniques became more sophisticated. By the 1960s the major issue connected with the use of the UCR was that they measured only "crimes known to police." Many criminologists recognized that for a variety of reasons, many victims did not report incidents to the police, and that the police did not record every criminal act brought to their attention. Until the early 1960s, one could only speculate on the level of under reporting and under recording.

In 1966 a pilot victimization study was conducted under the sponsorship of the Law Enforcement Assistance Administration of the Department of Justice. In 1972, as a result, the United States Bureau of Census began to conduct the largest survey of crime victimization ever undertaken. The survey involved 60,000 households selected randomly from a pool of 80 million families in the United States. Twice a year for three consecutive years, these families were visited and were interviewed personally about their experiences as victims of crime (currently these victim survey groups are changed every three years). The results showed that "for the crimes measured (rape, robbery, assault, burglary, theft), 36 million victimizations affecting 22 million households (about 25% of all U.S. households) occur each year, a level much higher than indicated by the number of crimes reported to the police" (Cole, 1992:15). The National Crime Surveys (NCS), as these studies are called, indicated that official FBI statistics underestimated actual victimization by 300 to 500 percent (Elias, 1986:38). NCS data, which presented a realistic assessment of the actual level of victimization in the United States, gave additional impetus to advocates of expanded services and financial help for crime victims.

### Victims of Crime and the Feminist Movement

After major successes during the late nineteenth and early twentieth century in regard to liberalized divorce laws, property rights for women, birth control clinics, and voting rights, feminists in post-World War II America saw their gains evaporating. In the resurgence of familism, many women gave up the work place for a place at home. As returning servicemen were reemployed, the salary gap widened between those men and the women who continued to work. Fewer women held legislative seats than previously; the number of faculty positions occupied by women in higher education decreased. No inroads into upper-echelon business and industrial management were made in the two decades after the war (Hunt, 1970:95).

Betty Friedan's *The Feminine Mystique*, published in 1963, sold 1.5 million copies. The book inspired the founding, in 1966, of the National Organization for Women (NOW). The major goal of this contemporary feminist organization was to challenge and remedy the discrimination faced by women in American society, particularly in education and employment. The organization also would have a dramatic impact on the social response to female victims of crime, especially victims of unreported domestic violence and rape (Karmen, 1990:34).

The first grassroots effort to assist sexual assault victims was made in 1972 by a group of feminists in Berkeley, California:

> It was here that the idea of a 24-hour hotline and the belief that victims needed alternative services to the criminal justice, hospital, and the mental health institutions, were born. BAWAR'S (Bay Area Women Against Rape) vision of services incorporated these ideas and implemented them along with direct counseling, public education, and rape prevention activity. The tiny handful of women...was composed of political activists and militant feminists who saw themselves as advocates of rape victims in the established institutions (Schwendinger and Schwendinger, 1983:9).

This program was followed rapidly by programs providing shelters for battered women and by victim assistance programs to deal with child abuse and neglect.

NOW had a significant impact on the treatment of female victims of crime. Its court challenges led to changes in the laws in many states, which make prosecution of offenders more of an option for women than in the past. Its educational work, emphasizing sexual equality, resulted in significant social change in a relatively short period. The impact of NOW on the actual operations of victims' assistance programs, however, has diminished. A current leader in the victims' movement describes the change:

> The feminist movement is responsible for the establishment of rape crisis centers and domestic violence shelters, and out of that I think it is clear that the victims' movement today is made up predominantly of women. But I think the impact of the National Organization for Women fell off sharply after that initial enthusiasm and that initial involvement, so that in today's world it simply does not have the same kind of impact on victims' assistance, per se, although clearly women are still in charge of most programs (Young, 1987:9).

## Crime Victim Compensation Programs

One of the most politically significant and dramatic advances in contemporary victim assistance was made in 1965, when the State of California began its own program to compensate crime victims in the absence of any private or governmental programs. Initially the state provided funds to innocent and needy victims of violent criminal acts and to dependents of murder victims. California's initiative was followed quickly by similar programs in New York State (1966), Hawaii (1967), Massachusetts and Maryland (1968), and New Jersey (1971). Miers suggests, in regard to the emergence of violent crime compensation boards (VCCBs), that:

a significant characteristic of the relationship between government and the individual during this period (the late sixties) was the "politicization" of the victim of crime. By this I mean that through media pressure and the influence of certain individuals in public office and elsewhere, victims of crimes of violence were converted into an identifiable and coherent group, with evident political potential....There is, in my view, little doubt but that political factors were the single most important determinant behind the introduction of victim compensation schemes (Miers, 1978:51).

Another expert on crime victims declares that the importance of the emergence of VCCBs should not be underestimated: "Although the civil rights and anti-war movements in the United States, and comparable movements elsewhere, helped promote a climate for considering victims generally, not until compensation programs arose in the late 1960's did crime victims really begin to emerge." (Elias, 1986:19).

By 1991, 45 states had established victim compensation programs (Mc Cormack, 1991:330). These programs reimburse victims of crime for their losses, pay significant out-of-pocket medical expenses, provide for long-term care for seriously injured victims, pay burial expenses, and provide other services. The programs vary as to fund-raising methods, eligibility requirements, and the size of the compensation awards.

### An Overview of Victim Assistance Programs

To understand the nature of the victims' assistance network in the United States, it might be helpful at this point to discuss briefly how the national, state, and local governments interact on behalf of crime victims.

At the national level, the government is headed by a president elected every four years. A bicameral congress considers and passes legislation for the entire country according to procedures established by a federal constitution. In 1984 the U.S. Congress passed the first major piece of crime victim legislation, the Victims of Crime Act. The Act was amended and improved in 1986 and 1988, and currently is funded through 1994 at $150 million per year. These funds mainly support state-level agencies and programs aiding victims of crime.

The United States is a confederation of autonomous states — 50 at the present time — each with its own governor and legislative body, its own constitution, a great degree of independence in establishing its governance, its own criminal and civil laws and taxing powers, and the authority to determine the nature and purposes of its social institutions. Over the years, all of the states have established and funded some amount of crime victim assistance. For example, almost all states have crime victim compensation boards to reimburse victims for financial losses resulting from criminal acts; all provide some funding for general victim services, aiding victims of sexual assault, helping victims of domestic violence, and other services.

The states are divided into counties for voting, taxation, court and trial processes, and other functions. Counties are composed of various municipalities, villages, townships, and other jurisdictions; each of these has executives, governing bodies, and limited power to pass local laws and administrative rules affecting their residents. The great majority of these local jurisdictions have victim assistance programs. Because of the number and diversity of these programs, coordination of effort is difficult at best; it depends heavily on the cooperation and the agreement of interests of the groups involved. Personal leadership at each level of operation (national, state, and local) is critical in influencing the ultimate delivery of victim services.

### Victim Assistance at the National Level

Since the mid-1960s the United States Congress has considered and rejected numerous bills to compensate victims of crime. Progress was not made at the national level until the Republican administrations of the 1980s embraced the victims' movement as a natural extension of their conservative philosophy opposing criminal offenders. Those administrations created the President's Task Force on Victims of Crime in 1982, and backed the 1982 Omnibus Victims of Crime Act and the 1984 Crime Victim Assistance Act (Elias, 1986:20). Despite its support however, the federal government has been consistent in its view that public safety and assistance to crime victims are ultimately state concerns. Therefore, none of the national legislation, then or since that time, has provided sufficient funding to fully address the problems of compensation or other forms of victim assistance.

The Victims of Crime Act of 1984 created the Office for Victims of Crime (OVC), which remains the most significant federal agency for victim assistance. As a result of the Act, fines and fees levied against persons convicted of federal crimes are spent to assist crime victims throughout the country. No centralized agencies exist in individual states to receive and distribute the funds from the OVC; rather, federal funds go directly to state agencies and programs that provide victim assistance according to a plan developed by the OVC. These funds in turn filter down to support victim assistance programs at the county level, including local municipal, town, and village programs.

### Assistance at the State Level

As noted above, states rather than the federal government have been in the vanguard of the victims' movement since the 1960s. The first major state legislation for compensating crime victims was passed in California in 1965 and was followed rapidly by similar legislation in other states. Crime victim compensation boards (their titles vary among states) continue to be administered centrally at the state level. In addition to federal funds provided by the OVC since 1984, states have raised their own funds to support the compensation boards through taxes, penalty assessments, or other means. In some cases, states support victim assistance programs which are administered by county-level prosecutors' offices. Various county programs also receive support funds from state agencies such as departments of mental health and family and social services.

**Assistance at the County (Local) Level**

Because most crime control and prosecutorial responsibilities are lodged at the county level, the local police, local prosecutors and courts, and local victims' advocates collectively provide the most direct and most significant assistance to crime victims. Many of the programs at this level tend to be victim-specific; they deal with a single group such as battered wives, abused or sexually molested children, rape victims, or geriatric victims. Their staffs tend to be a mix of professionals and volunteers working in close cooperation with criminal justice practitioners and hospital emergency room personnel. Among the most effective are the many Victim/Witness Assistance Programs. These are administered by county prosecutors' offices, which provide crime victims with support, monetary assistance, and legal advice.

**Crime Victim Leadership Organizations**

Many national (and state) organizations lobby for victims' rights and influence legislation on behalf of crime victims. Most prominent are the National Organization for Victims Assistance (NOVA), The National Victims Center (NVC), Mothers Against Drunk Driving (MADD), The National Committee for the Prevention of Child Abuse (NCPCA), and the National Coalition Against Sexual Assault (NCASA). These groups act as victim assistance coordinators for a vast network of volunteer, practitioner, and professional victim assistance programs at the national, state, and local levels. Their activities include public education, training, fund raising, lobbying, and information management.

Although they have no direct authority over the many victims' programs in the country, these professionally managed agencies have succeeded in coordinating the activities of the diverse victims' groups throughout the United States. Through their leadership over the years they have been able to bring together an array of public and private victims' programs and tie them into the network of state and federally funded programs. In addition, they have lobbied successfully at the federal and state levels for a variety of legislation benefiting victims. Generally these are private, nonprofit organizations that are supported by their members and by public and private grants and donations.

**A Time for Introspection**

Developments in crime victim assistance in the United States over the past 30 years have been truly remarkable. In the face of such progress, it is difficult to speak of shortcomings. Yet as the movement continues to mature, existing policy and/or operations should be reviewed and new or tangential directions should be charted in certain major, closely related areas.

## Developing a General Welfare Perspective

From its beginning, the victims' movement in the United States has been influenced by a retributive philosophy. In fact, it originated with groups that had a strong anti-offender bias (Karmen, 1984:20). It has been difficult to disengage from this legacy, which has caused tensions among otherwise supportive individuals. They view such a philosophy as lacking dimension and perhaps as counterproductive (Walker, 1989:167,170). At a workshop on violence and public health, Marvin Wolfgang advocated a more comprehensive commonweal perspective. He suggested that efforts to deal with deviant behavior (and its victims) should extend beyond the criminal justice system and the notion of deserved punishment:

> Tensions between justice and public tranquility and order were guiding concerns in the quest of the Violence Commission (1969) to understand and to prevent violence. In that analytical and philosophical context, violent disorder was dissected with the cutting instrument of criminal law and the system of criminal justice. Although various theories were used to reveal the causes of violence, the primary inquiry was from the viewpoint of violative and unlawful behavior.

> The Founding Fathers seemed prescient in their deliberations and constitutional framing. They inscribed another viewpoint and objective into this nation's first legal document; namely, the promotion of the general welfare....The disorders of violence are as much challenge to the general health and welfare of our nation as they are to the system of justice and law (Wolfgang, 1985:9).

By adopting such a general welfare perspective, advocates for crime victims' would include among their concerns the "offender/victims" — that is, offenders who themselves are victims of discrimination, racism, poverty, and related conditions. Promoting programs to assist these high-risk individuals would be consistent with the overall goals of victim advocacy: *to prevent victimization* as well as to support victims of violence. A strong commitment to helping individuals in these offender/victim groups would contribute directly to a reduction in victimization. The major caution, then, is that in the fervor to achieve a universal bill of rights for victims, the movement must not forget that many offenders are victims in their own right. A movement ideology that sponsors gains for crime victims at the expense of constitutional and human rights eventually may lose support.

## Victim Compensation Programs

Victims' advocates should be concerned about the fact that so few victims of crime actually are assisted by violent crime compensation boards. A major reason, it seems, is the symbolic nature of the political commitment to victims' assistance on the part of federal and state lawmakers, which results in seriously inadequate program funding. A 1991 national survey of VCCBs revealed:

> that a paucity of funds in almost all state programs accounts in part for limitations on the numbers and amounts of compensation awards. Many states have set the

> maximum award per victimization at unrealistically low levels, which obviate the original intent; those states which offer more generous benefits are in danger of overexpending their resources. North Carolina's VCCB is so hard pressed, for example, that it has been forced to disseminate funds on a first come, first served basis (Mc Cormack, 1991:338).(3)

The survey showed wide variations among the states in claims filed, awards made, and awards-to-claims ratios.

This study and others (Chappel, 1988; Elias, 1986; Friedman et al., 1982; Gattuso-Holman, 1976, Karmen, 1984) have pointed out that in addition to lack of funds, lack of information about the programs is a major reason why victims do not file claims. Chappel suggests, "Perhaps the most significant (limitation) of these (VCCBs) is the lack of public awareness of the very existence of the programs, a situation that can be explained in many jurisdictions by poor mechanisms devised to bring the programs to the attention of eligible crime victims" (1988:380). According to *Compensating Victims of Crime*, the 1992 report of the Office of Justice Programs of the National Institute of Justice, only 10 program directors said that "victims in their state were adequately informed about the compensation program... if programs made more victims aware of their rights to compensation, they likely would diminish the average claim paid to those victims, unless there were major increases in funding." The report also stated that "almost half the program directors said that existing funds for program administration were inadequate"; even if "better outreach efforts increased the number of claims, many states would be unable to process the increased case load in an efficient and timely manner" (NIJ, 1992:13,14).

The remoteness of most VCCBs from their clients also seems to contribute significantly to the low level of claims. Most state VCCBs have only one central office. If outreach is to be successful, more decentralized, community-based locations must be established in urban neighborhoods, where victimization is most prevalent. Again, in reference to the 1992 NIJ report cited above, researchers pointed to the decentralized, highly effective VCCB of Denver, Colorado, "in which separate victim compensation boards were established in each of the state's judicial districts, administered by local district attorney's (prosecutor's) office". The report mentions a number of bureaucratic objections to such programs. Supporters of such decentralized programs, however, believe that the administrators "would be more sensitive to victims' interests and needs and because compensation decisions would be made by local officials [they] would insure better coordination with locally delivered victim service programs".

**Victim/Witness Assistance Programs**

Victim/Witness Assistance Programs (VWAPs) administered by local prosecutors suffer from the same lack of legislative commitment as compensation boards (Roberts, 1990:107). Their problems are compounded by (1) the "functional" or system-facilitating nature of the programs — that is, the offer of assistance to victims who agree to cooperate in the prosecution of the offender — and (2) the fact that they provide virtually no outreach to crime victims whose crimes are not cleared by arrest. In regard to the first of these elements, Elias points out that:

> Within criminal justice, officials often consider victims as a threat or interference in their activities. And victim programs may be even more threatening, unless tailored to official objectives. Witness management schemes, for example, may promote official goals, but expensive victim assistance programs may drain scarce resources and thus be resisted....This suggests that only victim advocacy carefully tailored to parallel official goals will be likely to be successful, even if such schemes do not serve victim interests very well or perhaps at all (1986:238).

As to the second element, the lack of services to victims of uncleared crimes, VWAP coordinators in New Jersey reported, "It would be unusual for [us] to be provided with information concerning crimes that were not currently being handled by the prosecutor's office." The data in that report revealed that in the 21 New Jersey counties, slightly more than 100 victimizations connected with uncleared crime came to the attention of VWAP coordinators each month (Mc Cormack, 1992:8).

**Police and Crime Victims**

The policing establishment in the United States generally has not lived up to its potential for assisting crime victims. Of the approximately 15,000 state and local police departments in the country, only a handful have effective programs for post crime victim assistance. In an earlier version of this paper I cited a State of New Jersey survey of 'chiefs of police' conducted in 1988. In the lead question in the survey, the chiefs were asked whether, in addition to the normal crisis intervention response to reported crime, they had formal programs of victim assistance. Of the 51 responding agencies, 47 replied in the negative. The chiefs also were asked whether, in their opinion, coordinating immediate aftercare assistance to crime victims was an appropriate use of police resources. Forty-five said "no." The following statement was typical of the negative responses:

> There is no way that police agencies can take on any additional roles with respect to social services. We are already taxed with victims procedures, domestic violence programs, alcohol and drug dependency programs and there is no assistance from the state with respect to manpower or budget increases. They are living in a dream world — do more with less. These recent additional responsibilities defy all reason. Most chiefs of police feel that, in time, police work will have to be returning to general police work and will designate social agencies to deal with social problems. We are being dumped on because we work 365 days a year and around the clock. It is more economical to throw things in the direction of law enforcement.

On the basis of this survey and more than 40 years of research and experience with policing nationwide, it is clear to me that police view victims as an added burden on their already overtaxed resources rather than as an opportunity to enrich their jobs and perform a vital service to their communities. Victims' advocates should focus more attention on the police as a prime source of victim assistance. They are the first at the scene of a crisis, and with proper indoctrination and training can significantly affect the impact of victimization. One of the surest ways for the police to achieve the professional status they seek is through this type of community service. Perhaps the victims' movement should sponsor such recognition more aggressively in return for a more responsive role in victims' affairs on the part of the police.

## Summary

The major areas of concern described above must be addressed if the victims' movement is to continue to grow and mature. To reach its full potential and to expand on its remarkable achievements since the 1960s, the movement must seek out issues that will augment its political base. By embracing a wider spectrum of national victim concerns — particularly those related to victims in lower socioeconomic groups — and by assuming a general welfare position rather than a retributive stance, victims' advocacy will attract a wider constituency. The Office for Victims of Crime points the way in its "Report to Congress: April 1990". It suggests that new challenges are arising, which were not addressed in the original or amended forms of The Victims of Crime Act. These include hate crimes resulting in murder, rape, assault, and vandalism against persons of a particular race, religion, or sexual orientation. The report also highlights the epidemic of drugs and violence and recommends that victims' advocates show concern for the impact of such crimes on residents of the affected neighborhoods. In addition, the report suggests that the emergence of new populations of drug-addicted babies and the lack of victim assistance programs in high-crime neighborhoods should be concerns of the victims' movement. These new initiatives are essential if the victims' movement in the United States is to realize its potential to serve society's victims fairly and effectively.

## REFERENCES

Chappel, D. 1988. "The implementation of victims' rights in North America." In M.C. Bassiouni (Ed.) *Nouvelles estudes penales: International protection of victims*. Toulouse, France: Eres, pp. 377-384.

Cole, G.F. 1983. *The American system of criminal justice*, third edition. Monterey, CA: Brooks/Cole Publishing Company.

Department of Justice, Office of Justice Programs. 1992. *Compensating crime victims: A summary of policies and practices*. Washington, DC: U.S. Government Printing Office.

Department of Justice, Office for Victims of Crime. 1990. *Victims of crime act of 1984 as amended: A report to Congress by the Attorney General.* Washington, DC: U.S. Government Printing Office.

Elias, R. 1986. *The politics of victimization: Victims, victimology and human rights.* New York, NY: Oxford University Press.

Friedman, Kenneth, Helen Bischoff, Robert Davis, and Andresa Person. 1982. *Victims and helpers: Reactions to crime.* Washington, DC: National Institute of Justice.

Gattuso-Holman, Nancy A. 1976. "Criminal sentencing and victim compensation legislation: Where is the victim?" In Emilio C. Viano (Ed.) *Victims and society.* Washington, DC: Visage, pp. 363-367.

Hunt, Morton. 1970. "Up against the wall, male chauvinist pig." *In From Playboy: The sexual revolution.* Chicago, IL: Playboy Press, pp 93-103.

Karmen, Andrew. 1990. *Crime victims: An introduction to victimology*, 2nd edition. Monterey, CA: Brooks/Cole.

Mc Cormack, Robert J. 1988. *Police chief's survey on crime victim assistance: State of New Jersey.* Trenton State College, unpublished.

_____. 1991. "Compensating victims of violent crime." *Justice Quarterly*, Volume 8, Number 3, September, Washington, DC, pp.329-346.

_____. 1992. "Outside the victims system: Crimes 'not cleared by arrest' or 'downgraded'. " Paper presented at the Annual Meeting of the American Society of Criminology, New Orleans, Louisiana, November.

Miers, David. 1978. *Responses to victimization: A comparative study of compensation for criminal violence in Great Britain and Ontario.* Abingdon, Oxon: Professional Books Limited, p. 51.

Roberts, Albert R. 1990. *Helping crime victims: Research, policy and practice.* Newbury Park, CA: Sage Publications, Inc.

Schwendinger, Julia R., and Herman Schwendinger. 1983. *Rape and inequality.* Beverly Hills, CA: Sage Publications, Inc..

Siegel, Larry J., and Joseph J. Senna. 1991. *Juvenile delinquency: Theory, practice and law*, St. Paul, MN: West Publishing Company.

United States. 1982. *President's task force on victims of crime: Final report.* Washington DC: U.S. Government Printing Office.

Time Magazine. 1986. "Growing pains at 40," March 19.

Walker, Samuel. 1992. *The police in America: An introduction.* New York, NY: Mc Graw-Hill, Inc..

Wolfgang, Marvin E. 1985. "Interpersonal violence and public health care: New Directions, new challenges." In U.S. Department of Health and Human Services, *Surgeon General's workshop on violence and public health report.* Washington, DC: DHHS, pp.9-18.

Young, Marlene. 1987. "Who's looking out for victims." Interview by Robert McCormack for *Law Enforcement News*, New York, NY, November 24.

# Radical Victimology:
# A Critique of the Concept of
# Victim in Traditional Victimology

Marilyn D. McShane
Frank P. Williams III

*Traditional victimology has not yet tapped the potential of radical criminology to assist in the explanation of social reactions to crime and crime victims. From the theoretical perspective of the radical framework it is possible to explore society's preference for truly innocent victims and the limited ability of the system to avenge them (i.e., through victim assistance programs). Other avenues of analysis from this perspective include the role of the victim in furthering the interests of police and prosecution agencies, as well as the interests of the media and capitalist business enterprises. A radical victimological approach can also be used to analyze the extended victimization of the offender's family by the criminal justice system.*

Interest in victims of criminal offenses is by no means new (von Hentig, 1948). In the 1970s, however, a new area called *victimology* emerged and its advocates proclaimed that it would be able to provide a more interdisciplinary and coherent approach to the topic than ever before. Through the 1980s the new field proliferated and established itself as a fixture in criminology and criminal justice. The subject matter of the new victimology lent itself to political and public interest and, we will argue, was coopted by those interests.

As victimology matured, much of the literature became focused on the concept of victims' rights. Concurrently, the public began to recognize "victims" and raise cries of outrage in response to media coverage of poorly treated victims. Amplifying the effect of this movement was the emergence of crusading victim's groups focused on singular crimes (drunken driving, missing children, and rape, for instance) and specific needs. One of the proposed solutions to the plight of the victim was victim compensation. Unfor-

MARILYN D. McSHANE:Associate Professor, Department of Criminal Justice, California State University, San Bernardino. FRANK P. WILLIAMS III:Professor and Chair, Department of Criminal Justice, California State University, San Bernardino.

CRIME & DELINQUENCY, Vol. 38 No. 2, April 1992 258-271

tunately, the benefits of compensation measures quickly faded as victims "discovered painfully that the recovery of money from a grudging bureaucracy was not the cure-all for the difficulties they experienced" (Geis 1990, p. 252). One of the consequences of their dissatisfaction was an attempt to give victims a more significant role in the criminal justice process. However, this new focus had the effect of precipitating a concentration on the offender and the criminal justice system, rather than on the victim. (See Murphy [1990], Smith [1988], and Umbreit [1989] for further discussion of the role of the victim, the criminal justice system, and the offender.)

In the discussion that follows, we argue that current images of victimology tend to involve the state rather than the victim. Further, those images have served a conservative crime control agenda and have increased the power of the state in criminal proceedings.

## RADICAL VICTIMOLOGY

In a 1983 essay David Friedrichs postulated that radical criminology and victimology had great potential for reciprocal influence. He suggested a search for ways to blend and empirically test some of their common theoretical propositions. Calling for a study of victims from a radical perspective, Friedrichs introduced the term radical victimology. Phipps (1986) also saw commonalities and contended that radical criminology could mature via the empirical research of victimization surveys. Both approaches eschew an isolated focus on the victim (or on the victim-offender relationship) and instead seek an analysis of the role of the victim within the criminal justice system. In short, they ask what the victim represents and symbolizes in the criminal justice system. Young (1986, p. 23) also uses the term radical victimology in referring to the necessity of determining the risk and effect of crime on citizens.

This essay responds to Friedrichs's and Phipps's calls for an expansion of the traditional victimological perspective. We do not, however, intend to limit ourselves to a particular form of radical criminology; to do so would narrow the approach and our purpose is to provide as much scope as possible. Rather than presenting a complete radical perspective, we will offer the general directions of such a position and provide some exemplary areas in which such work would be fruitful. Particular spheres of concern include the definition of victim; an understanding of the victim's assigned role in our criminal justice system; and the use and abuse of victims by the politico-economic system, the criminal justice system, politicians, and the media.

## DEFINITION OF THE VICTIM

Victims probably had their greatest say in and influence on dispositions of offenders prior to the emergence of systems of law. Victims and their relatives controlled the extent of retribution and, consequently, the extent of their satisfaction with the punishment meted out to the offender. The threat of blood feuds was high enough, however, to require societal intervention. Law, or the intervention of a third party as Hoebel (1954) defined it, began the process of restricting the role of the victim. With the advent of such notions as the "King's Peace," the victim began to fade from his or her key role in the criminal process and, in a move calculated to reinforce central authority, the state took over the role of the victim. True, individual victims showed up to testify at trials, or gave information to the criminal justice system in a variety of ways, but they were no longer the accusers and prosecutors who brought the offender to justice.

In addition to being banished from a major role in the criminal process, victims lost the important right to determine the essence of a transgression and the state began to use law to define offenses independent of the victim's sense of harm. From the perspective of traditional victimology, this point marked the beginning of neglect of the victim. As Zehr and Umbreit (1982, p. 64) have said, "victim neglect is not simply a result of indifference, it is a logical extension of a legal system which defines crime as an offense against the state."

The state's historically increasing indifference to victims is reflected in the changing criminal justice role it assigns to them. One reflection of this indifference is found in the modification of the victim's role from a person who has been harmed in some way to one who provides emotional credibility to the prosecution. In this fashion the state ignores actual harm and instead focuses on the offender, exacting the price for transgressing the legal codes. Such a process, where the victim is concerned, lacks satisfaction and reduces him or her to a secondary role. Real harm has thus been subordinated to theoretical conceptions of *legal* harm and the definition of a victim becomes an artificial one. Unfortunately, the traditional (system-oriented) definition of victim used in victimology is entirely created by law and the legal process. Some criminologists, however, have noted this restriction.

While victimology was still young, Richard Quinney (1972) criticized traditional state definitions of crime, criminals, and victims. At the same time, other radical criminologists began extending definitions of crime beyond those behaviors incorporated in criminal statutes to various forms of immoral activities and behaviors, particularly those committed in the name of capitalism and the state (Taylor, Walton, and Young 1973; Quinney 1974;

Krisberg 1975). Similarly, they enlarged the concept of victim to include those who suffered at the hands of the state (Schwendinger and Schwendinger 1970).

Radical discussions of this period identified new groups as victims, but they stopped short of developing the theme of the traditional victim as someone whose victimization continues within the criminal justice processing system. Instead, this latter notion was developed by victimologists. As a result, system victimization was denied a structural foundation and, instead, was discussed in a fashion that seemed to imply that this second victimization was a mistake of ignorance. Such an oversight could easily be remedied by specialized training of criminal justice personnel and by increasing the availability of victim's programs. In short, the definition of victim remains the same, albeit now we intend to include them within the system.

## THE INNOCENCE OF THE VICTIM

The images conveyed by official definitions of the victim are composed largely of middle-class symbolism. These images of the victim partake of an understanding of crime, and the criminal process, from a distance. Removed from the reality of crime as an endemic feature of American life, most middle-class citizens can only understand crime, and their own victimization, as irrational, senseless phenomena. From such a perspective, victims are merely innocent bystanders who are swept into this maelstrom of irrationality.[1] They cannot appreciate crime as a major contributor to an underground economy, a relief from the frustrations of living without means in a property-oriented society, or even as a form of excitement. For the middle class, the victim and offender are part of a strict dichotomy, a mutually exclusive set of categories. The offender cannot be viewed as victim, nor can the victim be viewed as offender.

Black's (1983) discussion of crime as "self-help" calls into question the purity of the victim/offender dichotomy. His conception suggests that at least some offenders and victims can be thought of as participants in a dynamic, ongoing interaction. At any point, participants can be called the victim or the offender, depending on the stage of the interaction. For instance, in an ongoing relationship, one of the actors may be taking retribution (Black's "self-help") on the other actor for an earlier "victimization." At that particular point, the earlier victim becomes the present offender and the earlier offender the present victim. If the interaction continues, the positions may again be exchanged. From this perspective, our popular conception of victims is derived from a simplistic middle-class framework where all victims are innocent characters in a morality play. This framework requires that victims do not participate in offenses and that the victim-offender relationship remains static. For example, the middle-class conception of an assault is one where a victim is irrationally done bodily harm by an offender who seems not to care about the inviolate rights of others.

Katz's (1988) recent work affirms that some offenders even seem to recognize and cultivate such an image of "irrationality" in their behavior.[2] Middle-class citizens may have difficulty in conceiving of a system where offenders and victims trade places as they act, react, and retaliate in an emergent drama of the sort commonly played in lower-class communities. Under these latter circumstances, the intervention of the criminal justice system itself is required to supply the labels of victim and offender. Until that intervention, there are no victims and offenders in the usual sense of the terms. In short, the two categories may be mixed and reciprocal until such time as the police appear. Typical public, and official, conceptions cannot capture the richness of this interplay and present a mythically pure and stereotypical vision of the victim.

A critical function of this artificiality is that it tends to subvert any search for root causes of crime, while restricting the public view of the nature of crime.[3] Because of the perception that victims and offenders do not share attributes, the public tends to explain crime by reference to characteristics, imputed or real, of the offender. Thus, the causes of crime are viewed as individual problems, such as a lack of discipline, irresponsibility, a lack of concern for others, or some other defect of character or genetics. The background factors of crime are either ignored or become secondary to those factors that capture the "real essence" of the offender.

We suggest that this problem breeds an emphasis on "garden-variety" street crime and deflects attention away from white-collar crime. Victims of white-collar crimes tend to be either nonsterotypical or diffuse in nature. Moreover, the offenders (financiers, corporate executives, evangelists) share attributes with the image of the middle-class victim rather than the image of the street criminal. Indeed, the imagery is so powerful that even when crimes of the powerful come before our legal system, they are most often handled outside of the criminal arena as civil lawsuits. When the Ivan Boeskys, the executives of Bank of Commerce and Credit International, and the Jim Bakkers of the world are indicted or convicted of crimes, the public can become incensed yet, in the next moment, will not incorporate their ilk in decrying the "problem of crime."

The stereotypical victim/offender dichotomy simply is not capable of incorporating the true complexity of crime, but such versions are dominant among the public and the media. How, then, does this image come to be and

what purposes does it serve? We believe that one answer lies in the maintenance of social order.

## IMAGES OF THE VICTIM AS ORDER-MAINTAINING

One of the critical problems for any social order is the maintenance of
exemplars. Durkheim's classic discussion of the order-maintaining role of
deviance and crime captures the flavor of that dilemma well. Without crime
and deviance, Durkheim (1965) maintained, a society would be unable to
define the boundaries of acceptable behavior. Because members of society
define behavior boundaries in an emergent fashion, a lack of exemplars
would, ironically, result in a deterioration of social order. Durkheim did not,
however, discuss the role of social imagery in defining exemplars.

A crucial part of social imagery is a clear distinction between those outside
and those inside moral boundaries. Otherwise there is no explicit lesson to
be learned, no clarification of the moral order. Where crime is concerned,
this means that participants in the event must be assigned independent
images. In the ideal, an offender must partake of an image that exemplifies
evil and, conversely, the victim must exemplify moral purity. Because real
situations do not always convey such a clear separation as does the ideal,
imagery becomes even more important as an order-maintaining device.

From this perspective, the earlier discussion of victim/offender brings into
question the value of real-life crime events for the maintenance of social
order. Thus, imagery is a social *enhancement* that assists in the separation of
victim/offender participants. But how does such imagery develop? One answer is that particular forms of social order are bound up with particular
images of the victim/offender. Political-legal frameworks underlying and
supporting a social order require certain roles to be played as transgressors
and victims. Should these roles be in question, or should they become
intermixed, those maintaining the social order must intervene to redefine the
roles and their boundaries. Failure to keep the roles separate may result in
challenges to the legal system, law, and ultimately to the political-legal order
itself. Imagery, then, is boundary-maintaining and necessary to the existence
and maintenance of any social order.

## THE UTILITY OF VICTIMS FOR THOSE WHO MAINTAIN ORDER

Once the concept and image of victim is fixed, social order is not only
maintained but actors within order-maintaining systems may benefit from

the victim's presence. As long as the victim is "pure," those manipulating the victim may also partake of that symbolism and enhance their positions. This is possible in individual cases within the legal system, in generalized cases within the system, and outside of the system as part of the political arena. We will now provide some examples of this function of the victim.

### The Criminal Justice System

Victim assistance programs provide excellent empirical insight into the utility of the victim for the criminal justice system. (See Peter Finn and Beverly Lee [1988] for a discussion of the use of victim-witness assistance programs.) A study of current programs demonstrates the extent to which their activity aids the prosecution's (political) response to crime.

An analysis of the components of various victim-witness assistance programs yields evidence that there is an overwhelming emphasis on the offender. That which is passed off as victim assistance is, in reality, predicated on the needs of the prosecution rather than on the needs of the victim. The major aspects of these programs include:

> *Victim notification*: notifying victims of the status of court proceedings involving the offender, such as plea negotiations, sentencing and parole decisions;
> *Victim impact statements*: informing the judge of the physical, financial and emotional impact of the crime on the victim, or the victim's survivors, to be used in consideration of the offender's sentence;
> *Court orientation*: providing information on the operation of the criminal justice system and emphasizing the victim's or witness' responsibilities in court to assist in the prosecution of the defendant;
> *Transportation*: transporting witnesses or victims to and from court, so that their presence may be used in the trial to help convict the defendant;
> *Escorting*: accompanying victims or witnesses to the courtroom and sitting with them during proceedings against the defendant.

At this point skeptics might argue that some of the services provided by victim-assistance programs, such as restitution and counseling seem to directly benefit the victim. However, under close and critical scrutiny, the evidence suggests that even the most personal of services are heavily motivated toward securing the assistance of victims in the prosecution. As Finn (n.d., p. 3) explains in a pamphlet on victim-assistance programs, "unless their emotional needs are met, many victims will either not testify — and thereby force the prosecutor to drop the case — or they will testify so poorly that the prosecutor loses the case. Thus, many prosecutors have come to value these programs' ability to prepare victims and witnesses." If this is not enough

216

evidence of prosecutorial emphasis, then consider that victim-assistance programs may choose to serve only those victims who report the crime, or whose case is prosecuted (Villmoare and Benevenuti 1988, p. 61).

Another multi-motive assistance package is help with filing a civil lawsuit against an attacker. Attorneys who aid in this process may have their fees paid out of a victims' fund; however, the victims may see little, if any, money from a judgement in their favor against the typical indigent offender. Thus attorneys have instituted a self-perpetuating process that provides them with work, while providing many victims with a false sense of legal recourse.

Victim compensation is another punitive tool used by the courts to exact a punishment on the offender. (For a discussion of victim compensation programs, see Karmen [1990, pp. 306-22].) Offenders will often not remain under supervision (a probation status normally required during which payments are made) long enough to make a substantial financial contribution toward the victim's loss. As Friedrichs (1983, p. 288) suggests, "compensation laws may be regarded as a strategic device to promote legitimacy, to demonstrate that the state is taking measures to aid crime victims" and he hints that these "expenditures on behalf of victims of crime are quite negligible within the context of the economy as a whole." Moreover, Friedrichs's comments concerning legitimacy are exemplified by victim compensation programs that screen out any victims who are not "morally blameless" (Miers 1978).

For law enforcement, the needs of victims are a means by which additional resources may be garnered. The organization is able to expand into specialized units such as rape units, domestic violence units and, even more recently in Los Angeles, a unit to protect victims of obsessive people (Nikos 1991).[4] These units are used to reflect the sincerity of the organization before citizen groups (and the city/county council) and thus provide political support. Further, although such specialized units directly assist in the acquisition of additional resources, when the rationale for their existence is obviated, the personnel assigned to the unit are merged into the department's general manpower allocations.

### Legislative Process

According to Elias (1983; 1986), victims have been coopted and manipulated by legislators for personal, ideological, and political gain. A close, critical analysis of victims' legislation lends credence to Elias's conclusion. Victims' initiatives help to create and then perpetuate biased definitions of crime and justice that become part of the rhetoric of legislative campaigns and law enforcement patterns. Groups and bills that focus attention on street crime and "Willie Horton" types of offenders[5] receive financial aid and philosophical guidance from the government and others interested in "conservative crime politics" (Elias 1986).

In 1982, California legislators lined up to be associated with the Roberti-Imbrecht-Rains-Goggin Child Sexual Abuse Prevention Act. The problem here was that the act was given an inappropriate title, a practice that an assistant in the California Attorney General's Office (Iglehart 1990) recently admitted was a misleading, but common, ploy to gain voter's support. In reality, this popular legislation did nothing to *prevent* child sexual abuse, it simply instituted harsher punishments for those caught molesting children, extended the statute of limitations for filing charges and provided funds for police and prosecutors to be trained in handling cases. A politician's claim that he or she had supported such an act would hardly constitute support of victims or the prevention of child abuse. Aside from legislative political gain, the act allowed judges and prosecutors to reap the political benefits of appearing to "get tough" and impose new harsher penalties in an area where their predecessors had failed.

Likewise, the California Child Protection Act of 1984 was equally misnamed. This act did nothing to directly protect children. Instead, it allowed the state to confiscate property derived from the profits of child pornography and the cameras, film and lights used in such a criminal enterprise. This act also eliminated the need to prove intent in prosecuting the crime so that it would be easier to obtain convictions. The value of such a piece of legislation was not wasted on prosecutors who could assert that they had aggressively increased convictions for child pornography. Legislators in this case were eager to point out that they were first in protecting children.

Finally, California voters recently passed another misnamed referendum. Passing it off as the Crime Victims Justice Reform Initiative, the creators of this complicated piece of legislation offered victims little, if anything. The initiative was a collection of bills that had already been individually rejected by the legislature. The thrust of the act was a series of shortcuts in the judicial process designed to improve the records of judges and prosecutors at a time when the public was high on expectations and short on patience with the courts. Legislators who supported the initiative were attempting to ride the wave of law and order embraced by the voting public. Faced with spending caps on their own campaigns, political candidates backed this legislation with their excess funds. Thus, they were able to successfully campaign on a single popular issue while avoiding legal limitations on campaign spending. Both the candidates and the "victims" bill benefited from their association with provictim propaganda. Meanwhile, the primary message that caught people's attention was that their chances of becoming a victim were greater than ever before and that something needed be done about it.

## Media Exploitation

The media interpretation of the victim is an emotional presentation to which most citizens are very vulnerable; thus it amounts to exploitation. Unless a person has had a very significant experience or impression to counteract the media's image of criminal victimization, that image often becomes reality. Invariably, strong emotional imagery is a crucial part of crime news. First, stories show victims to be "just like you and me." Then, the victimizing event is described in sufficient detail to allow consumers to feel some small part of what the victim endured. This, in turn, creates an "identification through shared experience," bonding the consumer with the victim. The victim-story usually ends with how the victim's life has been changed forever, leaving the consumer with a very potent image that the victim will never be the same (normal or happy) again. Media tradition also demands a haunting implication that it could happen again; the consumer might even be next.

The latent goal of any story is, of course, to sell the newspaper, magazine, or program to the public. If the context of the story is good versus evil, so much the better. There is, however, little market for stories in which victims and offenders interchange roles. Good and evil become mixed, metaphors are difficult to achieve, and the message value of the story is unclear. Therefore, media portrayals of victims are uniformly dependent on, and partake of, official definitions of the victim.

## Capitalist Enterprise

Victimization and crime prevention is big business, with purveyors of security and self-protection devices targeting victims as well as citizens' fears of becoming victims. And, as with most forms of enterprise in capitalist systems, government either directly or indirectly encourages consumerism. For instance, the government of both England and Wales recently blamed citizens for rising rates of property crime by accusing them of failing to guard their possessions (Bivens 1991). A similar position, supported in this country by insurance practices, encourages people to invest in target hardening as a major approach to crime prevention. As Karmen (1984, p. 10) explains,

> Businesses have rediscovered victims as an untapped market for goods and services. After suffering through an unpleasant experience, many victims become willing, even eager, consumers and search for products that will protect them from any further harm.

219

The outspoken approval by law enforcement agencies of target hardening as a crime prevention technique is a key element in the purveying of private merchandise. Victims are given tips on crime prevention so that the chances of future victimization are decreased and law enforcement-sanctioned neighborhood watch programs purvey information on ways to target-harden homes to be burglar-proof. Security alarm companies advertise systems to protect homes and businesses and, in some cases, promise that the systems will be hard-wired directly into the police station. Ironically, citizens will often spend more on the alarm systems than they would lose in burglaries, especially so if they have insurance. Thus the image of victim is a critical component of the capitalist enterprise.[6]

## EXTENDED VICTIMIZATION BY THE SYSTEM

A final direction we would like to pursue requires an atypical extension of the victim concept and is related not to the traditional victim but to the offender. Although older sociological work pointed out that novice offenders could be victimized by the system (see Sudnow 1965 and Newman 1956 as examples), no one has dealt with the potential adverse effect of an indirect labeling process that takes place for the offender's family and friends. Some have, however, noted that those close to the offender suffer from that association. In a study of Chicano gangs, Zatz (1989) reported that Chicano males who had not been in trouble with the law but who had brothers or friends in gangs, were treated by the police as if they were also gang members. This observation is not new, and occurs frequently in the criminological literature. In addition, the nonacademic police literature contains references to acquaintances, colleagues, friends, and siblings in similar terms.

We suggest that there is a systematic form of negative labeling that takes place among close associates of offenders. This labeling process constitutes victimization of those individuals by the criminal justice system and the public. The process of "guilt by association" results in a reaction to close associates *as if they, too, partake of the same evil nature as that ascribed to the offender*. It may be that families experience the greatest effect. Because of popular myths and misconceptions, both public and system assume that criminality can, and does, run in families. Thus, if a single sibling or parent (or even a close relative) becomes a client of the criminal justice system, all other family members will fall under closer scrutiny. While we have no direct evidence, we would hypothesize that this phenomenon applies more strictly to males than females and, certainly, more to the young than the old. In addition, we suspect that the entire process is sensitive to class position as well.

220

Radical victimology should be prepared to examine the effects generated by this form of systematic victimization. Certainly, one can expect that offender-associates who come under close scrutiny by the criminal justice system will experience a loss of status, fewer opportunities, and diminished life chances. In fact, we would predict that the total experience is criminogenic.[7]

## SUMMARY

The perspective we have presented here proposes to extend victimology into neglected areas. The perspective is necessarily critical, focusing on the criminal justice system more than the victim and on public representations of the victim. Traditional victimology is not currently offering a critique of its conceptions nor its own, often self-serving, use of the victim. Neither is it prepared to define victims in any other context than the straightforward, legalistic conception of victim. As a result, expansion of victimology is not only needed, it is required in order for the discipline to proceed in a critical manner.

It is not likely that traditional victimology will embrace the images presented in this essay. On the other hand, those who have a passing interest in the field will probably be more receptive.[8] In short, we are challenging the existing paradigm and expect those new to, or not now within, victimology to do the majority of the work of expanding the field. Without this work, victimology promises to remain, albeit unwittingly, a pawn of the state and the political process. The examples we present here are just that, exemplars of the type of analysis and direction of critical inquiry that would benefit the field. We mean this presentation to neither be all-encompassing nor limiting for a new radical victimology perspective. We hope that this essay will generate some degree of interest and we await fresh and, certainly, more thoughtful contributions.

## NOTES

1. This should be contrasted with the common attribution of rationality to the offender. When discussing abstract crime, the public appears to view the subject as irrational; when discussing *offenders* the public appears to adopt a view of rationality. The latter is, of course, a product of the contemporary ideology of blaming and making the offender responsible for purposeful action. So, too, are contemporary criminological theories engaged in this attribution of rationality.

2. There is some question about the viability of Katz's empirical data. However, the insights he offers are more pertinent here. The conception of an offender who purposefully cultivates an

image of irrationality to achieve dominance over a victim is replete with irony given the public conception of irrational acts of violence by rational offenders.

3. After reading an earlier draft, Don Gibbons suggested to us that "evil offender" views could be seen as serving the interest of the powerful. Clearly this is a point deserving of a good deal of elaboration, but we give it superficial treatment here because of a desire to keep the commentary focused on the victim.

4. The creation of this latter special unit is not surprising given that some of the city's most powerful constituents are actors and actresses who are potential victims of obsessive fans.

5. Willie Horton was an inmate in Massachusetts who received a furlough in 1988. Originally convicted of rape, he committed another rape while on furlough. The incident was highly publicized by the Bush For President campaign as an attack on the Democratic presidential candidate, Dukakis, who was then governor of Massachusetts.

6. The element of victim imagery that most facilitates the crime prevention industry is the notion that crime events are irrational and random. In this way, everyone is a potential victim of the absolute worst crime scenario. Security alarm companies are then able to sell the most expensive possible system. Similarly, companies and retailers make a substantial profit on the sale of auto alarm and antitheft systems.

7. Although not a full explanation for the criminality traditionally associated with siblings and close friends, this new victimological thrust presents a reasonable dimension of the problem. Moreover, such a dimension allows the same predictions as have been associated with genetic and cultural transmission theories of criminality. Over a period of time, an indirect system-victimization explanation can also account for the relationship between minority/ethnic groups and crime rates.

8. Kuhn (1970) has noted that a careful examination of the history of science points to a relationship between discovery and novel perspectives and those who are new to, or uncommitted to, the discipline. In this case we are suggesting that traditional victimologists have too much invested in the status quo to perceive that other areas require investigation or that the concept of victim can be profitably broadened.

## REFERENCES

Bivens, Matt. 1991. "England, Wales Crime Rates Increase; Victims Get Partial Blame." *San Bernardino Sun*, March 28, sec. A, p. 12.

Black, Donald. 1983. "Crime as Social Control." *American Sociological Review* 48:34-45.

Durkheim, Emile. 1965. *The Rules of the Sociological Method* (S. A. Solovay and J. H. Mueller trans.). New York: Free Press. (Original work published 1895)

Elias, Robert. 1983. *Victims of the System: Crime Victims and Compensation in American Politics and Criminal Justice*. New Brunswick, NJ: Transaction Books.

―――. 1986. *The Politics of Victimization*. New York: Oxford University Press.

Finn, Peter. n.d. "Victims." *Crime File Study Guide*. Washington, DC: National Institute of Justice.

Finn, Peter and Beverly Lee. 1988. *Establishing and Expanding Victim-Witness Assistance Programs*. Washington, DC: National Institute of Justice.

Friedrichs, David. 1983. "Victimology: A Consideration of the Radical Critique." *Crime & Delinquency* 29:283-94.

Geis, Gilbert. 1990. "Crime Victims: Practices and Prospects." Pp. 251-68 in *Victims of Crime*, edited by A. Lurigio, W. Skogan, and R. Davis. Newbury Park, CA: Sage.

Hoebel, E. Adamson. 1954. *The Law of Primitive Man*. Cambridge, MA: Harvard University Press.

Iglehart, Richard. 1990. "The Impact of Proposition 115 — The Crime Victims Initiative." Keynote Speech delivered to the Association of Criminal Justice Researchers, Claremont, CA, October.

Karmen, Andrew. 1984. "The Rediscovery of Crime Victims." Pp. 5-21 in *Order Under Law*, 3rd ed., edited by R. Culbertson and R. Weisheit. Prospect Heights, IL: Waveland.

———. 1990. *Crime Victims: An Introduction to Victimology*. Pacific Grove, CA: Brooks Cole.

Katz, Jack. 1988. *Seductions of Crime: The Moral and Sensual Attractions of Doing Evil*. New York: Basic Books.

Krisbreg, Barry. 1975. *Crime and Privilege*. Englewood Cliffs, NJ: Prentice-Hall.

Kuhn, Thomas S. 1970. *The Structure of Scientific Revolutions*, 2nd ed. Chicago: University of Chicago Press.

Miers, D. 1978. *Responses to Victimization*. Abington, England: Professional Books.

Murphy, Jeffrie. 1990. "Getting Even: The Role of the Victim." Pp. 209-25 in *Crime, Culpability, and Remedy*, edited by E. F. Paul, F. Miller, and J. Paul. Cambridge, MA: Basil Blackwell.

Newman, Donald. 1956. "Pleading Guilty for Considerations: A Study of Bargain Justice." *Journal of Criminal Law, Criminology and Police Science* 46:780-90.

Nikos, Karen. 1991. "New Police Unit to Protect Victims of Obsessive People." *Los Angeles Daily News*, February 16, sec. B, p. 7.

Phipps, Alan. 1986. "Radical Criminology and Criminal Victimization: Proposals for the Development of Theory and Intervention." Pp. 97-117 in *Confronting Crime*, edited by R. Matthews and J. Young. Beverly Hills, CA: Sage.

Quinney, Richard. 1972. "Who is the Victim?" *Criminology* 10:314-23.

———. 1974. *Critique of Legal Order*. Boston: Little, Brown.

Schwendinger, Herman and Julia Schwendinger. 1970. "Defenders of Order or Guardians of Human Rights?" *Issues in Criminology* 7:72-81.

Smith, Brent. 1988. "Victims and Victims' Rights Activists: Attitudes Toward Criminal Justice Officials and Victim-Related Issues." *Criminal Justice Review* 13:21-27.

Sudnow, David. 1965. "Normal Crimes: Sociological Features of the Penal Code in a Public Defender's Office." *Social Problems* 12:255-76.

Taylor, Ian, Paul Walton, and Jock Young. 1973. *The New Criminology: For a Social Theory of Deviance*. New York: Harper & Row.

Umbreit, Mark. 1989. "Crime Victims Seeking Fairness, Not Revenge: Toward Restorative Justice." *Federal Probation* 53:52-57.

Villmoare, Edwin and Jeanne Benvenuti. 1988. *California Victims of Crime Handbook*. Sacramento, CA: McGeorge School of Law, University of the Pacific.

von Hentig, Hans. 1948. *The Criminal and His Victim*. New Haven, CT: Yale University Press.

Young, Jock. 1986. "The Failure of Criminology: The Need for a Radical Realism." In *Confronting Crime*, edited by R. Matthews and J. Young. London: Sage.

Zatz, Marjorie. 1989. "Chicano Youth Gangs and Crime: The Creation of a Moral Panic." *Contemporary Crises* 11:129-58.

Zehr, Howard and Mark Umbreit. 1982. "Victim Offender Reconciliation: An Incarceration Substitute." *Federal Probation* 46:63-68.

*Robert F. Meier and Terance D. Miethe*

# Understanding Theories of Criminal Victimization

**ABSTRACT**

Current theories of victimization have generated a sizable body of empirical research, mostly within the last two decades. The two most widely known perspectives, lifestyle-exposure and routine activities theories, have been the object of much current thinking and empirical testing, but their maturation has been hampered by many of the same problems impeding theories of criminality. These include inadequate attention to variation by type of crime, compartmentalized thinking, poor links between theory and data, inadequate measures of key concepts, and failure to specify clearly functional relationships between sets of variables. Many of these problems can be addressed by closer examination of the interrelationships among victims, offenders, and criminal situations. Victimization theories should be incorporated into comprehensive integrated theories of crime.

Victimization theories are now a common feature of criminological work, but it has not always been so. In spite of their obvious appeal, perspectives on victim behavior have only recently gained sufficient scholarly respectability to join forces with the mainstay of the criminological arsenal, theories of offender behavior. Work that has incorporated victim perspectives, such as Wolfgang's (1958) research on homicide and especially Amir's (1971) related work on rape, encountered political difficulty because it appeared that the victim bore some responsibility for the crime. This was an idea that smacked of "blaming the victim," a cornerstone of liberal crime control ideology and some-

Robert F. Meier is professor and chair of sociology at Iowa State University. Terance D. Miethe is associate professor of criminal justice at the University of Nevada at Las-Vegas

thing to be avoided at all scholarly cost, even truth. But the impediments to a defensible notion of victim involvement in crime were more long-standing than this, and even relatively unenlightened criminologists must surely have known that no picture of predatory crime can ever be complete without information about the victim of these offenses. Only in the last two decades have victimization theories generated empirical, as well as anecdotal, support, most notably in the form of lifestyle-exposure (Hindelang, Gottfredson, and Garofalo 1978) and routine activities theories (Cohen and Felson 1979). This long road to respectability is hard to explain, but the high (or low) points can at least be identified.

In this essay, we argue that the current popularity of and support for victimization surveys is well deserved but that investigators must also consider the major limitations of the theoretical and empirical work that has been done on victimization. Although it is beyond the scope of this essay to provide a complete critique of victimization studies, we do note that much previous research has suffered from a number of problems, including the use of inadequate measures of key concepts, few statistical controls, and the absence of multilevel models and contextual effects that could provide alternative explanations for the results of victimization research. We also note that, while some versions of victimization theories suggest that victims and offenders are tied together in a broader social ecology of crime, these theories do not provide testable propositions about the conditions of offending and victimization to permit adequate predictions of crime. In spite of these problems, we are encouraged about the current status of victimization surveys.

We begin our analysis by examining the historical context of victimization theories in Section I. We also identify major sources of information concerning these theories, predominantly victimization surveys. Section II identifies major current theories of victimization with particular attention to lifestyle theories and routine activities theories. Alternative models of victimization are identified in Section III, and major concepts used in victimization theories are examined in Section IV with an eye toward improving conceptual clarity. Section V discusses what we consider to be major problems with victimization theories. The context of crime plays an important role in modeling victimization, and its effects are discussed in Section VI. We discuss the prospects of integrating theories of victimization with theories of criminality in Section VII. Conclusions are offered in Section VIII.

## I. Historical Foundations for Current Victimization Theories

The use of such expressions as "the victim-offender problem" (Mac-Donald 1939), "the duet frame of crime" (Von Hentig 1948), "the penal couple" (Ellenberger 1955), and, more generally, "the victim-offender relationship" (Von Hentig 1940; Schafer 1968; Schultz 1968) clearly indicates the significance of crime victims to the understanding of crime. Garofalo (1914) was one of the first to note that a victim may provoke another into attack, whereas Mendelsohn (1956) developed a victim typology that distinguishes victims who are more culpable than their offenders from those who are considered totally guiltless. Von Hentig (1948) described general classes of crime victims (e.g., the young, females, the old, the mentally defective, the depressed, the acquisitive, the lonesome and heartbroken) and some of the characteristics associated with these personal attributes that increase their vulnerability to crime.

Such a list of phrases is not a history, and it would be incorrect to claim that modern victim theories are merely the latest variants in a long lineage of earlier victim theories. These early writers did not propose theories, and even some of the concepts they used were primitive. Furthermore, it is speculative at best to attempt to sketch a victim theory ancestry since there seem to be few connections among these early works. Although it is difficult to trace the origins of any particular theoretical perspective, two fairly recent research traditions appear to be the antecedents to current theories of victimization. These include research on victim precipitation and the development of victimization surveys.

### A. Victim Precipitation

The first systematic study of victim involvement in crime was conducted in the late 1950s by Marvin Wolfgang. The term he introduced, "victim precipitation," became a popular descriptor for all direct-contact predatory crime (e.g., murder, assault, forcible rape, robbery). When applied to homicide, victim precipitation is restricted to those cases in which "the victim is the first in the homicide drama to resort to physical force against the subsequent slayer" (Wolfgang 1958, p. 252; see also Wolfgang 1957). A similar definition is used in the case of aggravated assault except that insinuating language or gestures might also be considered provoking actions (Curtis 1974; Miethe 1985). Victim-precipitated robbery involves cases in which the victim has acted without reasonable self-protection in the handling of money, jewelry, or other valuables (Normandeau 1968; Curtis 1974), whereas this concept in forcible rape applies to "an episode ending in forced sexual intercourse in which the victim first agreed to sexual relations, or clearly invited them verbally or through gestures, but then retracted before the act" (Amir 1967; Curtis 1974). Under each of these definitions, there is an explicit time ordering of events in which victims initiate some type of action that results in their subsequent victimization.

Previous studies using police reports suggest some level of victim involvement in a large proportion of violent crimes. The extent of victim precipitation, however, varies widely by type of offense. Estimates of victim precipitation range from 22 to 38 percent for homicide, 14 percent for aggravated assault, between 4 and 19 percent for rape cases, and about 11 percent of armed robberies are characterized by carelessness on the part of the victim (see, for review, Curtis 1974). These figures are best considered low estimates of the rate of victim involvement because of the fairly restrictive definition of victim precipitation for some crimes (i.e., murder, assault) and the large number of cases with incomplete information. The national survey of aggravated assaults reported by Curtis (1974), for example, had insufficient data for determining the presence of victim precipitation in 51 percent of the cases. Nonetheless, the importance of the notion of victim precipitation is clearly revealed in many cases of homicide where who becomes labeled the victim and who the offender (Wolfgang 1957) is a matter of chance or circumstance.

There are several reasons why previous research on victim-precipitated crime was influential in the emergence of current theories of victimization. First, the prevalence of victim precipitation signified the importance of victims' actions in explaining violent crime but also brought attention to the less direct ways by which citizens contribute to their victimization. These less direct forms of victim involvement would include such acts as getting involved in risky or vulnerable situations, not exercising good judgment when in public places, leaving property unprotected, and interacting on a regular basis with potential offenders.

Second, the notion of victim precipitation, by definition, attributes some responsibility for crime to the actions of its victims. That victim-precipitation researchers had to deal directly with such an unpopular public and political stance may have made it easier for subsequent scholars to examine victim culpability and how the routine activities and lifestyles of citizens provide opportunities for crime. Thus, current theories of victimization may have benefited greatly from the prior work on victim precipitation.

The implication of blame in victim-precipitation analyses has inhibited full development of the concept. When Wolfgang's student Menachim Amir (1971) adopted the concept in a study of forcible rape that parallels Wolfgang's research on homicide, it caused a major political controversy. Amir, like Wolfgang, used official police reports in the city of Philadelphia; he also used the subculture of violence as a unifying theoretical notion to explain this crime. But Amir was not sufficiently sensitive to the differences between murder and rape in using the idea of victim precipitation. While it is neither counterintuitive nor politically contentious to acknowledge that murder victims sometimes strike the first blow or otherwise provoke a violent response, it was politically aberrant to suggest that rape victims were provocative, at least in the same sense. In suggesting the nature of victim precipitation in rape, Amir reported that 20 percent of the victims had a prior record for some sort of sexual misconduct (usually prostitution or juvenile intercourse) and another 20 percent had "bad reputations." Wolfgang's research offered a promising idea to further explore the relationship between offender and victim, but Amir's study blunted the promise by not developing the idea beyond Wolfgang's pioneering work.

Actually, Amir was either too far ahead, or too far behind, his times. The 1970s were politically charged in criminology as well as in society at large with much concern about victim blaming and women's rights. Research on rape would shortly be done correctly only by women. The idea that men had anything reasonably objective to say about rape was not given much credence. Surely this overstates the matter, but there is no mistaking the fact that there were very few male authors on rape, and Amir himself took an academic assignment in Israel never really to publish on rape again. The concept of victim precipitation remained comatose under the feminist assault never to resurface, even for homicide.

In fairness, the concept of victim precipitation was never really defined very well, and Amir's application of the concept to include "bad reputation" was a serious mistake scientifically. Such an indicator clearly smacked of subjectivity, and no validity checks were made of the Philadelphia Police Department records in which this phrase appeared.

## B. Victimization Surveys

The second major contributor to the emergence of current victimization theories is the development of large-scale victimization surveys. Prior to the advent of victimization surveys in the late 1960s and early 1970s, official reports on crimes known to the police and self-reports of offending were the only systematically available data on criminal activities. However, neither of these sources give any systematic information about the actions and characteristics of crime victims. Although it is possible to understand crime without directly surveying its victims (e.g., by interviewing offenders about their choice of crime sites, doing observation studies of areas with high rates of crime), victim surveys provide information about aspects of the criminal event that is not routinely collected from other sources.

There were three early studies: one by Reiss of business victimization; Biderman's study in Washington, D.C.; and Ennis's survey through the National Opinion Research Center (NORC) (President's Commission on Law Enforcement and Administration of Justice 1967, pp. 38–43). These surveys, thoroughly reviewed by Sparks (1982), paved the way for more systematic studies. Of these initial efforts, one deserves more than passing comment.

The first national project was sponsored by the President's (Lyndon Johnson) Commission on Law Enforcement and Administration of Justice. The report was published in the commission proceedings the following year, and the findings were startling even to criminologists, let alone citizens (Ennis 1967). This first systematic survey of victims used a probability sample of nearly ten thousand households. The major conclusions included the findings that forcible rape was three and a half times more frequent than the reported rate, burglaries were three times the reported rate, and robbery was 50 percent higher than the reported rate. Thus, not only were most crimes underreported to a significant degree, the extent of underreporting varied from crime to crime. This meant that official estimates of crimes were not only "off" by some factor but that the degree to which they were off was variable and could not be estimated without separate surveys for each crime category.

The largest current victimization survey, the National Crime Victimization Survey (NCS), involves yearly reports based on surveys of from between 59,000 and 72,000 U.S. households in which questions are asked to identify personal attributes of crime victims and characteristics of the offense. The interviews are conducted by Bureau of the Census personnel, and the results are coordinated by the Department of Justice. Actually, the NCS is a series of surveys rather than a survey at a single point in time. The NCS series involves probability samples of households that are interviewed a maximum of seven times at six-month intervals. Started in 1973, the NCS series involves interviews with persons over twelve years of age. Persons who move out of a household are not followed to their new address, but, if a new family or person moves into a sampled housing unit between waves, they are interviewed as part of the series. Skogan (1990) outlines the major changes in the implementation of the NCS series.

Even at their earlier stages of development, victimization surveys addressed fundamental questions about crime. Victim surveys represent an alternative barometer of the extent and distribution of crime. They also identify factors associated with reporting crime to the authorities, and they yield detailed information about the consequences of crime for the victim. For present purposes, however, the major contribution of victimization surveys is that they provide detailed information about the ecology of crime (e.g., where it occurred, type of injury, victim-offender relationship) and about the demographic characteristics of victims. It is the distribution of crime and the characteristics of victims identified in victimization surveys that are the social facts to be explained by current theories of victimization.

## II. Current Major Theories of Victimization

Like theories of the behavior of criminals, theories of the behavior of crime victims are many and variable. Some, like the notion of victim precipitation, are little more than an idea, let alone a scientific concept. Others either are little more than victim typologies (Von Hentig 1948; Mendelsohn 1956) or highlight the distribution and characteristics of individuals who have repeat or multiple victimization experiences (Nelson 1980; Gottfredson 1981; Sparks 1981; Skogan 1990). Two major theories considered here are more sophisticated and have been the object of substantial empirical testing. The two most advanced theories are the lifestyle-exposure perspective and the routine activities theory.

There are points of conceptual and explanatory overlap between them, but they each offer a distinctive view of the role of victims in the crime process.

### A. Lifestyle-Exposure Theories of Victimization

One of the first systematic theories of criminal victimization was the lifestyle-exposure approach developed by Hindelang, Gottfredson, and Garofalo (1978) less than twenty years ago. This theory was originally proposed to account for differences in the risks of violent victimization across social groups, but it has been extended to include property crime, and it forms the basis for more elaborate theories of target-selection processes.

The basic premise underlying the lifestyle-exposure theory is that demographic differences in the likelihood of victimization are attributed to differences in the personal lifestyles of victims. Variations in lifestyles are important because they are related to the differential exposure to dangerous places, times, and others—that is, situations in which there are high risks of victimization. A graphic representation of this theoretical perspective is presented in figure 1.

From this perspective, an individual's lifestyle is the critical factor that determines risks of criminal victimization. Lifestyle is defined in this context as "routine daily activities, both vocational activities (work, school, keeping house, etc.) and leisure activities" (Hindelang, Gottfredson, and Garofalo 1978, p. 241). People's daily activities may naturally bring them into contact with crime, or they merely increase the risk of crime that victims experience. Time spent in one's home generally decreases victim risk, while time spent in public settings increases risk.

Differences in lifestyles are socially determined by individuals' collective responses or adaptations to various role expectations and structural constraints (see fig. 1). Both ascribed and achieved status characteristics (e.g., age, gender, race, income, marital status, education, occupation) are important correlates of predatory crime because these status attributes carry with them shared expectations about appropriate behavior and structural obstacles that both enable and constrain one's behavioral choices. Adherence to these cultural and structural expectations leads to the establishment of routine activities patterns and associations with others similarly situated. These lifestyles and associations, in turn, are expected to enhance one's exposure to risky or vulnerable situations that increase individuals' chances of victimization. Several

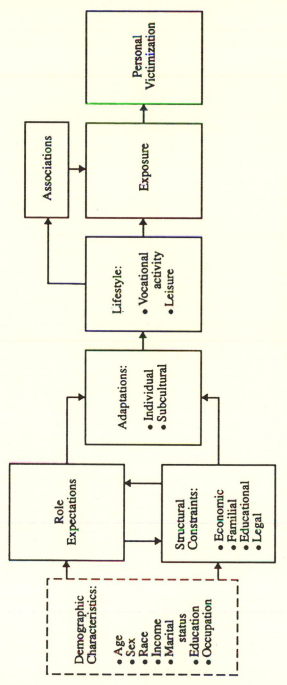

FIG. 1.—A lifestyle-exposure model of victimization. Source: adapted from Hindelang, Gottfredson, and Garofalo (1978)

233

examples should clarify the basic logic underlying this lifestyle-exposure model.

1. *Gender.* Despite major efforts to promote gender equality in American society, there remain fundamental differences in role expectations and structural opportunities for men and women. Gender stereotyping results in gender differences in such basic activities as where and with whom time is spent, the degree of supervision in daily activities, the likelihood of having contact with strangers, and exposure to risky and dangerous public places. For example, females spend a greater proportion of their time inside the home because as adolescents they are more closely supervised than males, and as adults they are more likely to assume housekeeping and child-rearing responsibilities (Hindelang, Gottfredson, and Garofalo 1978). Greater familial responsibilities and the systematic denial of educational and economic opportunities may severely impede women's participation in public life. Furthermore, even when engaged in public activity, women's routine activities are more likely to take place in the presence of friends and intimate others than in isolation. These role expectations and structural impediments are assumed to increase private domestic activities among women, increase supervision of their public behavior, decrease their exposure to high-risk persons and places, and subsequently decrease their relative risks of criminal victimization. Males, by contrast, are traditionally socialized to be active in the public domain, assertive and aggressive in social situations, have fewer restrictions on their daily lives, and spend more time away from a protective home environment. Accordingly, gender differences in traditional lifestyles are said partly to explain the higher victimization risks of men.

2. *Income.* Another strong determinant of lifestyle and exposure to crime is economic resources, such as income. As a fundamental aspect of stratification, income determines whether structural conditions either enable or constrain various aspects of social life. Low income severely restricts one's choices in regard to housing, transportation, associations with others, and leisure activities. Individuals' abilities to move out of crime-prone environments, live in apartments or homes with elaborate security measures (e.g., security guards, video surveillance, burglar alarms), avoid contact with potential offenders, and undertake leisure activities in safer areas are limited when living under conditions of economic deprivation. As family income increases, there is greater flexibility to adjust one's lifestyle to select the area in which to live, the mode of transportation for daily activities, the amount of

time spent in private versus public places, and the type of leisure activities (Hindelang, Gottfredson, and Garofalo 1978). The greater choices afforded persons with higher economic resources allow them to more easily avoid risky and vulnerable situations. Thus, by patterning the nature of social life, income is a lifestyle characteristic that is expected to lead to differential risks of victimization.

3. *Empirical Predictions.*   From a lifestyle-exposure perspective, differences in risks of violent victimization by gender, high-income, and other status characteristics are attributed to differences in lifestyles that increase individuals' exposure to risky and vulnerable situations. Given that victimization risks are not uniformly distributed across time and space, lifestyles are assumed to affect the probability of victimization because different lifestyles are associated with differential risks of being in particular places, at particular times, under particular circumstances, and interacting with particular kinds of persons. Accordingly, persons who are younger, male, not married, low income, and black should have higher risks of violent victimization than their counterparts because each group is said to engage in more public activity (especially at night), spend less time with family members, or associate more frequently with persons who have offender characteristics. Under this theoretical model, individuals' risks of property victimization should also be higher among those social groups (e.g., young, male, single persons) who spend more time engaged in public activity because such persons would be less able to protect their dwelling from crime.

If a lifestyle-exposure theory is an adequate explanation for differential risks of predatory victimization, several outcomes would be expected. First, if demographic differences in victimization risks are due to differences in lifestyles and routine activities, the impact of each demographic variable (e.g., age, gender, race, social class) should decrease in importance once separate measures of lifestyles and routine activities are included as control variables. Second, persons with the configuration of status characteristics commonly recognized as having the most vulnerable lifestyles (i.e., young, single, low-income, black males) should have a greater risk of victimization than any other configuration, and their exact opposites (i.e., older, married, high-income, white females) should have the lowest relative risks. Third, given increases in efforts to promote gender and racial equality in all institutional domains over the last two decades, differences in victimization risks by these factors should decrease over time. In other words, smaller differences in victimization risks by gender and race would be expected over time if there were fewer group-specific role expectations and fewer structural obstacles that impede the life chances of persons within each of these groups.

While these hypotheses from lifestyle-exposure theories are relatively straightforward, they have not been adequately examined. In fact, only the first hypothesis has been examined empirically. The results of previous research (Miethe, Stafford, and Long 1987; Kennedy and Forde 1990) indicate that some demographic differences in victim risks (e.g., gender and age differences) can be attributed to differences in individuals' routine activities and lifestyles. Differences in victimization risks by configuration of status characteristics or changes over time in demographic predictors of victimization risks have not been investigated.

## B. Routine Activity Theory

The routine activity perspective developed by Cohen and Felson (1979) has many similarities with the lifestyle-exposure theory. Both emphasize how patterns of routine activities or lifestyles in conventional society provide an opportunity structure for crime. Each theory also downplays the importance of offender motivation and other aspects of criminality in understanding individuals' risks of victimization and the social ecology of crime. These theories are also representative of a wider "criminal opportunity" perspective because they stress how the availability of criminal opportunities is determined, in large part, by the routine activity patterns of everyday life (Cohen 1981; Cohen and Land 1987). The fundamental differences between these theories are in terminology and in the fact that routine activity theory was originally developed to account for changes in crime rates over time whereas lifestyle-exposure theory was proposed to account for differences in victimization risks across social groups. Over the past decade, however, each theory has been applied across units of analysis and in both cross-sectional and longitudinal designs.

According to Cohen and Felson (1979, p. 589), structural changes in routine activity patterns influence crime rates by affecting the convergence in time and space of three elements of direct-contact predatory crimes: motivated offenders, suitable targets, and the absence of capable guardians against a violation. As necessary elements, the lack of any of these conditions is sufficient to prevent criminal activity. Furthermore, Cohen and Felson (1979) note that increases in crime rates could occur without any increase in the structural conditions that motivate offenders to engage in crime as long as there has been an increase in the supply of attractive and unguarded targets for victimization. Their argument about how crime rates can increase even if offender motivation remains constant is important because it allows them to account for the apparent contradiction underlying most theories of criminality that crime rates continued to rise throughout the 1960s and 1970s in the United States even though conditions that foster criminality (e.g., unemployment, racial segregation, economic inequality) were decreasing.

From this perspective, routine activities are defined as "any recurrent and prevalent activities that provide for basic population and individual needs" (Cohen and Felson 1979, p. 593). Similar to the notion of lifestyle, these routine activities include formalized work, leisure, and the ways by which humans acquire food, shelter, and other basic needs or desires (e.g., companionship, sexual expression). Drawing from work in human ecology (e.g., Hawley 1950), Cohen and Felson (1979) argue that humans are located in ecological niches with a particular tempo, pace, and rhythm in which predatory crime is a way of securing these basic needs or desires at the expense of others. Potential victims in this environment are likely to alter their daily habits and take evasive actions that may persuade offenders to seek alternative targets. It is under such predatory conditions that the routine activities of potential victims are said both to enhance and to restrict the opportunities for crime.

1. *Social Change and Routine Activities.*   The basic premise underlying routine activity theory is that various social changes in conventional society increase criminal opportunities. For example, given the assorted costs for stealing items with great weight (e.g., their theft requires more physical energy, they are harder to conceal), it is not surprising that burglars are most attracted to items that are easily portable and have high resale value (e.g., cash, jewelry, electronic equipment). Accordingly, any changes in manufacturing or production activities that decrease the size or increase the demand for expensive durable goods (e.g., televisions, tape decks, VCRs, home computers, compact disk players) are expected to increase the attractiveness of these goods for victimization. Similarly, increases over time in the level of safety precautions taken by the public would apparently decrease crime rates by reducing the accessibility of potential crime targets to would-be offenders. Such changes, of course, might also result in alternative outcomes such as no net reduction in crime rates because crime

237

is being displaced to other objects, victims, or times depending on the structural conditions.

Of the various social changes in routine activities that have occurred over the last four decades, Lawrence Cohen, Marcus Felson, and their colleagues have placed primary importance on changes in sustenance and leisure activities away from domestic life and family-based living arrangements. A basic proposition underlying this theory is that any decrease in the concentration of activities within family-based households will increase crime rates (Cohen and Land 1987). There are several ways by which such social changes are assumed to increase criminal opportunities. First, a rise in single-person households or households consisting of unrelated persons requires a greater supply of durable consumer goods and other merchandise that are considered attractive property to steal. Such a duplication of consumer goods is unnecessary in family-like living arrangements. Second, increases in nonfamilial activities and households decrease the level of personal guardianship over others. The mere presence of a spouse, child, or other relative in a household provides greater protection for individuals and their property than is true of persons who live alone, and living with other relatives also increases the likelihood that public activities will be undertaken in groups. Third, increases in nonfamily households alter the location of routine activities from a private domain to a public domain, thereby also increasing one's exposure to risky and vulnerable situations. Thus, changes in domestic activities and living arrangements may increase the supply of attractive crime targets, decrease the level of guardianship, and consequently increase criminal opportunities.

Although applicable to various social science disciplines, there are several reasons why routine activity theory is especially attractive to sociologists. First, this theoretical approach clearly highlights the symbiotic relationship between conventional and illegal activity patterns. Illegal activities are presumed to "feed on" the routine activities of everyday life (Felson and Cohen 1980; Messner and Blau 1987). Second, this theory identifies a fundamental irony between constructive social change and crime rates. Specifically, many social changes that have improved both the quality and equality of social life in the United States (e.g., increased labor force participation and educational attainment among women, increases in out-of-home leisure activities) are the same factors predicted to increase rates of predatory crime. Third, both routine activity and lifestyle-exposure theory attempt to explain crime, not in the actions or numbers of motivated offenders, but in the activities and lifestyles of potential victims. Accordingly, these approaches have more relevance to a wider range of sociologists than most theories because they ignore the sources of criminal motivation and other major topics in traditional criminology (i.e., you do not have to be a criminologist to understand these theories) and direct attention to how the habits, lifestyles, and behavioral patterns of ordinary citizens in their daily lives create an environment for predatory crime.

2. *Applying Routine Activities.*   Over the last decade, routine activity theory has been used to explain aggregate rates and individuals' risks of victimization, changes in crime rates over time, and the social ecology of crime. Each of these applications focuses on how the nature of nonhousehold activity influences one's exposure to crime. For example, Cohen and Felson (1979) examine the relationship between crime rates and the "household activity ratio" (i.e., the sum of the number of married female labor force participants and the number of nonhusband/nonwife households divided by the total number of households). Felson and Cohen (1980) investigate the impact of increases in the rate of primary households on increasing burglary rates over time. Arguing that high rates of unemployment lead to decreases in nonhousehold activity, Cohen, Felson, and Land (1980) also apply this approach to study how unemployment rates and the household activity ratio influence temporal changes in rates of robbery, burglary, and automobile theft. Messner and Blau (1987) examine the relationship between crime rates for standard metropolitan statistical areas (SMSAs) in the United States and measures of the volume of household activity (i.e., size of television viewing audience) and nonhousehold activity (i.e., the supply of sport and entertainment establishments). Miethe, Hughes, and McDowall (1991) use this perspective to examine how measures of guardianship, nonhousehold activity, and target attractiveness influence offense-specific crime rates and changes in crime rates in 584 U.S. cities for the three decades from 1960 to 1980. Finally, Messner and Tardiff (1985) apply routine activity theory to examine the social ecology of urban homicide.

Most previous studies using the individual or household as the unit of analysis can be interpreted as tests of both routine activity and lifestyle-exposure theories. Cohen and Cantor (1980), for example, examine how characteristics of individuals and their lifestyles (e.g., income, age, race, major daily activity, household size) influence risks of residential burglary and personal larceny. Cohen, Kluegel, and Land

(1981) evaluate whether measures of exposure, guardianship, proximity to motivated offenders, and target attractiveness mediate the impact of income, race, and age on individuals' risks of predatory victimization. The impact of measures of nonhousehold activity, target suitability, and guardianship on individuals' risks of victimization has also been examined in other studies (e.g., Clarke et al. 1985; Lynch 1987; Maxfield 1987; Miethe, Stafford, and Long 1987; Sampson and Wooldredge 1987; Massey, Krohn, and Bonati 1989; Kennedy and Forde 1990). In the only study that uses longitudinal data on individuals, Miethe, Stafford, and Sloane (1990) explore the interrelationships between changes in the level of nonhousehold activity, guardianship patterns, and temporal changes in individuals' risks of personal and property victimization. The utility of this theoretical formulation for predicting multiple victimizations was also suggested by other researchers (Gottfredson 1981; Sparks 1981).

3. *Empirical Predictions.* Although studies vary widely in terms of their units of analysis and measurement of key concepts, the predictive validity of routine activity theory rests ultimately on the empirical observation of three outcomes. First, routine activity patterns that indicate greater levels of nonhousehold activity should increase individuals' risks and aggregate rates of predatory crime by increasing potential victims' visibility and accessibility as crime targets. Second, routine activity patterns that indicate higher levels of self-protection or guardianship should decrease individuals' risks and aggregate rates of predatory crime. Third, persons and property with higher subjective or material value to offenders should have higher risks of victimization than less attractive crime targets. Taken together, a routine activity approach predicts the greatest risks for predatory crime when potential victims have high target suitability (i.e., high visibility, accessibility, and attractiveness) and low levels of guardianship.

## III. Alternative Theoretical Models

Lifestyle-exposure and routine activity theories have been the most widely applied perspectives to account for individuals' risks and aggregate rates of criminal victimization. However, other work has attempted to integrate these perspectives more directly, derive a clearer conceptual framework for explaining the process of target selection, and examine the context-specific effects of routine activities and lifestyles on risks of criminal victimization.

## A. A Structural-Choice Model of Victimization

Miethe and Meier (1990) examined the feasibility of integrating routine activity and lifestyle-exposure theories into what is called a "structural-choice" theory of victimization. Consistent with other work (Cohen, Kluegel, and Land 1981), we argued that current theories of victimization highlight the importance of physical proximity to motivated offenders, exposure to high-risk environments, target attractiveness, and the absence of guardianship as necessary conditions for predatory crime.

Two central propositions were derived from routine activity and lifestyle-exposure theories. First, routine activity patterns and lifestyles each contribute to the creation of a criminal opportunity structure by enhancing the contact between potential offenders and victims. Second, the subjective value of a person or object and its level of guardianship determine the choice of the particular crime target. In combination, these propositions imply that "routine activities may predispose some persons and their property to greater risks, but the selection of a particular crime victim within a sociospatial context is determined by the expected utility of one target over another" (Miethe and Meier 1990, p. 245). Under this revised theoretical model, proximity and exposure are considered "structural" features (because they pattern the nature of social interaction and predispose individuals to riskier situations), whereas attractiveness and guardianship represent the "choice" component (because they determine the selection of the particular crime target within a sociospatial context).

There are several reasons why this "structural-choice" model may be a useful integration of current victimization theories. First, the revised model emphasizes both macrodynamic forces that contribute to a criminal opportunity structure (as identified by routine activity theory) and microlevel processes that determine the selection of particular crime victims (as implied by lifestyle-exposure theory).

Second, the structural-choice model retains the view that exposure, proximity, attractiveness, and guardianship are necessary conditions for victimization, meaning that the absence of any of these factors is sufficient to eliminate predatory crime.

Third, the structural-choice model follows closely the distinction between "predisposing" and "precipitating" factors. Specifically, both characterizations assume that living in particular environments increases one's exposure and proximity to dangerous situations, but whether a person becomes a crime victim depends on their presumed subjective utility over alternative targets.

Fourth, the structural-choice perspective emphasizes the context-specific effects of routine activities and lifestyles on risks of predatory crime. For example, target attractiveness and guardianship may have little impact on victimization risks for residents of areas with a low criminal opportunity structure because, by definition, such environments are not conducive to predatory crime in the first place. Alternatively, geographical areas with a high concentration of offenders may have such a high criminal opportunity structure that all residents, regardless of their perceived attractiveness or level of guardianship, are equally susceptible to criminal victimization.

## B. Conceptualizing Target-Selection Processes

Both routine activity and lifestyle-exposure theories are designed to explain crime rates and why particular groups of individuals have higher risks of victimization than others. Differences in victimization risks for different demographic groups (e.g., males, young persons, nonwhites, the low income) are attributed to differences in lifestyles and routine activities that enhance persons' exposure to risky times, places, and potential offenders. However, neither of these approaches develops an adequate microlevel theory to account for the selection of particular crime targets within a particular sociospatial context. This is the case because both theories pay little attention to factors associated with criminality and offender motivation. Offender motivation is either assumed to be constant or there is no explicit reference to what motivates people to commit crime (Cohen and Land 1987).

A closer examination of these theories, however, reveals two specific images of criminality. First, an implicit assumption underlying these criminal opportunity theories is that offender motivation is at least partially caused by the lack of external physical restraints. Criminal intentions are translated into actions when there is a suitable person or object for victimization and "an absence of ordinary physical restraints such as the presence of other people or objects that inhibit, or are perceived to inhibit, the successful completion of direct contact predatory crime" (Cohen and Land 1987, p. 51). In this image, offenders are in some sense constantly motivated to commit crimes, and crime is explained only in mechanisms of restraint (Hirschi 1969). Second, offenders are assumed to make choices, no matter how rudimentary, in the selection of targets for victimization. It is this rational conception of criminal behavior underlying current victimization theories that, in our opinion, offers the most promise in explaining target-selection processes.

From the perspective of a "reasoning criminal" (Cornish and Clarke 1986), offenders seek to benefit themselves by their criminal behavior and select victims who offer a high payoff with little effort or risk of detection. The decision to get involved in crime and the subsequent choice of particular crime victims are influenced by the constraints of time, ability, energy, limited information, and the availability of alternatives, both conventional and unconventional. Nonetheless, it is hardly outrageous to assume that most offenders engage in some level of planning and foresight and adapt their behavior to take into account situational contingencies (Cornish and Clarke 1986). Through the selective filtering and processing of information, the rational offender is said to select from a pool of potential victims those targets that are thought to offer the greatest net rewards.

Interviews with convicted offenders reveal that many personal and situational factors are considered in the selection of crime targets. Burglars, for example, report that the risks of detection (i.e., the likelihood of getting caught), the potential yield or reward, and the relative ease with which the home can be entered are the critical factors in selecting targets for victimization (Bennett and Wright 1985). Similar aspects of the physical environment and victim characteristics are considered by other offenders (e.g., robbers, muggers) when selecting crime targets (Cornish and Clarke 1986).

Hough (1987) has developed a conceptual framework for explaining target selection that clarifies the importance of routine activities and lifestyles in this process. According to Hough (1987, p. 359), this revised conceptual scheme takes it as axiomatic that, if members of one group are selected as crime targets more frequently than another, they must meet at least one of three conditions: they must be exposed more frequently to motivated offenders (proximity), be more attractive as targets in that they afford a better "yield" to the offender (reward), or be more attractive in that they are more accessible or less defended against victimization (absence of capable guardians). This theoretical approach is diagramed in figure 2. The virtue of this perspective for understanding criminal victimization is that it clearly states that differences in proximity, attractiveness, or guardianship can account for differences in individuals' risks of victimization and that persons who possess each of these characteristics are especially vulnerable to crime.

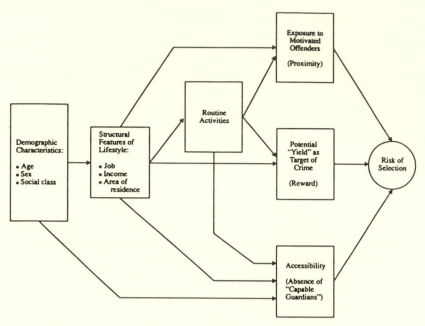

FIG. 2.—A target-selection model. Source: adapted from Hough (1987)

Consistent with both routine activity and lifestyle-exposure theory, these differences in target-selection factors are determined by individuals' routine activities and lifestyles.

Although a model that incorporates both structural and choice elements clarifies the role of routine activities and lifestyles in target-selection processes, the model is still limited in several respects. First, while it is reasonable to predict that criminal victimization is most likely under conditions of proximity, reward, and no guardianship, the model does not specify which factor is most important. Second, while interviews with convicted offenders suggest that target-selection factors may vary widely for different types of predatory crime (Bennett and Wright 1985; Carroll and Weaver 1986; Cornish and Clarke 1986; Feeney 1986; Walsh 1986), the model does not capture these crime-specific differences. Third, even within particular types of crime (e.g., among muggers), there appear to be major differences in factors associated with target selection, such as those found between novice and seasoned offenders (Cornish and Clarke 1986). These within-crime differences are also not directly incorporated in the revised model. Nonetheless, the conceptual framework outlined by Hough (1987) is a major improvement over the original formulations of routine activity and lifestyle theories.

## IV. Major Concepts in Victimization Theories

Although the terminology differs across studies, the central concepts underlying theories of victimization are essentially the same: proximity to crime, exposure, target attractiveness, and guardianship. Indeed, the major difference among victimization theories is the extent to which these concepts are interrelated.

### A. *Proximity to Crime*

Physical proximity to high-crime areas is a major factor that increases victim risk. Proximity is best represented as the physical distance between areas where potential targets of crime reside and areas where relatively large populations of potential offenders are found (Cohen, Kluegel, and Land 1981, p. 507). Living in a high-crime area increases the likelihood of frequent contact with offenders and thus increases one's risks of victimization. That persons spend a majority of their time around the home and that offenders tend to select victims in close proximity to their residences (Hindelang, Gottfredson, and Garofalo 1978) further increase the adverse consequences of living in a high-crime area.

Both theories of criminality and research in the spatial ecology of crime identify characteristics of high-crime areas. Macrosociological theories of criminality (e.g., social disorganization, anomie, differential social organization) suggest that high-crime geographical areas have high levels of population turnover, ethnic heterogeneity, and low socioeconomic status. However, the work on deviant places and "hot spots" (Stark 1987; Sherman, Gartin, and Buerger 1989) indicates that even within a large geographical area with a high crime rate (e.g., neighborhood, subdivision, a side of town) there is variation in the amount of crime. From this perspective, some places (e.g., bars, convenience stores, adult bookstores, apartment complexes) are more dangerous than others because they attract people for whom crime is more likely, provide more targets for victimization, and have a diminished capacity for social control. Living near major transportation arteries, fast-food restaurants, bus stops, schools, and other places that attract larger numbers of strangers would also increase one's vulnerability to crime for similar reasons.

Common measures of physical proximity used in previous research include place of residence (e.g., rural or urban resident), socioeconomic characteristics of the area (e.g., income level, unemployment rate, racial composition), and the perceived safety of the immediate neighborhood (Cohen, Kluegel, and Land 1981; Hough 1987; Lynch 1987; Sampson and Wooldredge 1987). The average rate of offending in an individual's immediate neighborhood is probably the best single indicator of proximity, but self-report or official measures of offending are rarely available at the neighborhood level of observation. Studies using the British Crime Survey (Sampson and Wooldredge 1987; Miethe and Meier 1990) are notable exceptions. As discussed shortly, the absence of multilevel research designs in a variety of settings has been a major limitation in previous research and has limited the development of measures of offending rates in models of victimization risks.

There is substantial empirical support for the relationship between proximity and increased risks of victimization. For example, we found in our study of British residents (Miethe and Meier 1990) that persons who lived in inner-city areas perceived their neighborhoods to be unsafe at night and that persons who lived in areas with higher levels of offending had higher risks of burglary, personal theft, and assault victimization. Using a seven-category variable based on the income of neighborhoods and urban-rural residence, Cohen, Kluegel, and Land (1981) found that persons who lived in central cities and low-income areas had higher risks of assault, burglary, and personal larceny than persons who live in other types of areas. Given high levels of residential segregation in the United States based on status characteristics, the observed association between particular demographic factors (e.g., low income, being single, being nonwhite, high residential mobility) and individuals' risks of victimization may also be attributed to the proximity of these social groups to pools of motivated offenders (Hindelang, Gottfredson, and Garofalo 1978; Smith and Jarjoura 1989). However, as discussed below, it is important to note that such findings are also consistent with other major components of victimization theories.

## B. Exposure to Crime

While proximity reflects the physical distance between large numbers of offenders and victims, "exposure to crime" is indicative of one's vulnerability to crime (Cohen, Kluegel, and Land 1981). A building or dwelling has higher exposure to burglary if it is detached from other units, has multiple points of entry, and is located on a corner lot. Persons are exposed to higher risks of personal theft and assault when placed in risky or vulnerable situations at particular times, under particular circumstances, and with particular kinds of persons. Usually, such exposure can result from the routine activities and lifestyles of persons. For example, risks of personal victimization are assumed to be directly related to the amount of time spend in public places (e.g., streets, parks) and, especially, public places at night (Hindelang, Gottfredson, and Garofalo 1978, p. 251). Furthermore, frequent contact with drinking establishments, bus depots, public transit, convenience stores, shopping malls, and other dangerous public places also increases one's exposure to crime (Sherman, Gartin, and Buerger 1989).

Exposure has usually been measured in terms of the level and nature of nonhousehold activity. One such common measure is the individual's primary daily activity (e.g. Cohen and Cantor 1980, 1981; Cohen, Kluegel, and Land 1981). Persons who are employed or are in school have greater exposure to crime because they spend more time away from home and they are more often in public places. More detailed indicators of this concept include the average number of evenings per week spent outside the home for leisure activities and the average number of hours per week the dwelling is unoccupied during the day or night (Sampson and Wooldredge 1987; Massey, Krohn, and Bonati 1989). When applied to the study of crime rates, measures of exposure have included the household activity ratio (Cohen and Felson 1979) and aggregate rates of television viewing, the supply of entertainment establishments (e.g., commercial cinemas, profit-making sport activities, opera and symphony orchestra companies), public transportation, female labor force participation, and retail sales from eating and drinking establishments.

Increases in nonhousehold activity are associated with higher crime rates in some studies (e.g., Cohen and Felson 1979; Felson and Cohen 1980; Cohen, Kluegel, and Land 1981) but not in others (Miethe, Hughes, and McDowall 1991). Increases in individuals' level of daytime and nighttime activity outside the home over time do not necessarily lead to increased risks of violent or property victimization, although cross-sectional analyses generally reveal that victimization risks are higher for persons who have higher levels of activity outside the home (Hough 1987; Sampson and Wooldredge 1987; Massey, Krohn, and Bonati 1989; Kennedy and Forde 1991).

Studies of the physical characteristics of burgled households and interviews with known offenders also suggest that the visibility and accessibility of attractive targets influence risks of victimization (Reppetto 1974; Waller and Okihiro 1978; Bennett and Wright 1985; Walsh 1986; Hough 1987). Unfortunately, little research has examined how active participation in particular types of routine activities (e.g., bar visits, visiting places where teenagers "hang out") influences risks of violent victimization.

## C. Target Attractiveness

A central assumption underlying current victimization theories is that particular targets are selected because they have symbolic or economic value to the offender. However, crime targets are also attractive to offenders when they are smaller in size (i.e., more portable) and there is less physical resistance against attack or illegal removal (Cohen, Kluegel, and Land 1981). Under a structural-choice model of victimization, it is the differential value or subjective utility associated with crime targets that determines the source of victimization within a social context (Miethe and Meier 1990, p. 250).

A variety of indicators of target attractiveness have been employed. In the original work on routine activity theory, Cohen and Felson (1979) compared the theft rate for portable and movable durables (e.g., electronic components, television sets, radios, automobiles and their accessories) with their overall circulation rate. The decreased size of these durable goods from the early 1960s through the mid-1970s also corresponds with increases in official crime rates in the United States. However, the supply of many of these portable durable goods (e.g., televisions, radios, car tape players, phonograph cartridges) may not be a good indicator of target attractiveness for studies of crime rates over time when one considers that the reduced costs and increased availability of many of these items may lead to their devaluation as "attractive" crime targets. As a general proxy for purchasing power and the supply of expensive goods, median family income and the gross national product are aggregate measures of target attractiveness that are not susceptible to such a devaluation over time.

The major measures of target attractiveness at the individual level of analysis have been the ownership of expensive and portable consumer goods (e.g., videocassette recorders, color television sets, bicycles, motorcycles), carrying cash and jewelry in public, family income, and social class (Sampson and Wooldredge 1987; Miethe and Meier 1990). As a measure of economic attractiveness, family income is commonly recognized as a proxy of this concept because it can be immediately recognized by offenders in most cases (e.g., through the geographical location of a dwelling within a city, its exterior condition, or the general appearance of the individual). In the case of expressive acts of interpersonal violence, it has been difficult to think of an unambiguous measure of target attractiveness.

Similar to the findings of research on exposure, findings on the effects of target attractiveness have not been consistent. Higher risks of victimization for persons with higher income are observed in some studies but not in others (Cohen and Cantor 1980, 1981; Cohen, Kluegel, and Land 1981; Hough 1987; Miethe and Meier 1990; Miethe, Stafford, and Sloane 1990). Persons who carry larger sums of money while in public places have a greater net risk of assault victimization, but ownership of a videocassette recorder was found either to decrease or to have no significant impact on individuals' risks of burglary (Sampson and Wooldredge 1987; Miethe and Meier 1990). Studies of crime rates for geographic areas also yield inconsistent results about the relationship between economic conditions and crime rates (Cohen, Felson, and Land 1980; Cohen 1981; Stahura and Sloan 1988; Miethe, Hughes, and McDowall 1991). Clearly, the effects vary according to the indicator chosen, suggesting that more conceptual attention must be devoted both to exposure and target attractiveness.

### D. Capable Guardianship

The final major component of current victimization theories involves the ability of persons or objects to prevent the occurrence of crime. Guardianship has both social (interpersonal) and physical dimensions. Social guardianship includes the number of household members, the density of friendship networks in the neighborhood, and having neighbors watch property or a dwelling when the home is unoccupied. The availability of others (e.g., friends, neighbors, pedestrians, law enforcement officers) may prevent crime by their presence alone or through offering physical assistance in warding off an attack. Physical guardianship involves target-hardening activities (e.g., door/window locks, window bars, burglar alarms, guard dogs, ownership of firearms), other physical impediments to household theft (e.g., street lighting, guarded public entrances), and participation in collective activities (e.g., neighborhood watch programs, home security surveys). Regardless of its particular form, the availability of capable guardianship is deemed important because it indicates increased "costs" to would-be offenders (e.g., greater effort, greater risk of detection and apprehension) and thus should decrease the opportunity for victimization.

A review of previous research on guardianship activities reveals several general trends. First, target-hardening efforts are widespread in the United States and may be regarded as the most widespread and common forms of crime prevention. The majority of people in urban and suburban areas take routine precautions against crime such as locking doors and windows, using exterior lighting, and having neighbors watch their property (Dubow 1979; Skogan and Maxfield 1981; Miethe 1991). Collective crime prevention activities (e.g., property-marking projects, Neighborhood Watch) have also been organized throughout the country (Rosenbaum 1987, 1990).

Second, the success of guardianship activities has been mixed. Physical and social guardianship is associated with lower rates of victimization in several studies but not in others (Scarr 1973; Reppetto 1974; Lavrakas et al. 1981; Skogan and Maxfield 1981; Winchester and Jackson 1982; Yin 1986; Rosenbaum 1987, 1990; Miethe and Meier 1990). However, several authors (e.g., Mayhew 1984) argue that the use of cross-sectional designs has contributed to these inconsistent results because of what is called the "victimization effect." The victimization effect is the tendency for persons to take precautions as a consequence of being victimized. Because cross-sectional designs cannot determine the temporal ordering of victimization experiences and heightened awareness of crime prevention, an observed positive relationship may mask the deterrent effect of precautions on victimization risks.

Third, few studies of guardianship have exercised sufficient controls for other factors influencing victimization risks. Under such conditions, it is impossible to ascertain unambiguously whether differences between protected and unprotected residents are due to the deterrent effect of protective actions or to other factors (e.g., lifestyles, target attractiveness, proximity to high-crime areas) that also alter the likelihood of victimization.

## V.  Problems with Previous Evaluations of Victimization Theories

Although theories of victimization have been the object of much research, there are several recurring problems that preclude complete confidence in the results of this research. These involve inadequate measures of key concepts, the lack of sufficient statistical controls, and the failure to examine multilevel and context-specific models of victimization.

### A.  Inadequate Measures of Key Concepts

The development of clear empirical indicators of key theoretical concepts has been a major problem in the development of victimization theory. This is a problem in many theoretical areas in criminology, but the popularity of criminal opportunity theories of victimization makes this problem somehow more pressing than in areas where there is little research activity. We refer to this problem as one of *theoretical indeterminacy*, or the ability of the same indicator to serve more than one theoretical master. Consider the following alternative interpretations of the indicators of key concepts in victimization theories.

*Proximity* to motivated offenders is generally considered the physical distance between pools of offenders and victims, but this concept has usually been measured by the degree of population concentration (e.g., living in an urban versus rural area) and the socioeconomic characteristics of the geographical area. From this perspective, living in a large urban area and a low socioeconomic neighborhood are widely used as proxy measures of proximity (Cohen, Kluegel, and Land 1981; Hough 1987). However, it is easy to see that these variables may not only measure proximity but also a breakdown in social control, population heterogeneity, diminished economic opportunity, and other factors underlying traditional theories of criminality that attempt to explain the motivation of offenders. Using such indicators, higher victimization risks for persons who live in urban areas or low-income neighborhoods would not empirically distinguish theories of victimization from theories of criminality. Without greater conceptual refinement, it is hard to know what is being tested.

We have already mentioned that *exposure* to crime is usually indicated by the level of nonhousehold activity. Accordingly, persons who are employed outside the home or are going to school are assumed to be more exposed to crime than persons whose daily activities are more likely to take place around the home (e.g., unemployed, homemakers, retired, disabled). Yet such nonhousehold activities may actually be associated with "low exposure" because both work and school take place in a confined environment with a relatively high level of guardianship and supervision. However, only in the case of the Victim-Risk Supplement of the NCS and the British Crime Survey (BCS) are activities in particular public places (e.g., going to bars/taverns, taking public transit) included as variables that may be used to develop better measures of exposure to risky and vulnerable situations. Furthermore, without controlling for other factors, measuring exposure in this manner is consistent with some theories of criminality (e.g., differential association) that predict a relationship between nonhousehold activity and crime because of the acquisition of criminal norms, not because of greater risk of victimization.

When examining crime rates and social trends, Cohen and Felson (1979) used the "household activity ratio" as a measure of exposure. As defined earlier, this ratio is a composite index of the number of married women in the labor force and the number of nonhusband/nonwife households. Cohen and Felson (1979) assume that this ratio measures both the dispersion of the population away from households and the supply of durable goods susceptible to theft, but it is equally indicative of the prevalence of nontraditional families and reductions in social integration, ideas that are consistent with several theories of criminality as well as Cohen and Felson's theory of routine activities. In this sense, the positive association between crime rates and non-household activity could be due as much to social disorganization processes (e.g., problems of norm transmission and community control) or a breakdown of bonds to mainstream society (i.e., lower attachment, commitment, involvement and belief in conventional activity) as to increases in the supply of criminal opportunities from greater exposure and lower guardianship. If findings fit both sets of theories equally, then opportunity-based theories, while plausible, do not tell us anything unique about the social ecology of crime (Miethe, Hughes, and McDowall 1991, p. 168).

"Target attractiveness" is defined in terms of both its material and symbolic value to offenders (Cohen, Kluegel, and Land 1981). However, measures of individual ownership and the circulation of small but expensive durable goods (e.g., jewelry, audiovisual equipment) are not routinely available in the NCS yearly data or census reports. Thus, target attractiveness is usually measured by general economic conditions (e.g., family income, unemployment rate) even though such indicators may equally serve as surrogates for lower criminal motivation (because higher income and lower unemployment indicate greater legitimate economic opportunities) and greater exposure to crime (because higher income affords greater leisure activity outside the home).

The only available measure of guardianship in the NCS series and census data is the number of members in the household. Neither source provides measures of safety precautions and other types of guardianship on a routine basis. In the case of property crimes against the dwelling (e.g., burglary, vandalism, theft of property around the home), larger households should have lower victimization risks because the dwelling would be less likely to be unoccupied. As a measure of guardianship for violent crime, it must be assumed that the greater the household size, the less likely a person will be alone in a public place.

However, household size may also have a crime-enhancing effect as a result of the impact of household size on household crowding and, in turn, the possible adverse consequences of crowding on criminal motivation.

## B. The Use of Secondary Data

What these examples also show is that the reliance on secondary data has contributed to the use of inadequate measures of proximity, exposure, attractiveness, and guardianship. The proxy measures typically do not tap each dimension of the underlying concepts and have ambiguous meanings. Substantive inferences about the predictive utility of victimization theories are questionable under such conditions.

Indeed, we would argue that reliance on secondary data sources is one of the basic causes of measurement problems in studies of victimization. Given that victimization is such a rare event (only about 25 percent of U.S. households are "touched" by any crime each year and most of that is relatively minor), it is not surprising that the enormous costs of getting a large sample of particular types of crime victims and nonvictims prohibit many researchers from collecting their own data. However, the largest data source on individuals' victimization experiences, the yearly National Crime Victimization Survey series, was designed primarily to provide alternative estimates of the rate of crime rather than to test theories of victimization. The victim-risk supplement of the NCS data and the current NCS redesign are the only national data in this series that have potential for such theoretical analyses (Skogan 1990). Similarly, census data are the primary data source for studies of crime rates in geographical areas. Unfortunately, census data are collected primarily for political and administrative reasons. Thus, although both NCS data and census reports for various aggregate units are widely available, neither of these sources provides complete and unequivocal measures of the key concepts underlying victimization theories.

## C. The Use of Statistical Controls

Statistical control for other variables is virtually a requirement for causal inference in nonexperimental designs. Statistical control allows for an assessment of the net impact of one variable on another once adjustments are made for the variation shared between the primary independent variable and other predictor variables. Empirical studies of victimization processes, however, have rarely included measures of each major concept and component underlying victimization theories even though proximity, exposure, attractiveness, and lack of guardianship are considered *necessary* conditions for predatory crime. The failure to include adequate statistical controls for all relevant variables may seriously distort inferences about the substantive impact of each of these factors on victimization risks.

When measures of a particular concept have multiple meanings, statistical control is one way of disentangling and isolating the unique effects of each theoretical component. Given the pervasiveness of ambiguous measures of key concepts underlying theories of victimization, statistical control is especially important. Most measures of theoretical concepts used in studies of victimization have ambiguous meanings (Miethe, Hughes, and McDowall 1991). The following are examples. *Female labor-force participation* may represent either wider exposure, decreased guardianship, increased target attractiveness, or reduced criminal motivations resulting from rising economic resources. *Income* may represent target attractiveness, higher exposure from nonhousehold activity, or reduced criminal motivation. *Unemployment* may indicate criminogenic conditions, reduced circulation of money, and reduced levels of nonhousehold leisure activities. And *household size* may represent higher guardianship or increases in criminogenic conditions due to the adverse impact of household crowding. It is not possible to assess the adequacy of theoretical concepts when their presumed empirical indicators have multiple meanings. Previous evaluations of criminal opportunity theories have not included sufficient measures of key concepts or exercised sufficient statistical controls to isolate the unique impact of each theoretical component.

## D. *Level of Analysis and Model Specification*

Previous evaluations of theories of criminality and victimization have relied on what is called a "main effects" or "additive model." Under such a specification, the impact of a variable is assumed to be identical across levels of another variable. When applied to theories of victimization, the additive specification assumes that the impact of target attractiveness, for example, is the same for persons who vary in their exposure to crime and have different levels of guardianship. The impact of guardianship is likewise presumed to be the same across various social contexts. Regardless of where individuals live and their particular routine activities and lifestyles, increases in household size or the number of safety precautions are assumed to decrease risks of predatory crime.

However, the failure to examine whether variables have different effects across different contexts is a type of model misspecification that
may dramatically alter substantive conclusions about the predictive
validity of current theories.

There are various ways in which contextual effects can occur in
models of victimization. What is required are data that permit multilevel observation and sensitivity to alternative social contexts. Data
that do not permit the examination of multilevel relationships or the
estimation of separate models of victimization across different social
contexts are severely limited. Most aggregate data sources are restricted
to one level of analysis (e.g., individual, census tract, city, SMSA) and
do not contain measures of contextual variables. The opportunity to
perform contextual analyses is important because it may more clearly
specify the conditions under which proximity, exposure, target attractiveness, and guardianship alter individuals' risks and aggregate rates
of predatory crime. The results of the few studies using this approach
also suggest its utility as a research tool for testing theories of victimization (Sampson and Wooldredge 1987; Smith and Jarjoura 1989; Miethe
and McDowall 1993).

### VI. Contextual Effects in Models of Victimization
The context of crime is a particularly important dimension, and the
further development of victimization or opportunity-based theories of
crime may require greater sensitivity to contextual information. A fundamental aspect of predatory crime is that it occurs in a social context
in which there is a convergence of victims and offenders in time and
space. It is surprising that little research has incorporated aspects of
the social context directly into theories of victimization. To their
credit, routine activity and lifestyle-exposure theories acknowledge the
importance of exposure and proximity to risky or vulnerable situations
as necessary conditions for predatory crime. However, what is absent
is a clear specification of how aspects of the wider social context influence risks of victimization. There are several ways in which the social
context can both facilitate and constrain the occurrence of crime.

A major contribution of macrosociological theories of criminality is
that they identify the structural conditions associated with crime. For
example, population heterogeneity and density, residential mobility,
and low economic opportunity are identified as criminogenic forces
because they either increase cultural conflict, decrease economic resources, or hamper the development of effective mechanisms of social

control (Kornhauser 1978; Bursik 1988; Sampson and Groves 1989). One primary way in which these social forces generate a facilitating context for crime is by increasing the pool of potential offenders. The greater an individual's proximity to these criminogenic areas, the greater one's risks of victimization.

According to current theories of victimization, an alternative way in which the social context influences predatory crime is by increasing the supply of criminal opportunities. Because routine activities of everyday life are said to create criminal opportunities, geographical areas with high levels of public activity, expensive and portable consumer goods, and lower levels of physical guardianship are presumed to have higher rates of crime. Some persons, regardless of their own routine activities and lifestyles, may be more vulnerable than others to crime simply by living in these "crime-attractive" areas. The composition and structure of a neighborhood may influence individuals' victimization risks because both give off cues to would-be offenders about the potential yield and costs for engaging in crime in that geographical area.

Research on the crime-reduction benefits of safety precautions is an example of how elements of the wider social context influence individuals' risks of victimization. As a form of guardianship, it is widely assumed that taking safety precautions (e.g., locking doors, installing alarms, owning dogs) reduces risks of predatory crime. However, what is less clear is how a person's chances of victimization are influenced by the safety precautions taken by others in their immediate neighborhood. The safety precautions of others may either enhance or reduce an individual's risks of victimization. According to the arguments about *crime displacement* (Gabor 1981, 1990; Cornish and Clarke 1987; Miethe 1991), persons are negatively affected by the protective actions of others in their neighborhood because these actions are assumed to deflect crime to less protected others. Alternatively, a "free-rider" effect suggests that persons benefit from the social control activities of their immediate neighbors because these actions convey to would-be offenders an image that this area, in general, is a risky place to commit crime. Regardless of whether these safety precautions of others inhibit or enhance victimization risks, the major point is that the community context of crime control in both cases is said to alter individuals' risks of victimization substantially.

The assumption underlying contextual analyses is that victimization risks and its predictors vary by characteristics of the wider social context. These contextual effects can take various forms. First, living near "hot spots" for crime (Sherman, Gartin, and Buerger 1989) may be especially harmful because of proximity to areas with high concentration of offenders. Second, routine activities and lifestyles may have context-specific effects on victimization risks. For example, the crime-enhancing effects of exposure and proximity to motivated offenders may be important only in neighborhoods with low levels of informal and formal social control. When there are high levels of social integration and safety precautions in an area, these social control mechanisms may be of sufficient strength to deter crime and overwhelm the adverse effects of exposure and proximity to crime. Alternatively, the supply of expensive consumer goods in the immediate environment may influence the risks of property victimization even for residents who lack these possessions. As indicated by the conflicting predictions about displacement and free-rider effects, it may be unclear in other cases whether the same contextual factor impedes or enhances an individuals' risks of victimization. However, regardless of the particular type of contextual effect, what is important about multilevel models and contextual analysis is that victimization risks are seen as a function of both the routine activities of residents and the composition and structure of the wider geographical area.

It is difficult to overemphasize the potential import of including both measures of individuals' lifestyles and contextual variables in studies of victimization. First, a major premise of sociological theory is that social conditions enable and constrain human activity. Although not denying that individuals' lifestyles influence their vulnerability to crime, most sociological theories assume that the community context has a direct impact on victimization risks independent of individual characteristics. Second, it is possible that many of the presumed individual-level effects are actually reflective of community dynamics. For example, the strong impact of being young or unmarried on victimization risks is commonly attributed to the lifestyles of such persons. Yet the influence of these factors may simply reflect the tendency for both single persons and young adults to live in transitional neighborhoods with more potential offenders, lower internal social control, and high rates of public activity (see also Smith and Jarjoura 1989). Under these conditions, too much importance would be placed on these individual-level causes of victimization risks.

The importance of contextual factors has been empirically documented in several recent studies. For example, Miethe and McDowall

(1993) found that contextual factors had significant main and interactive effects on risks of both violent and property victimization. The impact of individuals' routine activities and lifestyles depends on the particular composition of the wider neighborhood. Sampson and Wooldredge (1987) found that personal risks of burglary were influenced by the level of family disruption, single-person households, and density of ownership of portable consumer goods (i.e., VCRs) in the wider community. Smith and Jarjoura (1989) found that risks of burglary were influenced by several neighborhood factors (e.g., racial heterogeneity, population instability, median income). Aspects of community composition and structure have been included in several additional studies of individuals' risks of victimization (e.g., Cohen, Kluegel, and Land 1981; Simcha-Fagan and Schwartz 1986; Sampson and Lauritsen 1990).

### VII. Prospects for Integrating Theories of Victimization and Theories of Offending

The development of theories of victimization requires the development of theories of offending. The objectives of theories of crime can only be attained with an understanding of the processes by which victims come to experience risk of crime and offenders come to be motivated to commit crime and of the social contexts that unite these parallel sets of processes. For these reasons, the theoretical objective in criminology should be identified as the development of defensible theories of crime, not just theories of victimization or just theories of offending.

The development of testable propositions about crime requires information about both victims and offenders. This information may involve data pertaining to group differences in offending and victimization (sometimes referred to as "structural" information) or to social psychological processes in offending and victimization (sometimes called "processual" information). These levels of observation and analysis have served criminologists well in the development of theoretical perspectives on both offending and victimization, but there has been no systematic attempt to formulate integrated theories of offending *and* victimization.

The prospects for such an integration are bright, but it must be admitted that previous efforts at theoretical integration in criminology have not been terribly successful. Several notable attempts in recent years have been made to integrate different theoretical traditions (Elliott, Ageton, and Cantor 1979; Pearson and Weiner 1985; Thornberry

1987), and there have been discussions about the issue of methods and desirability of theoretical integration in general (Hirschi 1979; Short 1979, 1985; Elliott 1985; Messner, Krohn, and Liska 1989). So far, the idea of theoretical integration has been applied only to theories of criminality, and theories of victimization have been relatively neglected.

The disadvantages of integrative efforts are initially conceptual and theoretical. That is, some perspectives do not lend themselves to integration because they make contradictory assumptions that cannot be reconciled. Cultural deviance and control theories, for example, have been said to contain irreconcilable differences in domain assumptions (Kornhauser 1978), which, if correct, would make any meaningful integration impossible. Several studies have attempted to unite variables from different theoretical traditions and have reported results as though they represented a unified perspective (Johnson 1979; Pearson and Weiner 1985). Such efforts are perhaps harmless (and perhaps even positive) unless they give the impression that the result of such efforts is a "new" rather than a logically recombined theory.

The problems of theoretical integration are significant (see also Meier 1989), but they may not be insurmountable. For one thing, there is no reason to believe that *any* theory of criminality and *any* theory of victimization make incompatible assumptions about the nature of crime or social reality. Furthermore, no theory of criminality makes explicit assumptions about victim processes that preclude integrative efforts; likewise, no theory of victimization makes any restrictive assumptions about offenders.

As a way of overcoming compartmentalized thinking, the integration of theories of criminality and victimization should improve substantially our understanding of crime. From their inception, theories of criminality (e.g., strain, social disorganization, differential association, social bond) have emphasized the structural and social psychological factors associated with criminal motivation, but they have ignored how the actions of potential crime targets condition the physical opportunities for victimization. The primary goal of these theories has been to explain the decision to engage in crime. In contrast, theories of victimization emphasize the causal role of personal characteristics that enhance the accessibility and attractiveness of crime victims, but these theories largely neglect sources of criminal motivation. By addressing both crime-commission and target-selection decisions, it is easier to see the value of an integrated perspective.

From an integrated perspective, crime is not simply what offenders do and what victims do. Rather, understanding crime from an integrated perspective requires an understanding of the social structure that surrounds both criminals and victims. It is that structure, or context, that creates both offender motivation and victim risk-taking. Integrated theories are theories sensitive to the nature and impact of that structure. Such theories are informed about offenders, victims, and structural facilitators that link them. Furthermore, such theories, if they are to be truly useful, will be testable and judged on their predictive validity. Traditional "isolationist" approaches that focus only on one component of the larger picture are necessarily limited and should be tolerated only insofar as they contribute to larger theoretical structures. Both more sophisticated offender and victim theories can make such a contribution.

## VIII. Conclusions

Current theories of victimization highlight the symbiotic relationship between conventional and illegal activities. Regardless of their particular terminology, routine activities and lifestyle-exposure theories emphasize how criminal opportunities develop out of the routine activities of everyday life. Routine activity patterns that increase proximity to motivated offenders, increase exposure to risky and dangerous situations, enhance the expected utility or attractiveness of potential crime targets, and reduce the level of guardianship are assumed to increase aggregate rates and individuals' risks of predatory crime. These criminal opportunity theories have been used to account for changes in crime rates in the United States over time, the level of crime in aggregate units (e.g., cities, SMSAs), differences in victimization risks for different social groups (e.g., males, single persons, younger people), and individuals' risks of victimization.

The results of previous studies give some indication of the explanatory power of these criminal opportunity theories. There is some evidence to support each of the major components underlying these theories (i.e., proximity, exposure, attractiveness, and guardianship). However, this supporting evidence is less impressive when the major limitations of previous work are acknowledged. That previous research has generally used inadequate proxy measures of key concepts, includes few statistical controls, and has not examined rigorously multilevel models and contextual effects casts doubt on the substantive conclusions from these studies.

While current theories of victimization suggest that victims and offenders are inextricably linked in an ecology of crime, they do not provide sufficient information about the conditions of offending to permit adequate predictions of crime. This is, of course, also a failing of theories of criminality that concentrate only on accounting for the pool of motivated offenders; the victim side of the equation is neglected. More adequate theories should be sought in the exploration of combinations of victim and offender theories and a sensitivity to the social contexts in which crimes are committed.

## REFERENCES

Amir, Menachem. 1967. "Victim-precipitated Forcible Rape." *Journal of Criminal Law, Criminology, and Police Science* 58:493–502.

———. 1971. *Patterns of Forcible Rape*. Chicago: University of Chicago Press.

Bennett, Trevor, and Richard Wright. 1985. *Burglars on Burglary: Prevention and the Offender*. Hampshire, England: Bower.

Bursik, Robert J., Jr. 1988. "Social Disorganization and Theories of Crime and Delinquency: Problems and Prospects." *Criminology* 26:529–51.

Carroll, John, and Frances Weaver. 1986. "Shoplifters' Perceptions of Crime Opportunities: A Process-tracking Study." In *The Reasoning Criminal: Rational Choice Perspectives on Offending*, edited by Derek B. Cornish and Ronald V. Clarke. New York: Springer-Verlag.

Clarke, Ronald, Paul Ekblom, Mike Hough, and Pat Mayhew. 1985. "Elderly Victims of Crime and Exposure to Risk." *Howard Journal of Criminal Justice* 24:1–9.

Cohen, Lawrence E. 1981. "Modeling Crime Trends: A Criminal Opportunity Perspective." *Journal of Research in Crime and Delinquency* 18:138–64.

Cohen, Lawrence E., and David Cantor. 1980. "The Determinants of Larceny: An Empirical and Theoretical Study." *Journal of Research in Crime and Delinquency* 17:140–59.

Cohen, Lawrence E., and David Cantor. 1981. "Residential Burglary in the United States: Lifestyle and Demographic Factors Associated with the Probability of Victimization." *Journal of Research in Crime and Delinquency* 18:113–27.

Cohen, Lawrence E., and Marcus Felson. 1979. "Social Change and Crime Rate Trends: A Routine Activity Approach." *American Sociological Review* 44:588–608.

Cohen, Lawrence E., Marcus Felson, and Kenneth C. Land. 1980. "Property Crime Rates in the United States: A Macrodynamic Analysis 1947–77 with Ex Ante Forecasts for the Mid-1980s." *American Journal of Sociology* 86:90–118.

Cohen, Lawrence E., James R. Kluegel, and Kenneth C. Land. 1981. "Social Inequality and Predatory Criminal Victimization: An Exposition and Test of a Formal Theory." *American Sociology Review* 46:505–24.

Cohen, Lawrence E., and Kenneth C. Land. 1987. "Sociological Positivism and the Explanation of Criminality." In *Positive Criminology*, edited by Michael Gottfredson and Travis Hirschi. Beverly Hills, Calif.: Sage.

Cornish, Derek B., and Ronald V. Clarke. 1986. *The Reasoning Criminal: Rational Choice Perspectives on Offending*. New York: Springer-Verlag.

———. 1987. "Understanding Crime Displacement." *Criminology* 25:933–43.

Curtis, Lynn. 1974. "Victim-Precipitation and Violent Crimes." *Social Problems* 21:594–605.

Dubow, Fred. 1979. *Reactions to Crime: A Critical Review of the Literature*. Washington, D.C.: U.S. Government Printing Office.

Ellenberger, T. 1955. "Psychological Relationships between the Criminal and His Victim." *Archives of Criminal Psychology* 2:257–90.

Elliott, Delbert. 1985. "The Assumption That Theories Can Be Combined with Increased Explanatory Power." In *Theoretical Methods in Criminology*, edited by Robert F. Meier. Beverly Hills, Calif.: Sage.

Elliott, Delbert, Suzanne Ageton, and R. J. Cantor. 1979. "An Integrated Theoretical Perspective on Delinquent Behavior." *Journal of Research in Crime and Delinquency* 16:3–27.

Ennis, Philip H. 1967. *Criminal Victimization in the U.S.* Field Survey 2. Report on a National Survey by the President's Commission on Law Enforcement and Administration of Justice. Washington, D.C.: U.S. Government Printing Office.

Feeney, Floyd. 1986. "Robbers as Decision-Makers." In *The Reasoning Criminal: Rational Choice Perspectives on Offending*, edited by Derek B. Cornish and Ronald V. Clarke. New York: Springer-Verlag.

Felson, Marcus, and Lawrence Cohen. 1980. "Human Ecology and Crime: A Routine Activity Approach." *Human Ecology* 8:389–406.

Gabor, Thomas. 1981. "The Crime Displacement Hypothesis: An Empirical Examination." *Crime and Delinquency* 26:390–404.

———. 1990. "Crime Displacement and Situational Prevention: Toward the Development of Some Principles." *Canadian Journal of Criminology* 32:41–73.

Garofalo, R. 1914. *Criminology*. Boston: Little, Brown.

Gottfredson, Michael. 1981. "On the Etiology of Criminal Victimization." *Journal of Law and Criminology* 72:714–26.

Hawley, Amos. 1950. *Human Ecology: A Theory of Community Structure*. New York: Ronald Press.

Hindelang, Michael S., Michael Gottfredson, and James Garofalo. 1978. *Victims of Personal Crime*. Cambridge, Mass.: Ballinger.

Hirschi, Travis. 1969. *The Causes of Delinquency*. Berkeley: University of California Press.

———. 1979. "Separate and Unequal Is Better." *Journal of Research on Crime and Delinquency* 16:34–38.

Hough, Michael. 1987. "Offenders' Choice of Targets: Findings from Victim Surveys." *Journal of Quantitative Criminology* 3:355–69.

Johnson, Richard E. 1979. *Juvenile Delinquency and Its Origins*. Cambridge: Cambridge University Press.

Kennedy, Leslie, and David Forde. 1990. "Routine Activity and Crime: An Analysis of Victimization in Canada." *Criminology* 28:137–51.

Kornhauser, Ruth. 1978. *Social Sources of Delinquency*. Chicago: University of Chicago Press.

Lavrakas, P. J., J. Normoyle, W. G. Skogan, E. J. Herz, G. Salem, and D. A. Lewis. 1981. *Factors Related to Citizen Involvement in Personal, Household, and Neighborhood Anti-Crime Measures*. Washington, D.C.: U.S. Government Printing Office.

Lynch, James P. 1987. "Routine Activity and Victimization at Work." *Journal of Quantitative Criminology* 3:283–300.

MacDonald, Robert. 1939. *Crime Is a Business*. Palo Alto, Calif.: Stanford University Press.

Massey, James L., Marvin D. Krohn, and Lisa M. Bonati. 1989. "Property Crime and the Routine Activities of Individuals." *Journal of Research in Crime and Delinquency* 26:378–400.

Maxfield, Michael G. 1987. "Household Composition, Routine Activity, and Victimization: A Comparative Analysis." *Journal of Quantitative Criminology* 3:301–20.

Mayhew, Pat. 1984. "Target-Hardening: How Much of an Answer?" In *Coping with Burglary*, edited by Ronald V. Clarke and Tim Hope. Boston: Kluwer-Nijhoff.

Meier, Robert F. 1989. "Deviance and Differentiation." In *Theoretical Integration in the Study of Deviance and Crime: Problems and Prospects*, edited by Steven F. Messner, Marvin D. Krohn, and Allen E. Liska. Albany, N.Y.: SUNY Press.

Mendelsohn, B. 1956. "The Victimology" (in French). *Etudes Internationales de Psycho-Sociologie Criminelle* 1956(3):25–26.

Messner, Steven F., and Judith R. Blau. 1987. "Routine Leisure Activities and Rates of Crime: A Macro-Level Analysis." *Social Forces* 65:1035–52.

Messner, Steven F., Marvin D. Krohn, and Allen E. Liska, eds. 1989. *Theoretical Integration in the Study of Deviance and Crime: Problems and Prospects*. Albany, N.Y.: SUNY Press.

Messner, Steven F., and Kenneth Tardiff. 1985. "The Social Ecology of Urban Homicide: An Application of the 'Routine Activities' Approach." *Criminology* 23:241–67.

Miethe, Terance D. 1985. "The Myth or Reality of Victim Involvement in Crime: A Review and Comment on Victim-Precipitation Research." *Sociological Focus* 18:209–220.

———. 1991. "Citizen-based Crime Control Activity and Victimization Risks: Examination of Displacement and Free-Rider Effects." *Criminology* 29:419–39.

Miethe, Terance D., Michael Hughes, and David McDowall. 1991. "Social Change and Crime Rates: An Evaluation of Alternative Theoretical Approaches." *Social Forces* 70:165–85.

Miethe, Terance D., and David McDowall. 1993. "Contextual Effects in Models of Criminal Victimization." *Social Forces* (forthcoming).

Miethe, Terance D., and Robert F. Meier. 1990. "Criminal Opportunity and Victimization Rates: A Structural-Choice Theory of Criminal Victimization." *Journal of Research in Crime and Delinquency* 27:243–66.

Miethe, Terance D., Mark C. Stafford, and J. Scott Long. 1987. "Social Differentiation in Criminal Victimization: A Test of Routine Activities/Lifestyle Theory." *American Sociological Review* 52:184–94.

Miethe, Terance D., Mark Stafford, and Douglas Sloane. 1990. "Lifestyle Changes and Risks of Criminal Victimization." *Journal of Quantitative Criminology* 6:357–76.

Nelson, James. 1980. "Multiple Victimization in American Cities: A Statistical Analysis of Rare Events." *American Journal of Sociology* 85:870–91.

Normandeau, Andre. 1968. "Trends and Patterns in Crimes of Robbery." Doctoral dissertation. University of Pennsylvania, Philadelphia.

Pearson, Frank S., and Neil Alan Weiner. 1985. "Toward an Integration of Criminological Theories." *Journal of Criminal Law and Criminology* 76:116–50.

President's Commission on Law Enforcement and Administration of Justice. 1967. *The Challenge of Crime in a Free Society*. Washington, D.C.: U.S. Government Printing Office.

Reppetto, Thomas A. 1974. *Residential Crime*. Cambridge, Mass.: Ballinger.

Rosenbaum, Dennis P. 1987. "The Theory and Research behind Neighborhood Watch: Is It a Sound Fear and Crime Reduction Strategy?" *Crime and Delinquency* 33:103–34.

———. 1990. "Community Crime Prevention: A Review and Synthesis of the Literature." *Justice Quarterly* 5:323–95.

Sampson, Robert J., and W. Bryon Groves. 1989. "Community Structure and Crime: Testing Social-Disorganization Theory." *American Journal of Sociology* 94:774–802.

Sampson, Robert J., and Janet L. Lauritsen. 1990. "Deviant Lifestyles, Proximity to Crime, and the Offender-Victim Link in Personal Violence." *Journal of Research in Crime and Delinquency* 27:110–39.

Sampson, Robert J., and John D. Wooldredge. 1987. "Linking the Micro- and Macro-Level Dimensions of Lifestyle-Routine Activity and Opportunity Models of Predatory Victimization." *Journal of Quantitative Criminology* 3:371–93.

Scarr, Harry A. 1973. *Patterns of Burglary*. Washington, D.C.: U.S. Government Printing Office.

Schafer, Stephen. 1968. *The Victim and His Criminal: A Study in Functional Responsibility*. New York: Random House.

Schultz, Lawrence. 1968. "The Victim-Offender Relationship." *Crime and Delinquency* 14:135–41.

Sherman, Lawrence W., P. R. Gartin, and M. E. Buerger. 1989. "Hot Spots of Predatory Crime: Routine Activities and the Criminology of Place." *Criminology* 27:24–55.

Short, James F., Jr. 1979. "On the Etiology of Delinquent Behavior." *Journal of Research on Crime and Delinquency* 16:28–33.

Short, James F., Jr. 1985. "The Level of Explanation Problem in Criminology." In *Theoretical Methods in Criminology*, edited by Robert F. Meier. Beverly Hills, Calif.: Sage.

Simcha-Fagan, Ora, and Joseph E. Schwartz. 1986. "Neighborhood and Delinquency: An Assessment of Contextual Effects." *Criminology* 24:667–99.

Skogan, Wesley G. 1990. "The Polls—a Review of the National Crime Survey Redesign." *Public Opinion Quarterly* 54:256–72.

Skogan, Wesley G., and Michael G. Maxfield. 1981. *Coping with Crime: Individual and Neighborhood Reactions.* Beverly Hills, Calif.: Sage.

Smith, Douglas A., and G. Roger Jarjoura. 1989. "Household Characteristics, Neighborhood Composition, and Victimization Risk." *Social Forces* 68:621–40.

Sparks, Richard F. 1981. "Multiple Victimization: Evidence, Theory, and Future Research." *Journal of Criminal Law and Criminology* 72:762–78.

———. 1982. *Research on Victims of Crime: Accomplishments, Issues, and New Directions.* Washington, D.C.: U.S. Government Printing Office.

Stahura, John, and John Sloan III. 1988. "Urban Satisfaction of Places, Routine Activities, and Suburban Crime Rates." *Social Forces* 66:1102–18.

Stark, Rodney. 1987. "Deviant Places." *Criminology* 25:893–908.

Thornberry, Terence P. 1987. "Toward an Interactional Theory of Delinquency." *Criminology* 25:863–92.

Von Hentig, Hans. 1940. "Remarks on the Interaction of Perpetrator and Victim." *Journal of Criminal Law, Criminology, and Police Science* 31:303–9.

Von Hentig, Hans. 1948. *The Criminal and His Victim.* New Haven, Conn.: Yale University Press.

Waller, Irvin, and Norman Okihiro. 1978. *Burglary: The Victim and the Public.* Toronto: University of Toronto Press.

Walsh, Dermot. 1986. "Victim Selection Procedures among Economic Criminals: The Rational Choice Perspective." In *The Reasoning Criminal: Rational Choice Perspectives on Offending*, edited by Derek Cornish and Ronald V. Clarke. New York: Springer-Verlag.

Winchester, S., and H. Jackson. 1982. *Residential Burglary: The Limits of Prevention.* Home Office Research Study no. 74. London: H.M. Stationery Office.

Wolfgang, Marvin. 1957. "Victim-precipitated Criminal Homicide." *Journal of Criminal Law, Criminology, and Police Science* 48:1–11.

Wolfgang, Marvin. 1958. *Patterns of Criminal Homicide.* Philadelphia: University of Pennsylvania Press.

Yin, Robert K. 1986. "Community Crime Prevention: A Synthesis of Eleven Evaluations." In *Community Crime Prevention: Does It Work?* edited by Dennis Rosenbaum. Criminal Justice System Annuals. Beverly Hills, Calif.: Sage.

Journal of Consulting and Clinical Psychology
1994, Vol. 62, No. 1, 111–123

# Psychological Distress Following Criminal Victimization in the General Population: Cross-Sectional, Longitudinal, and Prospective Analyses

Fran H. Norris and Krzysztof Kaniasty

Samples of 105 violent crime victims, 227 property crime victims, and 190 nonvictims provided normative data regarding levels of psychological distress following criminal victimization. At points approximately 3 months, 9 months, and 15 months postcrime, symptoms of depression, somatization, hostility, anxiety, phobic anxiety, fear of crime, and avoidance were assessed. Although crime victims showed substantial improvement between 3 and 9 months, thereafter they did not. Over the course of the study, violent crime victims remained more distressed than did property crime victims who, in turn, remained more distressed than nonvictims. Regression analyses revealed that the effects of crime could not be accounted for by precrime differences between victims and nonvictims in either social status or psychological functioning. However, lasting effects were often contingent on the occurrence of subsequent crimes.

Crime is viewed as one of the most serious domestic problems in the United States. The U.S. Bureau of Justice Statistics (Koppel, 1987) now estimates that 83% of the United States population will experience a violent crime at some point in their lives and that virtually all persons (99%) will experience a personal theft. Recent studies have shown that even crimes as serious as sexual assault are shockingly frequent (Kilpatrick & Resnick, 1992b; Koss, 1990; Koss, Gidycz, & Wisniewski, 1987). In short, over the course of life, U.S. citizens are more likely than not to become victims of crime.

These statistics are cause for serious concern regarding mental health in the United States. Crime victims, predominantly rape victims, have been shown to suffer from a variety of psychological problems. (For reviews, see Frieze, Hymer, & Greenberg, 1987; McCann, Sakheim, & Abrahamson, 1988; Steketee & Foa, 1987.) These reactions include but are not limited to depression, anxiety, hostility, fear, sexual dysfunction, physical illness, and posttraumatic stress (e.g., Atkeson, Calhoun, Resick, & Ellis, 1982; Bard & Sangrey, 1986; Burgess & Holmstrom, 1978; Davis & Friedman, 1985; Kilpatrick et al., 1985; Kilpatrick & Resnick, 1992b; Koss, Woodruff, & Koss, 1990; Siegel, Golding, Stein, Burnam, & Sorenson, 1990; Sorenson & Golding, 1990).

There is also considerable evidence that criminal victimization, certainly sexual assault, may produce problems that persist long beyond the initial trauma. In a now-classic study, Atkeson et al. (1982) obtained measures of depression 2 weeks,

Fran H. Norris, Department of Psychology, Georgia State University; Krzysztof Kaniasty, Department of Psychology, Indiana University of Pennsylvania.

This research was supported by Grant MH41579 to Fran H. Norris from the Violence and Traumatic Stress Research Branch of the National Institute of Mental Health.

Correspondence concerning this article should be addressed to Fran H. Norris, Department of Psychology, Georgia State University, University Plaza, Atlanta, Georgia 30303-3083.

and 1, 2, 4, 8, and 12 months after rape. Rape victims had significantly higher depression than did a matched control group of nonvictims for the first 4 months. At 8 and 12 months, however, there were no group differences. Sales, Baum, and Shore (1984) found a similar pattern among the rape victims they studied, except that they found a reactivation of symptoms more than 6 months after the initial assault. In a study of sexual assault victims who were identified during a large-scale survey of adolescents, Ageton (1983) found victims' anger, embarrassment, depression, guilt, and fear to still be evident after 3 years. Using a multidimensional measure of self-esteem, repeated assessments (from 6 days to 2 years), and a matched comparison group, Murphy et al. (1988) found that rape had a strong initial impact on self-esteem that lessened slowly over time. Rape victims have also exhibited intense fear, anxiety, and posttraumatic stress (Calhoun, Atkeson, & Resick, 1982; Kilpatrick, Resick, & Veronen, 1981; Kilpatrick & Resnick, 1992b) at points 1 year or more after the assault.

Whereas rape understandably has commanded the most research interest, it is apparent that crimes other than sexual assault may also have lasting psychological effects. From a larger probability sample, Kilpatrick and associates identified victims of various crimes such as assault, robbery, and burglary. Although an average of 15 years had passed since the crimes, victims showed a high prevalence of posttraumatic stress disorder (PTSD; Kilpatrick, Saunders, Veronen, Best, & Von, 1987) and other mental health problems (Kilpatrick et al., 1985). Across studies, it generally appears that rape victims are more symptomatic (or have longer recovery times) than assault victims, that assault victims (sexual or physical) are more symptomatic than robbery victims, and that violent crime victims (assault or robbery) are more symptomatic than property crime victims (e.g., Davis & Friedman, 1985; Lurigio & Resick, 1990; Resick, 1987; Skogan, 1987; Wirtz & Harrell, 1987a; 1987b).

Together, these studies appear to provide strong evidence that the effects of crime are both pervasive and persistent. On the other hand, it is not clear how accurately these findings from

267

samples that are predominantly nonrepresentative describe the general population of crime victims. That is, despite numerous studies, there is a paucity of normative data. Although there is a growing number of studies in which probability sampling procedures are used (e.g., Burnam et al., 1988; Kilpatrick et al., 1987; Kilpatrick & Resnick, 1992b; Koss et al., 1990; Sorenson & Golding, 1990), very few studies have simultaneously had all of the features necessary for researchers to examine the true extent of crime's psychological costs: a longitudinal design, comprehensive and repeated assessment of criminal events, and a sample that is both heterogeneous and representative.

This study was undertaken to address these two basic questions: How lasting and how ubiquitous are the psychological consequences of crime and violence? We collected three waves of data, at approximately 3 months, 9 months, and 15 months postcrime. Furthermore, we defined the event of interest to encompass violent crimes of all types and included samples of property crime victims and nonvictims for comparison purposes. Perhaps most important, these victims were sampled randomly, not because they either reported the crime or sought professional assistance. Victims, like nonvictims, were drawn from a large, probability sample of adults living in the state of Kentucky. The sample was heterogeneous in terms of sex, age, social status, and urbanicity. Kentucky's population is similar to that of the United States as a whole and thus should be neither especially hardy nor especially vulnerable to the impact of crime and violence. The nature of the study's sample and design let us derive normative data and explore the impact of various potential confounds on the findings obtained.

## Method

### Sample and Sampling Procedures

These data are from a three-wave panel study of criminal victimization conducted in the state of Kentucky. In January 1988, a statewide sample of telephone households was generated using random digit dialing procedures. A 5-item screening instrument was used to classify all contacted households ($N = 12,226$) into three groups (*violent, property,* and *nonvictim*) on the basis of crime incidence for the preceding 6 months.[1] Because the probability varied that a household would belong to a given category, the probability of selection for an interview also varied according to the screener classification. All households reporting violent crime were selected for an interview. To provide comparison samples of approximately equal size, we also selected 2 in 5 property households and 1 in 28 nonvictim households. The end result of this procedure was three samples, each approximately representative of its respective population in Kentucky.

We relied on both *informants* and *respondents.* The informant was the person who answered the phone. Given that the calls were placed at different times of day and night and on different days of the week, there seemed to be little reason to expect a randomly selected household member to be better informed about crimes than any other member. The advantages of randomly selecting the informant had to be weighed against the disadvantages of calling a different person to the phone (higher nonresponse) and having to enumerate all households including those not subsequently selected for the interview (i.e. because of the higher cost, fewer households could be screened).

Once a household was selected for the interview, we selected the actual respondent using procedures developed by Kish (1949). In nonvictim households, 1 person was selected randomly from all adults residing in that household. In violent and property households, the victim was selected. Only 8% of violent households and 25% of property households had more than 1 victim. In these cases, 1 respondent was selected randomly from all adult household members experiencing the incident. Among those selected, interviews were completed in 175 violent households, 328 property households, and 304 nonvictim households. These numbers correspond to response rates of 71% for violent and property households and 79% for nonvictim households.

Regardless of their initial screener classification, all respondents answered an 18-item crime incidence battery that was similar to, but revised from, the one used in the National Crime Survey (Lehnen & Skogan, 1984). This instrument was considerably more detailed than the 5-item screening instrument used for household selection. Although most persons (88%) were classified correctly by the initial screener, some persons switched categories on the basis of their interview data. For example, some persons selected from nonvictim households reported incidents when responding to this more detailed instrument. All subsequent classifications of individuals were based on results from the 18-item battery; that is, the screener was used only for the initial selection of households. Final ns were approximately the same: 171 violent crime victims, 338 property crime victims, and 298 nonvictims.

Six months after the first interview (Time 1 [T1]), and again 6 months after that, we attempted to reinterview all study participants by telephone. Time 2 (T2) response rates were reasonably high (80% for nonvictims, 85% for property crime victims, 82% for violent crime victims), as were those for Time 3 (T3; 83% for nonvictims, 82% for property crime victims, and 75% for violent crime victims). Altogether, 522 persons completed all three interviews and had complete data on all measures. As shown in Table 1, this "analysis sample" was comparable to the original T1 sample.

The analysis sample included 105 violent crime victims and 227 property crime victims. Respondents who answered "yes" to both property and violent crime items were classified as victims of violence.[2] Of violent crime victims (women and men combined), 54% had experienced threats or simple assaults (no weapon involved), 23% aggravated assault (weapon involved), 19% robbery, and 6% rape.[3] Fifty-five per-

---

[1] To establish contact with 12,226 households, it was necessary for us to complete 98 replicates of 224 randomly generated phone numbers. Each replicate provided a representative sample of telephone households in the state of Kentucky. The majority of calls to other than the successfully contacted households were placed to nonworking or nonresidential numbers. The refusal rate at this stage was less than 5%.

[2] One issue for classifying victims was how to treat persons with multiple crimes. A liberal estimate of the multiple crime rate is the proportion of victims endorsing more than 1 of the 18 crime items. More than 1 item was endorsed by 78% of the violent crime group and by 60% of the property crime group. These percentages overestimate multiple crimes because respondents may have been describing different aspects of the same incident. A more conservative estimate of the multiple crime rate is the proportion of respondents who acknowledge that the act described by a given item happened more than once. Of violent crime victims, 35% indicated that a particular act happened more than once. The most often repeated act was a threat of violence. Analyses that compared the repeated incidence group ($n = 37$) to the single incidence group ($n = 68$) revealed that the groups did not differ significantly in age, gender, education, urbanicity, marital status, or overall symptomatology. Among property crime victims, 23% reported a particular act (most often vandalism) more than once. Again, this repeated incidence group ($n = 52$) did not differ from the single incidence group ($n = 175$).

[3] Instruments similar to those used by the National Crime Survey have been criticized for failing to detect incidents of rape (e.g., Koss, Gidycz, & Wisniewski, 1987). Some of our changes were designed to

Table 1
*Analysis Sample Description and Comparison With Original (T1) Sample*

| Description of sample | T1 sample | Analysis sample | | | |
|---|---|---|---|---|---|
| | | Total | Violent | Property | No crime |
| Mean age (in years) | 38.70 | 39.06 | 32.32*** | 38.00*** | 44.06 |
| Mean education (in years) | 12.65 | 12.97 | 13.28* | 13.25** | 12.46 |
| Mean symptom score | 0.49 | 0.48 | 0.78*** | 0.46*** | 0.33 |
| % female | 59 | 58 | 52 | 58 | 63 |
| % married | 57 | 60 | 42*** | 60* | 71 |
| % urban | 53 | 55 | 53 | 60* | 50 |
| % prior crime | 40 | 44 | 53** | 47** | 35 |
| % violent crime at T1 | 21 | 20 | 100 | — | — |
| % property crime at T1 | 42 | 44 | — | 100 | — |
| % violent crime at T2 | — | 8 | 23*** | 5 | 3 |
| % property crime at T2 | — | 19 | 20*** | 26*** | 8 |
| % violent crime at T3 | — | 6 | 19*** | 3*** | 2 |
| % property crime at T3 | — | 19 | 20*** | 25*** | 10 |
| *n* | 807 | 522 | 105 | 227 | 190 |

*Note.* T1 = Time 1 (January–February 1988); T2 = Time 2 (July–August 1988); T3 = Time 3 (January–Feburary 1989). Dashes indicate that the sample characteristic is not applicable.
* Significantly different from no crime group, $p < .05$ ($F$ if mean, $\chi^2$ if %). ** Significantly different from no crime group, $p < .01$ ($F$ if mean, $\chi^2$ if %). *** Significantly different from no crime group, $p < .001$ ($F$ if mean, $\chi^2$ if %).

cent reported knowing the person who committed the crime. Among these acquaintance crime victims, 25 respondents identified the assailant as a relative or friend, but only 6 respondents indicated that this person was living with them at the time of the crime. Thus victims of domestic violence comprise only a small proportion of our violent crime sample, and it is possible that our screening procedures failed to detect them. Of property crime victims, 20% had experienced vandalism, 50% larceny (theft outside the home), and 30% burglary (theft from inside the home). Sixteen percent of these victims knew the perpetrator, but very few were living with him or her at the time of the crime (4 out of 227). These percentages are offered only to describe the analysis sample and should not be taken as population estimates.

As shown in Table 1, the groups differed in several ways. Relative to nonvictims, crime victims were younger, more educated, and more symptomatic. They were more likely to be single and, in the case of property crime, more likely to live in metropolitan areas. Respondents who reported crimes for the 6-month interval preceding T1 were more likely than other respondents to report crimes occurring prior to that interval as well. T1 victims were also more likely than nonvictims to report crimes at T2 and T3. We considered these confounds of crime with prior and subsequent crime when we assessed the unique effects of the focal crime.

## Interviewing Procedures

All interviewers (mostly women and Kentucky residents) received training in the conduct of interviews with crime victims. Special attention was paid to the importance of establishing rapport, being sensitive, and treating all information confidentially. For example, a standard procedure was for the interviewer to make sure that the respondent was alone at the time of the interview and to give him or her the opportunity to reschedule the interview at a later time. Respondents were also given an 800 number (the Attorney General of Kentucky's hot line) that they could call if they then or later became concerned about the study. Supervisors monitored interviewers regularly to make sure that each in-

terview was conducted in accordance with research and ethical guidelines.[4]

## Design

The design was longitudinal, encompassing three interviews at 6-month intervals. At each interview, respondents were questioned about

---

increase the sensitivity of the instrument. We asked all respondents, "In the past 6 months, did anyone beat up, sexually attack, or hit you?" Respondents who answered "no" were then asked, "Did anyone *try* to attack you in the past 6 months?" If they again said "no," they were asked, "Did anyone *threaten* to beat you up or attack you?" Whenever respondents answered "yes" to any of these questions, they were asked the following question: "Did this incident involve a (an attempted/a threat of) rape or sexual assault?" Finally, all respondents were asked, "Did anything else happen to you in the past 6 months that you thought was a crime? This could be anything, anytime, since the Fourth of July." If "yes," they were asked, "During this incident were you injured, attacked, or threatened or was an attempt made to injure or attack you?" Thus, there was more than one occasion at which a rape could have been detected. Nonetheless, it remains probable that we failed to detect some incidents. One way of assessing the instrument's accuracy is to use it to estimate crime rates. Our survey may be used to make such estimates when weights (inverse of the probability of selection) are applied to the data. Of our weighted female sample, 0.8% reported a threatened, attempted, or actual rape at T1. An additional and independent 0.8% reported such incidents at T2, for a total annual rate of 16 per 1,000 population. This estimate is far greater than that provided by the U.S. Department of Justice but is quite similar to those expected in surveys especially designed to study sexual aggression and victimization (Kilpatrick & Resnick, 1992a).

[4] An obvious limitation of telephone surveys is that they exclude persons who have no phones. Although the proportion of the population

their current symptoms and about any crimes occurring in the past 6 months. At T1 (January–February 1988) reports were elicited for crimes occurring "since the Fourth of July." The length of the interval bounded by the date of the crime and the date of the interview averaged 3.4 months and did not differ between violent and property crime victims, $F(1, 507) = 1.77$. At T2 (July–August 1988) and again at T3 (January–February 1989), reports were elicited for crimes occurring "since the last time you were interviewed."

## Measures

Seven potential consequences of crime were assessed at each wave. *Depression, somatization, hostility, anxiety,* and *phobic anxiety* were measured with the Brief Symptom Inventory (BSI) developed by Derogatis and Spencer (1982).[5] As used here, the labels *depression, anxiety,* and so forth reflect variations in measures of these states rather than diagnosed conditions. The BSI has been used successfully to assess psychological symptoms in a variety of community populations. The selected subscales had 28 items, a 1-month report period, and a 5-point response format ranging from *not at all* (0) to *several times a week* (4). The symptom score derived from these subscales had an alpha of .93. Internal consistency coefficients for the subscales were .85 for Depression, .81 for Somatization, .73 for Hostility, .79 for Anxiety, and .64 for Phobic Anxiety. Each scale score is the mean value of contributing items; the higher the score, the higher the symptoms.

We developed measures of two additional consequences, *fear of crime* and *avoidance behavior,* on the basis of previously existing measures (Ferraro & LaGrange, 1987; Norris & Johnson, 1988). All items had a 4-point response format ranging from *never* (0) to *often* (4). For the present analysis, however, they were recoded to give them the same potential range (0–4) as items on the BSI. Fear of crime was scored as the mean of six items that tap the extent to which respondents worry about being victimized by crime (e.g., "During the past 4 weeks did you worry that someone would try to rob you or to steal something from you?"). Avoidance behavior, scored as the mean of five items, referred to the extent to which the individual actually avoided other people or places because of the threat of crime (e.g., "During the past four weeks, how often did you stay away from certain types of people to avoid crime?"). At .75 and .76, alphas for the two measures were comparable to alphas for the BSI scales.

## Results

### Time 1 Symptom Profile

Before presenting the longitudinal data, we describe the symptoms initially exhibited by this sample. In Figure 1 the means on the seven symptom measures are shown for the violent crime, property crime, and no crime groups at T1. A multivariate analysis of variance (MANOVA) yielded a significant effect for crime, $F(14, 1024) = 7.35, p < .001$, thereby verifying visual impression that the three groups differed in their overall levels of psychological distress. In the analyses that follow, we consider these between-group differences in more detail, but here we address two broader issues. The first concerns the severity of effects. As shown, the no-crime group's means were virtually identical to the norms provided by Derogatis and Spencer (1982) for nonpatient adults (available for BSI scales only). Although below those established for psychiatric samples, the crime groups' means were well above the nonpatient norms. In the case of violent crime, group means exceeded the norms by no less than one standard deviation. Moreover, about 25% of the violent crime victims reported extreme distress ($T$ scores > 70)

on the BSI Depression, Hostility, and Anxiety scales. An additional 22–27% showed moderate distress ($T$ scores in the 61–70 range) on these same scales. For reference purposes, the distribution of $T$ scores for each sample and time point are provided in the Appendix.

The second issue concerns the specificity of effects. The scoring procedures we used enabled us to compare scale means across symptom domains as well as across groups (or time). In Figure.1, the various types of symptoms are shown in descending order (from left to right) according to the extent to which they were reported by the violent crime group. Two observations can be made. First, crime is associated with a relatively uniform elevation of symptoms rather than a specific symptom profile. Nonetheless, victims and nonvictims alike exhibited some types of symptoms considerably more often than they exhibited others. Fear of crime and avoidance behaviors were most common; somatization and generalized phobias were least common. Symptoms indicative of anxiety, depression, and hostility occurred at levels intermediate to these extremes.

Overall, these self-report data suggest that the symptoms experienced by crime victims were quite pervasive across diverse symptom domains. In most cases, these reactions were of moderate intensity and did not constitute psychiatric disorders. However, a substantial percentage of violent crime victims exhibited levels of symptoms indicative of clinically significant distress.

### Total Effects of Crime and Time

We tested the total effects of crime and time using multivariate analysis of variance (MANOVA) as the statistical technique. Crime (violent, property, and no crime) was the between-subjects factor. Time (T1, T2, T3, each 6 months apart) was the within-subjects factor. Of particular interest were the interactions between crime and time. To reduce the possi-

excluded is now very small (7%; U.S. Bureau of the Census, 1991), people who do not have telephones are likely to be poor, socially isolated, homeless, or transient. This underrepresentation of the disenfranchised population should be acknowledged. Nonetheless, the more expensive and time-consuming face-to-face surveys tend to produce a similar bias (Groves, 1987). More generally, telephone surveys compare very favorably with face-to-face surveys in producing valid and reliable data (Dillman, 1978; Quinn, Gutek, & Walsh, 1980). Studies have shown that telephone interviewing is very suitable for clinical assessments ranging widely in length and degree of topic sensitivity (Aneshensel, Frerichs, Clark, & Yokopenic, 1982; Seidner, Burling, Fisher, & Blair, 1990; Tausing & Freeman, 1988). Telephone interviews appear to be especially appropriate for victimization studies because they provide anonymity and counteract reluctance to answer personal and sensitive questions (Tuchfarber & Klecka, 1976). After reviewing research that used either telephone or face-to-face interviewing methods in studying physical abuse of women, Smith (1989) concluded that telephone surveys were "the method of choice" (p. 322).

[5] This 28-item version of the Brief Symptom Inventory is from *Brief Symptom Inventory (BSI): Administration, Scoring, and Procedures Manual-1* by L. Derogatis and P. Spencer, 1982, Redgewood, MD: Clinical Psychometric Research Incorporated. Copyright 1982 by Clinical Psychometric Research Incorporated. Adapted by permission.

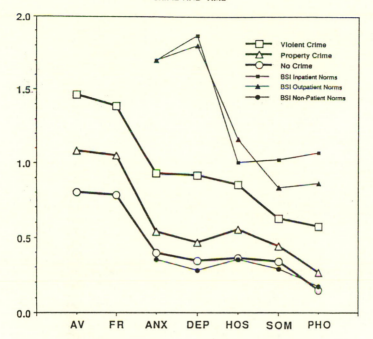

*Figure 1.* Mean levels of self-reported psychological distress shown at T1 by violent crime, property crime, and no-crime groups compared with nonpatient and psychiatric norms (see Derogatis & Spencer, 1982). AV = avoidance behavior; FR = fear of crime; ANX = anxiety; DEP = depression; HOS = hostility; SOM = somatization; PHO = phobic anxiety; BSI = Brief Symptom Inventory, Derogatis & Spencer, 1982; T1 = Time 1, January–February 1988.

bility of Type I errors, we tested univariate effects only when there was a significant multivariate $F$, and we examined the results of contrasts only when there was a significant omnibus $F$. Moreover, we restricted ourselves to conducting specific, orthogonal contrasts: For the crime factor, the means for the two crime groups were first compared with the means of the no-crime group (crime vs. no crime) and then to one another (violent vs. property). Similarly, for the time factor, the means for the later two time points were first compared with the initial means (T1 vs. T2 and T3) and then to one another (T2 vs. T3). The MANOVA results are summarized in Table 2. Sample means are shown in Table 3.

*Main effects.* When testing the main effects of crime, each dependent variable was equivalent to its average level across the three time points (e.g., depression was the average of T1 depression, T2 depression, and T3 depression). The multivariate effect of crime was highly significant, $F(14, 1024) = 7.04$, $p < .001$. As Table 2 shows, this effect was significant for each symptom measure. Contrasts revealed that the crime groups showed significantly higher symptoms than the no-crime group and that

the violent crime group showed significantly higher symptoms than the property crime group.

In this type of design, main effects of time indicate that there are differences among time points without regard to when they occurred. A multivariate effect of time was observed, $F(14, 2062) = 7.87$, $p < .001$: for the sample as a whole, symptoms declined over time (see Table 3). This improvement held for all self-reported symptoms. As indicated by the contrasts, the difference was largely between the first and the two later time points (T1 vs. T2, T3). Somatization, hostility, anxiety, and phobic anxiety showed additional but less strong differences between T2 and T3.

*Interactions.* A significant crime by time interaction indicates that groups differ in the course of their symptoms over time; for example, the symptoms of one group declined while those of another group remained stable. The crime by time interaction was significant in the multivariate test, $F(28, 4122) = 1.60$, $p < .03$, and in 4 of the 7 univariate tests (depression, anxiety, phobic anxiety, and avoidance behavior). For fear of crime, the effect approached significance, $p < .07$.

Table 2
*Univariate Effects of Crime and Time*

| Effect | Type of test and *df* | Depression | Somatization | Hostility | Anxiety | Phobic anxiety | Fear of crime | Avoidance behavior |
|---|---|---|---|---|---|---|---|---|
| Crime | $F(2, 519)$ | 31.45*** | 8.89*** | 29.67*** | 33.08*** | 20.98*** | 20.76*** | 14.85*** |
| Crime versus no crime | $t(519)$ | 6.06*** | 3.69*** | 6.98*** | 6.74*** | 5.19*** | 5.83*** | 4.74*** |
| Violent versus property | $t(519)$ | 6.39*** | 2.84** | 4.79*** | 6.00*** | 4.97*** | 4.03*** | 3.71*** |
| Time | $F(2, 1038)$ | 21.34*** | 5.22** | 17.74*** | 18.19*** | 23.99*** | 10.69*** | 15.81*** |
| T1 versus T2, T3 | $t(519)$ | 6.17*** | 2.62** | 5.17*** | 5.34*** | 5.83*** | 4.04*** | 5.26*** |
| T2 versus T3 | $t(519)$ | 1.48 | 1.93* | 2.77** | 2.03* | 3.29*** | 1.39 | 0.98 |
| Crime × Time | $F(4, 1038)$ | 3.46** | 0.70 | 1.69 | 3.45** | 5.29*** | 2.16 | 2.91* |
| Crime versus no crime | | | | | | | | |
| × T1 versus T2, T3 | $t(519)$ | 2.82** | — | — | 2.21* | 3.24*** | — | 3.06** |
| × T2 versus T3 | $t(519)$ | 0.08 | — | — | 1.28 | 1.10 | — | 1.13 |
| Violent versus property | | | | | | | | |
| × T1 versus T2, T3 | $t(519)$ | 2.75** | — | — | 2.26* | 2.41* | — | 0.61 |
| × T2 versus T3 | $t(519)$ | 0.65 | — | — | 2.15* | 2.56** | — | 0.09 |

*Note.* T1 = Time 1 (January–February 1988); T2 = Time 2 (July–August 1988); T3 = Time 3 (January–February 1989). Dashes indicate that the test was not performed because the omnibus *F* was not significant.
* $p < .05$. ** $p < .01$. *** $p < .001$.

The contrasts revealed that the interactions typically involved changes that occurred between the first and the two later measurements. When the crime groups were compared with the no-crime group, between-groups differences emerged with regard to how much change had occurred over this interval (T1 vs. T2, T3) in depression, anxiety, phobic anxiety, and avoidance. Likewise, the violent and property groups differed with regard to the amount of change each showed in depression, anxiety, and phobic anxiety over this same interval of time. Violent crime victims were the only group that continued to decline between T2 and T3, and this change was limited to anxiety and phobic anxiety. Despite these changes, the groups retained their same rank order throughout the study period (see Table 3). This pattern is also evident in the normed distributions presented in the Appendix.

In summary, both crime and time had significant effects on the symptoms reported by this sample. Across time, crime victims, especially violent crime victims, experienced levels of symptoms much higher than those of nonvictims. Initially, crime victims showed clear signs of recovery, that is, they showed declines that could eventually "return" them to a state of well-being comparable to that possessed by nonvictims. For the most part, however, these declines leveled off between T2 and T3, thus providing little evidence that crime victims would thereafter continue to improve.

### Unique Effects of Crime Over Time

For longitudinal analyses, mean data have incomparable descriptive appeal. One can easily see both the overall differences between groups and the changes each group exhibits over time. Here, these data are all the more appealing because each group

Table 3
*Means on Study Measures by Time and Crime*

| Time | Group | Depression M | Depression SD | Somatization M | Somatization SD | Hostility M | Hostility SD | Anxiety M | Anxiety SD | Phobic anxiety M | Phobic anxiety SD | Fear of crime M | Fear of crime SD | Avoidance behavior M | Avoidance behavior SD |
|---|---|---|---|---|---|---|---|---|---|---|---|---|---|---|---|
| T1 | Violent | 0.91 | 0.88 | 0.62 | 0.73 | 0.85 | 0.73 | 0.93 | 0.81 | 0.57 | 0.84 | 1.39 | 0.84 | 1.46 | 0.97 |
| | Property | 0.46 | 0.57 | 0.44 | 0.58 | 0.55 | 0.53 | 0.54 | 0.52 | 0.26 | 0.48 | 1.05 | 0.76 | 1.08 | 0.89 |
| | No crime | 0.34 | 0.48 | 0.34 | 0.52 | 0.36 | 0.42 | 0.39 | 0.45 | 0.14 | 0.30 | 0.78 | 0.68 | 0.80 | 0.84 |
| T2 | Violent | 0.69 | 0.70 | 0.59 | 0.76 | 0.71 | 0.64 | 0.79 | 0.67 | 0.44 | 0.75 | 1.22 | 0.82 | 1.26 | 1.01 |
| | Property | 0.37 | 0.48 | 0.40 | 0.56 | 0.49 | 0.53 | 0.46 | 0.49 | 0.18 | 0.40 | 0.95 | 0.70 | 0.92 | 0.87 |
| | No crime | 0.31 | 0.47 | 0.32 | 0.50 | 0.34 | 0.42 | 0.35 | 0.40 | 0.14 | 0.30 | 0.77 | 0.66 | 0.89 | 0.89 |
| T3 | Violent | 0.64 | 0.70 | 0.50 | 0.63 | 0.63 | 0.60 | 0.68 | 0.59 | 0.31 | 0.64 | 1.19 | 0.85 | 1.21 | 0.94 |
| | Property | 0.36 | 0.45 | 0.38 | 0.50 | 0.43 | 0.51 | 0.46 | 0.47 | 0.17 | 0.38 | 0.90 | 0.68 | 0.87 | 0.87 |
| | No crime | 0.28 | 0:41 | 0.30 | 0.55 | 0.30 | 0.34 | 0.34 | 0.41 | 0.10 | 0.28 | 0.76 | 0.65 | 0.78 | 0.80 |

*Note.* T1 = Time 1 (January–February 1988); T2 = Time 2 (July–August 1988); T3 = Time 3 (January–February 1989). The three time points correspond, on the average, to points 3 months, 9 months, and 15 months postcrime.

was approximately representative of its respective population in Kentucky. Thus, it seemed particularly worthwhile to observe them as they naturally evolved. Nonetheless, we cannot infer causality to the crimes themselves because victims differed from nonvictims in many ways. These differences included not only initial age, marital status, and education but also exposure to other crimes. Furthermore, the MANOVAs could not establish that the postcrime means differed from the precrime symptom levels.

To overcome these limitations, we reanalyzed the data using multiple regression as the statistical technique. The dependent variables were again self-reported measures of depression, somatization, hostility, anxiety, phobic anxiety, fear of crime, and avoidance behavior. To provide results parallel to the MANOVAs, we performed two separate series of regressions. The first series was conducted on the total sample ($n = 522$) using dummy-coded (0, 1) measures of T1 crime, T2 crime, and T3 crime. On these variables, a score of 1 indicated that a crime, of any type, had occurred in the 6 months preceding the referenced time point; for example, a score of 1 on T2 crime indicated that a crime had occurred between T1 and T2. (In this sample, 64% experienced T1 crimes, 26% experienced T2 crimes, and 24% experienced T3 crimes.) Thus, the effects of these variables were comparable to the crime vs. no crime contrasts examined in the MANOVA results. To provide results comparable to the violence vs. property contrasts, we conducted a second series of regressions using only victim data ($n = 332$) and dummy-coded (0, 1) measures of T1 violence, T2 violence, and T3 violence. (In this victim sample, 32% experienced T1 violence, 12% experienced T2 violence, and 9% experienced T3 violence.)

The regressions were conducted hierarchically. Background variables (age, sex, education, marital status, urbanicity, and prior crime) were entered in the first step. T1 crime (or T1 violence) was entered in the second step. When predicting T2 and T3 symptoms, we then entered measures of subsequent crime and T1 symptoms in that order. This sequence allowed us to determine (a) whether crime has effects on symptoms independent of its confounds with demographic status and prior crime, (b) whether long-term effects of the initial crime are mediated by subsequent crime, and (c) whether crime shows effects on postcrime symptoms when precrime symptoms are controlled.

*Crime versus no crime.* The regressions conducted for the total sample are presented in Table 4. For all dependent measures, the variance in symptoms explained by the set of background variables was significant, ranging from 3% to 16%. These variables were least predictive of somatization and most predictive of hostility. The results show that, even with the effects of demographics and prior crime controlled, T1 crime had significant effects on all T1 symptoms (see Table 4, Time 1, Step 2).

Likewise, T1 crime made significant contributions to all T2 symptom outcomes (see Table 4, Time 2, Step 2). Although sometimes remaining significant, the effects always declined in strength when T2 crime was controlled (Table 4, Time 2, Step 3). For example, in the equation for T2 anxiety, the beta for T1 crime was .14 before but .09 after T2 crime was entered (which itself had a highly significant beta of .24). Thus some part (but

not all) of the lasting consequence of crime was mediated by subsequent exposure to crime. In the final step, T1 symptoms were entered into each equation. From these results, we can observe that T1 crime had no additional effect on T2 symptoms beyond that explained by T1 symptoms. T2 crime, however, had significant effects even with precrime symptoms controlled. This held for all types of symptoms.

Up to a point, the T3 regressions showed a similar pattern of results. Usually the betas for T1 crime were initially significant (Table 4, Time 3, Step 2) but fell to nonsignificant levels when the T2 and T3 crime variables were entered (Table 4, Step 3, Step 4). The effects of T3 crime were generally of insufficient magnitude to remain significant when precrime symptoms were controlled (Table 4, Step 5).

In summary, these results indicate that both the short-term and the long-term effects of crime were independent of background differences between victims and nonvictims. Long-term effects, however, were often contingent on the occurrence of subsequent crimes; the longer the time span, the more important this mediating effect became. It also appears that crimes must achieve some critical level of severity before effects can be demonstrated in prospective designs.

*Violent versus property.* The results of these regressions are presented in Table 5. Background variables explained about the same amount of variance (3–17%) in the victim sample as they had in the total sample. At T1, with status and prior crime controlled, violence generally predicted more variance in this victim sample than had crime in the total sample. These results substantiate the earlier findings that violent crime victims were more symptomatic than were property crime victims.

At T2, violence again significantly predicted all symptom domains (see Table 5, Step 2). Many of these effects continued to be quite strong even when T2 violence was accounted for (Table 5, Step 3), suggesting that the long-term effects of violence are less contingent on subsequent exposure to crime than are long-term effects of other crimes. This is not to say that the longer term effects of violence were not somewhat mediated by subsequent violence; most of the betas did decline when T2 violence was entered. T2 violence itself had quite strong effects. In 6 of 7 equations, these effects were observed even when precrime symptoms were controlled (Table 5, Step 5).

By T3, T1 violence explained no variance in somatization but continued to show significant effects on the other symptom measures (Table 5, Step 2). By this time, more of the effects of T1 violence were accounted for by subsequent violence (Table 5, Steps 3 and 4). On hostility, for example, an initial beta for T1 violence of .11 dropped first to .07 and then to .01 as the T2 and T3 measures of violence were entered into the equation. However, for many symptoms—especially depression and fear—T1 violence had effects that were independent of subsequent violence. The effects of T3 violence at T3 were usually weaker than those of T2 violence at T2. Yet prospective effects were demonstrated for depression, hostility, anxiety, and fear.

Altogether, these analyses provide ample evidence that violent crime has effects that are strong and lasting. Equally independent of confounds with demographic status and prior crime, these effects were less (though still somewhat) contingent on exposure to subsequent crimes. Moreover, violence was a

273

Table 4

*Results of Hierarchical Regressions: Standardized Betas for Crime by Step (Total Sample)*

| | Time 1 | Time 2 | | | | Time 3 | | | |
|---|---|---|---|---|---|---|---|---|---|
| Step | 2 | 2 | 3 | 4 | 5 | 2 | 3 | 4 | 5 |
| **Depression** | | | | | | | | | |
| 1. Background variables[a] | | | | | | | | | |
| 2. T1 Crime | .12** | .09* | .05 | — | .00 | .11** | .08 | .06 | .02 |
| 3. T2 Crime | | | .21*** | — | .10** | | .17*** | .16*** | .07 |
| 4. T3 Crime | | | | — | — | | | .09* | .05 |
| 5. T1 Depression | | | | | .60*** | | | | .54*** |
| **Somatization** | | | | | | | | | |
| 1. Background variables[a] | | | | | | | | | |
| 2. T1 Crime | .14** | .12** | .08 | — | .02 | .12** | .09* | .08 | .02 |
| 3. T2 Crime | | | .20*** | — | .12*** | | .14*** | .13** | .06 |
| 4. T3 Crime | | | | — | — | | | .08 | .03 |
| 5. T1 Somatization | | | | | .61*** | | | | .58*** |
| **Hostility** | | | | | | | | | |
| 1. Background variables[a] | | | | | | | | | |
| 2. T1 Crime | .15*** | .13** | .09* | — | .02 | .13** | .08 | .06 | .01 |
| 3. T2 Crime | | | .18*** | — | .09* | | .21*** | .19*** | .13** |
| 4. T3 Crime | | | | — | — | | | .12** | .08* |
| 5. T1 Hostility | | | | | .56*** | | | | .45*** |
| **Anxiety** | | | | | | | | | |
| 1. Background variables[a] | | | | | | | | | |
| 2. T1 Crime | .15*** | .14*** | .09* | — | .03 | .13** | .08 | .08 | .02 |
| 3. T2 Crime | | | .24*** | — | .13*** | | .20*** | .19*** | .09* |
| 4. T3 Crime | | | | — | — | | | .08 | .05 |
| 5. T1 Anxiety | | | | | .58*** | | | | .54*** |
| **Phobic anxiety** | | | | | | | | | |
| 1. Background variables[a] | | | | | | | | | |
| 2. T1 Crime | .16*** | .11* | .05 | — | −.02 | .10* | .05 | .05 | −.02 |
| 3. T2 Crime | | | .26*** | — | .12*** | | .20*** | .20*** | .06 |
| 4. T3 Crime | | | | — | — | | | .05 | .02 |
| 5. T1 Phobic Anxiety | | | | | .62*** | | | | .61*** |
| **Fear of crime** | | | | | | | | | |
| 1. Background variables[a] | | | | | | | | | |
| 2. T1 Crime | .25*** | .19*** | .16*** | — | .02 | .15*** | .12** | .11* | −.02 |
| 3. T2 Crime | | | .16*** | — | .10** | | .13** | .12** | .07 |
| 4. T3 Crime | | | | — | — | | | .08 | .05 |
| 5. T1 Fear | | | | | .62*** | | | | .58*** |
| **Avoidance behavior** | | | | | | | | | |
| 1. Background variables[a] | | | | | | | | | |
| 2. T1 Crime | .18*** | .12** | .08 | — | −.02 | .11* | .08 | .06 | −.03 |
| 3. T2 Crime | | | .18*** | — | .09** | | .13** | .13** | .05 |
| 4. T3 Crime | | | | — | — | | | .09* | .02 |
| 5. T1 Avoidance | | | | | .69*** | | | | .69*** |

*Note.* T1 = Time 1 (January–February 1988); T2 = Time 2 (July–August 1988); T3 = Time 3 (January–February 1989). Dashes indicate that the step was not applicable at Time 2.
[a] In Step 1, age, education, sex, marital status, urbanicity, and prior crime were entered together. Thus all effects shown in this table are independent of the effects of these background variables.
* $p < .05$. ** $p < .01$. *** $p < .001$.

Table 5

*Results of Hierarchical Regressions: Standardized Betas for Violence by Step (Crime Victims Only)*

| | Time 1 | Time 2 | | | | | Time 3 | | | |
|---|---|---|---|---|---|---|---|---|---|---|
| Step | 2 | 2 | 3 | 4 | 5 | 2 | 3 | 4 | 5 |
| | | | | | | | | | | |
| *Depression* | | | | | | | | | | |
| 1. Background variables[a] | | | | | | | | | | |
| 2. T1 Violence | .22*** | .21*** | .17*** | — | .05 | .21*** | .20*** | .15** | .04 |
| 3. T2 Violence | | | .19*** | — | .13** | | .03 | .02 | −.04 |
| 4. T3 Violence | | | | — | | | | .19*** | .19*** |
| 5. T1 Depression | | | | | .61*** | | | | .58*** |
| | | | | | | | | | | |
| *Somatization* | | | | | | | | | | |
| 1. Background variables[a] | | | | | | | | | | |
| 2. T1 Violence | .13* | .13* | .10 | — | .04 | .07 | .06 | .05 | −.01 |
| 3. T2 Violence | | | .12* | — | .09* | | .05 | .05 | .02 |
| 4. T3 Violence | | | | — | | | | .07 | .03 |
| 5. T1 Somatization | | | | | .58*** | | | | .57*** |
| | | | | | | | | | | |
| *Hostility* | | | | | | | | | | |
| 1. Background variables[a] | | | | | | | | | | |
| 2. T1 Violence | .15** | .12* | .08 | — | .01 | .11* | .07 | .01 | −.03 |
| 3. T2 Violence | | | .16** | — | .10* | | .17*** | .15** | .11 |
| 4. T3 Violence | | | | — | | | | .24*** | .18*** |
| 5. T1 Hostility | | | | | .53*** | | | | .44*** |
| | | | | | | | | | | |
| *Anxiety* | | | | | | | | | | |
| 1. Background variables[a] | | | | | | | | | | |
| 2. T1 Violence | .22*** | .23*** | .18*** | — | .07 | .15** | .12* | .07 | −.03 |
| 3. T2 Violence | | | .18*** | — | .12*** | | .15** | .14** | .08 |
| 4. T3 Violence | | | | — | | | | .18*** | .13** |
| 5. T1 Anxiety | | | | | .57*** | | | | .57*** |
| | | | | | | | | | | |
| *Phobic anxiety* | | | | | | | | | | |
| 1. Background variables[a] | | | | | | | | | | |
| 2. T1 Violence | .20*** | .20*** | .16** | — | .06 | .12* | .09 | .07 | −.02 |
| 3. T2 Violence | | | .18*** | — | .09* | | .12* | .12* | .03 |
| 4. T3 Violence | | | | — | | | | .06 | .02 |
| 5. T1 Phobic anxiety | | | | | .63*** | | | | .65*** |
| | | | | | | | | | | |
| *Fear of crime* | | | | | | | | | | |
| 1. Background variables[a] | | | | | | | | | | |
| 2. T1 Violence | .21*** | .18*** | .15** | — | .03 | .18*** | .16** | .13* | .02 |
| 3. T2 Violence | | | .14** | — | .10* | | .09 | .08 | .05 |
| 4. T3 Violence | | | | — | | | | .13* | .11* |
| 5. T1 Fear | | | | | .60*** | | | | .56*** |
| | | | | | | | | | | |
| *Avoidance behavior* | | | | | | | | | | |
| 1. Background variables[a] | | | | | | | | | | |
| 2. T1 Violence | .17** | .16** | .14** | — | .04 | .18*** | .17*** | .15** | .06 |
| 3. T2 Violence | | | .11* | — | .04 | | .03 | .02 | −.04 |
| 4. T3 Violence | | | | — | | | | .08 | .07 |
| 5. T1 Avoidance | | | | | .68*** | | | | .66*** |

*Note.* T1 = Time 1 (January–February 1988); T2 = Time 2 (July–August 1988); T3 = Time 3 (January–February 1989). Dashes indicate that the step was not applicable at Time 2.

[a] In Step 1, age, education, sex, marital status, urbanicity, and prior crime were entered together. Thus all effects shown in this table are independent of the effects of these background variables.

* $p < .05$.  ** $p < .01$.  *** $p < .001$.

sufficiently powerful stressor to evidence effects in prospective analyses that included precrime measures of psychological state.

## Discussion

Our study began about 3 months (on the average) after the crimes occurred. Previous research indicates that much of victims' initial distress would have dissipated by that time (e.g., Atkeson et al., 1982; Frank & Stewart, 1984; Kilpatrick & Calhoun, 1988). Yet, after 3 months, the victims in this study showed pervasive symptomatology across diverse domains, including depression, anxiety, somatization, hostility, and fear. All victims exhibited a similar profile of symptoms, but violent crime victims were clearly the most severely distressed. Although victims' symptoms declined from these levels over the next 6 months, they soon leveled off. After 9 months, there was little evidence that crime victims would continue to improve. After 15 months, which is where our study ends, violent crime victims were still more symptomatic than were property crime victims who, in turn, were still more symptomatic than nonvictims.

Taking advantage of the representativeness of these samples, we have provided normative data (see Appendix) against which other individuals or samples may be compared. As discussed by Kendall and Grove (1988), the use of normative comparisons may help outcome studies improve their "convincingness": "Normative comparisons, where once troubled and disordered clients are compared to meaningful and representative nondisturbed reference groups, provide a yardstick by which to gauge how far clients have progressed" (p. 156). One does not need to establish that no one in the client group is distressed—just that the group approximates a normal group. As shown in the Appendix, even nonvictim populations have some proportion with abnormal (>70) $T$ scores (typically 2–5%). Whereas nonvictim data provide one standard for assessing victim recovery, data from similarly disturbed but clinically untreated victim groups provide another. Although time alone produced considerable movement toward normality, at no point did these victims resemble nonvictims; for example, even at T3, 16% of violent crime victims still had depression scores above 70. Using these data, an evaluator could assess whether a particular intervention accelerated the recovery of crime victims or fostered a degree of recovery greater than the norm.

Similarly, normative comparisons could help to identify subgroups of victims that are at particular risk for profound and prolonged distress. For example, in our sample, 35% of victims of the most serious violent crimes (aggravated assault, rape, robbery; $n = 48$) showed abnormal $T$ scores on T1 depression. As summoned by the American Psychological Association's Task Force on Victims of Crime and Violence (Kahn, 1984), data such as these could be useful for justifying new victim programs or for deciding where to allocate all-too-scarce resources.

To establish norms, one does not necessarily need to make causal inferences regarding the source of the observed distress. Yet, to the extent that we can identify causes, it is clearly desirable to do so. Whether these between-group differences in self-reported distress were the result of the crimes themselves cannot be known for sure. Nevertheless, most of the evidence is consistent with this specific interpretation. In accordance with the findings of Burnam et al. (1988), the regression analyses revealed that the symptoms shown by victims could not be attributed to differences between groups on such factors as age, sex, education, and marital status. Furthermore, as did Skogan's (1987) prospective study of victimization and fear, these results suggested that postcrime symptoms were higher than could be explained by precrime symptoms. Indeed, on 13 of 14 tests, T2 crime and violence had significant effects on T2 symptoms even when precrime (T1) symptoms were controlled. Even at T3, prospective effects were demonstrated in 1 of 7 crime analyses (hostility) and in 4 of 7 violence analyses (fear, hostility, anxiety, and depression). Methodologically, this is an important demonstration in a field of inquiry where baseline data are almost always lacking.

On the other hand, a meaningful proportion of victims' lasting symptomatology was explained by subsequent exposure to crime and violence. Burgess and Holmstrom (1978) likewise found that rape victims with subsequent victimizations had longer recovery times. In general, victims of multiple rapes have shown poorer outcomes (Burnam et al., 1988; Cohen & Roth, 1987; Frank & Stewart, 1984; Frazier, 1991; Koss, 1990; Resick, 1987). The present study suggests that these rape-specific findings hold for other crimes as well. In fact, the less severe the first crime (e.g., property vs. violent), the more significant these mediating effects became. Clinically, this finding has vital implications. Treating the victim without "treating" the environment may do little to hasten the course of recovery. Spouse abuse is an obvious and compelling example, but even for other crimes, clinical assessments should include an assessment of risk for future victimization.

Other research conducted on this sample (Norris & Kaniasty, 1992) suggests a starting point for such an assessment of risk. In a series of logistic regressions, we attempted to predict subsequent (T2 or T3) nonacquaintance crimes of larceny, burglary, and violence from initial (T1) measures of precautionary behavior, personal victimization, county crime rates, fear of crime, and numerous sociodemographic variables (e.g., age, sex, household composition, type of dwelling). Consistent with previous studies (e.g., Koss & Dinero, 1989; Norris & Johnson, 1988), prior victimization was the best predictor of subsequent victimization—larceny and burglary as well as violence. It is important to note, however, that although we measured four different aspects of precautionary behavior, none had any predictive value. Victims of crime were neither more nor less cautious than others. Thus victims' behavior was not to blame, and we should be careful not to give that impression to either the victim or the public at large. These findings imply that "victim control" (i.e., blaming) models are inappropriate as a basis for either public policy (e.g., Koss, 1990; Norris & Johnson, 1988) or psychological treatment (e.g., Frazier, 1991; Meyer & Taylor, 1986).

The other notable finding from this analysis (Norris & Kaniasty, 1992) was that fear of crime was also a very consistent predictor of subsequent crime. That is, respondents who were most worried about becoming crime victims were, in fact, most likely to become crime victims. This finding may simply indicate that individuals know something about their own risk status that is not captured by sociological variables. If valid, this interpretation has implications for the long-standing controversy regarding the rational versus irrational nature of fear (e.g., Garofalo & Laub, 1978; McPherson, 1978). Moreover, it should remind us that victims' professed fears have an environmental as well as intrapsychic base. If so, clinicians may be uniquely situated to discern the rational from the irrational fear and to identify the circumstances in an individual victim's life that place him or her at subsequent risk.

Unfortunately, at present, only a small proportion of crime victims receive professional help (Golding, Stein, Siegel, Burnam, & Sorenson, 1988; Norris, Kaniasty, & Scheer, 1990). Efforts to reach out to victims and provide services to them are sorely needed. However, one has to question whether the present corps of service providers is equipped to bear this burden alone. The very magnitude of the problem implies, first, that clinical psychologists should receive more training in the areas of victimization and trauma than traditionally has been provided. Second, it implies that placing clinical interventions in the context of crime prevention may open new avenues for community support and funding of treatment programs. Third, it implies that clinicians should explore ways to expand their reach through broader based interventions designed to address violence and fear at the community as well as at the individual level (e.g., Koss & Harvey, 1991; Roark, 1987).

Any of these initiatives would complement the growing movement in this country toward viewing violence as a public health (as opposed to criminal justice) issue. Recently, public health officials have identified violence as comparable in importance to previous epidemics and as equally unacceptable. As discussed by Rosenberg and Fenley (1991), this shift toward seeing violence as unacceptable (rather than inevitable) is the first step in enlisting the public health structure (including medicine, psychology, and social services) to help change the social norms. The key elements of a public health approach are surveillance, the setting of specific objectives, the development and implementation of prevention strategies, and interdisciplinary collaboration—activities that are already familiar to many, if not most, applied psychologists. As this perspective takes hold, no group of professionals could find themselves more on the forefront of efforts to address the crime problem than clinical and consulting psychologists.

## References

Ageton, S. (1983). *Sexual assault among adolescents*. Lexington, MA: Heath.

Aneshensel, C., Frerichs, R., Clark, V., & Yokopenic, P. (1982). Measuring depression in the community: A comparison of telephone and personal interviews. *Public Opinion Quarterly, 46*, 110–121.

Atkeson, B., Calhoun, K., Resick, P., & Ellis, E. (1982). Victims of rape: Repeated assessment of depressive symptoms. *Journal of Consulting and Clinical Psychology, 50*, 96–102.

Bard, M., & Sangrey, D. (1986). *The crime victim's book* (2nd ed.). New York: Brunner/Mazel.

Burgess, A., & Holmstrom, L. (1978). Recovery from rape and prior life stress. *Research in Nursing and Health, 1*, 165–174.

Burnam, M., Stein, J., Golding, J., Siegel, J., Sorenson, S., Forsythe, A.,

& Telles, C. (1988). Sexual assault and mental disorders in a community population. *Journal of Consulting and Clinical Psychology, 56*, 843–850.

Calhoun, K., Atkeson, B., & Resick, P. (1982). A longitudinal examination of fear reactions in victims of rape. *Journal of Counseling Psychology, 29*, 655–661.

Cohen, L., & Roth, S. (1987). The psychological aftermath of rape: Long-term effects and individual differences in recovery. *Journal of Social and Clinical Psychology, 5*, 525–534.

Davis, R., & Friedman, L. (1985). The emotional aftermath of crime and violence. In C. Figley (Ed.), *Trauma and its wake: The study and treatment of post-traumatic stress disorder* (pp. 90–112). New York: Brunner/Mazel.

Derogatis, L., & Spencer, P. (1982). *Brief Symptom Inventory (BSI): Administration, scoring and procedures manual-1*. Redgewood, MD: Clinical Psychometric Research Incorporated.

Dillman, D. (1978). *Mail and telephone surveys: The total design method*. New York: Interscience.

Ferraro, K., & LaGrange, R. (1987). The measurement of fear of crime. *Sociological Inquiry, 57*, 70–101.

Frank, E., & Stewart, P. (1984). Depressive symptoms in rape victims: A revisit. *Journal of Affective Disorders, 7*, 77–85.

Frazier, P. (1991). Self-blame as a mediator of postrape depressive symptoms. *Journal of Social and Clinical Psychology, 10*, 47–57.

Frieze, I., Hymer, S., & Greenberg, M. (1987). Describing the crime victim: Psychological reactions to victimization. *Professional Psychology: Research and Practice, 18*, 299–315.

Garofalo, J., & Laub, J. (1978). The fear of crime: Broadening our perspective. *Victimology: An International Journal, 3*, 242–253.

Golding, J., Stein, J., Siegel, J., Burnam, M., & Sorenson, S. (1988). Sexual assault history and use of health and mental health services. *American Journal of Community Psychology, 16*, 625–644.

Groves, R. (1987). Research on survey data quality. *Public Opinion Quarterly, 51*, S156–S172.

Kahn, A. (Ed.). (1984). *Victims of crime and violence: Final report of the APA Task Force on Victims of Crime and Violence*. Washington, DC: American Psychological Association.

Kendall, P., & Grove, W. (1988). Normative comparisons in therapy outcome. *Behavioral Assessment, 10*, 147–158.

Kilpatrick, D., Best, C., Veronen, L., Amick, A., Villeponteaux, L., & Ruff, G. (1985). Mental health correlates of victimization: A random community survey. *Journal of Consulting and Clinical Psychology, 53*, 866–873.

Kilpatrick, D., & Calhoun, K. (1988). Early behavioral treatment for rape trauma: Efficacy or artifact? *Behavior Therapy, 19*, 421–427.

Kilpatrick, D., Resick, P., & Veronen, L. (1981). Effects of a rape experience: A longitudinal study. *Journal of Social Issues, 37*, 105–122.

Kilpatrick, D., & Resnick, H. (1992a, August). *Etiological factors in development of crime-related post-traumatic stress disorder*. Paper presented at the meeting of the American Psychological Association, Washington, DC.

Kilpatrick, D., & Resnick, H. (1992b). PTSD associated with exposure to criminal victimization in clinical and community populations. In J. Davidson & E. Foa (Eds.) *Posttraumatic stress disorder in review: Recent research and future directions*. Washington, DC: American Psychiatric Press.

Kilpatrick, D., Saunders, B., Veronen, L., Best, C., & Von, J. (1987). Criminal victimization: Lifetime prevalence, reporting to police, and psychological impact. *Crime and Delinquency, 33*, 479–489.

Kish, L. (1949). A procedure for objective respondent selection within the household. *American Statistical Association Journal, 44*, 380–387.

Koppel, H. (1987). *Lifetime likelihood of victimization*. Washington, DC: Bureau of Justice Statistics.

Koss, M. (1990). The women's mental health research agenda: Violence against women. *American Psychologist, 45,* 374–380.

Koss, M., & Dinero, T. (1989). Discriminant analysis of risk factors for sexual victimization among a national sample of college women. *Journal of Consulting and Clinical Psychology, 57,* 242–250.

Koss, M., Gidycz, C., & Wisniewski, N. (1987). The scope of rape: Incidence and prevalence of sexual aggression and victimization in a national sample of higher education students. *Journal of Consulting and Clinical Psychology, 55,* 162–170.

Koss, M., & Harvey, M. (1991). *The rape victim: Clinical and community interventions*. Newbury Park, CA: Sage.

Koss, M., Woodruff, W., & Koss, P. (1990). Relation of criminal victimization to health perceptions among women medical patients. *Journal of Consulting and Clinical Psychology, 58,* 147–152.

Lehnen, R., & Skogan, W. (1984). *The National Crime Survey: Working papers: Vol. 2. Methodological studies*. Washington, DC: U.S. Department of Justice, Bureau of Justice Statistics.

Lurigio, A., & Resick, P. (1990). Healing the psychological wounds of criminal victimization: Predicting postcrime distress and recovery. In A. Lurigio, W. Skogan, & R. Davis (Eds.), *Victims of crime: Problems, policies, and programs* (pp. 50–68). Newbury Park, CA: Sage.

McCann, L., Sakheim, D., & Abrahamson, D. (1988). Trauma and victimization: A model of psychological adaptation. *The Counseling Psychologist, 16,* 531–594.

McPherson, M. (1978). Realities and perception of crime at the neighborhood level. *Victimology: An International Journal, 3,* 321–328.

Meyer, C., & Taylor, S. (1986). Adjustment to rape. *Journal of Personality and Social Psychology, 50,* 1226–1234.

Murphy, S., Amick-McMullan, A., Kilpatrick, D., Haskett, M., Veronen, L., Best, C., & Saunders, B. (1988). Rape victims' self-esteem: A longitudinal analysis. *Journal of Interpersonal Violence, 3,* 355–370.

Norris, F., & Johnson, K. (1988). The effects of "self-help" precautionary measures on criminal victimization and fear. *Journal of Urban Affairs, 10,* 161–181.

Norris, F., & Kaniasty, K. (1992). A longitudinal study of the effects of various crime prevention strategies on criminal victimization, fear of crime, and psychological distress. *American Journal of Community Psychology, 20,* 625–648.

Norris, F., Kaniasty, K., & Scheer, D. (1990). Use of mental health ser-

vices among victims of crime: Frequency, correlates, and subsequent recovery. *Journal of Consulting and Clinical Psychology, 58,* 538–547.

Quinn, R., Gutek, B., & Walsh, J. (1980). Telephone interviewing: A reappraisal and a field experiment. *Basic and Applied Psychology, 1,* 127–153.

Resick, P. (1987). Psychological effects of victimization: Implications for the criminal justice system. *Crime and Delinquency, 33,* 468–478.

Roark, M. (1987). Preventing violence on college campuses. *Journal of Counseling and Development, 65,* 367–371.

Rosenberg, M., & Fenley, M. (1991). *Violence in America: A public health approach*. New York: Oxford University Press.

Sales, E., Baum, M., & Shore, B. (1984). Victim readjustment following assault. *Journal of Social Issues, 40,* 117–136.

Seidner, A., Burling, T., Fisher, L., & Blair, T. (1990). Characteristics of telephone applicants to a residential rehabilitation program for homeless veterans. *Journal of Consulting and Clinical Psychology, 58,* 825–831.

Siegel, J., Golding, J., Stein, J., Burnam, M., & Sorenson, S. (1990). Reactions to sexual assault: A community study. *Journal of Interpersonal Violence, 5,* 229–246.

Skogan, W. (1987). The impact of victimization on fear. *Crime and Delinquency, 33,* 135–154.

Smith, M. (1989). Woman abuse: The case for surveys by telephone. *Journal of Interpersonal Violence, 4,* 308–324.

Sorenson, S., & Golding, J. (1990). Depressive sequelae of recent criminal victimization. *Journal of Traumatic Stress, 3,* 337–350.

Steketee, G., & Foa, E. (1987). Rape victims: Post-traumatic stress responses and their treatment: A review of the literature. *Journal of Anxiety Disorders, 1,* 69–86.

Tausing, J., & Freeman, E. (1988). The next best thing to being there: Conducting the clinical research interview by telephone. *American Journal of Orthopsychiatry, 58,* 418–427.

Tuchfarber, A., & Klecka, W. (1976). *Measuring crime victimization: An efficient method*. Washington, DC: The Police Foundation.

U.S. Bureau of the Census. (1991). *Statistical abstract of the United States: 1991* (111th ed.). Washington, DC: U.S. Government Printing Office.

Wirtz, P., & Harrell, A. (1987a). Assaultive versus nonassaultive victimization: A profile analysis of psychological response. *Journal of Interpersonal Violence, 2,* 264–277.

Wirtz, P., & Harrell, A. (1987b). Victim and crime characteristics, coping responses, and short- and long-term recovery from victimization. *Journal of Consulting and Clinical Psychology, 55,* 866–871.

Appendix

T-Score Distributions on Brief Symptom Inventory Scales by Sample and Time

| | | | | Percentage of sample falling in range | | | | | | | | |
|---|---|---|---|---|---|---|---|---|---|---|---|---|
| | Upper bound of range[a] | | | No crime | | | Property crime | | | Violent crime | | |
| Scale | T score | Percentile | Raw score | T1 | T2 | T3 | T1 | T2 | T3 | T1 | T2 | T3 |
| Depression | 50 | 50 | 0.17 | 58 | 60 | 59 | 45 | 56 | 53 | 22 | 31 | 35 |
| | 60 | 84 | 0.61 | 18 | 23 | 26 | 27 | 21 | 25 | 27 | 23 | 29 |
| | 70 | 98 | 1.48 | 19 | 14 | 13 | 21 | 19 | 18 | 27 | 31 | 20 |
| | 80 | 100 | 4.00 | 4 | 4 | 3 | 7 | 5 | 4 | 25 | 15 | 16 |
| Somatization | 50 | 50 | 0.14 | 60 | 60 | 67 | 51 | 54 | 48 | 38 | 41 | 41 |
| | 60 | 84 | 0.59 | 22 | 23 | 20 | 26 | 24 | 32 | 28 | 29 | 33 |
| | 70 | 98 | 1.66 | 16 | 13 | 9 | 17 | 17 | 18 | 24 | 22 | 20 |
| | 80 | 100 | 4.00 | 2 | 4 | 4 | 6 | 5 | 3 | 11 | 9 | 6 |
| Hostility | 50 | 50 | 0.27 | 59 | 68 | 68 | 37 | 50 | 56 | 31 | 29 | 34 |
| | 60 | 84 | 0.60 | 24 | 20 | 22 | 37 | 25 | 23 | 18 | 32 | 29 |
| | 70 | 98 | 1.31 | 13 | 7 | 9 | 18 | 17 | 15 | 27 | 22 | 25 |
| | 80 | 100 | 4.00 | 4 | 5 | 2 | 8 | 8 | 6 | 25 | 17 | 12 |
| Anxiety | 50 | 50 | 0.28 | 47 | 52 | 50 | 37 | 42 | 44 | 19 | 20 | 25 |
| | 60 | 84 | 0.67 | 36 | 35 | 37 | 36 | 36 | 37 | 35 | 37 | 39 |
| | 70 | 98 | 1.37 | 13 | 10 | 10 | 19 | 15 | 14 | 22 | 29 | 25 |
| | 80 | 100 | 4.00 | 5 | 3 | 3 | 8 | 8 | 5 | 24 | 14 | 11 |
| Phobic Anxiety | 50 | 50 | 0.00 | 72 | 73 | 77 | 62 | 71 | 71 | 42 | 56 | 57 |
| | 60 | 84 | 0.30 | 13 | 15 | 15 | 15 | 12 | 13 | 19 | 10 | 17 |
| | 70 | 98 | 0.88 | 12 | 9 | 4 | 13 | 12 | 11 | 17 | 17 | 17 |
| | 80 | 100 | 4.00 | 3 | 3 | 4 | 10 | 5 | 5 | 22 | 17 | 9 |

[a] The upper bound of the range is based on the average score of the no-crime group across the three time points (T1 = Time 1, January–February 1988; T2 = Time 2, July–August 1988; T3 = Time 3, January–February 1989).

Revised June 15, 1992
Revision received February 16, 1993
Accepted March 9, 1993 ■

# ADVICE TO CRIME VICTIMS:
## Effects of Crime, Victim, and Advisor Factors

R. BARRY RUBACK
*Georgia State University*

There is consistent evidence from a variety of sources that crime victims' reporting decisions are influenced by others. The present studies extended this prior work by surveying two statewide stratified random samples ($n_s$ = 817 and 832). In Study 1, of 148 respondents who said a family member had been a victim of sexual assault, domestic assault, or robbery, only 65% said that they had advised the victims to report the crime, and women were significantly more likely to advise reporting domestic assault than were men. In both Study 1 and Study 2, respondents were asked about the appropriateness of reporting specific crimes to the police. Based on both within- and between-respondent questions, it appears that reporting advice is contingent on several factors: the seriousness of the offense, the gender of the victim, the victim-offender relationship, and the gender of the respondent.

C rime victims often consult with others, and the advice they receive strongly influences their decision to call or not to call the police. For example, the initial studies of police delay in responding to crimes found that the major source of delay was not police but citizens, because they often spoke with someone before calling the police (Spelman & Brown, 1981; Van Kirk, 1978). Additional findings from interviews with victims of rape, robbery, burglary, and theft

AUTHOR'S NOTE: *An earlier version of this article was presented at the annual meeting of the American Society of Criminology, Phoenix. This research was supported in part by the Georgia Statistical Analysis Bureau, which is funded by the Criminal Justice Coordinating Council through SAC-I funds received from the Bureau of Justice Statistics, U.S. Department of Justice. Study 2 was supported by the Applied Research Center at Georgia State University. Address all correspondence to R. Barry Ruback, Department of Psychology, Georgia State University, Atlanta, GA 30303.*

CRIMINAL JUSTICE AND BEHAVIOR, Vol. 21 No. 4, December 1994 423-442

indicated that a substantial proportion spoke with someone else before calling the police (Ruback, Greenberg, & Westcott, 1984). Moreover, there is substantial evidence that victims are influenced by their conversations with others. Interview studies suggest that many crime victims receive advice from others and are likely to comply with this advice (Greenberg, Ruback, & Westcott, 1983). In addition, experimental research indicates that crime victims follow the advice they receive, even if this advice comes from a stranger (Greenberg & Ruback, 1992).

Given that advisors play an important role in victims' decisions, it is important to understand the factors they use when determining what is the appropriate advice to give. The two studies described here investigated three types of factors: the crime, the victim, and the advisor. With regard to crime, the studies tested advice as a function of the type of crime, because crime seriousness is the single best predictor of reporting (Skogan, 1984). Data from the National Crime Victimization Survey (Bureau of Justice Statistics, 1994) consistently indicate that, the greater the harm suffered, the more likely a crime is to be reported. Thus reporting is more likely if the crime involved interpersonal violence rather than theft, if it was completed rather than attempted, if the property taken was of greater rather than lesser value, if a weapon was involved, and if the victim was more seriously injured. Thus the hypothesis was that advisors would be more likely to recommend that a crime be reported the more serious the crime was.

In addition to crime seriousness, factors about the victim also are likely to affect the type of advice that victims receive. One factor about the victim is the victim's gender. Based on traditional gender roles in society that consider females as more vulnerable than males, it would be expected that crimes against females would be viewed as more unjust than crimes against males. Consistent with that hypothesis, data from 1992 (Bureau of Justice Statistics, 1994) indicated that crimes of violence against females were more likely to be reported (56.3%) than were crimes of violence against males (45.0%). Thus one would expect advisors to be more likely to advise reporting crimes against women than against men.

In addition to the victim's gender, another factor that is likely to affect advisors' judgments about the appropriateness of reporting a crime is the relationship between the victim and the offender. Because individuals are more likely to think that they are safe with nonstrangers than with strangers, being victimized by a nonstranger should be more violative of individuals' sense of moral order and justice than being victimized by a stranger. Consistent with that notion, data from a rape crisis center in Atlanta indicated that rape victims were significantly more angry when they had known the offender previously than when the offender was a stranger (Greenberg & Ruback, 1992). However, although there has been some debate about whether victims still use this factor when deciding whether or not to report their victimization to the police (Bachman, 1993; Ruback, 1993), results from that and other studies all indicate that crimes are less likely to be reported the closer the relationship between the victim and the offender. This consistent finding probably results from victims' determination that other factors, such as fear of retaliation from the offender, outweigh the general principle that more serious crimes should be reported. Based on this prior research on reporting, it is reasonable to hypothesize that advisors will be less likely to advise reporting a crime if the offender was a relative or friend rather than a stranger.

In addition to factors about the crime and the victim, it is also likely that who the advisor is makes a difference in terms of the type of advice given. For example, there is evidence that female victims experience greater fear than do male victims (e.g., Davis & Friedman, 1985; Maguire, 1980). That being the case, it is reasonable to hypothesize that female advisors would be more likely to advise reporting than would male advisors.

Crime seriousness, victim gender, victim-offender relationship, and advisor gender have been previously tested as predictors of advice to victims in cross-national studies by Greenberg and Ruback (1992). Subjects in these studies were given items from the study of crime seriousness by Wolfgang, Figlio, Tracy, and Singer (1985) and were asked to judge on a continuum whether the appropriate action was to call the police or to handle the matter privately. In three countries (India, Nigeria, and Thailand), the seriousness of the crime, the gender of the victim, and the victim-offender relationship (i.e., whether or not they were related) were significant predictors of normative standards regarding reporting. However, those findings were not true for a U.S. sample, probably because seriousness was not directly measured, as it was in the other countries. In addition, a second study of college students in India indicated that subjects thought it was more appropriate to report crimes committed by strangers than by relatives and crimes involving female victims rather than male victims (Ruback, Gupta, & Kohli, in press). The latter study also found a strong participant gender effect, such that females, compared to males, believed it was more appropriate to report the crimes.

Although these prior findings are suggestive of the importance of crime, victim, and advisor factors in terms of the type of advice victims are likely to receive, the Greenberg and Ruback (1992) and Ruback et al. (in press) studies involved nonrepresentative groups (i.e., high school and college students), and most of the samples involved individuals in foreign countries. It may be that findings would be different if a representative sample of American adults was used.

In addition, the prior studies did not investigate how these variables combine to affect the ultimate advice given. Rather than being additive, it may be that these factors interact with one another. In particular, it is reasonable to hypothesize a curvilinear relationship between crime seriousness and factors about the victim: That is, for crimes of low seriousness, there should be little ambiguity regarding the appropriate action, because almost no one would think that they should be reported. Similarly, for crimes of high seriousness, there should be little ambiguity regarding the appropriate action, because virtually everyone would think that they should be reported. Only for crimes of moderate seriousness would there be ambiguity, and for those crimes, other factors, such as the gender of the victim, would be important additional pieces of information to help resolve the ambiguity.

These hypotheses were tested in the present studies with both actual crime reports and simulations. The studies used two statewide stratified random-sample telephone surveys. The first study was conducted as part of a victimization survey, and the second study was conducted as part of a quarterly statewide poll in Georgia.

## STUDY 1

The first study used a telephone survey to investigate social influence on victims by asking about actual victimizations and presenting respondents with simulated situations. Telephone surveys employing random-digit dialing are probably the most cost-effective way to collect quality data (Lavrakas, 1987), because response rates are generally much better when respondents are contacted by telephone than in person, especially when questions are personal.

The telephone survey was conducted by the Applied Research Center at Georgia State University. Households were sampled from a database purchased from Survey Samplings Inc., a Connecticut-based company that maintains a database containing all active telephone exchanges. The company identifies all working exchanges (the first three numbers of the seven-digit telephone number) and working blocks (the fourth and fifth numbers). Each working exchange is assigned to the specific county in which it is used. The sample for the state of Georgia was stratified by county population, so that the chance of a person from any particular county being included in the sample was proportional to the number of residents in that county compared to the state population. The company then selected the sample for the state by randomly generating the last two digits for the working exchanges and working blocks. From this pool of numbers, businesses were eliminated. This methodology ensured that the final sample would include both new and unlisted telephone numbers. According to Survey Samplings, Inc., recent telephone surveys have had cooperation rates of 54% in the Southeast, somewhat lower than for other parts of the country. Cooperation is also generally lower in big cities than in suburban and rural areas.

Although a sample is the only feasible way to study victimizations and to assess attitudes, it must be noted that there are potential problems with using random-digit dialing. First, individuals who cannot be reached may be systematically different from those who are included in the study. For example, Groves and Kahn (1979) found that people without telephones were likely to live in single-adult households, to be less educated, to be poorer, to be minorities, and to be employed in an occupation that is nonprofessional and nonmanagerial. Although more people have telephones now than when that study was conducted, there is still some bias in using telephones. For the present study, individuals who do not have a telephone are undoubtedly less well-off and probably more transient than individuals who do have telephones. If these individuals are more likely to be and to know victims of crime, this bias would lead to an underestimate of the true number of victimizations in the state, although this bias probably does not affect other questions in the survey regarding advice to victims.

## METHOD

*Respondents.* The sample consisted of 817 residents of Georgia, 317 males and 500 females, who ranged in age from 18 to 83 ($M = 42.8$, $SD = 16.4$). In the final sample, 130 of Georgia's 159 counties were represented. As would be expected from a statewide stratified sample, about half of the sample lived in the metropolitan Atlanta area.

The majority of telephone calls did not result in a completed interview because of nonworking numbers. Other households were not included because no one answered the telephone, even after the household was called eight times. Of the 1,727 households contacted, 817 (47.3%) completed the interview, slightly less than the typical response rate, but not surprising given the sensitive nature of the questions. In terms of the survey, it might be that persons who were interested in criminal justice issues or who had been victimized were more likely to agree to the interview. If this is true, then crime victims might be overrepresented in the final sample. It is unknown whether this bias equals or outweighs the countervailing bias resulting from using telephone interviews.

The sample was four-fifths Caucasian, one-sixth African American, and 2% other (Asian, Hispanic, Native American). A small number of respondents (.6%) did not give their race. Almost all of the sample (88%) had a high school diploma, and 31% had at least a college degree. Annual household incomes ranged from less than $7,500 (7.1% of the sample) to more than $75,000 (11.1% of the sample). Most of the sample (40.1%) had annual incomes between $25,000 and $50,000. Compared to the statewide population, the sample had a higher percentage of women, included a higher percentage of Caucasians, and was better educated.

*Procedure.* Trained interviewers called each of the households identified in the sample pool of numbers. When someone in the home was reached, the interviewer read a brief statement introducing the study as being sponsored by the Georgia Criminal Justice Coordinating Council, a state agency that reports directly to the governor. The interviewer then asked for the person over 18 in the household who had the most recent birthday (see Henry, 1990), a procedure that controls for the fact that in telephone surveys it is generally easier to reach women than men and to reach older than younger individuals (Lavrakas, 1987). When the person with the most recent birthday came to the telephone, the interviewer described the study, asked if the individual understood what was involved, and then asked for the person's consent to participate. When that introduction was completed and consent was given, the interview began. The interviews were conducted during the last 2 weeks of July and the first week of August 1992. On the average, interviews took about 19 minutes to complete.

*Instrument.* Respondents were asked whether they had been a victim of robbery, attempted robbery, aggravated assault, attempted assault, sexual assault, burglary or attempted burglary, or theft or vandalism of property. If they said they had been a victim of a crime in the prior year, they then were asked who the offender was (stranger, acquaintance, well-known person, family member), what was the first action they took after the crime (called the police, talked to someone, some other action), and whether or not they reported the crime to the police. In addition, respondents were asked if anyone in their family had ever been a victim of unwanted sexual activity, assault, or robbery and whether they had advised this family member to call the police.

There were also seven questions that asked respondents about whether they would advise a relative to report seven different victimization scenarios ($10 robbery without a weapon, $10 robbery with a lead pipe, sexual assault by an unknown offender, sexual assault by a boyfriend, assault on an elderly female relative, man assaults his wife, man assaults a family member) to the police. These questions about normative beliefs were taken from studies by Greenberg and Ruback (1992). Also asked were questions on a 5-item scale assessing fear of crime (alpha = .77) and a 15-item scale assessing precautionary behavior (Norris & Kaniasty, 1992; alpha = .70). The final group of questions asked respondents about demographic and descriptive information (race, education, age, size of household, income, sex, zip code, and county of residence).

287

**RESULTS**

*Actions after a victimization.* Respondents were asked whether they had been the victim of any of several completed or attempted crimes. Of the 817 respondents, 32% suffered some victimization, violent or nonviolent, during the prior year (the percentage may be 3 points higher or lower due to sampling error). Consistent with other studies, males had higher victimization rates than did females, and Blacks had higher victimization rates than did Whites. Black males had the highest victimization rates, whereas White females had the lowest victimization rates. After the crime was over or the crime was discovered, 52% of the victims said that they reported immediately, whereas 21% said that they spoke with someone else first, and 27% took some other action. Victims' first action was not related to their fear of crime or precautionary behavior. Eventually, 63% reported their victimization to the police.

Victims' first actions were initially analyzed in terms of the type of crime involved. For 170 person crimes (robbery, attempted robbery, assault, attempted assault, sexual assault), 37% of the victims reported immediately, 17% spoke with someone else first, and 46% took some other action. For 284 property crimes (burglary, theft, vandalism), 61% of the victims reported immediately, 23% of the victims spoke with someone else first, and 16% took some other action. A $3 \times 2$ comparison of victims' first action taken after the crime (report, talk with someone, other action) by type of crime (person vs. property) was significant, $\chi^2(2) = 47.61, p < .001$. As the above percentages suggest, property crime victims were most likely to call the police first, whereas person crime victims were most likely to take some other action.

Victims' first actions also were analyzed in terms of whether the offender was a stranger or a nonstranger. These analyses were conducted separately for person crimes and for property crimes. Both analyses were significant, $\chi^2(2) = 6.08, p < .05$, and $\chi^2(2) = 11.11, p < .01$, for person and property crimes, respectively. As can be seen in Table 1, for both person and property crimes, if the offender was a stranger rather than a nonstranger, victims' first action was more likely to be reporting the crime and less likely to be talking with someone or

TABLE 1:    Victims' First Actions by ( Percentages) Type of Crime and Victim-Offender Relationship (Study 1)

| Victim-Offender Relationship | n | First Action | | |
| --- | --- | --- | --- | --- |
| | | Report | Talk to Someone | Other Action |
| Person crimes | | | | |
| Stranger | 83 | 45 | 11 | 45 |
| Nonstranger | 87 | 30 | 23 | 47 |
| Property crimes | | | | |
| Stranger | 200 | 66 | 22 | 12 |
| Nonstranger | 84 | 48 | 26 | 26 |

NOTE: Percentages may not add to 100 because of rounding.

taking some other action. If the offender was a nonstranger, victims' first action was more likely to be talking with someone or taking some other action rather than reporting to the police.

*Advice to others.* In addition to asking respondents whether they had been victimized during the prior year, we also asked them whether anyone in their household had ever been a victim of sexual assault, domestic assault, and robbery. For sexual assault, 49 respondents reported a victimization in their family, and 28 (57%) of these victims had been advised to report. For domestic assault, 48 respondents reported a victimization in their family, and 32 (67%) of these victims had been advised to report. For robbery, 51 respondents reported a victimization in their family, and 36 (71%) of the victims had been advised to report.

For each of these three crimes, a 2 × 2 (Race of Respondent × Gender of Respondent) analysis of variance (ANOVA) was conducted on the type of advice given. For sexual assault and robbery, there was no significant effect. For domestic assault, there was a significant effect for gender of respondent, $F(1, 38) = 4.28, p < .05$, with females ($M = 1.82$) being significantly more likely to recommend reporting than males ($M = 1.50$).

*Normative beliefs.* To try to understand respondents' beliefs about reporting crimes to the police, we presented them with seven different scenarios and asked them if they would advise a family member who was so victimized to report the crime. Correlations between respondents' ratings and their demographic characteristics (age, income, education), attitudes (fear of crime, perception of disorder in the neighborhood, judgments of the police), precautionary behaviors, and victimizations in the prior year revealed few significant effects, and even those that were significant were small. Thus, to emphasize what has been found before (e.g., Rich & Sampson, 1990), individual differences, including prior victimization, were not meaningful predictors of perceptions of actions in the criminal justice system.

In addition to the correlational analyses, the seven scenarios were also analyzed by a $2 \times 2 \times 2$ between respondents (Gender $\times$ Race $\times$ Urban/Rural Location) $\times 7$ within respondents repeated measures ANOVA. The only significant effect was the repeated measure, $F(6, 4494) = 22.33$, $p < .001$. Means and standard deviations for the items are presented in Table 2. Of particular interest is the comparison of the two items concerning a family member being beaten and two items concerning a female relative being forced to perform a sexual act. Within each of the pairs, in one item the offender had a relationship with the victim and in the other the offender was a stranger. For both pairs, when the offender was a stranger, respondents said that they would be significantly more likely to advise the victim to call the police than when the victim knew the offender. This result occurred even though the item of a man beating his wife is more serious (based on the ratings from Wolfgang et al., 1985) than is a stranger beating a family member.

DISCUSSION

The results of Study 1 indicated, consistent with other studies, that one-fifth of victims said that they spoke with someone immediately after the crime, although this percentage differed depending on the particular type of crime. Moreover, for both person and property crimes, victims were more likely to call the police immediately if the offender was a stranger than a nonstranger. In addition, only 65% of the respondents whose family members had been crime victims had advised the victims to call the police. Although there is error associated

TABLE 2:   Mean Reporting Scores for Seven Crime Scenarios (Study 1)

| Scenario | M | Seriousness |
|---|---|---|
| A person does not have a weapon. He threatens to harm your relative unless your relative gives him money. Your relative gives him $10 and is not harmed. | 3.51[a] (.71) | 5.38 |
| A person armed with a lead pipe robs your relative of $10. Your relative is injured and requires hospitalization. | 3.82[d] (.56) | 13.33 |
| A high school boy beats one of your elderly female relatives with his fists. She requires hospitalization. | 3.84 (.50) | 17.52 |
| An unknown man beats a family member with his fists. Your relative requires hospitalization. | 3.75[c] (.67) | 11.78 |
| A man in your family beats his wife with his fists. She requires hospitalization. | 3.70[b] (.68) | 18.32 |
| An unknown man forces a female relative to perform a sexual act with him. | 3.83[d] (.54) | 25.85 |
| A boyfriend forces a female relative to perform a sexual act with him. | 3.76[c] (.56) | |

NOTE: Reporting scores are on a 4-point scale ranging from *strongly advise not to report the crime* = 1 to *strongly advise to report the crime* = 4. Means not sharing a common superscript are significantly different according to a Newman-Keuls test ($p < .05$). Numbers in parentheses are standard deviations. The seriousness ratings are from Wolfgang et al. (1985).

with victim surveys (e.g., describing a crime that was outside the study period as being in the study period), that problem is not the crucial issue here because this part of the study was not intended as an estimate of victimization incidents in the state. Rather, it was intended to learn how victims and their potential advisors behave. However, there may be a potential bias of social desirability because some respondents might have given an answer that made them look more like good citizens. That is, they might have said that they reported or advised reporting a crime when they actually did not.

In addition to these data regarding actual victimizations, Study 1 also investigated all respondents' beliefs about the appropriate action to take following seven different victimization scenarios. With both assault and sexual assault, respondents thought it was more appropriate to report a crime committed by a stranger than the same crime committed by a relative.

One of the weaknesses of this study is that the manipulation was totally within subjects. It could be that respondents recognized the manipulation and gave the answers they thought the interviewer wanted to hear. The only way to correct for that possibility is to use a between-subjects experimental design so that respondents are not aware of the other conditions in the study. The next study included that modification.

## STUDY 2

The second study was conducted to replicate and extend the findings from the first study regarding the effects for victim-offender relationship and gender of respondent. In addition, the study was designed to test whether the gender of the victim was a significant determinant of reporting advice. Also, because a larger number of crimes was used, the hypothesis regarding crime seriousness interacting with other factors could be investigated. The data were collected as part of the Quarterly Georgia State Poll, conducted during two weeks in October 1993.

**METHOD**

*Respondents.* The sample consisted of 832 residents of Georgia, 333 males and 499 females, who ranged in age from 18 to 90 ($M =$ 41.4, $SD = 15.2$). Half of the sample lived in the metropolitan Atlanta area. The sample was 67% Caucasian, 22% African American, and 3% other (Asian, Hispanic, Native American). About 8% of the respondents did not give their race. Almost all of the sample (88%) had a high school diploma, and 29% had at least a college degree. Annual household incomes ranged from less than $15,000 (10% of the sample) to more than $75,000 (9% of the sample). Most of the sample (32%) had annual incomes between $25,000 and $50,000. Compared to the statewide population, the sample had a higher percentage of women and was better educated.

*Instrument.* From the Wolfgang et al. (1985) study, 20 scenarios were taken to represent a broad spectrum of seriousness, ranging from an obscene phone call (seriousness = 1.87) to trying to entice a minor into a car for immoral purposes (seriousness = 25.22). These 20 scenarios were then doubled to 40 by making the victim either a male or a female. One of the items, a man beats his wife, which was used in Study 1, was modified to a man beats his sister or a man beats his brother, to hold the gender of perpetrator constant while still manipulating the gender of the victim. The most direct comparison, comparing a man beating his wife to a woman beating her husband, was believed to be inappropriate and therefore was not used (see Browne, 1993).

Respondents were asked one of four sets of 10 questions concerning their advice to a criminally victimized family member. Each set of 10 crimes had the same gender victim and each of the sets was randomly assigned to respondents, so that there were slightly more than 200 respondents for each of the four versions. Within each set of 10 questions, the order was randomized for each respondent. Respondents made their judgments on a 10-point scale ranging from *handle the matter privately* = 1 to *report to the police* = 10.

In addition to the manipulation of the gender of the victim across all items, there were three other experimental manipulations. One of the manipulations was within subjects. The respondents were given an item involving an attack by a relative: "A man in your family beats his brother (sister) with his fists. He (she) requires hospitalization." They also were given an item involving an attack by a stranger: "An unknown man beats one of your male (female) relatives with his fists. He (she) requires hospitalization."

The other two manipulations were between subjects. Half of the respondents were given an item involving an attack by a relative: "A teenager beats his father (mother), one of your male (female) relatives with his fists. The father (mother) requires hospitalization." Or, they were given an item involving an attack by a stranger: "An unknown teenager beats one of your male (female) relatives with his fists. He (she) requires hospitalization." The final manipulation involved a man using his fists to beat a male or female youngster, who either was or was not his child.

**RESULTS**

Because of the nature of the design, the 40 items used in the four different questionnaires had to be analyzed using two multivariate analyses. The between-respondents factors were gender of respondent, gender of victim, and area of the state (metropolitan Atlanta or nonmetropolitan Atlanta). The repeated measure was the 10 crimes the respondents received. Thus one set of the multivariate analyses involved one set of 10 crimes and the other set of analyses involved the other 10 crimes. It was believed that if a factor was significant across both sets of analyses, the factor was truly important.

The only factor to be significant on both multivariate analyses was the gender of the victim, $F(10, 377) = 2.75$, $p < .01$, and $F(10, 351) = 2.63$, $p < .01$. Table 3 presents the seriousness rating based on the Wolfgang et al. (1985) study, overall means for the 20 items, the separate means for male and female victims, and the significant univariate $F$s.

Consistent with the idea that crimes of moderate seriousness are the most ambiguous with regard to what is the appropriate action to take, it should be noted that significant differences as a function of the gender of the victim did not appear for the least severe or the most severe crimes. That is, although crime seriousness mattered overall in terms of reporting norms, with respondents believing that for more serious crimes reporting was more appropriate, $r(17) = .77$, $p < .01$, that was not true when the crime was not at all serious or very serious.

*Experimental manipulations.* There were three experimental manipulations, one within respondents and the other two between respondents. In terms of the within-respondent manipulation, respondents were presented with two items involving a male beating a stranger and beating a relative, both of them requiring hospitalization. A $2 \times 2 \times 2$ (Gender of Victim × Gender of Respondent × Area of the State) between-respondents × 2 (Victim-Offender Relationship) within-respondents ANOVA revealed significant effects for gender of victim, $F(1, 370) = 14.25$, gender of respondent, $F(1, 370) = 7.99$, $p < .01$, victim-offender relationship, $F(1, 370) = 27.60$, $p < .001$, and the interaction of victim gender and relationship, $F(1, 370) = 9.16$, $p <$

TABLE 3:   Mean Reporting Scores for 20 Crime Scenarios, Overall and by Gender of Victim (Study 2)

| Crime Scenario | Seriousness | Reporting Score | | | F |
| | | All Victims | Male Victims | Female Victims | |
| --- | --- | --- | --- | --- | --- |
| Obscene phone call | 1.87 | 6.53 | 6.26 | 6.70 | |
| Pickpocketing of $10 | 3.29 | 6.79 | 6.53 | 7.04 | |
| Pickpocketing of $100 | 4.38 | 8.22 | 8.03 | 8.40 | |
| Stolen car | 4.45 | 8.75 | 8.61 | 8.98 | |
| Hand run over victim's body | 5.13 | 7.84 | 7.42 | 7.85 | 3.84* |
| Check forgery | 7.21 | 8.54 | 8.51 | 8.61 | |
| Teenage son beats parent | 7.93 (15.90) | 8.89 | 8.53 | 9.16 | 7.62* |
| Threat to injure | 9.29 | 8.77 | 8.38 | 9.16 | 15.06*** |
| Robbery of $10 with gun | 9.42 | 9.19 | 9.27 | 9.13 | |
| Break in and $1,000 stolen | 9.60 | 9.38 | 9.29 | 9.47 | |
| Unknown man beats person | 11.78 | 9.26 | 9.12 | 9.51 | 4.83* |
| Attempt to kill with gun | 16.39 | 9.38 | 9.16 | 9.60 | 5.72* |
| Stabbing | 17.14 | 9.33 | 9.15 | 9.56 | 6.09* |
| Man beats adult sibling[a] | — | 8.59 | 8.05 | 9.23 | 17.64*** |
| Intentionally shot | 18.97 | 9.64 | 9.53 | 9.72 | |
| Teenager beats person | — (19.48) | 9.27 | 9.07 | 9.54 | 3.19 |
| Sexual assault | — (20.07) | 9.35 | 8.95 | 9.67 | 14.63*** |
| Parent beats own child | 22.89 | 9.32 | 9.28 | 9.43 | 6.02* |
| Unknown man beats child | — | 9.31 | 9.13 | 9.46 | |
| Enticing young child | 25.22 | 9.33 | 9.24 | 9.45 | |

NOTE: Reporting scores are on a 10-point scale ranging from *strongly advise to handle the matter privately* = 1 to *strongly advise to report the crime* = 10. The seriousness ratings are from Wolfgang et al. (1985). No seriousness rating means that the crime was not included in the Wolfgang et al. (1985) study. Seriousness ratings in parentheses are for female victims only.
[a]. The seriousness of a man beating his wife (the basis for this item) was 18.32.
*$p < .05$; **$p < .01$; ***$p < .001$.

.01. Respondents believed that reporting was the appropriate action more for female victims ($M = 9.39$) than for male victims ($M = 8.54$), and female respondents ($M = 9.20$) thought reporting was more appropriate than did male respondents ($M = 8.57$). Respondents also thought it was more appropriate to report an assault committed by a stranger ($M = 9.27$) than by a relative ($M = 8.61$).

The interaction of victim gender and victim-offender relationship was due to the fact that reporting was judged to be least appropriate for males victimized by a relative ($M = 8.19$) and most appropriate for assaults involving females victimized by a stranger ($M = 9.50$), based on post hoc Newman-Keuls tests ($p < .05$). Intermediate between these two extremes, and significantly different from both, were assaults of females victimized by a relative ($M = 8.90$) and assaults of males victimized by a stranger ($M = 8.94$). These two conditions did not differ significantly from each other.

There were two between-respondents manipulations, one involving a teenager beating a male or female adult who was or was not his or her parent and the other involving a male adult beating a male or female youngster who was or was not his child. Both of these manipulations were analyzed using $2 \times 2 \times 2 \times 2$ (Gender of Victim × Victim-Offender Relationship × Gender of Respondent × Area of State) between-respondents analyses of variance.

The analysis of variance of the teenager beating an adult revealed significant effects for gender of the victim, $F(1, 772) = 10.01, p < .01$, victim-offender relationship, $F(1, 772) = 8.75, p < .01$, and gender of respondent, $F(1, 772) = 11.99, p < .001$. Respondents were more likely to recommend reporting for female victims ($M = 9.32$) than for male victims ($M = 8.82$) and for stranger attackers ($M = 9.29$) than for relative attackers ($M = 8.84$). Female respondents ($M = 9.29$) were more likely to recommend reporting than were male respondents ($M = 8.71$). None of the interactions was significant.

The analysis of variance of the adult male beating a youngster yielded a significant effect only for gender of respondent, $F(1, 779) = 5.51, p < .05$. Females ($M = 9.47$) were significantly more likely to believe that the crime should be reported than were males ($M = 9.11$). The absence of significant effects for gender of victim and victim-offender relationship is consistent with the general hypothesis that, at very high levels of crime seriousness, few other factors matter.

## DISCUSSION

Consistent with the results from Study 1, Study 2 indicated that the victim-offender relationship affects respondents' beliefs about the appropriateness of calling the police. In addition, the study suggested that the gender of the victim matters, particularly for crimes of moderate seriousness. That is, as others (e.g., Skogan, 1984) have found, crime seriousness affects the perceived appropriateness of reporting crime. What is suggested by this study is that, at very low or very high levels, seriousness alone seems to affect the perceived appropriateness of reporting crime. In contrast, at moderate levels of seriousness, other factors also seem to matter. It would be important to replicate this finding using a larger number of crimes that encompassed the entire spectrum of seriousness.

It would be important to learn if this possible curvilinear relationship is also true in terms of victims' search for advice, that is, whether victims are most likely to want advice about what they should do when they have been the victim of a crime of moderate seriousness. Although victims may be most desirous of advice for crimes of moderate seriousness, it may be, as Ruback et al. (1984) suggested, that victims are most susceptible to influence when the crime is of very low seriousness (because of confusion about the costs and benefits of reporting) or of very high seriousness (because of the heightened arousal and stress associated with being a victim of a serious crime). Future research should test for these hypothesized differences regarding desire for and susceptibility to advice from others.

## GENERAL DISCUSSION

For several reasons, the present research should increase our confidence that advisors to victims use the type of crime, the victim-offender relationship, and the gender of the victim in determining what kind of advice to give victims. First, these studies involved two representative samples of the general population, with the exception of the approximately 5%-10% who do not own telephones. Second, they involved both real and simulated victimizations. Third, for the simulations, there were both between- and within-subjects manipulations. Fourth, results were consistent across the studies and across methods. Finally, these results are consonant with results from other studies.

That advisors tailor their advice to victims depending on the type of crime, the gender of the victim, and the victim-offender relationship is consistent with the kinds of factors that police and prosecutors use in their arrest and charging decisions (Law Enforcement Assistance Administration, 1977a, 1977b). For example, a study of how child abuse cases were processed in eight jurisdictions found that the cases that were most likely to be taken to the criminal justice system involved female victims, victims under 15 years of age, Black perpetrators, perpetrators who were not relatives, and perpetrators who had a criminal record (Gray, 1993). In other words, it seems that advisors are acting as surrogate agents of the criminal justice system because they are making judgments about the appropriateness of reporting, perhaps by using the same information that police and prosecutors use or perhaps by anticipating how these agents will react to the specific facts of the victim's case.

In only about half of the cases in Study 1 did victims report the crime immediately to the police. In about a fifth of the cases, victims said that they spoke with someone first. That victims delay before calling the police is important because, for many crimes, waiting too long before reporting can mean the difference between being able and not being able to make an arrest (Spelman & Brown, 1981; Van Kirk, 1978). Not only is it important for others to advise victims if the crime is to be reported, but the initial support implicit in the advice to report may be important for the victim's long-term recovery from the crime. For example, if significant others are unsupportive of rape victims, then victims are likely to have significantly poorer social adjustment (Davis, Brickman, & Baker, 1991).

Even though the results of the simulations generally were consistent with the real advice, there are still questions about whether respondents' answers would actually translate into behavior. Specifically, there appears to be high social desirability in saying one would call the police, even for relatively minor crimes. Thus there is a need to look at actual victimizations, not just simulations. One way, perhaps, is to use qualitative interviews, even though there would be a problem finding nonreporters and the people who had advised them not to report.

The present studies looked only at the final decision to report or not to report an incident, a decision that is the culmination of three stages (Greenberg & Ruback, 1992): a determination that the incident is a crime, a judgment about the seriousness of the crime, and a conclusion about what should be done. Although the crime, victim, and advisor factors investigated here affected the final decision, it may be that they work differentially at the three stages. That is, these factors might work in one direction at one stage and in the opposite direction at a later stage. For example, as hypothesized earlier, being victimized by a relative might make the crime more serious, but less likely to be reported. Future research should look more closely at how crime, victim, and advisor factors affect definitions of what crimes are, judgments about the perceived seriousness of crimes, and decisions about what actions should be taken.

Given that gender of victim and gender of advisor effects were significant in many of the analyses here, it would be important to look further at subcultures and ethnic groups within the United States where the status difference between men and women is even larger than it is in the majority culture. The expectation would be, as in the earlier studies in India (Greenberg & Ruback, 1992; Ruback et al., in press), that these gender effects would be even stronger. Finally, it would be important to investigate how all of the factors proposed here—seriousness, victim factors, advisor factors, and offender factors—interact to determine advisors' advice to victims.

## REFERENCES

Bachman, R. (1993). Predicting the reporting of rape victimizations: Have rape reforms made a difference? *Criminal Justice and Behavior, 20,* 254-270.

Browne, A. (1993). Violence against women by male partners: Prevalence, outcomes, and policy implications. *American Psychologist, 48,* 1077-1087.

Bureau of Justice Statistics. (1994). *Criminal victimization in the United States, 1992.* Washington, DC: U.S. Department of Justice.

Davis, R. C., Brickman, E., & Baker, T. (1991). Supportive and unsupportive responses of others to rape victims: Effects on concurrent victim adjustment. *American Journal of Community Psychology, 19,* 443-451.

Davis, R. C., & Friedman, L. N. (1985). The emotional aftermath of crime and violence. In C. R. Figley (Ed.), *Trauma and its wake: The study and treatment of post-traumatic stress disorder* (pp. 90-112). New York: Brunner/Mazel.

Gray, E. (1993). *Unequal justice: The prosecution of child sexual abuse.* New York: Free Press.

Greenberg, M. S., & Ruback, R. B. (1992). *After the crime: Victim decision making.* New York: Plenum.

Greenberg, M. S., Ruback, R. B., & Westcott, D. R. (1983). Decision making by crime victims: A multimethod approach. *Law & Society Review, 17,* 47-84.

Groves, R., & Kahn, M. (1979). *Surveys by telephone: A national comparison with personal interviews.* New York: Academic Press.

Henry, G. T. (1990). *Practical sampling.* Newbury Park, CA: Sage.

Lavrakas, P. J. (1987). *Telephone survey methods: Sampling, selection, and supervision.* Newbury Park, CA: Sage.

Law Enforcement Assistance Administration. (1977a). *Forcible rape: A national survey of the response by police* (Vol. 1). Washington, DC: U.S. Government Printing Office.

Law Enforcement Assistance Administration. (1977b). *Forcible rape: A national survey of the response by prosecutors* (Vol. 1). Washington, DC: U.S. Government Printing Office.

Maguire, M. (1980). The impact of burglary upon victims. *British Journal of Criminology, 20,* 261-275.

Norris, F. H., & Kaniasty, K. (1992). A longitudinal study of the effects of various crime prevention strategies on criminal victimization, fear of crime, and psychological distress. *American Journal of Community Psychology, 20,* 625-648.

Rich, R. F., & Sampson, R. J. (1990). Public perceptions of criminal justice policy: Does victimization make a difference? *Violence and Victims, 5,* 109-118.

Ruback, R. B. (1993). The victim-offender relationship does affect victims' decisions to report sexual assaults. *Criminal Justice and Behavior, 20,* 271-279.

Ruback, R. B., Greenberg, M. S., & Westcott, D. R. (1984). Social influence and crime victim decision making. *Journal of Social Issues, 40* (1), 51-76.

Ruback, R. B., Gupta, D., & Kohli, N. (in press). Normative standards for crime victims: Implications for research and policy. In R. C. Tripathi (Ed.), *Psychology and social policy.* New Delhi: Sage.

Skogan, W. G. (1984). Reporting crimes to the police: The status of world research. *Journal of Research in Crime and Delinquency, 21,* 113-137.

Spelman, W., & Brown, D. K. (1981). *Calling the police: Citizen reporting of serious crime.* Washington, DC: Police Executive Research Forum.

Van Kirk, M. (1978). *Response time analysis: Executive Summary.* Washington, DC: Law Enforcement Assistance Administration.

Wolfgang, M. E., Figlio, R. M., Tracy, P. E., & Singer, S. I. (1985). *The national survey of crime severity.* Washington, DC: Bureau of Justice Statistics.

# LONG-TERM CONSEQUENCES OF VICTIMIZATION BY WHITE-COLLAR CRIME*

NEAL SHOVER
GREER LITTON FOX
University of Tennessee, Knoxville

MICHAEL MILLS
Quito, Ecuador

This paper reports analysis of ethnographic data collected from individuals who lost funds when a loan company collapsed largely because of criminal conduct by its officers and employees. We describe the range of victims' experiences and examine whether victimization affected confidence and trust in political and economic leaders and in prevailing political and economic institutions. The findings suggest that 1) the overall impact of victimization on individuals and families ranged from minimal, for a majority of victims, to severe; 2) loss of confidence in economic and political leaders increased, but long-term effects of institutional delegitimation were nonexistent to weak in most cases; and 3) the strongest delegitimation effects were produced by the actions of state officials who devised and implemented a plan to resolve financial problems caused by the company's collapse. Study design and data limitations mandate that our findings be interpreted very cautiously, but they point to the importance of victims' perceptions of procedural fairness as a possible determinant of delegitimation. They also suggest that victims' past experiences and the vocabularies they employ to make sense of institutional failure and personal misfortune may constrain the long-term individual-level delegitimation effects of victimization by white-collar crime.

Since the mid-1970s the victims' rights movement has emerged as a powerful force in America's response to crime. Testimony to the symbolic and political strength of this movement is the initiation of victim assistance and victim compensation programs in states across the nation and, more recently, in amendments to state criminal codes giving crime victims a voice in the prosecution and sentencing of offenders (Davis and Henley 1990; Elias 1993). Political activity has been matched by new interest in the impact of crime on its many victims. Investigators have documented the

* Support for this research was provided by the Social Science Research Institute and the Department of Sociology, University of Tennessee, Knoxville. Points of view or opinions expressed here do not necessarily reflect the policies or positions of the Institute. We thank three anonymous reviewers for helpful comments.

JUSTICE QUARTERLY, Vol. 11 No. 1, March 1994
© 1994 Academy of Criminal Justice Sciences

physical injuries, suffering, and financial loss caused by offenders and thereby have provided justification for victim compensation programs.

Investigators, however, largely have ignored problems faced by victims of white-collar offenders. Studies in this area lag far behind the more numerous and methodologically more sophisticated studies of street crime victims (Moore and Mills 1990). Survey procedures, for example, now are used routinely to examine the nature and aftermath of victimization by street offenders, but only limited efforts have been made to apply these procedures to victimization by white-collar offenders (e.g., Inter-University Consortium 1992; Levi 1992; Pearce 1990; President's Commission 1967). There are many excellent case studies of the effects of white-collar crime, but most are journalistic in approach, are descriptive in presentation, and feature sensational and therefore atypical criminal incidents (examples are found in Cullen, Maakestad, and Cavender 1987; Douglas and Johnson 1977; Ermann and Lundman 1992; Heilbroner 1972; Hills 1987; Hochstedler 1984; Johnson and Douglas 1978).

## THE PROBLEM

The past neglect of white-collar crime victims is ironic: the problems caused by street crime victimization can be severe, but white-collar crime also exacts a very heavy toll. Its legacy of death and illness is substantial, and no one disputes that aggregate annual monetary losses to white-collar criminals dwarf comparable losses to street offenders (Elias 1990; Hills 1987; Kusic 1989). Moreover, apart from the immediate impact of white-collar crime on individual victims, the wider *delegitimation effects* may be serious. Some 40 years ago Sutherland suggested that it may be harmful to the social fabric in ways uniquely its own. Because it violates trust, white-collar crime breeds distrust, lowers social morale, and "attack[s] the fundamental principles of American institutions" (Sutherland 1949:13).

Sutherland may have been the first to call attention to the costs of white-collar crime, but he is not alone (e.g., President's Commission 1967; Shichor 1989). Nor is he alone in suggesting that these costs may include the erosion of legitimacy for prevailing institutions and persons who hold high-level positions in those institutions. Edelhertz (1980:124) suggests that this effect may be "far more significant than mere dollar losses—no matter how great—because [it goes] to the very heart of the issue of integrity of our society and to that confidence in our private and public institutions that is essential to their usefulness and effectiveness in serving the public."

Observers have identified two potentially significant areas of delegitimation caused by white-collar crime. One is loss of confidence in *political* institutions, processes, and leaders. Crimes committed by public officials and agencies or with their acquiescence may damage the public faith in and regard for political leaders and institutions. The second potential effect is diminution of trust in business leaders and *economic* institutions. "Trust," as Shapiro (1984:2) notes, "is truly the foundation of capitalism." In its absence, "people would not delegate discretionary use of their funds to other entrepreneurs . . . [and] capitalism would break down as funds were stuffed into mattresses, savings accounts, and solo business enterprises rather than invested in the business ventures of American corporations." This may be true particularly when white-collar crime becomes integrated closely with the structure of legitimate business (Conklin 1977:7).

In view of the importance of these arguments, it is remarkable that the delegitimation effects of white-collar crime have been the focus of so little research. In one of the few investigations of this subject, Peters and Welch (1980) examined the electoral consequences of charges of official corruption. Analyzing data from five congressional elections held from 1968 to 1978, they found little apparent effect on voter turnout and election outcomes. In contrast to the aggregate-level approach taken by those authors, we present an individual-level analysis based on personal interviews with former investors in a financial loan institution that failed largely because of criminal conduct by its officers and employees. We pursue two objectives. First, we describe the array of effects experienced by victims, and suggest an interpretation. Second, we explore the personal and institutional delegitimation effects produced by the crime-facilitated collapse of the loan company. We conclude with brief interpretive comments that underscore the importance of sociohistorical and ideological contexts in constructing meanings of white-collar criminal victimization and the potential contributions of social science inquiry.

## BACKGROUND

The Southland Industrial Banking Corporation (SIBC), chartered in 1929, operated for many years as a small loan company in a southeastern state. Under a "grandfather" clause it was permitted to use the word *banking* in its name, even though other industrial loan and thrift companies were prohibited from doing so.

The business of SIBC, which some people referred to as a "bank impersonator," consisted of making loans to individuals and business entities. The most important source of funds for SIBC was money received through the sale of investment certificates; these were remarkably similar to certificates of deposit (CDs) offered by commercial banks and savings and loan institutions. Unlike CDs, the certificates of investment offered by SIBC were not insured, although they generally earned a higher rate of interest than similar accounts at commercial banks and savings and loans. SIBC grew during the 1970s, and eventually operated nine separate branches located in six counties in the eastern part of its home state. In February 1983, some 4,000 individuals and businesses held investment certificates or passbook accounts in SIBC totaling nearly $51 million (R.J. Fast, personal communication, May 28, 1991).

On March 10, 1983, three weeks after the collapse of a local bank whose operations were entangled with its own, SIBC filed a petition to reorganize under Chapter 11 of the Bankruptcy Code. The Federal Deposit Insurance Corporation (FDIC) conducted a special examination of SIBC's assets as of April 4, 1983 to determine whether SIBC might qualify for federal deposit insurance. FDIC revealed "gross mismanagement" of SIBC's resources, including numerous examples of abusive and extremely complicated insider dealings. A variety of state and federal criminal indictments were returned against officers and employees of SIBC. Subsequently the defendants were acquitted of some charges, were found guilty of others, and pleaded guilty to still others. Eventually H.C. Baker, SIBC's former president and the principal defendant in the case, was sentenced to 20 years' federal imprisonment.

The Bankruptcy Code vests in the bankruptcy judge substantial discretion in resolving Chapter 11 petitions (Lebowitz 1986). Once SIBC's Chapter 11 bankruptcy petition was filed, the fate of SIBC and its investors was largely in his hands. The bankruptcy judge is authorized either to oversee a plan for corporate reorganization (if one is submitted) or, alternatively, to order the liquidation of the failed institution and the distribution of its assets to creditors. In this instance, to represent the interest of investors and other creditors, the judge appointed a creditors' committee consisting of seven persons whose investments in SIBC were among the largest. A plan of reorganization was developed by a group of out-of-state investors, their attorneys, the bankruptcy trustee, and the creditors' committee. The plan called for formation of the East State Bank Corporation (ESBC) as successor in interest to SIBC, thus allowing it to be awarded SIBC's remaining assets. These assets, along with capital from the out-of-state investors, would be used to place ESBC on a sound financial footing. A liquidating trust also would be established to recover SIBC's outstanding loans and other debts, which then would be forwarded to ESBC. Underlying the reorganization plan was the assumption that with SIBC's assets as a foundation, with funds provided by the new investors, with the infusion of recovered funds from the liquidating trust, and with competent and honest new management, ESBC would succeed where SIBC had failed. This arrangement would allow ESBC eventually to repay SIBC's victimized depositors and would allow the out-of-state investors to realize a profitable return on their risk capital.

Under the terms of the plan of reorganization, which gained approval from all quarters, businesses and individuals with funds invested at the time of the collapse were defined and treated as "unsecured creditors," and were divided into three categories. Those with less than $1,000 invested or deposited in SIBC received full return of their funds; those with $1,001 to $5,000 invested received a three-year certificate of deposit for the full amount of their investment, albeit at a rate of interest lower than promised by SIBC. Those with more than $5,000 invested or deposited received a 10-year certificate of deposit for 30 percent of their investment; for the remaining 70 percent they received stock claims in the new bank and an interest certificate in the liquidating trust.

Ten years after the collapse of SIBC, these interest certificates have yielded no return to holders. The same is true of the stock claims; in view of the present financial condition of SIBC's successor, there is little chance that they will ever generate any income for victims (T. Du Voisin, personal communication, March 16, 1993). That is, persons with more than $5,000 invested in SIBC have received only 30 percent of their investment, with no guarantee that they ever will receive the remaining 70 percent. Because many of the investors are approaching old age, this outcome seems increasingly likely with the passing years.

The bankruptcy process and the plan of reorganization are central to understanding the outcome of the SIBC case and its impact on former investors. Not only could investors be subject to victimization through direct loss of funds that were tied up in investment certificates and passbook accounts at the time of the SIBC collapse (loss victimization); in addition, for some investors, the bankruptcy process itself became a second source of victimization (resolution victimization). From the outset, former investors and other interested parties were assigned legal statuses and definitions that distorted and (in a minority of cases) greatly intensified the impact of their loss victimization. Exercising his discretionary power (Treister 1986), the bankruptcy judge ruled that SIBC was insolvent 90 days before the bankruptcy petition was filed. He ruled further that depositors and investors who withdrew funds during this 90-day period were "preferential creditors," and ordered them to return the funds to the liquidating trustee. His decision was applied even to investors who redeemed investment certificates that happened to mature during the 90-day period. As a result, these investors could be treated in the same fashion as any who may have acted on "inside information" and who withdrew funds before the collapse. Those who failed to comply with the judge's order to return funds withdrawn during this period were subject to legal action by the liquidating trustee. The judge's "90-day ruling" affected some 1,000 individual account holders. Some of these persons returned their funds voluntarily; the remainder promptly were sued by the trustee.

The trustee obtained summary judgments against all but a fraction of the victims affected by the "90-day rule." He also sued for, and was awarded, interest on the disputed funds. Many victims who initially resisted the trustee's efforts to reclaim their funds eventually negotiated settlements with him, but actions against others remain unconcluded 10 years after the process began. These investors, opposed by the trustee's attorneys, met with nothing but frustration and unfavorable judicial decisions. Because of accumulating interest charges, the sums of money they owed the liquidating trustee eventually far exceeded their original SIBC accounts. The trustee is empowered by the Bankruptcy Code to scrutinize their assets— home, land, automobiles, wages, and the like—for recovery of the contested funds plus interest charges. Their property was subject to seizure by the trustee and could be sold at public auction to satisfy all or part of outstanding judgments. Property belonging to some former investors, in fact, was seized and sold; the wages of other investors were garnisheed; and liens were placed on property belonging to still others.

## METHODS AND DATA

Interview data for this study were collected during 1990-1991. To select a sample of SIBC victims we began by examining a list of the names, the 1983 addresses, and the amount of the deposits or investments of SIBC's former customers that was generated and maintained in the office of the U.S. Bankruptcy Court in the city where SIBC was based. Although it would have been desirable to collect data from a random sample of investors on the list, practical difficulties made this impossible: in the years after 1983, many investors either moved out of the area or died.

Taking care to include ample numbers of persons with large and small investments, and excluding investors who lived outside the immediate metropolitan area where SIBC had its headquarters, we selected approximately 300 names from the 1983 list. We then searched the telephone directory for their telephone numbers, telephoned those persons we could locate, explained the research project, and asked them to grant us a brief interview at a time and place convenient for them. Our selection of respondents was guided by the desire to include a wide range of investors. Investments by members of the interview sample ranged from $1,400 to $205,000 (mean = $33,251; median = $16,000). Of approximately 150 persons contacted, we eventually conducted interviews with 45 investors and two close relatives of now-infirm or deceased investors. The 47 respondents ranged in age from 26 to 89, and averaged 63 years of age. They had completed an average of 15 years of education. Although 69 percent were retired from employment when interviewed, most had spent their later working lives as blue-collar craftsmen, as owner/operators of small businesses, or as public-sector professionals. We do not know how closely the interview sample resembles the total group of former SIBC investors.

Employing qualitative research procedures, we developed an interview guide, used it during the interviews, and revised it several times during the course of the study in response to ongoing analysis. Topics covered included the history and extent of respondents' investments in SIBC, their reactions upon hearing that it had filed for bankruptcy protection, the effects of victimization and financial loss in specific areas of their lives and finances (e.g., physical health and medical care), and the impact of the experience on their respect for and confidence in prevailing economic and political institutions. We conducted the interviews by asking respondents questions designed to elicit their assessments retrospectively before 1983 and at the time of the interview.

Despite the passage of years, most respondents spoke readily about their reactions to the bankruptcy, although they seemed less clear in remembering the details of the process and of the settlement itself. Even so, we cannot rule out the possibility that selective, potentially biasing recall may have been operating when respondents reported their experiences. Nor can we state confidently that any negative recollections of the SIBC experience do not reflect period effects, particularly because we collected our data at a time when the mass media almost daily reported crimes in the savings and loan industry.

We continued contacting and interviewing victims until we were confident of our understanding of the victimization experience. During interviews with the first 29 respondents the interviewer recorded notes on a standardized form; the final 18 interviews were audio tape-recorded and later transcribed. During later interviews we also endeavored to include several standardized questions, such as: "Overall, is your confidence in American business leaders today greater, about the same, or less than it was [seven] years ago?" and "Why?"

To obtain a clearer picture of the range of variation and to determine how closely the interview sample approximated the universe of former SIBC accounts, we also selected from bankruptcy court records, after a random start, a systematic sample of 275 former savings accounts and investment certificates. The records contained no information except the amount of each account and the account holder's name and address. Accounts in the sample ranged in value from $.06 to $190,000 (mean = $9,922; median = $3,768). We used data from this sample of records to estimate the distribution of financial loss victimization among individuals who held SIBC accounts. Comparison of data from the records sample with the characteristics of the interview sample shows that the latter includes a greater number of larger investments, and therefore of investors who lost large sums of money when SIBC collapsed. Therefore the impact of sampling on our findings may be twofold: 1) the interview sample may yield a richer array of evidence of the most serious effects of loss victimization, and 2) to the extent delegitimation parallels loss victimization (i.e., increases with dollar loss), the interview data may be biased somewhat toward discovery of delegitimation effects.

We have no systematic data on the perspectives or experiences of those who declined to be interviewed. They did so for many reasons, chiefly lack of interest, advanced age, embarrassment about their investment in SIBC, and unwillingness to revisit unpleasant memories. One individual, for example, explained that "it's something in the past. Talking about it would just make me more bitter, fill me with hatred again. . . . There's not a thing in this world you can do about it now." If the refusals reflect discouragement, futility, and disgust with the system rather than mere lack of interest, we may underestimate the impact of white-collar crime victimization on delegitimation. Although we are not certain, we think that those for whom the issue was most salient were willing to talk with us; for most nonrespondents, we believe, the refusal to participate reflected caring too little about the matter rather than caring too much. Delegitimation is not a likely outcome for those for whom the episode was "no big deal."

All but two respondents were interviewed in their homes or workplaces. We also interviewed the bankruptcy trustee and a local attorney who represented investors in litigation over the plan of reorganization.

## FINDINGS

### Personal Effects

We found enormous variation in investors' reactions to the bankruptcy of Southland Industrial Banking Corporation and in its impact. This variation is evident, for example, in their attitudes toward the reorganization plan and settlement process. Most respondents did not contact or retain an attorney, voted to accept the plan and the settlement formulas it contained, and have managed more or less successfully to put the experience behind them. Other SIBC victims, however, actively sought to protect their interests throughout the various stages of the bankruptcy process; some refused to surrender to the bankruptcy trustee the funds they were ordered to return. For individual investors, the decision to accept or to resist the settlement process was one of two principal determinants of the long-term impact of the SIBC experience. The other was the victims' potential to recover financially from their losses. This potential is a function not only of the proportion of their total assets that they had invested in Southland Industrial Banking Corporation, but also of their age and earning power. Other things being equal, a 45-year-old individual can hope to eventually recover from financial losses that might destroy a 70-year-old. The importance of this variable is interesting, particularly in light of research showing that fear of crime varies by type of crime and is related directly to sensitivity to risk of victimization (Warr 1987). Elderly victims who had invested a large proportion of their assets in SIBC were especially *vulnerable* to the risk of fraud or other crimes committed by its officers. Although we collected no data on respondents' sensitivity to risk, it seems likely that it is related positively to their level of vulnerability, as measured here by size of potential financial loss from victimization. If we were to construct a continuum of victimization impact, we would place at one end of the continuum young persons with little invested in Southland Industrial Banking Corporation. At the other end would be older persons who had invested a large share of their assets in SIBC and those, including persons who had invested rather modest sums of money in

309

SIBC, who were financially unable to surrender their funds to the bankruptcy trustee or who refused to do so.

Of the 47 victims whose experiences we analyzed, 20 (43%) were inconvenienced to varying degrees by the collapse of SIBC. While its assets were tied up in bankruptcy proceedings, they were unable to cover student fees, pay for the funeral of a loved one, or complete a home remodeling project. Because most of these victims had invested less than $5,000, they eventually received full return of their funds. They generally did not take an active part in the legal proceedings surrounding the liquidation of SIBC; few attended the public meetings that were held by bankruptcy court personnel. They experienced few intense emotions surrounding any aspect of the SIBC reorganization:

> I was ticked off. I earned $3.35 an hour and saved every penny. And greedy people caused my money to be tied up. I had to borrow from my folks.

The victims either never knew or have forgotten all details of the reorganization plan; simply stated, they have long since put it behind them. Ten years after the bankruptcy process was concluded for them, most of the victims rarely think about their involvement with Southland Industrial Banking Corporation. According to information provided by a representative of the out-of-state investors who reorganized SIBC (R.J. Fast, personal communication, May 28, 1991), approximately 50 percent of all the accounts were worth less than $5,000. Analysis of data from the records sample of 275 former savings and investment accounts shows that 55 percent were worth $5,000 or less. Taken together, this information provides persuasive evidence that a majority of the SIBC victims received nearly full return of their financial losses and therefore probably did not suffer long or intensely.

Nineteen of the 47 interviewed victims (40.4%) were affected more severely by their SIBC victimization. Initially, they were surprised and concerned when SIBC's bankruptcy petition was reported by the local media, but most were optimistic that the institution and their investments would be salvaged:

> Q: Do you recall what your first reaction was when you learned that SIBC had filed for bankruptcy?
> A: Well, I didn't have too much of a reaction. I don't know, I just kept thinking that if everybody will stay calm, why maybe everything will come through. I believe that was my basic feeling.
> Q: Were you hopeful, then?
> A: Yeah, I was hopeful. I really was. I'd say that's one of the key words there, that I just had hopes, and felt like that maybe it would pull through.

One 74-year-old investor said that he did not "give it a whole lot of thought" because he assumed that "surely they'd find some way to pull it out, straighten it up." There seemed ample reason for optimism. In the days and weeks that followed the bankruptcy petition, newspaper stories suggested that investors might lose only a small proportion of their funds because of reorganization. As the reorganization process began, however, SIBC's financial condition became apparent, and the reactions changed. For many respondents, hope and optimism gave way to fear, worry, and depression. Others felt intense anger and bitterness. Although these emotions persisted in some cases for many months, eventually they were supplanted in most cases by the realization that the bulk of their funds would not be returned:

> Q:  Did your emotions change, at any time, as this case developed or unfolded?
> A:  Yeah. I couldn't tell you how long, but it come to the place where, you just started looking at it, I reckon what you'd say, in "reality" there. And [I] realized that it was gone.

Nearly all of these investors eventually received at least part of their invested funds, but some lost large sums of money in the reorganization process. Eventually they became resigned to their losses:

> I never had, we never had much money. We worked hard for what we had, you know. Fifteen thousand dollars was a lot of what we had. That's a lot of money, and it hurt.
> Q:  How long did it take you to get over that?
> A:  You don't ever get completely over it, you just accept it.
> Q:  Were you bitter, in the beginning?
> A:  Oh, *yes*! I was very bitter [and would be still] if it would do any good.

Like this victim, others remain angry today: "[T]hey took my money. We was beat out of it by the rich!"

Investors such as these still think occasionally about the SIBC case despite the passage of time, particularly when they must carefully weigh spending on activities or items that could be considered "extras" or frivolous. Some told us they cannot afford to air-condition their home, had waited longer than normal before painting the house, or had forgone long-distance travel. As one respondent told us, "It'd be nice to have the money, but I don't. So you just have to go on." When their thoughts return to the SIBC experience, they feel cheated, not only because of the loss of their funds but also because of their inability to enjoy life as they would wish. Some, for example, regret that they cannot help their children or grandchildren with fiscal matters. This group consists predominantly of

311

those who held investment certificates worth more than $10,000, approximately 30 percent of the accounts in our records sample.

In contrast with the investors we have discussed to this point, a smaller proportion of victims were devastated by their experiences with SIBC. They were stunned, became fearful, or grew severely depressed by the first news of the collapse of Southland Industrial Banking Corporation. A woman told us that "[w]hen [her father] heard about [it], he called me. He sounded real shaky." Another former investor told us, "I was shocked. I couldn't believe it. . . . I just couldn't believe it was possible, you know, that something like that could happen." Victims such as these suffered catastrophic financial or emotional loss caused by the collapse and reorganization of SIBC. They saw their financial plans wrecked, and their sense of fiscal security was deeply eroded or destroyed:

> The worst part about this whole experience was when [her father] . . . realized that the money he worked hard for, and saved all those years, was gone. My daddy told me, "I should have burned it all, given it to the poor, or squandered it." . . . From then on out he was just like a beaten-down person.

Despite the passage of years, the loss of funds continues to take a heavy toll in worry, depression, and despondency among those who survive. They live daily with uncertainty and fear about the future:

> Q: How often do you think about the SIBC experience?
> A: Oh my, every day. Every day. Every day for eight years. I go to bed with it. I get up with it. I think of it through the day. And my husband. . . . I haven't seen my husband smile in eight years. . . . I tell you, that SIBC just destroyed any happiness that we could have had. . . . Really, it destroyed our life. We're not happy people anymore.

For some respondents, the most severe blow they sustained in the collapse of SIBC was less financial than emotional and psychological. The sums of money they had invested in SIBC did not distinguish them significantly from most of their fellow victims, but they were notable for their resistance to the reorganization process and the bankruptcy trustee's actions.

Because of data limitations, we cannot explain why some victims resisted the trustee's actions while others acquiesced. The ranks of resisters include many who believe their actions reflect unswerving commitment to principles of democratic citizenship, values of personal liberty, and opposition to injustice. They are deeply resentful that their decisions made them targets of what one called "debt collector tactics" and potentially subjected them to the label "criminal" because of their failure to comply with court orders:

I don't feel like a free human being anymore. The bankruptcy court and the trustee has the power over our life. And to think that the government has such a power over you, it's terrible. And, really, its the United States government, the law that they have, that's doing it to people. And that's not right, because we're not *criminals*!

Despite the passage of years, these victims remain extremely angry and resentful. These emotions are intensified by the belief that they should have been permitted to contest judicial decisions and other issues before a jury of ordinary citizens rather than solely before the bankruptcy judge. Some lived for years with constant uncertainty about the future and with a level of stress that was heightened by its simultaneous effect on loved ones:

Q: What's been the impact of this experience with SIBC on your life today?
A: It's destroying us. It's destroying us. Especially my wife, especially my wife. She was trained to look up to and obey an authority figure. I don't necessarily agree with that. Sometimes the authority figures are wrong. So, as a result, she's a walking bag of nerves, very short tempered [and] despondent. And I've been the same way, by the way. I've had my ups and downs.

Friedman (1985:67) believes that recent decades have seen the emergence, from legislation, court decisions, and administrative rulings, of a norm of "total justice," a "general notion that catastrophes of all sorts 'earn' compensation for the victims, so long as the victim was not evil enough to deserve the blows of fate." Like many of the victims we interviewed, the resisters understand that state legislators and executives could have resuscitated SIBC and spared it from bankruptcy. Some are bitter about the officials' refusal to do so:

Q: Who do you blame for all of this, everything that has happened to you?
A: Well, naturally, [H.C. Baker]. But, you know, I blame the state of Tennessee, because they knew what [he was] doing. . . . And why didn't they do something? . . . I think [state banking officials] and [the governor] and all those people could have done something better than what they did with SIBC, letting it go into bankruptcy. . . . They could've had another form of liquidation. . . . I think we were let down by the government.

We cannot rule out the possibility that those who resisted the trustee simply believed it was the state's obligation either to compensate them or to provide a proper forum to contest the trustee's actions. Whatever their motives, however, those who resisted are informed and extremely critical about the bankruptcy process and

313

the trustee's actions. One respondent, suppressing her own bitterness, recounted that a principal party in the reorganization process acknowledged openly that "it's not right, it's just legal!"

Unquestionably the problems caused by resistance created enormous emotional stress. An 82-year-old widow, for example, told us she had difficulty sleeping for several months for fear that she would lose her home. Subsequently she settled with the trustee in order to gain some "peace of mind." Her experience is not unusual. Another widow, who unsuccessfully appealed the court's summary judgment against her, looked around her home during the interview and said "It's all I have. I have no money. This is all I have. Where can I come up with the money they're talking about?" Aware that her home could be seized and sold at auction to satisfy the judgment and also knowing that state law permits her only a $5,000 homestead exemption, she fears an indigent and homeless future: "Where can I go on $5,000? I can't live without this place. This is Ed's [deceased husband] and my home." Like all of the victims in this group, she endured inestimable, protracted psychological suffering. Drawing from records sample data and the data on legal actions taken by the trustee, we estimate that those who suffered most severely may account for as many as 15 percent of the 4,000 former investors in Southland Industrial Banking Corporation. They number eight, or 17 percent, of the interview sample.

## Delegitimation Effects

After exploring the personal impacts of victimization, we questioned the members of the interview sample to determine whether the experience had diminished their confidence in prevailing political and financial leaders and institutions. Did this series of white-collar crimes produce the delegitimation effects hypothesized by scholars? This question is not easy to answer, largely because our data lack strictly comparable information from all respondents, and thus will not permit us to disentangle confidently possible antecedents of declining trust in leaders and institutions. Some respondents, for example, gave unmistakable evidence of growing disenchantment with political leaders. A subsequent opinion poll of the state's adult population showed that their concerns were shared by a substantial number of their peers ("Results," 1991). Topics of critical evaluation by respondents included intercession by five U.S. senators—the "Keating Five"—in threatened federal regulatory action against a large savings and loan institution that subsequently collapsed, charges of criminal conduct by officials of the Department of Housing and Urban Development, and action by members of Congress to raise their annual salary during a time of national belt tightening. One respondent commented on

> . . . the complete arrogance, as I see it, of an organization [Congress] that passes itself [pay] raises when people are being laid off from work left and right, [their] inability to even address, to even admit that there is a problem. It's like the king with no clothes—the kid's story—he thinks everything is fine. And nobody's gonna tell him any different, except the children, who tell the truth.

Victims were particularly disappointed with government's response to the problems of Southland Industrial Banking Corporation. A clear majority ranked state banking regulators just behind SIBC's principal officers when apportioning blame for the collapse of SIBC. They faulted state officials especially for permitting SIBC to continue operating past the point when its freewheeling operating style and fiscal problems should have been apparent to competent regulatory overseers:

> I feel like the state of Tennessee banking department, or insurance department, I guess it was, didn't do a very good job. And [they] let that go on without doing something, they were remiss in what they should have done, you know. To me, it's negligence on their part, that it ever got that far.

Despite this backdrop of increasing dissatisfaction and frustration with political leaders, most victims reported little, if any, loss of support for political institutions which can be attributed solely to crime committed by SIBC officers. They distinguished between evaluations of specific political leaders and evaluations of political institutions; their decline in confidence in the former rarely extended to the latter. Pressed to explain why they did not suffer stronger persisting effects of institutional delegitimation, a number of respondents said "It [American institutions] may not be perfect but it's the best there is." Most vote as often today as before the collapse of SIBC, and no subjects attributed their decline in voting to that experience.

The story is entirely different, however, for those who were targets of actions by the liquidating trustee:

> Q: Do you feel the same way about the law today as you did before this incident?
> A: See, I never had much [experience] with the law. I never gave it much thought. . . . If I was speeding, and I was caught, hey, so I was speeding. I'd pay the fine. I don't hold the law in as high esteem as I used to. I don't think we were given any protection under the law, be it state or federal.

Similar comments were offered by another respondent:

> [Action by the bankruptcy trustee to seize his assets] was
> the first in a series of occurrences that . . . to a great extent
> changed my view of what this country really stands for. . . .
> [Previously] I believed much more readily in the philoso-
> phies, the theories that we have these basic rights that are
> inviolate. I don't believe that anymore. Now I believe that
> *money* rules. And occasionally public opinion can sway.

How did their experiences affect respondents' confidence in
business institutions and leaders? Here we elicited evidence of substantial disillusionment and declining confidence. The combination
of massive crime in the savings and loan industry (Calavita and
Pontell 1990) and Wall Street investment scandals has left the respondents confused and not so confident that financial institutions
and safeguards are in good hands. Just as when they discussed
confidence in political institutions and leaders, most respondents
did not always find it easy to distinguish the effects of victimization
from the overall effect of these contextual developments. As one
man stated, "You think about it more or less all together. They're
all out to make a fast buck. And they don't care how they get it,
legally or what." Several, however, distinguished carefully between
the effects of context and the impact of the SIBC experience as
causes for their admitted decline in confidence in American business leaders:

> Q:   Overall, is your confidence in American business lead-
> ers today greater, about the same, or less than it was seven
> years ago?
> A:   I'd say it's less than it was. Because the more I see,
> and the more I read, and the more I hear, it appears that—
> this savings and loan thing—the people that handle and
> loan money aren't "purists." They don't give a hoot
> whether they do it properly or improperly, as I see it. Now
> [that is] not caused from my experience [with SIBC], it's
> just developed that way.

Most respondents told us that the crimes of SIBC and the bankruptcy reorganization process served as "a focus" for growing concern or "sensitized" them to national political and economic
conditions that they found unsettling.

Like their assessments of political leaders and institutions, the
victims' loss of confidence in business leaders did not extend to
business institutions. We explored, for example, whether victimization affected their subsequent investment behaviors and their participation in financial institutions and processes. Does
victimization by white-collar crime cause victims to withhold investment and participation in economic institutions and markets?
The data suggest that in this case it did not, although victims reported that they now invest more cautiously by first "checking

things out more carefully" and by dispersing their investments throughout several institutions and programs. Nearly all subjects also said that they invest only in federally insured programs or institutions; this response attests either to their continuing faith in government or to their general unawareness of investment options. We can summarize by saying that loss of trust and confidence in political and financial leaders was commonplace, although institutional delegitimation was rare. The strength of delegitimation effects was influenced heavily by the severity of victimization impact and by the requirement that investors return funds to the bankruptcy trustee.

We suggest two reasons for failure to find evidence of widespread or persisting institutional delegitimation effects: 1) victims' tendency to individualize responsibility for institutional failure and personal misfortune, and 2) cohort or generational effects. Subjects' responses to questions about the shortcomings of political institutions reveal a distinct tendency to invoke individual-centered attributions of responsibility. The subjects spoke readily about the faults of individual officials who happen to occupy positions in state and federal government, but they generally reserved criticism of political institutions:

> Like I said, I don't have nearly the faith in the people who are holding positions now. I think we have the best system in the world. . . . It just depends on who is in positions of making decisions. I think, right now, just to be blunt about it, we've got a bunch of self-serving—I hesitate to use the word, but I'd love to. They're just self-serving [and] that's why they got into the positions they are in.

Even while we emphasize our respondents' tendency to fault individuals rather than institutions, we acknowledge that it may be related to important characteristics of the SIBC case. The crimes of SIBC were crimes of readily identifiable *individuals* whose families were known personally to many of its investors. The effects of white-collar crime, whether on individual well-being or on institutional legitimacy, may differ according to the specific nature of the crime. Crimes committed by large, remote, impersonal corporations, as in the Ford Pinto case (Cullen et al. 1987), for example, may produce stronger condemnation of institutions.

Perhaps it is noteworthy that the SIBC incident occurred in a region of the United States with a long tradition of political conservatism, whose inhabitants value and celebrate individual responsibility and self-reliance. Historically, for example, workers in this region resisted labor unions because they feared the unions would be a meddlesome force and would limit or interfere with employees'

317

prerogatives to work under conditions and terms of their own choosing. In light of this cultural heritage, individualistic interpretations of misfortune may be particularly appealing.

Whatever its sources, the tendency to individualize responsibility is evident also in responses to the question "Who is to blame for what happened to you?" We noted earlier that victims blame SIBC officers, state regulators, and political figures for the collapse of SIBC. Their apportionment of responsibility does not stop there, however; they reserve a major share for themselves:

> Q:   Has this experience affected the way you think about the government, in any way?
> A:   I don't think the government was to fault, I think we were. We were gullible. And we were greedy, because we wanted the big interest.
> Q:   You blame yourself?
> A:   I blame myself. . . . I should have known better. I've done business, I know better than that.

Another said simply, "I think I was greedy, in trying to get 'super maximum interest' on that money I had." Indeed, the words *greedy* or *greed* are used more often than any others in spontaneous self-attributions elicited in response to questions about responsibility for the incident:

> I'm disgusted with me, that I could have been such a dope, you know. And not really looked a little deeper and been a little more careful. . . . I should have been more careful. . . . And I should have been a little more responsible than I was, really. . . . [And] I'm still just kinda mad at Mr. Baker.

Ten years after the incident occurred, the self-blaming and embarrassment felt by some victims of the SIBC case borders on stigma:

> You know, we've never even told our kids that it happened. We would hate for them to know that we were that dumb.
> Q:   You've never told your kids?
> A:   No, we never have.
> Q:   Now you said, before I turned on the tape recorder, that you really don't want *anyone* to know?
> A:   That's right.
> Q:   You feel that bad about it, yourself?
> A:   I just feel *stupid*! That's the way I feel about it. I feel madder at myself than I do [at] Southland Industrial Banking . . .
> Q:   Did you go to any of the public meetings that were held?
> A:   No! We stayed away from them. We were afraid somebody would see us there.

Victims looked to the shortcomings of *individuals*, including themselves, and less to political and economic institutions as the primary cause of their misfortune.

Cohort effects also may contribute to respondents' tendency to avoid blaming institutions. The majority grew up during the Great Depression (Elder 1974), products of economically depressed circumstances, and their achievements in life surpassed their childhood prospects and expectations. They experienced a measure of success and mobility. Their generation also helped defeat the Axis powers in World War II. Several of our respondents served in World War II combat, returned to a grateful nation, and together with their peers set to work to manufacture and consume the products that fueled postwar prosperity. For them, as for most of their generation, the years of work and child rearing were the years of the "American celebration" (Mills 1958). In those years as well, political leaders waged a cold war with communist states, and encouraged citizens to define the American experience and American institutions as exemplars for all nations. Although our interview notes and transcripts contain no indication of any mention by respondents, most were interviewed at a time when the Soviet Union and its eastern European alliances, America's politically defined opponent through nearly all of their adult years, were disintegrating. We cannot speculate whether these developments affected their responses to victimization by Southland Industrial Banking Corporation, but it is doubtful that respondents' faith in and support for American institutions could be shaken easily.

## IMPLICATIONS AND INTERPRETATION

Most studies of criminal victimization not only focus on street crimes but also, because of limited follow-up, report only short-term effects. In our study of white-collar crime victims, we found enduring and pervasive effects, for some individuals, nearly a decade after their victimization. In this respect our findings echo those from studies of victims of personal violence, whose victimization often results in long-lasting trauma (Herman, Russell, and Trocki 1986; Kilpatrick, Amick, and Resnick 1990; Pynoos and Eth 1984; Resick 1990). Certainly we do not claim that the effects on most of the victimized investors in our study approach in seriousness or damage the effects suffered by victims of violence, but we can draw two implications. First, greater attention to long-term consequences of crime would yield a richer account of the costs of crimes of all sorts. Second, certain categories of white-collar crime—such as environmental devastation and disasters resulting from corporate negligence or malfeasance—might tend especially to generate long-term effects of victimization.

What do our findings imply for current theoretical constructions of the link between victimization by white-collar crime and delegitimation? They suggest that a perception of responsiveness and fair treatment by state officials may condition the severity of delegitimation effects. Many respondents believe that the bankruptcy judge acted with indifference to their individual claims and with disregard for substantive justice. They fault him, for example, for not making special arrangements to accommodate the large number of investors who sought to attend routine judicial proceedings in the case. These were held in the regular bankruptcy courtroom, which has severely limited seating capacity. From the outset, many victims felt that they were treated as little more than potentially lawless and disruptive irritants. To ensure that order was maintained during public informational meetings held by the bankruptcy court, U.S. marshals maintained surveillance throughout the hall. This security precaution offended some investors and angered others. Echoing their words and sentiments, one respondent who was devastated by the SIBC experience told us:

> I think we've been mistreated much worse by the people who have made decisions since [SIBC owners] went to jail than anything the [owners] did. . . . [T]his incident has opened my eyes to just how unfair things can be and how little concerned the people who are supposed to [resolve such matters] in a just manner seem to be about doing so.

Many SIBC investors were victimized twice: first by the collapse of SIBC itself and second by the official response. Our findings on this point are consistent with reports by others who have investigated the experiences of victims, both of street crime and of white-collar crime (Edelhertz 1980; Edelhertz and Rogovin 1980; Steele 1975). When victims of street crime, for example, seek assistance with or redress of their complaints, often they

> discover . . . that they [are] treated as appendages of a system appallingly out of balance. They learn that somewhere along the way the system has lost track of the simple truth that it is supposed to be fair and to protect those who obey the law while punishing those who break it. Somewhere along the way the system began to serve lawyers and judges and defendants, treating the victim with institutionalized disinterest (President's Task Force 1982:vi).

In this regard, apparently they are not alone. Vaughan and Carlo (1975:158) discovered that a group of citizens victimized by an appliance repairman "repeatedly expressed their indignation at being cheated and their frustration at being unable to get satisfaction from the offender, or from anyplace else." A study of fraud in California that victimized many elderly citizens pointed to the "callous indifference that the system demonstrates toward those whom it is particularly charged with assisting" (Geis 1976:15).

Ironically, victims with the most extensive contact with the official system for redress of injury often emerge from the experience more disillusioned and more disheartened than when they began (Casper 1972). One potential explanation is a belief that they generally were not treated satisfactorily by its various offices. In telephone interviews with 733 Chicago residents who had personal experience with the police or the courts in the previous year, respondents' perceptions of whether they were treated fairly explained most of the variance in their assessments of procedural justice (Tyler, 1988). Citizens' perceptions are shaped by several aspects of interaction between citizens and police or court personnel: authorities' effort to be fair; their honesty; whether their behavior is consistent with ethical standards; whether opportunities for representation are provided; the quality of the decisions made; whether opportunities to appeal decisions are offered; and whether the authorities' behavior shows bias. In the eyes of SIBC's victims, the bankruptcy process was unnecessarily formal, legalistic, closed to their effective participation, and therefore unfair.

The findings of our research suggest, further, that the delegitimation effects of victimization by white-collar crime are moderated by aspects of the cultural and ideological context in which it occurs. Particularly important may be the presence of values of individualism and ideologies that foster and support constructions of blame which almost exclusively emphasize failure on the part of the individual, often of the victim. We are not alone in finding evidence of this situation. In reviewing evidence from many public opinion polls over nearly three decades, Lipset and Schneider note that "the public has shown a tendency to personalize social problems, that is, to attribute them to inept leaders and corrupt powerholders. . . . [As a result] people lose faith in leaders much more easily than they lose confidence in the system" (1987:378-79). "Individualism," according to Bellah et al. (1985:142), "lies at the very core of American culture." An important consequence is that Americans generally lack a vocabulary to articulate the overarching moral or political implications and significance of their experiences. To the extent that victims of white-collar crime are limited by language to explanations expressed in terms of individual culpability, to that extent institutions are immune both to eroded confidence and to demands for reform.

A similar preference for individual-centered attributions of responsibility finds expression in victims' self-blaming, which other investigators also have reported. Interviews with victims of fraud showed that they are "conscious of the primacy of the *caveat emptor* principle in relation to commercial transactions" and the *prima facie* assumption of negligence" on their part (Levi 1991:5). They experienced great "concern about their own failings in being caught out, and about how foolish other people would think them if they discovered that they had been conned" (p.11). Victimization "was a blow not only to their pockets but also to their self-esteem and (where others had been told about it) to their social reputation" (p. 5). Walsh and Schram (1980) argue that the experiences of rape victims and victims of white-collar crime share several important characteristics—among others, that questions about guilt or responsibility often turn on the victim's behavior. Like rape victims, persons victimized by white-collar crime have been prepared by socialization and life experiences to accept these pervasive attributions of personal culpability. They often look inward to explain their misfortunes.

When political movements are aimed at promoting interpretations of victimization that apportion blame more evenly between individual and external causes, inevitably they confront obstacles. One of the most important of these obstacles is official refusal to acknowledge and validate the status of *victim* (Elias 1986, 1990). The President's Commission on Victims of Crime (1982) does not contain a single reference to white-collar crime or its victims. The National Crime Victimization Survey spends millions of dollars annually to collect data on street crime and its victims but shows little interest in collecting comparable data on white-collar crimes (Inter-University Consortium 1992). Continued neglect or indifference by social scientists towards mistreated or victimized groups also may play a part in denying legitimacy to them and their suffering. Currently the study of white-collar crime victimization is at the same stage as was domestic violence in the early 1970s. At that time, domestic violence was largely hidden from view by prevailing ideologies that denied or discounted the victims' suffering. Along the same lines, we have shown here that some victims of white-collar crime endure enormous long-term pain and suffering.

## REFERENCES

Bellah, R., R. Madsen, W.M. Sullivan, A. Widler, and S.M. Tipton (1985) *Habits of the Heart*. Berkeley: University of California Press.

Calavita, K. and H.N. Pontell (1990) "'Heads I Win, Tails You Lose': Deregulation, Crime, and Crisis in the Savings and Loan Industry." *Crime and Delinquency* 36:309-41.

Casper, J.D. (1972) *Criminal Justice: The Consumer's Perspective*. Washington, DC: U.S. Department of Justice.

Conklin, J.E. (1977) *Illegal but Not Criminal*. Englewood Cliffs, NJ: Prentice-Hall.

Cullen, F.T., W.J. Maakestad, and G. Cavender (1987) *Corporate Crime under Attack*. Cincinnati: Anderson.

Davis, R.C. and M. Henley (1990) "Victim Service Programs." In A.J. Lurigio, W.C. Skogan, and R.C. Davis (eds.), *Victims of Crime*, pp. 157-71. Newbury Park, CA: Sage.

Douglas, J.D. and J.M. Johnson, eds. (1977) *Official Deviance*. Philadelphia: Lippincott.

Edelhertz, H. (1980) "Appendix B: White Collar Crime." In H. Edelhertz and C. Rogovin (eds.), *A National Strategy for Containing White Collar Crime*, pp. 119-32. Lexington, MA: Heath.

Edelhertz, H. and C. Rogovin, eds. (1980) *A National Strategy for Containing White Collar Crime*. Lexington, MA: Heath.

Elder, G.H. (1974) *Children of the Great Depression*. Chicago: University of Chicago Press.

Elias, R. (1986) *The Politics of Victimization*. New York: Oxford University Press.
—— (1990) "Which Victim Movement? The Politics of Victim Policy." In A.J. Lurigio, W.G. Skogan, and R.C. Davis (eds.), *Victims of Crime: Problems, Policies, and Programs*, pp. 226-50. Newbury Park, CA: Sage.
—— (1993) *Victims Still: The Political Manipulation of Crime Victims*. Newbury Park, CA: Sage.

Ermann, M.D. and R.J. Lundman, eds. (1992) *Corporate and Governmental Deviance*. 4th ed. New York: Oxford University Press.

Friedman, L. (1985) *Total Justice*. Boston: Beacon.

Geis, G. (1976) "Defrauding the Elderly." In J. Goldsmith and S. Goldsmith (eds.), *Crime and the Elderly*, pp. 7-19. Lexington, MA: Heath.

Heilbroner, R.L., ed. (1972) *In the Name of Profit*. New York: Warner.

Herman, J., D. Russell, and K. Trocki (1986) "Long-Term Effects of Incestuous Abuse in Childhood." *American Journal of Psychiatry* 143:1293-96.

Hills, S.L., ed. (1987) *Corporate Violence*. Totowa, NJ: Rowman and Littlefield.

Hochstedler, E., ed. (1984) *Corporations as Criminals*. Beverly Hills: Sage.

Inter-University Consortium for Political and Social Research (1992) *Fraud Victimization Survey, 1990*. Ann Arbor: ICPSR.

Johnson, J.M. and J.D. Douglas, eds. (1978) *Crime at the Top*. Philadelphia: Lippincott.

Kilpatrick, D.G., A. Amick, and H.S. Resnick (1990) *The Impact of Homicide on Surviving Family Members*. Washington: National Institute of Justice.

Kusic, J.Y. (1989) *White Collar Crime 101 Prevention Handbook*. Vienna, VA: White Collar Crime 101.

Lebowitz, H.M. (1986) *Bankruptcy Deskbook*. New York: Practicing Law Institute.

Levi, M. (1991) "The Victims of Fraud." Paper presented at the second Liverpool Conference on Fraud, Corruption, and Business Crime, University of Liverpool.
—— (1992) "White-Collar Crime Victimization." In K. Schlegel and D. Weisburd (eds.), *White-Collar Crime Reconsidered*, pp. 169-92. Boston: Northeastern University Press.

Lipset, S.M. and W. Schneider (1987) *The Confidence Gap*. (Revised ed.). Baltimore: Johns Hopkins University Press.

Mills, C.W. (1958) *The Sociological Imagination*. New York: Oxford University Press.

Moore, E. and M. Mills (1990) "The Neglected Victims and Unexamined Costs of White Collar Crime." *Crime and Delinquency* 36:408-18.

Pearce, F. (1990) *Second Islington Crime Survey*. Kingston, Ont.: Queen's University.

Peters, J.G. and S. Welch (1980) "The Effects of Charges of Corruption on Voting Behavior in Congressional Elections." *American Political Science Review* 74:697-708.

President's Commission on Law Enforcement and Administration of Justice (1967) *The Challenge of Crime in a Free Society*. Washington, DC: U.S. Government Printing Office.

President's Task Force on Victims of Crime (1982) *Final Report*. Washington, DC: U.S. Government Printing Office.

Pynoos, R.S. and S. Eth (1984) "The Child as Witness to Homicide." *Journal of Social Issues* 40:87-108.

Resick, R.A. (1990) "Victims of Sexual Assault." In A.J. Lurigio, W.G. Skogan, and R.C. Davis (eds.) *Victims of Crime: Problems, Policies, and Programs*, pp. 69-86. Beverly Hills: Sage.

"Results of the Tennessee Poll." (1991) Knoxville *News-Sentinel*, November 17, p. A1.

Shapiro, S. (1984) *Wayward Capitalists*. New Haven: Yale University Press.

Shichor, D. (1989) "Corporate Deviance and Corporate Victimization: A Review and Some Elaborations." *International Review of Victimology* 1:67-85.

Steele, E.H. (1975) "Fraud, Dispute and the Consumer: Responding to Consumer Complaints." *University of Pennsylvania Law Review* 123:1107-86.

Sutherland, E.H. (1949) *White Collar Crime*. New York: Holt, Rinehart and Winston.

Treister, G.M. (1986) *Fundamentals of Bankruptcy Law*. Philadelphia: American Law Institute and American Bar Association.

Tyler, T.R. (1988) "What Is Procedural Justice? Criteria Used by Citizens to Assess the Fairness of Legal Procedures." *Law and Society Review* 22:103-35.

Vaughan, D. and G. Carlo (1975) "The Appliance Repairman: A Study of Victim Responsiveness and Fraud." *Journal of Research in Crime and Delinquency* 12:153-61.

Walsh, M.E. and D.D. Schram (1980) "The Victim of White-Collar Crime: Accuser or Accused?" In G. Geis and E. Stotland (eds.), *White-Collar Crime*, pp. 32-51. Beverly Hills: Sage.

Warr, M. (1987) "Fear of Victimization and Sensitivity to Risk." *Journal of Quantitative Criminology* 3:29-46.

# Cross-Site Analysis of Victim-Offender Mediation in Four States

## Mark S. Umbreit
## Robert B. Coates

*This article reports on the first cross-site analysis of victim-offender mediation programs in the United States, working with juvenile courts in Albuquerque, Austin, Minneapolis, and Oakland. A total of 1,153 interviews were conducted with victims and offenders. These included pre- and postmediation interviews and the use of two comparison groups. Court officials were interviewed and 28 observations of mediations were conducted. The vast majority of victims and offenders experienced the mediation process and outcome as fair and were quite satisfied with it. Mediation resulted in significantly greater satisfaction and perceptions of fairness for victims, as well as significantly higher restitution completion by offenders, than found in comparison groups. Some implications for juvenile justice policy are offered.*

Mediation of conflict between crime victims and offenders has received increased attention over the past two decades. Through the process of allowing certain crime victims to meet face-to-face with offenders in the presence of a trained mediator, the issues of both victim assistance and

**MARK S. UMBREIT:** Assistant Professor, School of Social Work, University of Minnesota. **ROBERT B. COATES:** Consultant/Senior Research Associate, Salt Lake City, Utah.

The data reported in this article were collected through research made possible by grants to the Minnesota Citizens Council on Crime and Justice from the State Justice Institute in Alexandria, Virginia; the Hewlett Foundation in Menlo Park, California; and the Conflict and Change Center at the University of Minnesota. The Citizens Council Mediation Services contracted with the School of Social Work at the University of Minnesota for the services of the Principal Investigator. Points of view expressed in this article are those of the authors and do not necessarily represent the official position of the State Justice Institute, the Hewlett Foundation, or the University of Minnesota. A special thanks is due to the staff and volunteers of the four victim-offender mediation programs at the Citizens Council Mediation Services in Minneapolis; the New Mexico Center for Dispute Resolution in Albuquerque; the Office of Prisoner and Community Justice of Catholic Charities/Oakland Diocese; and the Travis County Juvenile Court Department in Austin, Texas. Also, the authors' research assistants made an invaluable contribution: Madeline Brown, Andy Galaway, Deborah Johnson, Boris Kalanj, Autumn Riddle, Sarah Orrick, Cynthia Wright, Mike Schumacher, Laurie Smith, Becki Tovar. The restitution completion analysis reported in this study is based, in part, upon the methodology developed by Andy Galaway in a prior smaller study of cases at the Minneapolis program site.

CRIME & DELINQUENCY, Vol. 39 No. 4, October 1993 565-585
© 1993 Sage Publications, Inc.

offender accountability can be addressed. Victims can receive answers to questions they may have about the crime, express their concerns directly to the person who victimized them, and have direct influence on the penalty the offender will receive. Offenders have an opportunity to take direct responsibility for their actions, portray themselves as more than just "criminals," and make amends through negotiation and payment of restitution to their victims. Offenders also have influence over the nature and amount of the restitution component of their sanctioning (Umbreit 1985, 1986; Zehr and Umbreit 1982).

Although there were only a handful of victim-offender mediation programs in the late 1970s, there are currently more than 100 programs in the United States, 26 in Canada, 18 in England, 25 in Germany, 40 in France, 54 in Norway, and 20 in Finland. Austria has a federal policy of promoting the use of mediation with young offenders (Umbreit 1991a). The vast majority of victim-offender mediation programs in the United States work with juvenile offenders (Gehm 1990; Hughes and Schneider 1989), although a growing number work with adult offenders as well.

The purpose of such mediation sessions is not to simply address the offender's issues related to treatment or accountability, nor is the purpose to focus entirely upon meeting the needs of victims of crime. Rather, mediation is meant to benefit both parties by addressing emotional and informational needs, as well as restoring victim losses and the offender's ability to be a law-abiding member of the community.

The growth of victim-offender mediation and reconciliation programs in North America and Europe has occurred within the larger context of restorative justice theory (Umbreit 1991a; Wright 1991; Zehr 1990). Rather than viewing crime as an offense against the state, "restorative justice" emphasizes that crime is a violation of one person by another. The provision of opportunities for victims and offenders to be directly involved in resolving criminal conflicts through dialogue and negotiation whenever possible is a basic element of restorative justice theory. Establishing blame for past behavior is far less important than problem solving for the future, which can restore emotional and physical losses for all parties involved in crime, including victims, offenders, and the larger community.

From the perspective of restorative justice theory, harsh and costly punishment of the offender is less important than empowering victims in their search for closure (i.e., receiving important information, expressing their feelings, and moving on with their lives) through direct involvement in the justice process, impressing on offenders the real human impact of their behaviors, and compensating victims for their losses through restitution by the offender. Both victims and offenders are viewed as active players in resolving most criminal conflicts.

This article reports on the first large cross-site analysis of victim-offender mediation programs to occur in the United States involving multiple data sets, research questions, comparison groups, and multiple quantitative and qualitative techniques of analysis. The programs examined worked closely with juvenile courts in Albuquerque (NM), Austin (TX), the Minneapolis-St. Paul area (MN), and the Oakland-East Bay area (CA). Issues related to the mediation process and outcomes, client satisfaction, perceptions of fairness, restitution completion, and recidivism are examined.

Victim-offender mediation, referred to as victim-offender reconciliation by some programs, has grown considerably over the past nearly two decades. Although it appears to be making an important contribution to meeting the needs of many crime victims, offenders, and court systems, there are only a limited number of empirical studies that have evaluated its effectiveness. Several small studies have found that the mediation process had a positive impact upon both victims and offenders (Coates and Gehm 1989; Davis, Tichane, and Grayson 1980; Dignan 1990; Gehm 1990; Umbreit 1991b, 1990, 1989). This finding was confirmed in a large multisite study in England (Marshall and Merry 1990), as well as by the initial results of the current study (Umbreit and Coates 1992). No study to date, however, has examined the impact of victim-offender mediation upon successful completion of the offender's restitution obligation to his or her victim. Nor has any study in the United States used comparison groups to examine the impact of mediation upon victims and offenders in multiple sites representing different geographical regions of the country.

## *METHODOLOGY*

Random assignment of subjects into experimental and control groups was not possible because of ethical concerns of court officials and program staff. Therefore, a quasi-experimental design (Cook and Campbell 1979) was employed consisting of quantitative and qualitative data collection and analysis, involving multiple data sets, research questions, and comparison groups. A total of 1,153 interviews were conducted with crime victims and juvenile offenders: 304 premediation interviews, 432 postmediation interviews, and 417 interviews with persons in two comparison groups. The study focused on the following research questions. Who participates in mediation and why? How does the mediation process work? How do participants in mediation evaluate it? What do court officials think about mediation? What were the immediate outcomes of mediation? What is the impact of mediation on restitution completion? What is the impact of mediation on recidivism?

Attitudes of victims and offenders regarding a number of important issues in the mediation process were examined through the use of pre- and postmediation interviews. Client satisfaction and perceptions of fairness were examined through use of postmediation interviews and two comparison groups: (a) victims and offenders who were referred to the mediation program but did not participate in mediation ("referred/no mediation"); and (b) victims and offenders within the same jurisdiction who had been matched (with the mediation sample) on the offender variables of age, race, sex, and offense but who were never referred to the mediation program ("nonreferral"). Premediation interviews were conducted over the telephone up to a week before the mediation. Postmediation interviews were conducted with the subjects, usually at their homes, approximately 2 months after the mediation. Comparison group interviews were conducted over the telephone approximately 2 months after the case disposition date.

Restitution completion by offenders in victim-offender mediation programs as well as recidivism were analyzed through use of a comparison group (nonreferral) from the same jurisdiction; group members were matched on variables of age, race, sex, offense, and restitution amount. Offenders in this matched sample were ordered to pay restitution through the existing restitution program in the probation office.

All victims and offenders referred to the mediation programs during 1990-1991 were given the opportunity to participate in the study. Table 1 describes the subsamples for the mediation group and the two comparison groups.

Eleven data collection instruments for interviewing of juvenile offenders and their victims were developed. The interview schedules consisted of both open-ended and closed-ended items, including Likert-type questions. Program monitoring, which consisted of review of program files, mediated restitution agreements, interviews with staff and volunteers, and observations of mediation sessions, indicated that the mediation intervention was consistent across all four sites.

*PROGRAM SITES*

The programs in Albuquerque, Minneapolis, and Oakland were the three primary sites, whereas a fourth program, in Austin, was added later in the study and received a more limited range of analysis.

The three primary programs are operated by private nonprofit community-based organizations working closely with the juvenile court. Nearly all of the mediation cases were referred by the local juvenile court and probation

TABLE 1:    Samples of Individuals Interviewed (During Calendar Years 1990-1991)

| Program Site | Referred to Mediation | | Not Referred to Mediation (Comparison Group 2) | Total |
|---|---|---|---|---|
| | Participating | Nonparticipating (Comparison Group 1) | | |
| Albuquerque | | | | |
| Victims | 73 | 33 | 25 | 131 |
| Offenders | 65 | 36 | 28 | 129 |
| Minneapolis | | | | |
| Victims | 96 | 51 | 72 | 219 |
| Offenders | 81 | 40 | 71 | 192 |
| Oakland | | | | |
| Victims | 61 | 19 | 10 | 90 |
| Offenders | 56 | 19 | 12 | 87 |
| Austin | | | | |
| Victims | 50 | | | 50 |
| Offenders | 50 | | | 50 |
| Total | 532 | 198 | 218 | 948 |

NOTE: Many of the victims and offenders who participated in mediation were inter-viewed before and after the mediation, resulting in a total of 1,153 interviews.

staff. A relatively small number of cases were referred by the prosecuting attorney or police.

Several factors were considered in selecting these program sites. Private nonprofit organizations sponsor the majority of victim-offender mediation programs throughout the country, and most programs focus upon juvenile offenders (Hughes and Schneider 1989; Umbreit 1988). The three primary programs offered both regional and program development diversity. With a few notable exceptions, each victim-offender mediation program employed a very similar case management process with juvenile offenders and their victims.

## MEDIATION REFERRALS

A total of 5,458 victims and offenders were referred by the juvenile court to the four victim-offender mediation program sites during calendar years 1990 and 1991, representing 2,799 individual victims and 2,659 individual offenders. Of these referrals, 83% involved a property crime, such as vandal-

TABLE 2:    Referral Characteristics (2-Year Period, 1990-1991)

| Variable | Albuquerque | Austin | Minneapolis | Oakland | Total |
|---|---|---|---|---|---|
| Cases referred | 591 | 1,107 | 903 | 541 | 3,142 |
| Preadjudication | 76% | 98% | 72% | 91% | 85% |
| Postadjudication | 24% | 2% | 28% | 9% | 15% |
| Individual victims | 654 | 1,058 | 633 | 454 | 2,799 |
| Individual offenders | 604 | 1,087 | 658 | 310 | 2,659 |
| Types of offenses |  |  |  |  |  |
|    Against property | 73% | 81% | 89% | 87% | 83% |
|    Against people | 27% | 19% | 11% | 13% | 17% |
| Most frequent |  |  |  |  |  |
|   property offense | burglary | burglary | vandalism | vandalism | burglary |
| Most frequent |  |  |  |  |  |
|   violent offense | assault | assault | assault | assault | assault |

ism, theft, or burglary, and 17% involved a crime of violence, primarily minor assaults.

Of the total cases, 85% were referred to the four programs prior to formal adjudication as a diversion effort. As Table 2 indicates, the remaining cases (15%) were referred following formal adjudication by the juvenile court. Although the proportion of postadjudication referrals at individual sites varied from 2% in Austin to 28% in Minneapolis, the vast majority of cases at all sites represented preadjudication/diversion referrals.

The average age of offenders referred to the four mediation programs was 15, with a range of 7 to 18 years of age. Of the referrals, 86% were male and 14% were female. A very large proportion of case referrals (46%) represented minority youth, with Hispanics being the largest minority group referred. The vast majority of offenders referred to the mediation programs had no prior criminal convictions. The minority, who did have prior convictions, had two to six offenses. Table 3 indicates the characteristics of offenders at the four program sites.

## FINDINGS

### Client Expectations for Mediation

Victims and offenders who participated in mediation had varied expectations. Victims were most likely to indicate that recovering their loss and helping the offender were equally important. These expectations were fol-

TABLE 3:    Offender Characteristics (2-Year Period, 1990-1991)

| Variable | Albuquerque $n = 604$ | Austin $n = 1,087$ | Minneapolis $n = 658$ | Oakland $n = 310$ | Total $n = 2,659$ |
|---|---|---|---|---|---|
| Average offender age | 15 | 15 | 15 | 15 | 15 |
| Offender age range | 10-19 | 10-17 | 10-18 | 7-18 | 7-18 |
| Offender gender | | | | | |
| Male | 90% | 87% | 85% | 82% | 86% |
| Female | 10% | 13% | 15% | 18% | 14% |
| Offender race | | | | | |
| Caucasian | 30% | 31% | 70% | 64% | 54% |
| Black | 2% | 25% | 23% | 15% | 14% |
| Hispanic | 65% | 42% | 2% | 15% | 27% |
| Other minorities | 3% | 2% | 5% | 6% | 5% |

lowed in frequency by the opportunity to tell the offender the effect of the crime and finally by the opportunity to get answers to questions they had about the crime. Although only one in four victims indicated that they were nervous about the pending mediation session with the offender, nine out of ten victims believed that the mediation session would probably be helpful.

Offenders indicated that "making things right" was their primary expectation, followed in frequency by having the opportunity to apologize to the victim and, finally, by being able "to be done with it." Only one out of ten offenders indicated that they expected the mediation session to be less punishment than they would have otherwise received. Nearly half of the offenders stated that they were nervous about the pending session. Six out of ten indicated that they cared about what the victims thought of them and, like the victims, nine out of ten offenders believed that the mediation session would be helpful.

### Voluntary Participation in Mediation

The question of whether or not victims and offenders actually participated voluntarily in mediation is crucial to the integrity of the victim-offender mediation process. It is important that young offenders, particularly, have a choice about participating in the mediation process and directly contribute to the outcome because coercion to participate would likely cause anger that would in turn be reflected in their behavior in the meeting with the victims.

A major concern of the victim rights movement is the issue of choice, allowing victims various options to regain a sense of power and control in their lives. If the mediation process is imposed upon victims of crime, that experience itself could be further victimizing.

331

Although a very high proportion of both victims (91%) and offenders (81%) in the current study clearly felt that their participation in mediation was voluntary, an earlier study by Coates and Gehm (1989) found that many offenders did not experience their involvement in mediation as voluntary. Particularly because of the highly coercive nature of any justice system's interaction with an offender, one would expect that many offenders in mediation would feel coerced into it. Yet, eight out of ten offenders from the combined sites experienced their involvement in mediation as voluntary. There was, however, a statistically significant different found between program sites. The Minneapolis program site had the highest rating of voluntary participation for offenders (90%), whereas the Albuquerque program site had the lowest rating (71%). There was no similar significant difference for victims from the different sites.

## The Mediation Process

The three primary victim-offender mediation programs employ a similar four-phase process; intake, preparation for mediator, mediation, and follow-up. During the preparation phase, the mediator usually met separately with both parties to hear their version of what happened, to explain the program, and to schedule a date for mediation.

The agenda of the mediation session with victim and offender focuses first on the facts and feelings related to the crime. Offenders are put in the often uncomfortable position of having to face the person they victimized. They are given the opportunity to become known as a person and even to express remorse in a very personal fashion. Through open discussion of their feelings, both victim and offender have the opportunity to deal with each other as people, oftentimes from the same neighborhood, rather than as stereotypes. The second part of the session focuses on victim losses and negotiation of a mutually satisfying restitution agreement. Mediation sessions tend to last about an hour.

The follow-up phase consists of monitoring completion of the restitution agreement, intervening if additional conflict develops, and scheduling a follow-up victim-offender meeting when appropriate.

The three program sites accept referrals of juvenile offenders from probation officials, at both a preadjudication (diversion) and postadjudication level. Both staff and community volunteers serve as mediators. Each mediator receives approximately 20 to 25 hours of initial training in mediation skills and program procedures.

From the 28 observations of mediation sessions conducted at the three primary sites, it was found that the process described above was usually applied, although not always in such a clear sequence (opening statement, telling of stories, transition to restitution discussion and agreement). Also, there were a number of notable examples in which the mediation process appeared to be applied in a very routinized fashion, with unclear leadership and guidance by the mediator, including missed opportunities for facilitating the mediation in such a way that both victim and offender received the maximum possible emotional benefit.

Both parties in the mediation ranked the importance of specific tasks performed by mediators. Victims ranked leadership most important in a mediator. This was followed by "made us feel comfortable"; "helped us with restitution plan"; and "allowed us to talk." Offenders had a slightly different ranking, beginning with the ability of the mediator to make them feel comfortable, followed by "allowed us to talk"; "helped us with the restitution plan"; and "the mediator was a good listener."

### Immediate Outcomes

The most obvious immediate outcome for those victims and offenders who chose to participate in mediation was the highly probable successful negotiation of a restitution agreement. These agreements consisted of a variety of elements (Table 4), but most focused on payment of financial restitution by the offender to the victim. It was not unusual for agreements to include personal service to the victim or community service, both of which were likely to result from conversion of a specific dollar amount of loss into hours of work, usually at an approximate minimum wage rate. Some restitution agreements simply required an apology by the offender to the victim.

The majority of participants in the current study reported successful negotiation of restitution agreements (91% in Oakland to 99% in Albuquerque). Restitution contracts were not the only immediate outcome of the mediation program. After going through mediation, participants often reported other important outcomes. As indicated in Table 5, victims from across the sites were significantly less upset about the crime and less fearful of being revictimized by the same offender after they were able to meet in mediation. A common theme expressed was "It minimized the fear I would have as a victim because I got to see that the offender was human, too."

### Client Satisfaction With Mediation

Nearly 80% of the offenders in the mediation sample and the two comparison group samples indicated satisfaction with how the system handled their case, with no significant differences among groups. For offenders,

**TABLE 4:    Immediate Outcomes (2-Year Period, 1990-1991)**

| Variable | Albuquerque | Austin | Minneapolis | Oakland | Total |
|---|---|---|---|---|---|
| Number of Mediations | 158 | 300 | 468 | 205 | 1,131 |
| Successfully negotiated | | | | | |
| restitution agreements | 99% | 98% | 93% | 91% | 95% |
| Agreements with | | | | | |
| Financial restitution | 82 | 171 | 239 | 111 | 603 |
| Personal service | 57 | 21 | 31 | 36 | 145 |
| Community service | 29 | 130 | 107 | 39 | 305 |
| Total financial restitution | $23,542 | $41,536 | $32,301 | $23,227 | $120,606 |
| Average financial | | | | | |
| restitution | $287 | $243 | $135 | $209 | $200 |
| Total hours of personal | | | | | |
| service | 1,028 | 439 | 508 | 585 | 2,560 |
| Average hours of | | | | | |
| personal service | 18 | 21 | 16 | 16 | 18 |
| Total hours of community | | | | | |
| service | 1,073 | 4,064 | 1,937 | 588 | 7,662 |
| Average hours of | | | | | |
| community service | 37 | 31 | 18 | 15 | 25 |

**TABLE 5:    Emotional Impact of Mediation on Victims**

| | Premediation | | Postmediation | | |
|---|---|---|---|---|---|
| Combined Sites | Percentage | n | Percentage | n | |
| Upset about crime | 67 | (155) | 49 | (162) | $p = .0001^*$ |
| Afraid of being revictimized | | | | | |
| by offender | 23 | (154) | 10 | (166) | $p = .003^*$ |

*Finding of significant difference.

therefore, participation in mediation appears not to have significantly increased their satisfaction with how the juvenile justice system handled their case.

A significant difference (at the .05 level) was found, however, for victims (Table 6). Although 79% of victims in the mediation group indicated satisfaction, only 57% in the referred/no mediation group and 57% of victims in the nonreferral to mediation group indicated satisfaction. This greater sense of satisfaction among victims in the mediation group was reflected in statements such as, "It gave us a chance to see each other face-to-face and to

TABLE 6:    Victim Satisfaction With Case Processing by System: Mediation
Sample Compared With Two Comparison Group Samples

| Combined Sites | Victims | |
|---|---|---|
| | Percentage | n |
| Mediation sample (experimental group) | 79 | (204) |
| Referred/no-mediation sample (comparison group 1) | 57 | (95) |
| Probability of chance | $p = .0001^*$ | |
| Nonreferral sample (comparison group 2) | 57 | (104) |
| Probability of chance | $p = .0001^*$ | |

*Finding of significant difference.

resolve what happened"; "It reduced my fear as a victim because I was able
to see that they were young people"; and "I feel good about it because it
worked out well. I think the kid finally realized the impact of what happened
and that's not what he wants to do with himself."

Nine out of ten victims and offenders at all of the sites combined were
satisfied with the actual outcome of the mediation session, which was nearly
always a written restitution agreement. A frequent theme expressed among
offenders was "It was helpful to see the victim as a person and to have a
chance to talk with him or her and make up for what I did." There were no
major differences found between individual sites.

### Client Perceptions of Fairness

Aggregated data from all three sites indicated that the mediation process
was significantly more likely to result in victim's perceptions that cases were
handled fairly by the juvenile justice system. In the mediation group, 83% of
the victims stated they experienced fairness in the processing of their case,
compared to only 53% in the referred/no mediation group and 62% in the
nonreferral to mediation group.

When compared to similar offenders who were never referred to the
mediation program, juveniles who met their victim in mediation were also
significantly more likely to indicate that they experienced fairness in the
processing of their case. For offenders in mediation, 89% indicated that they
experienced fairness, compared to 78% in the nonreferral to mediation group.
When compared to other juveniles who were referred to the mediation
program but who did not participate, however, no statistically significant
difference was found in their experience of fairness in the processing of their
case by the system.

Consistent with a prior study (Umbreit 1988), when crime victims who participated in mediation were asked to rank their most important concerns related to fairness in the justice system, they identified "help for the offender" as the primary concern. This was followed by "pay back the victim for their losses" and "receive an apology from the offender." Juvenile offenders in mediation indicated that "pay back the victim for their losses" was their most important concern related to fairness in the justice system. This was followed by "personally make things right" and "apologize to the victim."

When the data on perceptions of fairness were examined within program sites, no significant differences were found among offenders. Victims in mediation were, however, considerably more likely to have experienced fairness at each of the three primary sites. Significant differences were found at the Albuquerque site between the mediation sample and referred/no mediation sample and at the Minneapolis site between the mediation sample and both comparison groups.

### Victim/Offender Attitudes About Mediation

Both victims and offenders identified a number of important issues related to the process of talking about the crime and negotiating restitution. Negotiating restitution was important to nearly nine out of ten victims at both a pre- and postmediation level. Actually receiving restitution, however, was important to only seven out of ten victims. The opportunity to directly participate in an interpersonal problem-solving process to establish a fair restitution plan was more important to victims than actually receiving the agreed-upon restitution.

Significant differences related to informational and emotional needs of the victim, as well as with the process of negotiating restitution, were found between pre- and postmediation group samples. Victims reported that it was more important to receive answers from the offender about what happened and to tell the offender how the crime affected them after, rather than before, the actual mediation session. This was also true with negotiating restitution with the offender during the meeting, even though actually receiving restitution was less important.

For offenders, there were no significant differences between the pre- and postmediation samples. Negotiating restitution, paying restitution, telling the victim what happened, and apologizing to the victim were important to nine out of ten offenders in both samples.

This finding does not, however, fully capture the impact that mediation had on the attitude of the offenders. Being held personally accountable for their criminal behavior, through a face-to-face meeting with their victims can trigger a significant change in the attitude of many juvenile offenders. This change is expressed in the following statements. "After meeting the victim I now realize that I hurt them a lot . . . to understand how the victim feels makes me different." Through mediation "I was able to understand a lot about what I did. . . . I realized that the victim really got hurt and that made me feel really bad." The importance of this change in the attitude of many offenders is reflected in a statement by a judge in the Oakland area, who stated that the main impact of victim-offender mediation is a "major learning experience for kids about the rights of others, with implications far beyond just the delinquent act."

### Juvenile Court Support for Mediation

Juvenile court officials at the three primary research sites uniformly supported the victim-offender mediation program in their jurisdiction. Although there were some skeptics of the mediation concept during the early development of the program, most notably at the Minnesota site, judges and probation staff are now strong supporters and have played an important role in helping the move toward institutionalizing these programs.

Judges at all three sites recognized that the emotional benefits of the program were even more important than simply the payment of restitution. A judge in Albuquerque stated, "Mediation helps these kids realize that victims are not just targets, they are real people." A Minnesota judge stated, "Victim-offender mediation humanizes the process . . . victims gain a sense of control and power . . . offenders learn the real human impact of what they have done." The importance of young offenders taking responsibility for their criminal behavior by compensating the victim was highlighted by a judge in the Oakland area who said, "Victim-offender mediation teaches kids that 'what I did affected real people' . . . paying restitution as a consequence for their behavior is part of growing up."

These sentiments were echoed by probation directors and line staff at the three sites. Probation staff were also often quick to add that the mediation programs relieved the pressure of their high caseloads, particularly in cases involving more complex issues of restitution determination and payment.

### Impact of Mediation on Restitution Completion

Restitution is increasingly being required of juvenile offenders in many courts throughout the United States. Whether or not restitution is actually

TABLE 7:    Restitution Completion by Offenders (Percentage of Restitution Completed)

|  | Minneapolis | | Albuquerque | | Total | |
|---|---|---|---|---|---|---|
| Sample | Percentage | n | Percentage | n | Percentage | n |
| Mediation sample | | | | | | |
| (experimental group) | 77 | (125) | 93 | (42) | 81 | (167) |
| Nonreferral matched sample | | | | | | |
| (comparison group) | 55 | (179) | 69 | (42) | 58 | (221) |
| Probability of chance | $p = .0001*$ | | $p = .005*$ | | $p = .0001*$ | |

*Finding of significant difference.

completed by the offender, however, is a critical issue because victims who have their expectations raised by court-ordered restitution and then never receive compensation by the offender can experience a "second victimization."

At the Minneapolis and Albuquerque program sites, court data related to actual completion of restitution were analyzed. The comparison groups for this analysis represented a sample of similar offenders from the same jurisdiction who were matched on the variables of age, race, sex, offense, and amount of restitution. As Table 7 indicates, offenders who negotiated restitution agreements with their victims through a process of mediation were significantly more likely to actually complete their restitution obligation than similar offenders who were ordered by the court to pay a set amount of restitution.

Representing the first study to examine the impact of face-to-face mediation on successful completion of restitution, this finding is critical. At a time when concern for serving the needs of crime victims continues to grow, the fact that victim-offender mediation can significantly increase the likelihood of victims being compensated, in some form, for their losses has very important implications for juvenile justice policymakers.

## Impact of Mediation on Recidivism

The question of whether the victim-offender mediation process reduced further criminal behavior (recidivism) by those offenders participating in mediation was examined at each of the three primary sites. The comparison group at each site consisted of similar offenders from the same jurisdiction who were matched on the variables of age, sex, race, offense, and restitution amount with offenders in mediation.

Juvenile offenders in the three mediation programs committed considerably fewer additional crimes (18% recidivism) within a 1-year period following the mediation than similar offenders in the court-administered restitution program (27% recidivism). They also tended to commit crimes that were less serious than the offense that was referred to the mediation program. The largest reduction in recidivism occurred at the Minneapolis program site, with a recidivism rate of 22% for the mediation sample compared to 34% for the comparison group sample.

Although it is important to know that the victim-offender mediation process appears to have had an effect on suppressing further criminal behavior, the finding is not, however, statistically significant. The possibility that this apparent effect of mediation occurred by chance cannot be ruled out. It should be pointed out that the comparison group used in this study consisted of similar offenders in a structured court restitution program involving no mediation, rather than similar offenders who had no restitution responsibility.

This finding of no significant impact of mediation on recidivism is consistent with two English studies of victim offender mediation (Dignan 1990; Marshall and Merry 1990). Structured restitution programs for juvenile offenders, however, have been found to have a significant impact on reducing recidivism (Schneider 1986).

For some, a finding of a nonsignificant impact of the mediation process upon further reducing offender recidivism (when compared to a structured court restitution program) may come as a disappointment. For others, including the authors, it comes as no surprise. It could be argued that it is naive to think that a time-limited intervention such as mediation by itself (perhaps 4 to 8 hours per case) would have a dramatic effect on altering criminal and delinquent behavior that is influenced by many other factors, including family life, education, chemical abuse, and available opportunities for treatment and growth.

## CONCLUSIONS

A substantial amount of quantitative and qualitative data was collected from a total of 1,153 interviews with crime victims and juvenile offenders in four states, reviews of program and court records, interviews with court officials and program staff, and observations of 28 mediation sessions. Although this multisite analysis of juvenile victim-offender mediation programs represented the largest study of its kind in North America, it also contained a number of important limitations. First, the necessity of using a quasi-experimental design, without random assignment of subjects into an experimental and control group, eliminated the ability to broadly generalize its conclusions to all victims and offenders in these four or similar mediation programs. Also, early in the study it became evident that the premediation interviews were conducted too far into the overall case management process. At the point of the premediation interview, subjects had already agreed to mediation and their expectations were quite high. This resulted in considerable less change between the pre- and postmediation measurements than initially anticipated. Yet, no acceptable earlier point of administering the premediation interview could be determined without significantly contaminating the normal case management process.

Although caution must be exercised in generalizing these conclusions to other subjects or programs, they do provide important insight into this growing international field of justice reform.

The victim-offender mediation programs in the four states enjoyed strong support from local juvenile justice officials. No significant differences in outcomes were found between the three private community-based programs and the one probation-administered program. Together, they made a significant contribution to enhancing the quality of justice experienced by juvenile offenders and victims. This conclusion is consistent with a number of previous studies (Coates and Gehm 1989; Dignan 1990; Marshall and Merry 1990; Umbreit 1991b, 1990, 1980).

The mediation process is meant to increase the active participation of crime victims in the justice process, as well as encouraging offenders to make amends and be held accountable directly to the person they victimized, not just to the state. The vast majority of offenders indicated that they voluntarily chose to participate in victim-offender mediation. Programs in this study appear to have done a better job of presenting mediation as a voluntary choice to the offender (81% of offenders) than indicated in prior research (Coates and Gehm 1989). Mediation was perceived to be voluntary by the vast majority of victims (91%) who participated in it. Still, a small number of victims (9%) felt that they were coerced into participating in the victim-offender mediation program. Whether this perception of coercion was a function of the program staff, mediators, court-related officials, or even parents (of juvenile victims) is unclear.

The mediation process resulted in very high levels of satisfaction with the juvenile justice system responses for both parties. The vast majority of crime victims and juvenile offenders in mediation also indicated that they experienced fairness in the manner in which their case was disposed of by the court. For victims, an even greater differential impact was found related to satisfaction and perceptions of fairness, when compared to victims who did not enter mediation.

Victims and offenders consistently indicated, across all four sites, that the mediation process had a strong impact on humanizing the justice system response to the crime and allowed them more active involvement in resolving the issues related to compensating victims for their losses. After meeting and talking with the young offender in the presence of a mediator, victims indicated a significant reduction in their sense of vulnerability and anger.

Juvenile offenders did not perceive victim-offender mediation to be a significantly less demanding response to their criminal behavior than other options available to the court. The use of mediation was consistent with the concern to hold young offenders accountable for their criminal behavior.

Victim-offender mediation had a significant impact on the likelihood of offenders (81%) successfully completing their restitution obligation to victims, when compared to similar offenders who completed their restitution (58%) in a court-administered structured restitution program without mediation. This study is the first in North America or Europe to examine the impact of mediation upon successful restitution completion.

Although this multisite analysis of victim-offender mediation identified a number of outcomes that enhance the quality of justice for both victims and offenders, several limitations of the intervention also emerged. Mediation is clearly not a "quick fix" for reduction of delinquency.

There was a small amount of data that suggests that the mediation process could, over time, become so routinized that it would lead to an impersonal atmosphere that could become a dehumanizing experience for participants. The spontaneity, vitality, and creativity of the mediation process must be preserved by effective training of mediators and monitoring of mediator performance and program outcomes.

As the field of victim-offender mediation expands and becomes more institutionalized, a danger exists that it might alter its model to accommodate the dominant system of retributive justice, rather than influencing the present system to alter its model to incorporate a more restorative vision of justice upon which victim offender mediation is based.

## IMPLICATIONS

A number of implications for juvenile justice policy and practice follow the conclusions that emerged from this extensive 2 1/2-year multisite study of victim-offender mediation in the United States.

341

Strong empirical grounding to the emerging practice theory of restorative justice is offered by this study. As the most visible, though not only, expression of restorative justice theory, victim-offender mediation provides a radically different way of responding to certain types of crime. Crime victims and juvenile offenders become active, rather than passive, participants in the justice process. The face-to-face mediation process breaths life into the rather abstract notion of juvenile offenders needing to be held accountable. Through mediation, offenders are held accountable in a clear and direct fashion to the person they victimized, not only to the state. Mediation also provides a mechanism for restoring emotional and material losses experienced by the victim, while offering offenders an opportunity to make amends in a very personal way. Both victims and offenders in mediation appear to experience justice in a more understandable, humane, and satisfying manner.

Victim-offender mediation should be more consistently integrated into the large national network of court-sponsored restitution programs. All restitution programs emphasize the importance of holding offenders accountable for their behavior by compensating victims for their losses. Although restitution is now frequently ordered by many juvenile courts throughout the country, it is not unusual for actual restitution completion rates in those same jurisdictions to be rather low. Being ordered by a judge to pay restitution, usually through payment to the court clerk, is often experienced as a fine to pay the court rather than an obligation to the person they victimized.

Mediation, on the other hand, offers a very active process in which the young offender is directly confronted with the realization of the victim as a person, rather than simply an object or target. In addition to talking about what happened and how both parties felt about it, the offender's restitution obligation is, in fact, negotiated with the victim. Likewise, after experiencing the offender as a person rather than simply a criminal, victims are often quite flexible in negotiating a plan for restitution that realistically considers the offender's ability to pay. There is strong evidence that victims of crime are more likely to actually be compensated if the restitution plan is negotiated by the offender and victim.

The "balanced approach" to juvenile probation (Bazemore 1992; Maloney, Romig, and Armstrong 1988) has received a good deal of attention over the past few years. Rather than getting caught in the dichotomy of either emphasizing rehabilitation or increasing levels of control and punishment of the offender, the balanced approach is grounded in the belief that the purpose and function of juvenile probation must address the needs and interests of the victim, the offender, and the community. No one party should benefit at the expense of the other two. A balance between the principles of community safety, accountability, and competency development for the juvenile is the goal.

However, reference to victim-offender mediation is notably absent from the literature on the balanced approach to juvenile probation. This multisite study of mediation programs provides persuasive evidence that the two concepts should more intentionally be joined. The accountability principle of the balanced approach should more actively embrace the practice of victim-offender mediation. Restorative justice theory can provide a larger value base and context to operationalize a balanced approach to probation.

Mediating conflict between interested crime victims and offenders should receive far more attention from the large network of victim advocacy groups throughout the United States. There is strong evidence that a victim's sense of vulnerability and anxiety can be reduced following a direct mediation session with the offender. Although "victim impact" statements have increasingly been used in courts throughout the United States during the past decade, they represent a passive form of victim input into the justice process. The process of victim-offender mediation is an active way to achieve the popular goals of empowering victims and involving them in the justice process. In mediation, victims can help shape part of the offender's penalty through negotiation of a mutually agreeable restitution plan.

Wider public policy consideration should be given to increasing the availability of victim-offender mediation services, perhaps even as a basic right for those victims of crime who would find it helpful, assuming the offender agrees to such a meeting and a credible victim-offender mediation program is available to both parties. Wider access to victim-offender mediation should include recognition that the process can be an appropriate intervention in a wide range of property offenses and minor assaults, including residential burglary and robbery, and with offenders with multiple priors as well as first-time offenders. Referral to mediation can be effective either as a diversion from prosecution or at a postadjudication level.

Programs in this study have even reported positive results in working with an occasional negligent homicide or vehicular homicide case, in which the mediation is held between the offender and the surviving family member(s). To restrict access to mediation to the very low end of criminal behavior, involving cases that may not have even been prosecuted or those that would have self-corrected on their own, is to severely underuse the demonstrated power of the mediation intervention to offer a greater sense of involvement and closure for the victim, while providing an active and understandable process of accountability for the offender.

Despite the growth of victim-offender mediation programs in North America and Europe over the past decade, and a growing body of research that indicates many positive benefits of this intervention, these programs still have limited impact in most jurisdictions. For this justice reform to move from the margins to the mainstream of how we understand and respond to crime in modern, industrialized democracies, the opportunity of mediation must become far more available to a wide range of victims and offenders involved in both property and violent crime.

## REFERENCES

Bazemore, Gordon. 1992. "On Mission Statements and Reform in Juvenile Justice: The Case of the 'Balanced Approach'." *Federal Probation* 56:64-70.

Coates, Robert B. and John Gehm. 1989. "An Empirical Assessment." Pp. 251-63 in *Mediation and Criminal Justice*, edited by M. Wright and B. Galaway. London: Sage.

Cook, Thomas D. and Donald T. Campbell. 1979. *Quasi-Experimental Design & Analysis Issues in Field Settings*. Boston, MA: Houghton-Mifflin.

Davis, Robert, M. Tichane, and D. Grayson. 1980. *Mediation and Arbitration as Alternative to Prosecution in Felony Arrest Cases: An Evaluation of the Brooklyn Dispute Resolution Center*. New York: VERA Institute of Justice.

Dignan, Jim. 1990. "Repairing the Damage: An Evaluation of an Experimental Adult Reparation Scheme in Lettering, Northamptonshire." Centre for Criminological and Legal Research, Faculty of Law, University of Sheffield, England.

Gehm, John. 1990. "Mediated Victim-Offender Restitution Agreements: An Exploratory Analysis of Factors Related to Victim Participation." Pp. 177-82 in *Criminal Justice, Restitution and Reconciliation*, edited by B. Galaway and J. Hudson. Monsey, NY: Criminal Justice Press.

Hughes, Stella P. and Anne L. Schneider. 1989. "Victim-Offender Mediation: A Survey of Program Characteristics and Perceptions of Effectiveness." *Crime & Delinquency* 35:217-33.

Maloney, Dennis, Dennis Romig, and Troy Armstrong. 1988. *Juvenile Probation: The Balanced Approach*. Reno, NV: National Council of Juvenile and Family Court Judges.

Marshall, Tony F. and Susan Merry. 1990. *Crime and Accountability, Victim Offender Mediation in Practice*. London: Home Office.

Schneider, Anne L. 1986. "Restitution and Recidivism Rates of Juvenile Offenders: Results From Four Experimental Studies." *Criminology* 24:533-52.

Umbreit, Mark S. 1985. *Crime and Reconciliation: Creative Options for Victims and Offenders*. Nashville, TN: Abingdon Press.

————. 1986. "Victim Offender Mediation and Judicial Leadership." *Judicature* 69:202-4.

————. 1988. "Mediation of Victim Offender Conflict." *Journal of Dispute Resolution* 85-105.

————. 1989. "Victims Seeking Fairness, Not Revenge: Toward Restorative Justice." *Federal Probation* 53:52-57.

————. 1990. "The Meaning of Fairness to Burglary Victims." Pp. 47-57 in *Criminal Justice, Restitution and Reconciliation*, edited by B. Galaway and J. Hudson. Monsey, NY: Criminal Justice Press.

————. 1991a. "Having Offenders Meet With Their Victim Offers Benefits for Both Parties." *Corrections Today Journal* (July):164-66.

————. 1991b. "Minnesota Mediation Center Gets Positive Results." *Corrections Today Journal* (August):194-97.

Umbreit, Mark S. and Robert B. Coates. 1992. "The Impact of Mediating Victim Offender Conflict: An Analysis of Programs in Three States." *Juvenile & Family Court Journal* 43:21-28.

Wright, Martin. 1991. *Justice for Victims and Offenders*. Philadelphia: Open University Press.

Zehr, Howard. 1990. *Changing Lenses: A New Focus for Criminal Justice*. Scottdale, PA: Herald Press.

Zehr, Howard and Mark Umbreit. 1982. "Victim Offender Reconciliation: An Incarceration Substitute?" *Federal Probation* 46:63-68.

# New Wine and Old Wineskins:
# Four Challenges of Restorative Justice*

*Daniel W. Van Ness***

> *And nobody puts new wine into old wineskins;*
> *if he does, the wine will burst the skins,*
> *and the wine is lost and the skins too.*
> *No! New wine, fresh skins.*
>
> *Mark* 2:22

A t the 1987 London conference on criminal law reform that led to the formation of the Society for the Reform of Criminal Law, Justice John Kelly of Australia delivered a remarkable address on the purpose of law.[1] Speaking to two hundred judges, legal scholars, and law reformers from common law countries, he laid aside his prepared comments and spoke with great feeling about the need for criminal law practitioners to see themselves as healers. A purpose of criminal law, he

---

** Special Counsel on Criminal Justice, Prison Fellowship, Washington, D.C., U.S.A.; B.A., Wheaton College 1971; J.D., DePaul University 1975; LL.M., Georgetown University 1993. I gratefully acknowledge the assistance of Dr. Karen Strong, David Carlson, Thomas Crawford, and Dr. Daniel Dreisbach.

[1] For a brief account of this conference, see Conference Report, *Reform of the Criminal Law*, 1 Crim. L.F. 91 (1989).

said, should be to heal the wounds caused by crime. Since "healing" is not a word frequently heard in legal gatherings, it was helpful that he illustrated what he meant.

Justice Kelly told of a case in which he had made a special effort to ensure that a rape victim felt vindicated. He had just sentenced the defendant to prison, but before calling the next case he asked the victim to approach the bench. Justice Kelly had watched the complainant throughout the proceedings, and it was clear that she was very distraught, even after the offender's conviction and sentencing. The justice spoke with her briefly and concluded with these words: "You understand that what I have done here demonstrates conclusively *that what happened was not your fault.*" The young woman began to weep as she left the courtroom. When Justice Kelly called the family several days later, he learned that his words had marked the beginning of psychological healing for the victim. Her tears had been tears of healing.

The view that justice should bring about healing is, in fact, an ancient concept, one that a growing number of commentators are developing for contemporary application under the rubric of "restorative justice." Advocates of restorative justice face legal and jurisprudential challenges, among these the challenge to abolish criminal law, the challenge to rank multiple goals, the challenge to determine harm rationally, and the challenge to structure community–government cooperation. This article will consider these four challenges in turn and suggest ways in which they might be addressed.

## ROOTS

We are used to thinking of criminal law as the means through which government prohibits criminal behavior and punishes criminals.[2] We take for granted the distinction between private and public wrongs, which separates the law of torts from criminal law, a distinction

---

[2]      *See, e.g.,* Kenneth Mann, *Punitive Civil Sanctions,* 101 Yale L.J. 1795, 1807 (1992).

ingrained in our common law tradition.[3] But there is another, older understanding of law that resists this duality, affirming that no matter how we administer the law, one of the primary goals of justice should be to restore the parties injured by crime.[4]

Early legal systems that form the foundation of Western law emphasized the need for offenders and their families to settle with victims and their families. Although crime breached the common welfare, so that the community had an interest in, and a responsibility for, addressing the wrong and punishing the offender, the offense was not considered primarily a crime against the state, as it is today. Instead, a crime was viewed principally as an offense against the victim and the victim's family.[5] This understanding was reflected in ancient legal codes from the Middle East, the Roman empire, and later European polities.[6] Each of these diverse cultures responded to what we now call

---

[3]      See, e.g., Atcheson v. Everitt, 98 Eng. Rep. 1142 (K.B. 1775), in which Lord Mansfield wrote: "Now there is no distinction better known, than the distinction between civil and criminal law; or between criminal prosecutions and civil actions." Id. at 1147.

[4]      In his highly regarded book on what he calls "primitive law," E. Adamson Hoebel wrote:

> The job [of primitive law] is to clean the case up, to suppress or penalize the illegal behavior and to bring the relations of the disputants back into balance, so that life may resume its normal course. This type of law-work has frequently been compared to work of the medical practitioner. It is family doctor stuff, essential to keeping the social body on its feet.

E. Adamson Hoebel, The Law of Primitive Man 279 (1968).

[5]      E.g., Marvin E. Wolfgang, Victim Compensation in Crimes of Personal Violence, 50 Minn. L. Rev. 223 (1965).

[6]      The Code of Hammurabi (c. 1700 B.C.) prescribed restitution for property offenses, as did the Code of Lipit-Ishtar (c. 1875 B.C.). Other Middle Eastern codes, such as the Sumerian Code of Ur-Nammu (c. 2050 B.C.) and the Code of Eshnunna (c. 1700 B.C.) required restitution even in the case of violent offenses. The Roman Law of the Twelve Tables (449 B.C.) required thieves to pay double restitution unless the property was found in their houses; in that case, treble damages were imposed; for resisting the search of their houses, they paid quadruple restitution. The Lex Salica (c. A.D. 496), the earliest existing collection of Germanic tribal laws, included restitution for

crime by requiring offenders and their families to make amends to victims and their families—not simply to insure that injured persons received restitution but also to restore community peace.[7]

This can be seen as well in the language of the Old Testament, where the word *shalom* is used to describe the ideal state in which the community should function.[8] This term signifies completeness, fulfillment, wholeness—the existence of right relationships between individuals, the community, and God.[9] Crime was understood to break *shalom*, destroying right relationships within the community and creating harmful ones. Ancient Hebrew justice, then, aimed to restore wholeness.[10] Restitution formed an essential part of this process, but restitution was not an end in itself. This is suggested by the Hebrew word for "restitution," *shillum*, which comes from the same root as *shalom* and likewise implies the reestablishment of community peace. Along with restitution came the notion of vindication of the victim and of the law itself. This concept was embodied in another word derived from the same root as both *shalom* and *shillum—shillem*. *Shillem* can be translated as "retribution" or "recompense," not in the sense of revenge (that word in Hebrew comes from an entirely different root) but in the sense of

---

crimes ranging from theft to homicide. The Laws of Ethelbert (c. A.D. 600), promulgated by the ruler of Kent, contain detailed restitution schedules that distinguished the values, for example, of each finger and fingernail. Daniel W. Van Ness, *Restorative Justice*, in *Criminal Justice, Restitution, and Reconciliation* 7, 7 (Burt Galaway & Joe Hudson eds., 1990).

[7]     Hoebel, *supra* note 4, at 279.

[8]     We must distinguish *shalom* from the irrational belief that the world is safe and just. Psychologist Melvin Lerner has argued that human beings need to believe that people basically get what they deserve and that the world is both safe and just, even when events suggest otherwise. This self-delusion, Lerner argues, is necessary in order for people to function in their daily lives. Melvin J. Lerner, *The Belief in a Just World* 11–15 (1980). But the Hebrew word *shalom* does not imply a delusional belief that all is well. To hold healing and *shalom* as goals for society's response to crime is to recognize that hurt and injustice do exist and that they must be healed and rectified.

[9]     G. Lloyd Carr, *Shalom*, in *Theological Wordbook of the Old Testament* 931 (R.L. Harris et al. eds., 1980).

[10]    Van Ness, *supra* note 6, at 9.

satisfaction or vindication.[11]  In short, the purpose of the justice process was, through restitution and vindication, to restore a community that had been sundered by crime.

This view of justice is not confined to the far distant past.  Many precolonial African societies aimed not so much at punishing criminal offenders as at resolving the consequences to their victims.  Sanctions were compensatory rather than punitive, intended to restore victims to their previous position.[12]  Current Japanese experience demonstrates a similar emphasis on compensation to the victim and restoration of community peace.[13]  The approach (as we will see later) emphasizes a process that has been referred to as "confession, repentance and absolution."[14]

For all of its tradition, the restorative approach to criminal justice is unfamiliar to most of us today.  For common law jurisdictions, the Norman invasion of Britain marked a turning point away from this understanding of crime.  William the Conqueror and his successors

---

[11]      How is it that a root word meaning "wholeness and unity, a restored relationship" could produce derivatives with such varied meanings?

> The apparent diversity of meanings . . . can be accounted for in terms of the concept of *peace being restored through payment* (of tribute to a conqueror, Joshua 10:1), *restitution* (to one wronged, Exodus 21:36), *or simple payment and completion* (of a business transaction, II Kings 4:7).
>      The payment of a vow (Psalms 50:14) completes an agreement so that both parties are in a state of *shalom.*  Closely linked with this concept is the eschatological motif in some uses of the term.  *Recompense for sin, either national or personal, must be given.  Once that obligation has been met, wholeness is restored* (Isaiah 60:20, Joel 2:25).

Carr, *supra* note 9, at 931 (emphasis added).

[12]      Daniel D.N. Nsereko, Compensating Victims of Crime in Botswana (paper presented at the Society for the Reform of Criminal Law Conference on "Reform of Sentencing, Parole, and Early Release," Ottawa, Ontario, Canada, Aug. 1–4, 1988).

[13]      *See, e.g.,* Daniel H. Foote, *The Benevolent Paternalism of Japanese Criminal Justice,* 80 Cal. L. Rev. 317 (1992).

[14]      John O. Haley, *Confession, Repentance, and Absolution,* in *Mediation and Criminal Justice* 195 (Martin Wright & Burt Galaway eds., 1989).

found the legal process an effective tool for establishing the preeminence of the king over the church in secular matters, and in replacing local systems of dispute resolution.[15] The Leges Henrici, written early in the twelfth century, asserted exclusive royal jurisdiction over offenses such as theft punishable by death, counterfeiting, arson, premeditated assault, robbery, rape, abduction, and "breach of the king's peace given by his hand or writ."[16] Breach of the king's peace gave the royal house an extensive claim to jurisdiction:

> [N]owadays we do not easily conceive how the peace which lawful men ought to keep can be any other than the queen's or the commonwealth's. But the king's justice . . . was at first not ordinary but exceptional, and his power was called to aid only when other means had failed. . . . Gradually the privileges of the king's house were extended to the precinct of his court, to the army, to the regular meetings of the shire and hundred, and to the great roads. Also the king might grant special personal protection to his officers and followers; and these two kinds of privilege spread until they coalesced and covered the whole ground.[17]

Thus, the king became the paramount victim, sustaining legally acknowledged, although symbolic, damages.

Over time, the actual victim was ousted from any meaningful place in the justice process, illustrated by the redirection of reparation from the victim to the king in the form of fines.[18] A new model of

---

[15]    Harold J. Berman, *Law and Revolution* 255–56 (1983).

[16]    *Leges Henrici Primi* 109 (L.J. Downer ed. & trans., 1972).

[17]    Frederick Pollock, *English Law before the Norman Conquest*, 14 Law Q. Rev. 291, 301 (1898).

[18]    In the hands of the royal administrators after the Conquest [the king's peace] proved a dynamic concept, and, as Maitland once expressed it, eventually the King's peace swallowed up the peace of everyone else. . . . Already by the time of Bracton, in the thirteenth century, it had become common form to charge an accused in the following terms: "Whereas the said B was in the peace of

crime was emerging, with the government and the offender as the sole parties.

## RESTORATION INTO SAFE COMMUNITIES OF VICTIMS AND OFFENDERS WHO HAVE RESOLVED THEIR CONFLICTS

Criminal justice policy today is preoccupied with maintaining security—public order—while trying to balance the offender's rights and the government's power.   These are, of course, vital concerns, but a restorative perspective on justice suggests that fairness and order should be only part of society's response to crime.

And, in fact, other emphases have emerged.   These include restitution,[19] victim's rights,[20] rehabilitation,[21] victim–offender reconciliation,[22] community crime prevention,[23] and volunteer-based services for offenders and victims.[24]   Some of these movements incorporate proposals

---

God and of our lord the King, there came the said N, feloniously as a felon," etc.

George W. Keeton, *The Norman Conquest and the Common Law* 175 (1966).

[19]      *See* Charles F. Abel & Frank A. Marsh, *Punishment and Restitution* (1984); *Criminal Justice, Restitution, and Reconciliation, supra* note 6; Stephen Schafer, *Compensation and Restitution to Victims of Crime* (1970).

[20]      *See From Crime Policy to Victim Policy* (Ezzat A. Fattah ed., 1983); President's Task Force on Victims of Crime, *Final Report* (1982); Steven Rathgeb Smith & Susan Freinkel, *Adjusting the Balance:  Federal Policy and Victim Services* (1988).

[21]      *See* Francis T. Cullen & Karen E. Gilbert, *Reaffirming Rehabilitation* (1982).

[22]      *See Criminal Justice, Restitution, and Reconciliation, supra* note 6; *Criminology as Peacemaking* (Harold E. Pepinsky & Richard Quinney eds., 1991); *Mediation and Criminal Justice, supra* note 14.

[23]      *See* Judith Feins et al., *Partnerships for Neighborhood Crime Prevention* (1983); Richard Neely, *Take Back Your Neighborhood* (1990); Wesley G. Skogan & Michael G. Maxfield, *Coping with Crime* (1981).

[24]      *See* Marie Buckley, *Breaking into Prison:  A Citizen Guide to Volunteer Action* (1974); M.L. Gill & R.I. Mawby, *Volunteers in the Criminal Justice System:   A*

for systemic change, but for others the criminal justice system is basically irrelevant other than to provide a framework in which (or around which) the programs can function. In any event, the current system's limitations of vision and of participants have begun to be addressed at least in piece-meal fashion.

Some writers have suggested a more comprehensive approach that combines many of these alternatives and that not only recognizes the wisdom of the ancient model but also seeks to apply that wisdom to the present realities of criminal justice. This effort has been championed by legal scholars and criminologists,[25] victim–offender reconciliation practitioners,[26] and adherents of various philosophical, political, and religious perspectives.[27] Several have called this approach "restorative justice"[28]—the overall purpose of which is the restoration into safe communities of victims and offenders who have resolved their conflicts.[29]

---

*Comparative Study of Probation, Police, and Victim Support* (1990); R.I. Mawby & M.L. Gill, *Crime Victims* (1987).

[25]      *E.g.*, Haley, *supra* note 14, at 195; Martin Wright, *Justice for Victims and Offenders* (1991).

[26]      *E.g.*, *Mediation and Criminal Justice*, *supra* note 14; Mark Umbreit, *Crime and Reconciliation* (1985); Howard Zehr, *Changing Lenses: A New Focus for Crime and Justice* (1990).

[27]      *E.g.*, Wesley Cragg, *The Practice of Punishment* (1992); Daniel W. Van Ness, *Crime and Its Victims* (1986); M. Kay Harris, *Moving into the New Millennium: Toward a Feminist Vision of Justice,* 67(2) Prison J. 27 (1987); Virginia Mackey, Restorative Justice (discussion paper available from the Presbyterian Criminal Justice Program, Lexington, Kentucky, United States, 1990).

[28]      The term "restorative justice" was probably coined by Albert Eglash, *Beyond Restitution,* in *Restitution in Criminal Justice* 91, 92 (Joe Hudson & Burt Galaway eds., 1977), where he suggested that there are three types of criminal justice: retributive justice based on punishment, distributive justice based on therapeutic treatment of offenders, and restorative justice based on restitution. Both the punishment and the treatment model, he noted, focus on the actions of offenders, deny victim participation in the justice process, and require merely passive participation by the offender. Restorative justice focuses instead on the harmful effects of offenders' actions and actively involves victims and offenders in the process of reparation and rehabilitation.

[29]      They have expressed this in different ways. Zehr, *supra* note 26, at 178–81, analogizes to a camera lens and suggests that there are two alternative lenses: retributive

The restorative model seeks to respond to crime at both the macro and the micro level—addressing the need for building safe communities as well as the need for resolving specific crimes.

How might a system of restorative justice achieve its goals? In what ways would such a system differ from current criminal justice practice? While this article is not intended to explore these questions exhaustively, several general comments can be made. First, restorative justice advocates view crime as more than simply lawbreaking, an offense against governmental authority; crime is understood also to cause multiple injuries to victims, the community, and even the offender.[30] Second, proponents argue that the overarching purpose of the criminal justice *process* should be to repair those injuries.[31] Third, restorative justice advocates protest the civil government's apparent monopoly over society's response to crime. Victims, offenders, and their communities also must be involved at the earliest point and to the fullest extent possible. This suggests a collaborative effort, with civil government responsible for maintaining a basic framework of order, and the other parties responsible for restoring community peace and harmony. The work of civil government must be done in such a way that community

---

justice and restorative justice. With regard to restorative justice, he explains that "[c]rime is a violation of people and relationships. It creates obligations to make things right. Justice involves the victim, the offender, and the community in a search for solutions which promote repair, reconciliation, and reassurance." *Id.* at 181.

Cragg, *supra* note 27, at 203, describes restorative justice as a process of "resolving conflicts in a manner that reduces recourse to the justified use of force."

Wright, *supra* note 25, agrees. The new model is one

> in which the response to crime would be, not to add to the harm caused, by imposing further harm on the offender, but to do as much as possible to restore the situation. The community offers aid to the victim; the offender is held accountable and required to make reparation. Attention would be given not only to the *outcome,* but also to evolving a *process* that respected the feelings and humanity of both the victim and the offender.

*Id.* at 112.

[30]     *See, e.g.,* Zehr, *supra* note 26, at 181–86.

[31]     *See, e.g.,* Wright, *supra* note 25, at 114–17 (proposing a system with the primary aim of restoring—or even improving—the victim's prior condition).

building is enhanced, or at least not hampered.[32]

The focus of restorative justice, then, is intentionally holistic. In a restorative paradigm, criminal justice is not merely a contest between the defendant and the state. Criminal justice must take into account, too, the rights and responsibilities of the victim and the community, as well as the injuries sustained by victim, offender, and community.

## CHALLENGES

Ultimately, whole new institutional structures are likely to emerge from the restorative approach, just as the rehabilitation model gave birth to penitentiaries, probation and parole systems, and juvenile courts,[33] and as the just deserts model of fairness in sentencing gave rise to determinate sentences and sentencing guidelines.[34] One such initiative is victim–offender reconciliation, which permits these two parties to meet with a trained mediator to discuss the crime and its aftermath and to develop a strategy to "make things right."[35]

There is great value in model programs such as victim–offender reconciliation: they explore new horizons in criminal justice theory, and they provide data with which to evaluate and modify not only the programs but the theory behind them as well.[36] But more than models is needed—there is a continuing need for analytical precision in understanding the new vision, articulating purposes and outcomes, developing

---

[32] *See* section *infra* entitled "The Challenge to Structure Community–Government Cooperation."

[33] *See* Edgardo Rotman, *Beyond Punishment* 21–57 (1990).

[34] *See* Dean J. Spader, *Megatrends in Criminal Justice Theory,* 13 Am. J. Crim. L. 157, 180–95 (1986).

[35] For an excellent description of victim–offender reconciliation programs, see Zehr, *supra* note 26, at 158–74.

[36] This phenomenon has been aptly described as "theory overtaking practice" in Wright, *supra* note 25, at 41–45.

strategies for accomplishing those purposes, and evaluating results.[37]

Legal scholars and jurists can offer an invaluable service here, since a number of legal and jurisprudential challenges to criminal law and procedure are raised by the suggestion that a fundamental purpose of criminal justice should be to promote restoration of those touched by crime. This article examines four such challenges: (1) the challenge to abolish criminal law, (2) the challenge to rank multiple goals, (3) the challenge to determine harm rationally, and (4) the challenge to structure community–government cooperation.

## The Challenge to Abolish Criminal Law

Currently, both the criminal law and the civil law of torts deal with intentional behavior by one person that violates the rights of another. In criminal cases, the offender is prosecuted by an agent of the government and punished; to convict, the prosecutor must prove the offender guilty beyond a reasonable doubt. In tort cases, the defendant–offender is sued by the plaintiff–victim and is required to pay damages or otherwise make right the harm done; the plaintiff must prove the defendant liable by a preponderance of the evidence.[38] But since the underlying harmful action is basically the same in criminal and tort cases, why are the two treated differently? The answer most often given is that while civil cases are concerned with the violation of individual rights, criminal cases are concerned with broader societal rights; criminal cases should not be initiated by victims, since vindication of public policy should not depend on an individual victim's decision to institute legal proceedings.[39]

---

[37]     It must be remembered that criminal justice history is filled with visionary people whose visions failed to be realized because they neglected to engage in the requisite analytical work. This phenomenon is neatly summarized in the title of Blake McKelvey's *American Prisons: A History of Good Intentions* (1977).

[38]     For an excellent discussion of the distinctions between what he calls the criminal justice and the civil justice "paradigm," see Mann, *supra* note 2, at 1803–13.

[39]     *But see id.* at 1812 n.61, where Mann argues that while this is the conventional argument for the paradigmatic distinction between criminal and civil justice, the practical

But as we have seen, excluding victims' interests from criminal cases is a relatively recent development. How does the emphasis in restorative justice on repairing the damage caused by crime affect our understanding of criminal law? Should a separate criminal law be maintained?

Randy Barnett and John Hagel, early proponents of restitution as a new paradigm of criminal justice, have argued for what would effectively be the end of criminal law, replacing it with the civil law of torts:

> A specific action is defined as criminal within the context of this theory only if it violates the right of one or more identifiable individuals to person and property. These individuals are the victims of the criminal act, and only the victims, by virtue of the past infringement of their rights, acquire the right to demand restitution from the criminal.
>
> This is not to deny that criminal acts frequently have harmful effects upon other individuals besides the actual victims. All that is denied is that a harmful "effect," absent a specific infringement of rights, may vest rights in a third party.[40]

Barnett and Hagel define crime by examining not the offender's behavior but the victim's rights, particularly "the fundamental right of all individuals to be free in their person and property from the initiated use of force by others."[41] They agree that there may be broader social goals but argue that settling the private dispute will "vindicate the rights of the aggrieved party and thereby vindicate the rights of all persons."[42] Barnett and Hagel conclude that, among other things, this means there can be

---

distinction is blurred by RICO statutes, which authorize private prosecution, and by SEC actions, in which the government is authorized to seek compensation for private individuals.

[40] Randy E. Barnett & John Hagel, *Assessing the Criminal*, in *Assessing the Criminal: Restitution, Retribution, and the Legal Process* 1, 15 (Randy E. Barnett & John Hagel eds., 1977).

[41] *Id.* at 11.

[42] *Id.* at 25.

no "victimless crimes."

But vindicating the rights of direct victims does not vindicate the rights of all other persons. Though the injuries are not easy to quantify, *secondary victims* are also injured by crime:

> [C]rime imposes three distinct kinds of costs on its indirect victims. There are, first, the *avoidance costs* that are incurred by anyone who takes steps to minimize his chances of becoming the direct victim of crime. Installing locks and burglar alarms, avoiding unsafe areas, and paying for police protection, whether private or public, all fall into this category. Indirect victims may also have to pay *insurance costs*—costs that increase as the rate of crime in an area increases. And, finally, "as crime gives rise to fear, apprehension, insecurity, and social divisiveness," indirect victims are forced to bear the *attitudinal costs* of crime.[43]

Interestingly, these costs directly affect the right to be free in person and property that Barnett and Hagel espouse. This suggests that the first rationale for maintaining criminal law is that civil law fails adequately to vindicate the rights of secondary victims.

Second, criminal law offers more than vindication of individual rights. It also provides a controlled mechanism for dealing with those accused of crossing the boundaries of socially tolerable behavior. In a thoughtful and disturbing essay entitled "Retributive Hatred," Jeffrie Murphy notes that crime arouses "feelings of anger, resentment, and even hatred . . . toward wrongdoers."[44] He argues that criminal justice should restrain these feelings. "Rational and moral beings . . . want a world, not utterly free of retributive hatred, but one where this passion is both respected and seen as potentially dangerous, as in great need of reflective

---

[43]     Richard Dagger, *Restitution, Punishment, and Debts to Society,* in *Victims, Offenders, and Alternative Sanctions* 3, 4 (Joe Hudson & Burt Galaway eds., 1980) (citations omitted).

[44]     Jeffrie G. Murphy, Retributive Hatred: An Essay on Criminal Liability and the Emotions 2 (paper presented at a conference on "Liability in Law and Morals," Bowling Green State University, Bowling Green, Ohio, United States, Apr. 15–17, 1988).

and institutional restraint."[45] While one may argue with his description of the desires of "rational and moral beings," few would dispute that the retributive impulse must be restrained.

Third, there are procedural advantages to governmentally prosecuted criminal cases. The experience of European countries that permit varying degrees of victim participation in the prosecution of criminal cases bears this out.[46] The victim typically lacks the expertise, financial resources, and time to prosecute. Furthermore, the goals of consistency, fairness, and efficiency can best be pursued by coordinated governmental action, since public prosecutors can weigh decisions in light of stated policies and rely on the help of investigatory agencies. Moreover, prosecutors are presumably less influenced than are victims by personal motivations such as revenge.[47]

In summary, maintaining the criminal law is desirable inasmuch as it provides an effective method of vindicating the rights of secondary victims, it restrains and channels in acceptable ways retributive emotions in society, and it offers procedural efficiencies in enforcing public values.

## The Challenge to Rank Multiple Goals

Given that the overall purpose of restorative justice is to resist crime by building safe and strong communities, this goal can be achieved only when multiple parties (victims, offenders, communities, and governments) pursue multiple goals (recompense, vindication, reconciliation, reintegration, atonement, and so forth). Is it possible for so many parties

---

[45]      *Id.* at 31.

[46]      *See, e.g.,* Matti Joutsen, *Listening to the Victim: The Victim's Role in European Criminal Justice Systems,* 34 Wayne L. Rev. 95 (1987).

[47]      *But see* Abraham S. Goldstein, *Defining the Role of the Victim in Criminal Prosecution,* 52 Miss. L.J. 515, 555 (1982). Governmental prosecution of offenses also has its limitations: the prosecutor administers an agency of government with its own administrative, political, investigative, and adjudicative objectives, any of which can lead prosecutors to focus less on a just resolution of the particular case and more on the effective use of limited resources. In addition, political forces may lead prosecutors to cater to, rather than restrain, retributive impulses in the community.

to pursue so many goals in such a way as to achieve restoration?

The current criminal justice system faces the challenge of balancing multiple goals,[48] usually expressed as deterrence, incapacitation, rehabilitation, and retribution (desert). The first two can be classified as utilitarian, with the focus on crime control. The third can either be similarly classified or be justified as a social value in and of itself. The last limits the nature and extent of the sentence, emphasizing proportionality. Paul Robinson has suggested that the attempt to pursue these four goals raises questions at two levels. First, does any one of them (such as crime control or proportionality) take precedence as an overarching goal of criminal justice? Second, which of the goals have priority when they cannot all be accommodated (when, for example, rehabilitation is prevented by a sentence sufficiently harsh to deter others)?[49]

At first glance, this confusion appears to grow geometrically under the restorative justice model, which adds such goals as recompense and vindication. But, in fact, the more holistic perspective of restorative justice may actually help society successfully manage multiple goals because it identifies restoration as the overarching goal of criminal justice.

How can the goals of deterrence, incapacitation, rehabilitation, and retribution be organized so that they help achieve the overarching purpose of restoration? Robinson, a former member of the U.S. Sentencing Commission, has explored approaches that permit multiple goals to interact with each other in a principled and consistent way. He proposes that a first step is to clarify which goals *determine* the sentence and which simply *limit* the nature or duration of the sentence.[50] A "determining goal" requires that certain features be included in the sentence; it recommends a sentence. A "limiting goal," in contrast, requires that certain features be excluded.[51] So, for example, rehabilitation as a determining goal might produce a recommendation of an indefinite period of treatment, whereas desert as a limiting goal would

---

[48]     Paul H. Robinson, *Hybrid Principles for the Distribution of Criminal Sanctions,* 82 Nw. U. L. Rev. 19 (1987).

[49]     *Id.* at 25–28.

[50]     *Id.* at 29–31.

[51]     *Id.*

establish maximum and minimum periods of time.

Although this approach was designed to rank sentencing purposes under the current paradigm, it could be adapted by restorative justice advocates. For example, with regard to specific crimes, the determining goal of the criminal justice process would be resolution of the conflict; community safety would be a limiting goal only. This means that restitution would be presumed and that sentences providing for incarceration, which effectively precludes or substantially delays restitution (since most offenders are impoverished and few prison industry programs exist), should be used solely as a last resort. Any social controls imposed on the offender should not unduly obstruct the determining goal of resolution.

Likewise, with reference to crime as a community phenomenon, the determining goal of the community and the government would be safety, with specific strategies limited by the need appropriately to resolve individual crimes when they occur. Similar analysis is needed in considering the other subsidiary goals: recompense and redress through the formal criminal justice system; rehabilitation and reconciliation through community-based programs. The challenge is to prioritize restorative outcomes over procedural goals. The test of any response to crime must be whether it is helping to restore the injured parties.

### The Challenge to Determine Harm Rationally

The current paradigm of criminal justice gives scant attention to the harm resulting from the offense and focuses instead on the offender's actions and state of mind. The extent of harm to victims and their neighbors is, with some exceptions, ignored. When this form of injury is considered in offenses such as theft, it is only to establish the seriousness of the crime (misdemeanor versus felony), and the inquiry is typically limited to whether the property was worth more or less than a specific statutory amount.[52]  Under recent sentencing and parole guidelines, the extent of harm also has been considered to determine the

---

[52]     *See, e.g.,* Ill. Ann. Stat. ch. 720, § 5/16-1(b) (1993) (providing that theft of property under $300 is a misdemeanor, and over that amount a felony).

length or severity of the sentence,[53] but again the categories are broad and general, and typically they are used to determine the amount of punishment as opposed to the amount of reparation.

In a restorative justice model, however, victim reparation is a determining goal. Consequently, calculating the amount of loss sustained by victims assumes great importance; to do such calculations, there must first be clarity about the kinds and extent of harms to be considered. This means that three categories of issue will need to be addressed: the kinds of victim to be reimbursed, how harms should be quantified, and how questions of disparity should be addressed.

## WHAT KINDS OF VICTIMS SHOULD BE REIMBURSED?

Most people would intuitively define the victim as the person directly harmed by the offense—the person whose house was burglarized, for example. That person is certainly the primary victim. But others are also affected adversely by crime. Family members and neighbors may suffer increased fear, as well as direct and indirect financial costs. The criminal justice system (and the community as well) may be called on to expend resources. An employer may lose money because of the absence of a victim who is at court or in the hospital. And so on.

Which victims should be considered for reparation? The answer to this question may vary depending on the offense. For example, immediate family members of a homicide victim might be made eligible to recover the costs of psychiatric counseling, while members of a theft victim's family might not. But at a minimum, two groups of victims should always be eligible for restitution: the direct victim and the community, with the direct victim having priority over all secondary victims, including the community.

Alan Harland and Cathryn Rosen have made an excellent case for differentiating direct victims from their communities and, therefore, for treating restitution differently from community service:

> [U]nlike victim restitution that is based upon (and limited by) a case-by-case determination of victim injuries, the "harms" on

---

[53]     E.g., Albert W. Alschuler, *The Failure of Sentencing Guidelines*, 58 U. Chi. L. Rev. 901, 908–15 (1991).

which the offender's community service liability is predicated are far less specific, and the metric against which the amount of service owed is assessed tends to be no less arbitrary than the amount of a fine, probation, incarceration, or any other penal rather than compensatory sanction . . . . [I]t is perhaps not unreasonable to question whether community service has any claim at all to be part of the presumptive norm of restitution, and to ask why it is useful to continue to treat the two sanctions as merely different examples of a uniform concept.[54]

Harland and Rosen are right on all counts. But while this does not necessarily preclude the use of community service as a form of reparative sanction, it does require that we clarify the nature and extent of the harm done to the community, as well as the most appropriate means for the offender to repair that harm.

## How Do We Quantify the Harm That Should Be Repaired?

While society incurs indirect costs as a result of crime, it is impossible to quantify with absolute accuracy the indirect costs related to a particular crime. But it is reasonable and necessary to make an effort at approximating these costs. Here the concept of "rough equivalences" developed by Norval Morris and Michael Tonry might be helpful.[55] They argue that pure equivalence between similar offenders is neither possible nor desirable. Instead, Morris and Tonry propose that the ideal should be to achieve "a rough equivalence of punishment that will allow room for the principled distribution of punishments on utilitarian grounds, unfettered by the miserable aim of making suffering equally painful."[56]

A similar approach could be taken in relating reparative sentences to levels of harm. While Harland and Rosen are right that such a system

---

[54]     Alan T. Harland & Cathryn J. Rosen, *Impediments to the Recovery of Restitution by Crime Victims*, 5(2) Violence & Victims 127, 132 (1990).

[55]     Norval Morris & Michael H. Tonry, *Between Prison and Probation: Intermediate Punishments in a Rational Sentencing System* (1990).

[56]     *Id.* at 31.

is more arbitrary than case-by-case restitution, it is certainly less arbitrary than current, entirely punitive sanctions. Criteria must be established and applied uniformly throughout the entire sentencing structure within a jurisdiction. Great Britain did this several years ago by devising guidelines for restitution. Ironically, they look a great deal like the Anglo-Saxon King Ethelbert's restitution schedules promulgated fourteen hundred years ago:

> Under guidelines sent to the country's 27,710 magistrates, attackers can be forced . . . to compensate their victims by the punch. Sample penalties: $84 for a simple graze, $168 for a black eye, $1,428 for a broken nose, $2,940 for a fractured jaw, and as much as $13,440 for a serious facial scar. Said Home Office Minister John Patten: "I am anxious that the victims get a better deal."[57]

Two things should be noted about the modern British approach: it restricts compensable harms to direct victims and it uses rough equivalences for the amount of restitution to be ordered.

While it is neither feasible nor, perhaps, desirable to attach monetary values to every conceivable type of harm, a serious effort to grapple with the issue is necessary. Otherwise, types and amounts of reparation may be simply arbitrary and no different in nature from the abstract "fine," except for who receives the money. If victims are to be paid back, and if offenders are to see their reparation as linked to the specific harm done, then restitution, like community service, should be as closely related to the particular injury as possible.

### How Do We Avoid Unwarranted Disparity?

This leads us directly into the question of disparity—whether particular offenders or victims will receive orders for restitution that are not comparable to those given to other offenders or victims. Disparity can happen in several ways.

---

[57]     *World Notes: Socking It to the Bad Guys,* Time, Oct. 3, 1988, at 43; *see* Home Office Circ. No. 85/1988; Magistrates' Ass'n of England and Wales, *Sentencing Guidelines* at iv (1992).

First, if each offender is sentenced according to the type of offense alone, the restitution order may fail to reflect the actual harm caused, because similar offenders committing similar crimes can bring about dramatically different injuries. Consider two burglaries in which a vase is stolen—if one is from a five-and-ten-cent store while the other is an authentic Ming, treating the offenders alike because their actions were similar would have a disparate effect on the two victims.

Second, if each offender is sentenced according only to the actual harm caused, then similar illegal conduct may result in dramatically different sentences. In the preceding example, the offender who stole the Ming vase could take years to repay the victim, while replacing the dime-store vase would be a matter of days or hours. Both victims and offenders would therefore receive significantly different treatment.

Finally, differing circumstances on the part of victims and offenders may lead to a disparate effect even when the offense and the financial loss are the same. Wealthy offenders may be able to complete their sentences simply by writing a check, while impoverished offenders may have to work long and hard to satisfy the judgment. Similarly, wealthy victims may have far less trouble recovering from crime than those who are without adequate financial resources.

Of course, not all disparity is wrong, nor is it possible to avoid it entirely. However, justice requires that victims and offenders be treated consistently, and that as much as possible outcomes not fall more heavily on some than on others for social, economic, or political reasons.

The earlier discussion on balancing multiple goals may offer guidance here. Should the emphasis be on *consistency* in dealing with offenders' actions or on victims' *harms?* This question calls for a prioritization of goals. Since restoration is the determining goal, the issue of fairness becomes a limiting goal.[58] Therefore, in a restorative justice system, guidelines outlining minimum and maximum amounts of restitution might be established for particular offenses. These would be related to typical losses of primary and secondary victims. If an agreement were not reached through negotiation, victims would present evidence of their actual losses to the sentencing judge, who would then

---

[58]          In the United States, it is likely that constitutional provisions requiring equal protection and prohibiting cruel and unusual punishment would yield this result.

set an amount within the pertinent range.[59]  If the actual loss were less than the minimum established, the victim would receive only the actual loss, and the balance would be set aside into a victim compensation fund for those victims whose loss exceeded the range.

A similar approach might help address the issue of economic imbalance between otherwise comparable offenders.  The Swedish "day fine" approach, which bases the sanction on the offender's daily wages, multiplied by a figure that represents the seriousness of the offense, could be adopted here as well.[60]  Once again, the determining goal would be reparation to the victim, and fairness would be a limiting goal.  Under this approach, one offender might actually be ordered to pay less than the indicated amount of restitution, with the balance made up from a compensation fund; another offender might be required to pay more, with the excess going into that fund.

### The Challenge to Structure Community–Government Cooperation

Under restorative justice, it is argued, civil government and the community cooperate both in enabling the victim and the offender to resolve the crime successfully and in building safe communities.  Is this kind of cooperation feasible?  Two concerns have been raised in this connection.

First, can community-based programs be linked with agencies of the criminal system without losing their restorative values?  This concern has been sparked by the experience of some reconciliation and mediation programs in the United States and England, which started with visionary objectives and then found those goals being redirected by a much larger criminal justice system with its own—and different—vision.  For example, a reconciliation program may begin to be measured by the *number* of offenders it diverts from prison, rather than by the peacemak-

---

[59]  "[G]iving offenders opportunities to demonstrate a willingness to accept responsibility for their offences is not incompatible with treating like cases alike and assuring that sentences arrived at reflect in appropriate ways the gravity of the offences committed."  Cragg, *supra* note 27, at 216.

[60]  Martin Wright, *Making Good: Prisons, Punishment, and Beyond* 87–88 (1982).

ing results of the mediation.[61]

Howard Zehr, a pioneer in reconciliation program development, has suggested three reasons that dependence on the criminal justice system can distort the vision of such programs: the criminal justice system's interests are retributive not restorative; its orientation is with the offender not the victim; and its inclination when challenged is self-preservation.[62] To these could be added the observation that the procedures of traditional criminal justice systems are coercive, which tends to mitigate against reconciliation or mediation.[63]

A second concern is that community–government collaboration will result in expanded state control. This is the well-known problem of net widening, and it happens in subtle ways.[64] Suppose, for example, that to develop credibility a community-based diversion program agrees to accept referrals of minor offenses from the local court. The court may respond by referring cases that are so minor they would have been dismissed otherwise. If offenders who fail to comply with the reconciliation agreement are then brought back before the judge and sentenced to jail or prison, the unintended effect of this arrangement, which was designed to be an *alternative* to incarceration, may actually be that more offenders are locked up.[65]

---

[61]     Zehr, *supra* note 26, at 232–36.

[62]     Dependence on the criminal justice system is one of three forces that Zehr argues can lead to distortion of vision; the other two are nongovernmental. They include the "dynamics of institutionalization"—such as the need for easily quantified and achieved administrative goals and measurements to justify the organization's existence; the tendency for programs to take on the values of their funding sources; differences between the goals of leaders and staff; and the difficulty of building "prophetic" functions into the organization's structure. The second of these is the design and operation of the program. If goal conflicts are not identified and resolved early on, they carry the potential of diverting the organization from a visionary mission. A succession of seemingly small policy decisions may change the long-range direction of the organization. *Id.* at 233–35.

[63]     Cragg, *supra* note 27, at 199.

[64]     *See, e.g.,* Thomas G. Blomberg, *Widening the Net: An Anomaly in the Evaluation of Diversion Programs,* in *Handbook of Criminal Justice Evaluation* 572 (Malcolm W. Klein & Katherine S. Teilmann eds., 1980).

[65]     *See, e.g.,* Christa Pelikan, *Conflict Resolution between Victims and Offenders in Austria and in the Federal Republic of Germany,* in *Crime in Europe* 151, 164–65 (Frances

But government does not exist apart from society; it is part of society, with specific powers and interests. This observation suggests that community–government cooperation must be fluid and dynamic in keeping with the nature of society itself. And it permits us to draw certain conclusions about what can make the cooperation effective. First, such an undertaking requires that both parties share the same overarching goal, and not just *any* goal. It is likely even now that government and community share the common goal of security. If the mutual goal is to be restoration of the victim, as well as of community safety, then a significant political and public education campaign lies ahead. This is true in the community, as well as in the governmental sphere.

Second, influence flows both ways. Thus, community programs themselves have affected the structure and the goals of the criminal justice system. Peter Kratcoski has outlined a pattern of evolving volunteer activity in criminal justice. At the outset, private groups set up new programs. These programs then have to turn to government assistance when services outstrip existing private resources. At some point, however, the government begins to underwrite the program fully, using volunteers to fill in gaps.[66] An example is the probation system, which grew out of a volunteer program initiated by John Augustus in 1842. Eventually the program was absorbed into the criminal justice system, but with a continuing mission to help offenders.[67]

Third, although government and community must seek the same overarching goal, they also play different roles not only in responding to individual offenders and victims but also in establishing community safety. Both of these objectives must be pursued with equal vigor.

---

Heidensohn & Martin Farrell eds., 1991). Pelikan describes a pilot program in which prosecutors were granted discretionary authority to divert juvenile offenders into a mediation program, as well as the steps taken to avoid net widening.

[66]     Peter C. Kratcoski, *Volunteers in Corrections,* 46(2) Fed. Probation 30 (1982).

[67]     A report several years ago from the Missouri Probation and Parole Department stated that it viewed its mission as helping the community determine its goals for offenders under supervision and then helping the community achieve them. On this program, see Steve German, *Knowledge Is Not Enough:  Addressing Client Needs in Probation and Parole,* in *Community Corrections* 15, 17 (Amer. Correctional Ass'n 1981).

While the obstacles to accomplishing this collaboration are daunting, we can be encouraged by reports from Japan. According to John Haley, criminal justice in that nation operates on two tracks. One is similar to the formal criminal justice system found in Western nations:

> Paralleling the formal process, however, is a second track to which there is no Western analogue. A pattern of confession, repentance and absolution dominates each stage of law enforcement in Japan. The players in the process include not only the authorities in new roles but also the offender and the victim. From the initial police interrogation to the final judicial hearing on sentencing, the vast majority of those accused of criminal offenses confess, display repentance, negotiate for their victims' pardon and submit to the mercy of the authorities. In return they are treated with extraordinary leniency; they gain at least the prospect of absolution by being dropped from the formal process altogether.[68]

To illustrate this leniency, Haley notes that prosecutors proceed in only about 5 percent of all prosecutable cases. The vast majority of such cases are handled in uncontested summary proceedings in which the maximum penalty is a fine of $1,000-1,350. By the time cases have reached this point, the offender has demonstrated remorse, paid restitution, and secured the victim's pardon. Haley concludes:

> In this respect the West, not Japan, should be considered remarkable. The moral imperative of forgiveness as a response to repentance is surely as much a part of the Judeo-Christian heritage as the East Asian tradition. . . . Whatever the reason, unlike Japan Western societies failed to develop institutional props for implementing such moral commands. Instead the legal institutions and processes of Western law both reflect and reinforce societal demands for retribution and revenge.[69]

---

[68] Haley, *supra* note 14, at 195 (citation omitted).

[69] *Id.* at 204. Other observers have written about the distinctive role of apology and settlement in how the Japanese respond to crime. *See, e.g.,* Foote, *supra* note 13;

For a pattern like Japan's to develop in Western justice systems, victims and offenders (as well as the formal criminal justice system) will need to work together. But what if they fail to interact in the cooperative and voluntary way Haley describes? Clearly they cannot be forced to participate in community-based, informal mechanisms for repairing injuries; only the government is authorized to use this kind of force to secure participation in the criminal justice system.

Current criminal justice procedures are highly coercive for both victims and offenders. They are built on the reasonable assumption that not all defendants will willingly take part in the trial process or voluntarily complete their sentences. But they are also predicated on the assumption that not all *victims* will cooperate in the prosecution of their offenders; unwilling victims may have to be subpoenaed to testify at trial.

Restorative justice, with its emphasis on full and early participation of the parties in addressing the injuries caused by crime, places a premium on *voluntary* involvement. For offenders, this demonstrates willingness to assume responsibility for their actions. For victims, it reduces the likelihood that they will be victimized a second time by the formal or informal responses to crime. When such involvement is not forthcoming, however, what should happen? How this question is answered depends to a certain extent on whether the uncooperative party is the victim or the offender.

An uncooperative offender will need to have sufficient coercion applied to ensure participation in the criminal justice system. However, it should be the least amount of coercion necessary, and voluntary assumption of responsibility should be encouraged. Of course, there is no such thing as completely voluntary action in a coercive environment (as when an offender agrees to restitution during a victim–offender reconciliation meeting conducted before sentencing). But assumption of responsibility by the offender should be encouraged.

Victims may also choose to participate or not in the process. If they choose not to, they should be permitted to waive any rights they may have to pursue restitution as a part of the criminal case. The offender should then be required to make compensation payments to the

Hiroshi Wagatsuma & Arthur Rosett, *The Implication of Apology: Law and Culture in Japan and the United States*, 20 Law & Soc'y Rev. 461 (1986).

victim compensation fund. However, there may be situations in which the actual and potential injuries to the community may necessitate the victim's involvement in order to secure a conviction. Under such circumstances, the government should have the authority (as it does today) to subpoena the victim as a witness. Yet even this should be done in a context that will be as protective and supportive as possible, in order that the victim's participation, though coerced, will still contribute to a measure of restoration.

## CONCLUSION

Dissatisfaction with the current paradigm of criminal justice is leading to new programs with different visions. Some, such as restitution, can be incorporated into existing structures. Others, such as victim–offender reconciliation, point to a possible new approach to criminal justice—restorative justice. In some ways, restorative justice is simply a new application of an ancient vision. It is new wine from old vines. But those of us who celebrate the harvest are advised to remember the parable of new wine and old wineskins. Before we begin to pour—before we insert restorative features into familiar responses to crime—we would do well to reflect on what the consequences may be.

This article has considered four likely consequences: the challenge to abolish criminal law, the challenge to rank multiple goals, the challenge to determine harm rationally, and the challenge to structure community–government cooperation. Although each challenge is significant, I have argued that all can be effectively addressed. Indeed, they must be if criminal justice is to become—using Justice John Kelly's image—a means of healing the wounds of crime.

# Acknowledgments

Bachman, Ronet and Dianne Cyr Carmody. "Fighting Fire with Fire: The Effects of
  Victim Resistance in Intimate Versus Stranger Perpetrated Assaults Against
  Females." *Journal of Family Violence* 9 (1994): 317–31. Reprinted with the
  permission of Plenum Press.

Buzawa, Eve S. and Thomas Austin. "Determining Police Response to Domestic
  Violence Victims: The Role of Victim Preference." *American Behavioral
  Scientist* 36 (1993): 610–23. Reprinted with the permission of Sage
  Publications, Inc.

Davis, Robert C. and Barbara E. Smith. "The Effects of Victim Impact Statements on
  Sentencing Decisions: A Test in an Urban Setting." *Justice Quarterly* 11
  (1994): 453–69. Reprinted with the permission of the Academy of Criminal
  Justice Sciences.

Esbensen, Finn-Aage and David Huizinga. "Juvenile Victimization and Delinquency."
  *Youth and Society* 23 (1991): 202–28. Reprinted with the permission of Sage
  Publications, Inc.

Fattah, Ezzat A. "From Crime Policy to Victim Policy: The Need for a Fundamental
  Policy Change." *International Annals of Criminology* 29 (1991): 43–60.
  Reprinted with the permission of the Societe de Criminologie.

Freedy, John R., Heidi S. Resnick, Dean G. Kilpatrick, Bonnie S. Dansky, and Ritchie
  P. Tidwell. "The Psychological Adjustment of Recent Crime Victims in the
  Criminal Justice System." *Journal of Interpersonal Violence* 9 (1994): 450–68.
  Reprinted with the permission of Sage Publications, Inc.

Jacobs, James B. and Barry Eisler. "The Hate Crime Statistics Act of 1990." *Criminal
  Law Bulletin* 29 (1993): 99–123. Reprinted with the permission of the publisher, *Criminal Law Bulletin*, a division of Research Institute of America, Inc.

Lynch, James P. and David Cantor. "Ecological and Behavioral Influences on Property
  Victimization at Home: Implications for Opportunity Theory." *Journal of
  Research in Crime and Delinquency* 29 (1992): 335–62. Reprinted with the
  permission of Sage Publications, Inc.

Marshall, Chris E. and Vincent J. Webb. "A Portrait of Crime Victims Who Fight
  Back." *Journal of Interpersonal Violence* 9 (1994): 45–74. Reprinted with the
  permission of Sage Publications, Inc.

Mc Cormack, Robert J. "United States Crime Victim Assistance: History, Organization and Evaluation." *International Journal of Comparative and Applied Criminal Justice* 18 (1994): 209–20. Reprinted with the permission of the Department of Administration of Justice, Wichita State University.

McShane, Marilyn D. and Frank P. Williams III. "Radical Victimology: A Critique of the Concept of Victim in Traditional Victimology." *Crime and Delinquency* 38 (1992): 258–71. Reprinted with the permission of Sage Publications, Inc.

Meier, Robert F. and Terance D. Miethe. "Understanding Theories of Criminal Victimization." *Crime and Justice: A Review of Research* 17 (1993): 459–99. Reprinted with the permission of the University of Chicago Press.

Norris, Fran H. and Krzysztof Kaniasty. "Psychological Distress Following Criminal Victimization in the General Population: Cross-Sectional, Longitudinal, and Prospective Analyses." *Journal of Consulting and Clinical Psychology* 62 (1994): 111–23. Copyright (1994) by the American Psychological Association. Reprinted by permission.

Ruback, R. Barry. "Advice to Crime Victims: Effects of Crime, Victim, and Advisor Factors." *Criminal Justice and Behavior* 21 (1994): 423–42. Reprinted with the permission of Sage Publications, Inc.

Shover, Neal, Greer Litton Fox, and Michael Mills. "Long-Term Consequences of Victimization by White-Collar Crime." *Justice Quarterly* 11 (1994): 75–98. Reprinted with the permission of the Academy of Criminal Justice Sciences.

Umbreit, Mark S. and Robert B. Coates. "Cross-Site Analysis of Victim-Offender Mediation in Four States." *Crime and Delinquency* 39 (1993): 565–85. Reprinted with the permission of Sage Publications, Inc.

Van Ness, Daniel W. "New Wine and Old Wineskins: Four Challenges of Restorative Justice." *Criminal Law Forum* 4 (1993): 251–76. Reprinted with the permission of Rutgers University School of Law, Camden.